Advance Praise for
Vital Questions Facing
Disability Studies in Education

"By raising key questions, this collection of essays effectively frames the most important issues that currently affect special and general education practice. The authors cogently address the political nature of disability language and the demeaning representation of the disabled in educational discourses. Using such concepts as 'historical evasions,' 'educational sites of resistance,' 'school hierarchy,' 'disrupting normalcy,' 'fallacies of misconceptions and misunderstandings,' 'teaching to trouble,' 'transgressing noncrossable borders,' and 'deconstructing difference,' the authors apply postmodern and poststructual analyses to make sense of complex educational systems. Yet, despite the theoretical sophistication of the essays, the result is a surprisingly accessible and practical book."

Ellen Brantlinger, Professor, Special Education Program Area;
Department of Curriculum and Instruction;
Indiana University, Bloomington

"Professors Danforth and Gabel have performed a needed service to education and to disability studies by bringing these fields together in a wonderfully coherent and intellectually energizing volume. The editors skillfully articulate a set of focal questions that frame and inspire the book's chapters while advancing the reader's grasp of key issues. More than twenty authors and co-authors address these questions in clear, variegated, and stimulating essays that represent the perspectives of theorizing scholars, teachers working in schools, professors engaged in teacher preparation, students, people with direct experience of disability, family members, and sometimes, all of the above. Danforth and Gabel have succeeded in spanning intellectual and practical domains to present a broad range of ideas that interrogate reigning deficit-models of education. This book reminds us that good questions are often the best mechanisms to provide direction to our thinking and even to spark empowering transformation. In asking critically important questions and presenting an impressive array of responses, this book is a bracing call for professional and social responsibility to rebuild our most foundational beliefs about teaching, students, and humanity."

Carol J. Gill, Associate Professor,
Department of Disability and Human Development;
University of Illinois at Chicago

Vital Questions Facing
Disability Studies in Education

Disability
Studies in
Education

Susan L. Gabel and Scot Danforth
General Editors

Vol. 2

PETER LANG
New York • Washington, D.C./Baltimore • Bern
Frankfurt am Main • Berlin • Brussels • Vienna • Oxford

Vital Questions Facing
Disability Studies in Education

EDITED BY
Scot Danforth and Susan L. Gabel

PETER LANG
New York • Washington, D.C./Baltimore • Bern
Frankfurt am Main • Berlin • Brussels • Vienna • Oxford

Library of Congress Cataloging-in-Publication Data

Vital questions facing disability studies in education /
edited by Scot Danforth, Susan L. Gabel.
p. cm. — (Disability studies in education; vol. 2)
Includes bibliographical references and index.
1. People with disabilities—Education. 2. Disability studies.
I. Danforth, Scot. II. Gabel, Susan L. (Susan Lynn). III. Title. IV. Series.
LC4019.V57   371.9071—dc22   2006008941
ISBN 978-0-8204-7834-0
ISSN 1548-7210

Bibliographic information published by **Die Deutsche Bibliothek**.
Die Deutsche Bibliothek lists this publication in the "Deutsche
Nationalbibliografie"; detailed bibliographic data is available
on the Internet at http://dnb.ddb.de/.

"Ramping Minds" cover image courtesy of Dan Wilkins, www.thenthdegree.com

Cover design by Lisa Barfield

The paper in this book meets the guidelines for permanence and durability
of the Committee on Production Guidelines for Book Longevity
of the Council of Library Resources.

Printed in the United States of America

For Barbara.

S.L.G.

For MaryEllen and Hope, who fill my heart each day.

S.D.

Table of Contents

**How Can Disability Studies in Education Contribute
to Current Issues and Debates About Language and the
Representation of Disability?**

**How Can Disability Studies Inform Our Understanding
of Contemporary Political Debates in Education, Particularly
in Their Relevance to Disabled Students?**

**How is Disability Studies in Education (Ir)relevant
to the Practical Interests, Experiences, and Goals
of Disabled People in Schools?**

**How Can Disability Studies in Education Be Relevant
to the Practical Concerns of Teachers?**

**In What Ways is Disability Studies (Ir)relevant
to Local, State, and National Policy?**

How Does Disability Studies in Education Contribute to Conversations About the Relationships Among School, Family, and Community?

How Can Disability Studies Inform the Development and Use of Advanced Educational Technologies?

Why Teach Disability Studies in Education?

How Can Disability Studies in Education Influence Education at the International Level?

How Can Disability Studies in Education Contribute to the Ongoing Education Conversation About Race, Ethnicity, Gender, Religion, Class, Sexual Orientation and Other Social Constructs?

Acknowledgments

As editors, we have enjoyed the support of many colleagues in preparing this book. We are particularly grateful to the authors, whose chapters reveal the rich array of scholarship in disability studies in education. Most of these authors participated in the development of the "vital questions" that are addressed here. We appreciate their commitment to and consideration of the future of disability studies in education. Thanks, also, to the members of the Disability Studies in Education special interest group in the American Educational Research Association, who keep disability studies in education alive and cause it to thrive.

Finally, we thank the editorial and production teams at Peter Lang, who have tirelessly and patiently worked with us to produce this volume.

Before It Had a Name: Exploring the Historical Roots of Disability Studies in Education

Steven J. Taylor

Like the area of inquiry on which it is based—Disability Studies—Disability Studies in Education existed before it had a name. That is to say, the key themes underlying Disability Studies in Education can be traced back many years before it was identified as an area of inquiry or associated with professional groups, conferences, and scholarly publications. Of course, in earlier times, some of these themes were not fully developed, and their implications not completely explored. Yet, an understanding of the intellectual forbearers of Disability Studies in Education can help us understand more clearly the foundational ideas underlying this area of scholarship.

Neither Disability Studies nor Disability Studies in Education represents a unitary perspective. Scholarship in these areas includes social constructionist or interpretivist, materialist, postmodernist, poststructuralist, legal, and even structural-functionalist perspectives and draws on disciplines as diverse as sociology, literature, critical theory, economics, law, history, art, philosophy, and others. Despite this diversity, there are key themes or core ideas underlying Disability Studies. I discuss one of these here: the idea that disability is a social phenomenon. In the remaining discussion, I briefly explore the origins of this idea. My review is not intended to be comprehensive; rather, my intention is merely to discuss some of the works that brought us to where we are today.

Central to a Disability Studies perspective is the assumption that disability is a social construction or, if one prefers, creation. In contrast to clinical, medical, or therapeutic perspectives on disability, Disability Studies focuses

on how disability is defined and represented in society. From this perspective, disability is not a characteristic that exists in the person so defined, but a
construct that finds its meaning in social and cultural context. Although there
are important differences among what are referred to as the social model of
disability, the social constructionist view of disability, the minority group
model, and other frameworks, they share in common an understanding of
disability as a social phenomenon.

The idea that disability is a social phenomenon can be traced back at
least to the 1960s sociological theories of "deviance" and "stigma." The
labeling theory of deviance (Becker, 1963; Erikson, 1962) focused attention
on how society creates deviants by labeling certain persons as "outsiders."
As Becker (1963) wrote:

> . . .*social groups create deviance by making the rules whose infraction constitutes*
> *deviance*, and by applying those rules to particular people and labeling them as out-
> siders. From this point of view, deviance is *not* a quality of the act a person com-
> mits, but rather a consequence of the application by others of rules and sanctions to
> an "offender." The deviant is one to whom that label has been applied; deviant be-
> havior is behavior that people so label. (p. 9)

Labeling theory was soon applied to people defined as disabled or handicapped in society. Scheff (1966) examined the labeling processes associated
with being diagnosed as mentally ill. Scott's (1969) *The Making of Blind
Men* challenged the notion that the personality and other characteristics
associated with blind people are inherent in being blind. Rather, Scott argued, blind people are socialized into playing a social role:

> The major thesis of this book has been that blindness is a learned social role.
> People whose vision fails will learn in two contexts the attitudes and behavior pat-
> terns that the blind are supposed to have, in their personal relationships with those
> with normal vision and in the organizations that exist to serve and to help blind peo-
> ple. (p. 117)

Mercer (1965, 1973) applied labeling theory to people defined as mentally retarded. Her influential 1973 book *Labeling the Mentally Retarded*
started with a statement of her basic thesis:

> The questions "Who are the persons in a community who are really mentally
> retarded? What is the right prevalence rate?" are nonsense questions, questions that
> are not capable of being answered. Persons have no names and belong to no class

until we put them in one. Whom we call mentally retarded, and where to draw the line between the mentally retarded and the normal, depends upon our interest and the purpose of our classifications. (p. 1)

Long before Disability Studies scholars distinguished between the medical model of disability and the social or minority group model of disability, Mercer made the distinction between a clinical perspective and social system perspective on mental retardation. From the clinical perspective, mental retardation was a pathological condition existing within the individual that could be objectively diagnosed by trained professionals using standardized instruments. From a social system perspective, mental retardation was a social role played by individuals in specific social systems in which they participated: "From a social system perspective, the term mental retardate does not describe individual pathology but rather refers to the label applied to a person because he occupies the position of mental retardate in some social system" (Mercer, 1973, pp. 27–28).

Closely related to labeling theory was Goffman's (1961) dramaturgical analysis of stigma in his influential book with that title. According to Goffman, a stigma was a condition that discredited a person's social identity. He distinguished among three major types of stigma, those associated with physical differences, those associated with presumed blemishes in individual character, and those associated with race, nation, or religion. Goffman's analysis focused on how people managed actual or potentially stigmatizing conditions in their relations with others.

Labeling theory and Goffman's *Stigma* had an immediate and profound influence on the helping professions in disability and especially in the fields of mental health and mental retardation. These theories resonated with the critique of institutional psychiatry as a vehicle for social control by psychiatrists Szasz (1961, 1970a, 1970b) and Laing (1967). Goffman's (1963) *Asylums*, a devastating analysis of the effects of mental hospitals and other "total institutions," also supported critics of involuntary commitment and treatment.[1]

In the latter part of the 1960s, leaders in the field of mental retardation began to translate sociological concepts into a philosophy of caring for people with mental retardation. In 1969, the President's Committee on Mental Retardation (PCMR) published an influential book, *Changing Patterns in Residential Services for the Mentally Retarded* (Kugel and Wolfensberger, 1969).

Established by President John F. Kennedy as the President's Panel on Mental Retardation in 1962, PCMR intended *Changing Patterns* to serve as a resource in formulating recommendations on residential care to the President and the nation (Kugel, 1969). The book included invited contributions from American and international leaders, including two chapters by Burton Blatt (1969a, 1969b) based on his 1966 photographic expose of institutions.

Changing Patterns contained two chapters by Bengt Nirje, then Executive Director of the Swedish Association for Retarded Children. In the first chapter, "A Scandinavian Visitor Looks at US Institutions," Nirje (1969a) described his observations during visits to institutions and confirmed Blatt's reports. Nirje's (1969b) second chapter, "The Normalization Principle and Its Human Management Implications," was more important.

The concept of normalization was developed in Scandinavia and incorporated into a 1959 Danish law governing services for people with mental retardation (Bank-Mikkelson, 1969). Until Nirje's *Changing Patterns* chapter, it had not been systematically defined and explained (Wolfensberger, 1972). Nirje (1969b) provided the following definition: "the normalization principle means making available to the mentally retarded patterns and conditions of everyday life which are as close as possible to the norms and patterns of the mainstream of society" (p. 181).

In the introduction to *Changing Patterns*, Kugel (1969) wrote regarding the normalization principle:

> This construct has never been fully presented in the American mental retardation literature, but it is of such power and universality as to provide a potential basis for legal and service structures anywhere. Indeed, the editors of this book view the normalization principle as perhaps the most important concept that has emerged in this compendium (p. 10).

Various contributors to *Changing Patterns* approached mental retardation from the perspective of the sociology of deviance. Dybwad (1969), the past executive director of the Association for Retarded Children (now The Arc of the United States), described normalization as a sociological concept: "The normalization principle draws together a number of other lines of thought on social role, role perception, deviancy, and stigma that had their origin in sociology and social psychology" (p. 386). Wolfensberger's (1969) history of the origin and nature of institutions started with a review of the "role perceptions" of people with mental retardation (for example, as sick) and explained:

> Social scientists in the recent past have elaborated a concept of great importance to the understanding of the behavior and management of retarded persons. The concept is that of deviance. A person can be defined as deviant if he is perceived as being significantly different from others in some overt aspect, and if this difference is negatively valued. An overt and negatively valued characteristic is called a "stigma." (p. 65)

Dunn (1969) used language to describe institutions that could have come from labeling theorists in sociology in his chapter in *Changing Patterns*: "Frequently, they have been operated on the medical model which views mental retardation as a disease, and has an emphasis on labeling and determining etiology; and once one has viewed mental retardation as a disease and affixed a label to an individual, one has a built-in, self-fulfilling prophecy" (p. 214).

Three years after *Changing Patterns*, Wolfensberger (1972) published another influential and widely read book, *The Principle of Normalization in Human Services*. In this book, Wolfensberger (1972) elaborated on the dimensions of normalization and offered a reformulated definition: "Utilization of means which are as culturally normative as possible, in order to establish and/or maintain personal behaviors and characteristics which are as culturally normative as possible" (p. 28). In later work, Wolfensberger (1983, 1998) promoted "social role valorization" as a refined version of the normalization principle.

Sociological theories of labeling and stigma led not only to a questioning of institutions but of special education as well. Dunn, a contributor to *Changing Patterns*, published a 1968 article, "Special education for the mildly retarded—Is much of it justifiable?" in which he questioned the legitimacy of special education. Dunn's article is still cited by critics of inclusion (Kavale and Forness, 2000) as the beginning of "ideological" attacks on segregation in the schools.

In 1969, PCMR and the U.S. Bureau of Education for the Handicapped sponsored a conference that resulted in a report titled *The Six-Hour Retarded Child*. The report was consistent with Mercer's studies that showed that many children placed in special education, especially those from minority groups, were only "retarded" during school hours and functioned perfectly well at home and in their communities. The report began with the following quote: "We now have what may be called a 6-hour retarded child—retarded from 9 to 3, five days a week, solely on the basis of an IQ score, without regard to his adaptive behavior, which may be exceptionally adaptive to the situation and community in which he lives." Thus, the report did not merely endorse the development of more precise diagnostic techniques, but recognized that the determination of mental retardation depended on social context and environment.

By the 1970s, critiques of labeling in special education became widespread. In 1975, Hobbs published a major two volume edited series titled *Issues in the Classification of Children* that examined the labeling of children by schools and other social institutions. The inside jackets of the volumes described their purpose:

> What happens when children are classified *delinquent, retarded, hyperkinetic, mentally ill,* or *emotionally disturbed*? What treatment are they likely to receive? What will their experiences be in schools, the courts, or hospitals? What effect does classification have on their families? Are labels for children applied and used fairly? How do they affect children's behavior, their opinions of themselves, and their future? To find the answers, ten federal agencies joined to sponsor the Project on Classification of Exceptional Children. This milestone book, the report of the project's task forces, examines current classification procedures—often harmful, biased, or inadequate—and provides the foundation for new public policy, effective legislation, and improved professional practice.

Although many of the chapters in these volumes merely offered revised and more precise classification systems, Rains et al. (1975), Rhodes and Sagor (1975), and others directly challenged labeling itself and school and societal structures that placed certain children in the role of outsiders.

Many of the earliest critiques of labeling in special education focused on people with mild mental retardation and other disabilities. Increasingly in the 1970s, the critiques shifted to the constructs of mental retardation, disability, and handicaps themselves. In an article based on the abbreviated life history of a man labeled mentally retarded, Bogdan and Taylor (1976) wrote, "mental retardation is a social construction or a concept which exists in the minds of the `judges' rather than in the minds of the 'judged'...A mentally retarded person is one who has been labeled as such according to rather arbitrarily created and applied criteria" (p. 47). Bogdan and Biklen (1977) coined the term "handicapism" to describe the widespread prejudice and discrimination against people with disabilities based on their labels:

> Our purpose is to introduce the concept of *handicapism* as a paradigm through which to understand the social experience of those who have previously been known as mentally ill, mentally retarded, deaf, crippled, alcoholic, addict, elderly, deformed, deviant, abnormal, disabled, and handicapped. Handicapism has many parallels to racism and sexism. We define it as a set of assumptions and practices that promote the differential and unequal treatment of people because of apparent or assumed physical, mental, or behavioral differences. (p. 14)

As Gabel (2005) notes, the term ableism is more commonly used today to refer to the sentiments and practices described by Bogdan and Biklen.

Today, labeling theory, Goffman's theory of stigma, and normalization seem overly simplistic, one-sided, and inadequate. Labeling and stigmatization are not inevitable (Bogdan and Taylor, 1989). Disability is not merely a label forced on people so defined; it can also be an identity and source of pride (Linton, 1998; Longmore, 2003). People with disabilities are not passive agents who willingly accept societal beliefs, attitudes, and stereotypes; they also can resist or even ignore the sentiments of the broader culture (Gabel, 2005; Taylor, 2000). Normalization tended to dismiss self-determination and to promote conformity or assimilation[2].

Yet labeling theory and the theory of stigma shifted the focus away from the presumed deficits of people with disabilities to the social and cultural contexts in which disability is constructed. The critiques of labeling, stigmatization, and the medicalization of deviance and the medical model (Conrad and Schneider, 1992) provided a solid foundation for what has come to be known as the interdisciplinary area of inquiry of Disability Studies. It is not a coincidence that the Society for Disability Studies was originally founded by Irving Zola and other sociologists as the Section of Chronic Illness, Impairment, and Disability of the Western Social Science Association in 1982.

An understanding of disability as a social phenomenon has important implications for educational policy and practice. Enter Disability Studies in Education. What distinguishes Disability Studies in Education from Disability Studies generally is a practical concern with schooling practices. In contrast to a traditional special education perspective and consistent with a Disability Studies perspective, Disability Studies in Education examines disability in social and cultural context. Constructions of disability are questioned and special education assumptions and practices are challenged.

To regard disability as a social construction or creation is not to deny human variation. Human beings differ in many ways. Variations according to ability do not need to be valued negatively or wrapped in stereotypes and stigma. Disability is not viewed as a condition to be cured but rather as a difference to be accepted and accommodated. It is a social phenomenon through and through.

References

Bank–Mikkelson, N. E. (1969). A metropolitan area in Denmark: Copenhagen. In R. B. Kugel and W. Wolfensberger (Eds.), *Changing patterns in residential services for the mentally retarded* (pp. 227–254). Washington, DC: President's Committee on Mental Retardation.

Becker, H. (1963). *Outsiders: Studies in the sociology of deviance.* New York: Free Press.

Blatt, B. (1969a). Purgatory. In R. B. Kugel and W. Wolfensberger (Eds.), *Changing patterns in residential services for the mentally retarded* (pp. 34–49). Washington, DC: President's Committee on Mental Retardation.

————.(1969b). Recommendations for institutional reform. In R. B. Kugel and W. Wolfensberger (Eds.), *Changing patterns in residential services for the mentally retarded* (pp. 173–177). Washington, DC: President's Committee on Mental Retardation.

Blatt, B. and Kaplan, F. (1966). *Christmas in purgatory: A photographic essay on mental retardation.* Boston: Allyn and Bacon.

Bogdan, R., and Biklen, D. (1977). Handicapism. *Social Policy, 7*(4), 14–19.

Bogdan, R., and Taylor, S. J. (1976). The judged, not the judges: An insider's view of mental retardation. *American Psychologist, 31*(1), 47–52.

————. (1989). Relationships with severely disabled people: The social construction of humanness. *Social Problems, 36*(2), 135–148.

Conrad, P., and Schneider, J. W. (1992). *Deviance and medicalization: From badness to sickness* [Expanded ed.]. Philadelphia: Temple University Press.

Dunn, L. M. (1968). Special education for the mildly retarded—Is much of it justifiable? *Exceptional Children, 35,* 5–22.

————. (1969). Small, special–purpose residential facilities for the retarded. In R. B. Kugel and W. Wolfensberger (Eds.), *Changing patterns in residential services for the mentally retarded* (pp. 211–226). Washington, DC: President's Committee on Mental Retardation.

Dybwad, G. 1969. Action implications, U.S.A. today. In R. B. Kugel and W. Wolfensberger (Eds.), *Changing patterns in residential services for the mentally retarded* (pp. 383–428). Washington, DC: President's Committee on Mental Retardation.

Erikson, K. T. (1962). Notes on the sociology of deviance. *Social Problems, 9*, 307–314.

Gabel, S. (2005). Disability Studies in education. In S. Gabel (Ed.), *Disability Studies in education: Readings in theory and method.* New York: Peter Lang Publishers.

Goffman, E. (1961). *Asylums: Notes on the management of a spoiled identity.* Boston: Prentice-Hall.

———. (1963). *Stigma: Notes on the management of spoiled identity.* Englewood Cliffs, NJ: Prentice-Hall, Inc.

Hobbs, N. (Ed.). (1975). *Issues in the classification of children: A sourcebook on categories, labels and their consequences, Volume II* [The Jossey-Bass Behavioral Science Series]. San Francisco: Jossey-Bass Publishers.

Kavale, K. A., and Forness, S. R. (2000, September/October). History, rhetoric, and reality: Analysis of the inclusion debate. *Remedial and Special Education, 21*(5), 279–296.

Kugel, R. B. (1969). Why innovative action? In R. B. Kugel and W. Wolfensberger (Eds.), *Changing patterns in residential services for the mentally retarded* (pp. 1–14). Washington, DC: President's Committee on Mental Retardation.

Kugel, R. B., and Wolfensberger, W. (Eds.). (1969). *Changing patterns in residential services for the mentally retarded.* Washington, DC: President's Committee on Mental Retardation.

Laing, R. D. (1967). *The politics of experience.* New York: Ballantine Books.

Linton, S. (1998). *Claiming disability: Knowledge and identity* [Cultural Front]. New York: New York University Press.

Longmore, P. K. (2003). *Why I burned my book and other essays on disability.* Philadelphia: Temple University Press.

Mercer, J. R. (1965). Social system perspective and clinical perspective: Frames of reference for understanding career patterns of persons labeled as mentally retarded. *Social Problems, 13*(1), 18–34.

———. (1973). *Labelling the mentally retarded: Clinical and social system perspectives on mental retardation.* Berkeley: University of California Press.

Nirje, B. (1969a). A Scandinavian visitor looks at U.S. institutions. In R. B. Kugel and W. Wolfensberger (Eds.), *Changing patterns in residential services for the mentally retarded* (pp. 51–57). Washington, DC: President's Committee on Mental Retardation.

———. (1969b). The normalization principle and its human management implications. In R. B. Kugel and W. Wolfensberger (Eds.), *Changing patterns in residential services for the mentally retarded* (pp. 179–195). Washington, DC: President's Committee on Mental Retardation.

President's Committee on Mental Retardation. (1969, August). *The six–hour retarded child: A report on a conference on problems of education of children in the inner city, Airlie House, Warrenton, VA.* Washington, DC: Author.

Rains, P. M., Kitsuse, J. I., Duster, T., and Freidson, E. (1975). The labeling approach to deviance. In N. Hobbs (Ed.), *Issues in the classification of children: A sourcebook on categories, labels and their consequences, Volume I* [The Jossey-Bass Behavioral Science Series] (pp. 88–100). San Francisco: Jossey-Bass Publishers.

Rhodes, W. C., and Sagor, M. (1975). Community perspectives. In N. Hobbs (Ed.), *Issues in the classification of children: A sourcebook on categories, labels and their consequences, Volume I* [The Jossey-Bass Behavioral Science Series] (pp. 101–129). San Francisco: Jossey-Bass Publishers.

Scheff, T. J. (1966). *Being mentally ill: A sociological theory.* Chicago: Aldine Publishing Co.

Scott, R. A. (1969). *The making of blind men: A study of adult socialization.* New York: Russell Sage Foundation.

Szasz, T. S. (1961). *The myth of mental illness: Foundations of a theory of personal conduct.* New York: Delta.

———. (1970a). *Ideology and insanity: Essays on the psychiatric dehumanization of man.* Garden City, NY: Anchor Books, Doubleday and Company, Inc.

———. (1970b). *The manufacture of madness: A comparative study of the Inquisition and the mental health movement.* New York: Delta.

Taylor, S. J. (2000). "You're not a retard, you're just wise": Disability, social identity, and family networks. *Journal of Contemporary Ethnography, 29*(1), 58–92.

Wolfensberger, W. (1969). The origin and nature of our institutional models. In R. B. Kugel and W. Wolfensberger (Eds.), *Changing patterns in residential services for the mentally retarded* (pp. 59–171b). Washington, DC: President's Committee on Mental Retardation.

————. (1972). *The principle of normalization in human services.* Toronto: National Institute of Mental Retardation.

————. (1983). Social Role Valorization: A proposed new term for the principle of normalization. *Mental Retardation, 21*(6), 234–239.

————. (1998). *A brief introduction to Social Role Valorization: A high-order concept for addressing the plight of societally devalued people, and for structuring human services* (3rd ed.). Syracuse, NY: Training Institute for Human Service Planning, Leadership and Change Agentry, Syracuse University.

Notes

[1] Foucault's *Madness and Civilization* would later become influential, but this was not translated into English until 1979. In Disability Studies, Foucault was not widely cited until the 1990s.

[2] Normalization does not necessarily mean that people with disabilities should be made "normal." Wolfensberger's (1972) formulation placed equal emphasis on changing society and service systems, on the one hand, and changing individuals, on the other. It is true that Wolfensberger's notion is incompatible with the concepts of disability culture and disabled identity (Linton, 1998). The Scandinavian version of normalization (Nirje, 1969) had subtle, but important differences from Wolfensberger's version. For Nirje and others, normalization meant that human services should stop treating people with disabilities in abnormal ways.

Introduction

Scot Danforth and Susan L. Gabel

Within the broad thicket of cultural meanings about disability and education, ranging from old fashioned notions of tragedy to more progressive concepts of independence or interdependence (Reindal, 1999), laced with ever-present professional discourses of helpfulness, power, and science, there is a constant need for critical analyses that doubt the sincere company line, critique the mundane play of power, and press the professions and the community to experiment with new forms of participation, solidarity, and equality. In these ways, scholars of disability studies in education (DSE) are intellectual and practical watchdogs of democracy, demanding social critics and creative inventors of new ways of living and learning together in diverse communities. The critical watchdog role presses for educational innovation and pedagogical creativity that exceeds current notions of progressive teaching practice, calling for a thorough reexamination of our assumptions about humanity, community, and self. This critical watchdog task requires a continuous interrogation of rarely questioned assumptions about what disability is; what disabled persons need, want, and deserve; and the responsibilities of education and educators in relation to such matters. Moreover, it demands an expansive moral imagination about how a diversity of persons can live together in communities of equality, solidarity, and respect.

Educational conversations about what disabled persons need, want, and deserve often turn toward inclusion and the strategies that create equal opportunity. Prominent in the current vocabulary of inclusive practice is "accommodation," a term that ideally represents what we hope disability studies in education will achieve. In common use, an accommodation is typically an alteration in the standard practices, materials, and processes in a P–12 general classroom in order to better support the presence and learning of a disabled student. At best, an accommodation provides a substantial improvement in the physical, intellectual, and practical accessibility of the learning experience. At worst, it is a legalistic tweaking of minor elements that leaves the ableist status quo reified. A second definition of the term, and the one that speaks to our hopes for disability studies in education, is a meaning drawn from the root verb *accommodate,* which suggests a concept of even greater hope and utility: "change to suit a new purpose" (www. dictionary.com).

Changing to suit a new purpose describes both what disability studies means to disabled persons and to social organizations such as schools or society. Each must change to seek a new purpose. The new purpose is the development of democratic, inclusive, accessible communities where biological and cultural diversities are not construed as deficits demanding remediation, illnesses requiring treatment. The new purpose is one of group identity empowerment for disabled persons as disability shifts in meaning from a social problem requiring tactics of individual modification and personal adjustment to an oppressed group with a history, an identity, and a just cause.

What disability studies in education provides in light of this new purpose are intellectual and practical tools, forms of thought and action that nurture a deeper awareness among educators about disability rights, inclusive participation, and disability identity. In most hopeful form, this deeper awareness is a moral imagination for teaching, learning, and relating to one another that combines countercultural critique with an ethos of democratic solidarity. It is an understanding that involves but goes beyond mere pedagogical practices and arrangements to challenge educators at the level of personal and communal ethics, asking troubling yet hopeful questions about who we are and who we are together.

Development of Disability Studies in Education in the United States

This volume grows out of that troubling sensibility and a renewed understanding of democratic schooling in a diverse society. This volume also grows out of the recent development of disability studies in education as a scholarly field in the United States. We trace a brief narrative of this development in order to help readers understand how scholars have worked together to cultivate the scholarship of disability studies in education.

In 1999, we co-founded a new Special Interest Group in the American Educational Research Association (AERA) called Disability Studies in

Education (DSE). The membership of this group grew over 400% in the first five years as curriculum theorists, special educators, educational technologists, policy researchers, educational historians, and many more quickly found disability studies in education scholarship to be relevant to the current needs of educators and researchers.

We believe that the dramatic interest in DSE among educational scholars and practitioners has coalesced for multiple reasons. One aspect of this growing interest in disability studies in education (DSE) arises from a strong sense of disenchantment with the kind of disability research which has become status quo in education. For example, educational research has long perpetuated the myth of the need for distinctions between research about disabled students and research about all other students. The objectification of disabled and labeled students and the scientized reification of deficit constructs and identities—always the targets of a somewhat ignored strand of educational critique—have become a gathering point for sustained protest among critical scholars (Danforth, 1997; Danforth and Rhodes, 1997, Gallagher, 1998; Gallagher et al., 2004). Inseparable from this concern is the evident failure of special education researchers to wholeheartedly support the cause of inclusive education. There is an obvious dearth of special education inquiries about teaching practices, organizational dynamics, and, particularly, educational policies that further the development of more inclusive and egalitarian schools. One must question the basis for this by asking whether special education theory and research have become a technology of power in the Foucauldian sense.

Another source of the growing interest in DSE builds from an awareness that the critical educational research traditions—areas that ask serious and deep questions about power, identity, and justice—have left something out. The standard critical trinity of class, race, and gender, even if fortified by constructs such as sexual orientation or immigrant status, fails to provide relevant, persuasive insight into the dynamics of power and identity within public schools by ignoring the most vulnerable students (those with significant cognitive impairment, for example) or by adding-on disability without fully exploring the ways in which disability transforms arguments about power, identity, and justice. Disability has been a vital, missing ingredient in most of these analyses, and this absence has left critical researchers with a thin and unsatisfying recipe.

A third reason for the expansion of interest in DSE is the experiences of teachers and other professionals who witness first-hand the many ways that disability has become synonymous with second-class citizenship, exclusion, derision, and a lesser form of educational provision. Captured within bureaucratic systems and hyper-professionalized schemes of interpretation, students with disabilities and disability labels remain an oppressed class within public schools. Many teachers who work closely with these students and attempt to battle the institutional and attitudinal barriers of social asymmetry and suffering know how disabling schools and school systems are. Many teachers refuse to hide behind the bureaucratic authority; refuse to comfort themselves with professional rituals of testing, diagnosis, and placement; and refuse to accept the furthering of social injustice within acceptable professional standards and practices. These critical professionals clamor for ways of thinking about disability and schooling that can propel radical social change and hunger for direction and support. As a special interest group in AERA and as a growing body of literature, disability studies in education has become one of their sources of nurturance and guidance in their deeply egalitarian cause.

In the past decade, disability studies in education has grown from an obscure sub-discipline into a recognized field of educational study as scholars and practitioners have come to value social interpretations of disability (Gabel, 2005). This has occurred against a cultural background that generally equates disability with individual tragedy and a professional environment that reflexively construes disability within a medicalized framework of individual deficit and dysfunction. This book is an effort to promote an educational literature that speaks back against the medicalized and tragic notions that often dominate cultural and professional discourses, thereby opening pathways for social and political modes of inquiry and forging outlines of professional practices reconceived.

What characterizes disability studies in education? Answering this question in a comprehensive and satisfactory way is an overwhelming task, perhaps an impossible one at this time. Disability studies in education scholarship takes on many forms within many areas of educational research. From our limited perspective at this point in time, we describe disability studies in education as an intellectual and practical tradition that bursts forth at the intersection of *disability studies* and educational research, creating a general orientation to disabilities as social and political phenomena within activities of education, schooling, and learning.

We view disability studies in the broadest frame possible, drawing from the critical sociology tradition of the United Kingdom (e.g. Barnes, 1991; Finkelstein, 1980; Oliver, 1990, 1992); the feminist literature on disability (e.g. Morris, 1996; Thomas, 1999); the humanities scholarship common in North America (e.g. Longmore and Umanksy, 2001; Mitchell and Snyder, 1997, 2000; Snyder et al., 2002; Thomson, 1997); the growing field of disability arts (e.g. Crutchfield and Epstein, 2000); and a variety of social sciences (e.g. Zola, 1982).

We recognize that constructing disability studies as located solely within basic disciplines (e.g., humanities, sociology, the arts) tends to ignore the contributions of scholars in applied fields and the ways in which applied scholarship contributes to and is influenced by disability studies. It also privileges the traditional disciplines while minimizing the value of applied scholarship, thus perpetuating the age-old hierarchies of the academy. We anticipate that future publications will explore the ways in which educational research has been present within disability studies since its inception.

At the intersection of disability studies and educational research, disability studies in education scholars investigate *what disability means*; how it is interpreted, enacted, and resisted in the social practices of individuals, groups, organizations, and cultures. Closely allied with this interpretive focus is an on-going political examination, an analysis of what Thompson (1990, p. 7) calls "meaning in the service of power"; the ways that cultural orientations, practices, and discourses construe disability and disabled identities along hierarchies of value that are closely connected to asymmetries of access, opportunity, and economic standing. This leads us to view disability studies in education as an ideological ally to queer studies, critical theory, critical race theory, feminist scholarship, ethnic identity or nationality-based traditions of scholarship, and other educational literatures that bring identity and power to the forefront of social analysis.

Disability studies in education also draws from a tradition perhaps best described as *critical special education*. Within the profession, a small group of scholars have fervently produced a critical research and practical literature illuminating social inequalities of disability, race and class (Dunn, 1968; Brantlinger, 2001; Ferri and Connor, 2005) and critiquing the authoritarian professional epistemologies that silence both the perspectives of disabled persons and the development of non-deficit orientations to disability (Heshusius, 1982, 1984, 1988, 1989; Iano, 1986, 1987; Poplin, 1987, 1988; Skrtic, 1986).

Although critique has been a basic characteristic of disability studies in education, a more recent trend has been to explore new ways of thinking and talking about, as well as enacting, practice. One early struggle, discussed at length in some of our early DSE conferences, is the problem of translating theory into practice and, alternatively, allowing practice to inform theory. Recently, we have seen an increase in published work by disability studies in education scholars who are exploring the applications of disability theorizing to teacher education (Ware, 2001), work with children (Baglieri and Knopf, 2004; Marigage, et al., 2004; Reid and Valle, 2004), curriculum theory (Selden, 2000; Kliewer and Fitzgerald, 2001; Baker, 2002; Gabel, 2002), and policy (Slee and Allan, 2001) and we believe these hold promise for the future of our field because without an impact on practice and policy, disability studies in education will not realize its goals of socio-political structural change in education. Without structural change, without a change in the basic practices and policies associated with disabled students, how can we say that we have succeeded in our goals, other than to say we and others like us think differently?

In this book, our overall goal is to demonstrate multiple flavors of DSE in the current moment by opening up a series of problematic questions concerning disability and education that demand our attention, that yearn for open and ongoing dialogue among scholars, students, families, teachers, and educational leaders. While DSE is most ostensibly an intellectual specialty area, we contend that it requires its practitioners and invites professional educators and nonprofessional members of the community to engage with enduring issues of identity, status, power, and access within everyday life activities in schools and communities. DSE offers a series of activated conceptual tools that pry open the prosaic problematics of the conventional, the customary, and the comfortable, promoting a process of analytic abrasion that exposes the injustices, asymmetries, and hidden sufferings that exist within circles of the ordinary and routine. It is a protest literature that provides a critical social analysis of oft-unexamined concerns and cries out for advocacy, action, and dramatic reform of educational institutions, norms, and practices. Done well, DSE leaves readers with a nagging sense of discomfort with the reified status quo, a lingering pang of guilt for accepting what went unnoticed before, and a flicker of anger over the customs, complacencies, and good intentions that mask social injustices on a daily basis. As a literature of critique and action, DSE seeks to both provoke and inspire readers by pointing to the darkened places within educational professions, institutions, and practices—evidencing oppression, suffering, and inequality in action—while also cultivating an intellectual and practical dialogue that shines new light and offers new democratic promises for the lives, learning experiences, and schooling of disabled persons.

Process and Structure of the Book

The structure of this book consists of a series of broad, provocative questions about disability and education. We began this project by asking our colleagues in the Disability Studies in Education Special Interest Group of the American Educational Research Association to help us pose important questions. Our requirement was that each question must be broad enough to allow for variety of thoughtful responses and also practical enough to probe current problems within P–12 schools (or schools that serve children through high school graduation), universities, and other places of learning. We gathered many proposed questions from our colleagues, and then we began to narrow them down through a process of elimination, combination, and reconstitution. In no way is the resulting series of questions exhaustive of DSE present or future, nor would we argue that our (re)constitution of the questions is the best. We view the questions as creating a framework for continuing current dialogues and initiating new conversations about problems that matter. The ten questions simultaneously look to the history of disability studies and disability research in education, solicit a snapshot of the present moment in disability studies in education, and encourage a vision of the future developments in the field.

Once the questions were solidified, we solicited two essay responses from leading scholars in the field. We gave our essayists great latitude in selecting topics or issues residing under the general umbrellas of their questions. This allowed the authors to grab hold of a specific topic of investigation within the scope of the broad question without having to attempt to write a traditional textbook-style chapter that thinly and authoritatively covers a topic from A to Z.

We also encouraged authors to find and use their own voice, to take on the writing style that they feel is most appropriate to their purposes. The result is a book containing variety of writing styles ranging from some fairly traditional academic writing to narratives of personal experience and some poetic verse.

Vital Questions

Question #1: How can disability studies in education contribute to current issues and debates about language and the representation of disability?
Some scholars have viewed disability studies in applied fields as an attempt to reclaim the hijacked social identities of the disabled from the public and the professionals who provide services to the disabled (e.g., special educators and rehabilitation counselors). In their most immediate form, these concerns play out in discussions of the use of language when talking or writing about disabled people (e.g., disability-first or person-first usage) or when representing disability in other ways (e.g., through art or the curriculum). Beneath these language and representation concerns reside a complex tangle of questions about epistemology, subject position, identity, the politics of representation, and fundamentally, ableism.

Question #2: How can disability studies inform our understanding of contemporary political debates in education, particularly in their relevance to disabled students?

Debates about the purpose and role of public education in America are over a century old, but in recent years, the so-called "culture wars" have heated up. These debates place children at risk of being caught in the middle while society at large argues about how students should be educated, and to what social and moral ends. Culture war conflicts over the education of disabled students have primarily taken place in isolation from broader educational conversations, usually occurring within the sub-field of special education. Issues of contention have focused on inclusion vs. continuum of services; positivist empirical research vs. interpretive, critical, and postmodern approaches; and legal/political policy stances vs. moral/philosophical positions. The contribution of disability studies to these on-going discussions within education and within the sub-field of special education remains undefined.

Question #3: How is disability studies in education (ir)relevant to the practical interests, experiences, and goals of disabled people in schools?

Increasingly, scholarship in disability studies has become "academic" in the narrowest sense of the term. This might be a phase in the natural evolution of the emergence and institutionalization of a new field of inquiry. However, as a whole, disability studies in the United States has been criticized for its lack of relevance to the lives of disabled people. In addition, as often happens in any area of inquiry, the language used by scholars is not accessible to non-academics, including many disabled people. Instead of being a medium of social change, disability studies sometimes follows its own agenda. Through establishing a conversation between disability studies and practical lives, this question asks what disability studies in education can do to avoid falling into the trap of irrelevance that results from a-practical theorizing.

Question #4: *How can disability studies in education be relevant to the practical concerns of teachers?*

While educators might adhere to the constructivist and democratic values related to American schooling in general, they are often steeped in tradition-alism's technical rationality when it comes to disabled students. This approach is antithetical to the progressive constructionism version of the social model of disability. This question asks what, if anything, can disability studies in education do to address the practical concerns of people working with "real students" in "real schools." In what ways, if at all, does disability studies inform pedagogy and practice? Traditionally, the general aim of special educators has been to either increase levels of functioning in areas of identified deficit or to alleviate the practical impact of impaired functioning. The inclusion movement has complicated matters by often importing this double goal into the general education classroom while also attempting to provide access to the general curriculum. The challenge to disability studies is to address the real needs of students and teachers. Simultaneously, we must contend with both the general classroom curriculum, the public school organization and culture, and the traditional special education focus on remediation and functional skills.

Question #5: *In what ways is disability studies (ir)relevant to local, state, and national policy?*

Of necessity, policy must be concerned with accountability, political realities, fiscal constraints, and many other issues that feel abstract to practitioners at the micro-level. Someone is always tinkering with school reform and
the policies it generates, but whether policies change incrementally or radically, we need to explore ways of critically analyzing their consequences for
disabled students. It is unclear whether a young field of academic inquiry
like disability studies can even have an impact on macro-policy levels. At the
same time it seems plausible that disability studies could contribute to the
policy arena by offering new and creative ways of approaching policy problems. This question explores where and when we should start influencing
policy and what the policy goal(s) should be. This is one of the most difficult
questions we face.

*Question #6: How does disability studies in education contribute to the
conversations about the relationships among school, family, and community?*

Disability studies often privileges the voices of those closest to the disability
experience, primarily the disabled and their families and loved ones. This
stance can lead to conflicts about who is authorized to speak for disabled
students when educational decisions must be made. Disability studies needs
to find a way to communicate its values to schools, families, and communities so that such conflicts are minimized and disabled students are free to
speak for themselves. The conceptual, experiential, and perspectival gaps
that exist between the disabled, parents of disabled students, and educational
institutions offer a rich but problematic terrain for disability studies examination.

*Question #7: How can disability studies inform the development and use of
advanced educational technologies?*

It is important that disability studies participate in a sustained critical and
practical examination of the purposes and uses of technology in education,
particularly when those technologies are used with disabled students (e.g.,
assistive or augmentative devices). The disability studies value of allowing
disabled people to "speak" for themselves becomes complicated when speaking for oneself entails the use of assistive or augmentative technologies. This
is particularly true when those technologies require the support of non-

disabled communication partners. When viewed from disability studies perspectives, these dilemmas of educational technology can be understood differently and alternative ways of making decisions with/for/by students can be generated.

Question #8: Why teach disability studies in education?

Disability studies in education needs to consider ways in which it can and should affect the teacher education curriculum in which disability is still considered a deficit that needs to be fixed, alleviated, or remediated. This is a consideration involving complex questions of teaching methods, classroom management, personal attitudes, and interpersonal morality. If we take to heart the underlying messages of disability studies, then how are we to prepare teachers to use educational practices that are categorized as intervention, therapy and instructional remediation? For example, should we and, if so, how can a teacher prepare a blind child to use all of his/her residual vision without undermining the message that blindness is not a defect? Or how can we consider giving a student with paraplegia a wheelchair when this decision assumes there is something "wrong" with crawling rather than walking? Is functional skill training always in conflict with the disability studies perspective? If it is not, then how do teacher educators prepare pre-service teachers to make decisions about when (and how) to address functional limitations? And what are the roles and responsibilities of the general and special educator in these decisions?

Question #9: How can disability studies in education influence education at the international level?

As educators, it is increasingly important for us to be aware of what is happening in the world. Immigration, cross-cultural experiences, international communication technologies, and globalization confront American schools on a regular basis. This increases the potential for tension and conflict since disability is valued based on cultural beliefs and practices. How, if at all, is disability studies affecting education in countries around the world? As important is the question of whether globalization is importing Western notions about disability and education to cultures where native practices are more liberatory for disabled people. What can the United States, and other

Western nations, learn from educators in the East or South who apply disability studies to their everyday practice?

Question #10: How can disability studies in education contribute to the ongoing educational conversation about race, ethnicity, gender, religion, class, sexual orientation and other social constructs?

Theorists use social constructs or categories as analytic and interpretive tools to develop nuanced understandings of the politics, policies, and practices of education. Traditionally, and despite the evident interaction between disability and other identity categories, most educational theorists have ignored disability as a social construct. The assumption has been that special education researchers will focus on disability in education. Yet with few exceptions, special education researchers have struggled little with the complexities and ambiguities of social categories, giving little attention to the processes and practices that actively construct disability types in the public schools, and perhaps paying even less attention to the interactions of power and identity across categories of race, class, gender, etc.

References

Baglieri, S., and Knopf, J. H. (2004). Normalizing difference in inclusive teaching. *Journal of Learning Disabilities*, *37,6*, 525–529.

Baker, B. (2002). The hunt for disability: The new eugenics and the normalization of school children. *Teachers College Record*, *104, 4*, 663–703.

Barnes, C. (1991). *Disabled people in Britain and discrimination*. Calgary: University of Calgary Press.

Brantlinger, E. (2001). Poverty, class, and disability: A historical, social, and political perspective. *Focus on Exceptional Children, 33, 7*, 1–19.

Crutchfield, S. and Epstein, M. J. (2000). *Points of contact: Disability, art, and culture*. Ann Arbor: University of Michigan Press.

Danforth, S. (1997). On what basis hope? Modern progress and postmodern possibilities. *Mental Retardation, 35, 2*, 93–106.

Danforth, S. and Rhodes, W. C. (1997). Deconstructing disability: A philosophy for inclusion. *Remedial and Special Education, 18, 6*, 357–66.

Dunn, L M. (1968). Special education for the mildly retarded: Is much of it justifiable? *Exceptional Children, 35*, 5–22.

Ferri, B. A. and Connor, D. J. (2005). Tools of Exclusion: Race, Disability, and (Re)segregated Education. *Teachers College Record, 107, 3*, 453–474.

Finkelstein, V. (1980). *Attitudes and disabled people: Issues for discussion.* New York: International Exchange of Information in Rehabilitation.

Gabel, S. (2002). Some conceptual problems with critical pedagogy. *Journal of Curriculum Inquiry, 32*, 177–201.

———. (2005). Introduction, in S. Gabel (Ed.), *Disability studies in education: Readings in theory and method,* pp. 1–20. New York: Peter Lang.

Gallagher, D. J. (1998). The scientific knowledge base of special education: Do we know what we think we know? *Exceptional Children, 64, 4,* 493–502.

Gallagher, D. J., Heshusius, L., Iano, R. P., and Skrtic, T. M. (2004). *Challenging orthodoxy in special education: Dissenting voices.* Denver: Love.

Heshusius, L. (1982). At the heart of the advocacy dilemma: A mechanistic world view. *Exceptional Children, 49*, 6–13.

———. (1984). Why would they and I want to do it? A phenomenological-theoretical view of special education. *Learning Disability Quarterly, 7*, 363–368.

———. (1988). The arts, science, and the study of exceptionality. *Exceptional Children, 55*, (1) 60–65.

———. (1989). The Newtonian mechanistic paradigm, special education, and contours of alternatives: An overview. *Journal of Learning Disabilities, 22*, 403–415.

Iano, R. P. (1986). The study and development of teaching: With implications for the advancement of special education. *Remedial & Special Education, 7*, 5, 50–61.

———. (1987). Rebuttal: Neither the absolute certainty of prescriptive law nor a surrender to mysticism. *Remedial & Special Education, 8*, 1, 52–61.

Kliewer, C., and Fitzgerald, L. M. (2001). Disability, schooling, and the artifacts of colonialism. *Teachers College Record, 103, 3*, 450–470.

Longmore, P. K. and Umanksy, L. (2001). *The new disability history: American perspectives.* New York: New York University Press.

Mariage, T. V., Paxton–Buursma, D. J., and Bouck, E. C. (2004). Interanimation: Repositioning possibilities in educational contexts. *Journal of Learning Disabilities 37, 6*, 534–549.

Mitchell, D. T. and Snyder, S. L. (2000). *Narrative prosthesis: disability and the dependencies of discourse.* Ann Arbor: University of Michigan Press.

———. (1997). *The body and physical difference: discourses of disability.* Ann Arbor : University of Michigan Press.

Morris, J. (1996). *Encounters with strangers: Feminism and disability.* London: Women's Press.

Oliver, M. (1990). *The politics of disablement: A sociological approach.* New York : St. Martin's Press.

———. (1992). Changing the social relations of research production. *Disability₁ Handicap and Society*, 7, 2, 101–115.

Poplin, M. S. (1987). Self-imposed blindness: The scientific method in education. *Remedial and Special Education, 8*, 6, 31–37.

———. (1988). Holistic/constructivist principles of the teaching/learning process: Implications for the field of learning disabilities. *Journal of Learning Disabilities, 21*, 401–416.

Reid, D. K., Valle, J. W. (2004). The discursive practice of learning disability: Implications for instruction and parent–school relations. *Journal of Learning Disabilities*, *37, 6*, 466–478.

Reindal, S. V. (1999). Independence, dependence, interdependence: some reflections on the subject and personal autonomy. *Disability and Society, 14, 3*, 353–367.

Selden, S. (2000). Eugenics and the social construction of merit, race and disability. *Journal of Curriculum Studies, 32, 2*, 235–252.

Skrtic, T. M. (1986). The crisis in special education knowledge: A perspective on perspective. *Focus on Exceptional Children, 18*, 1–16.

Slee, R., and Allan, J. (2001). Excluding the included: A reconsideration of inclusive education. *International Studies in Sociology of Education, 11, 2*, 173–191.

Snyder, S. L., Brueggemann, B. J., Thomson, R. G. (2002). *Disability studies: Enabling the humanities.* New York: Modern Language Association of America.

Thomas C. (1999). *Female forms: Experiencing and understanding disability.* Buckingham: Open University Press

Thompson, J. B. (1990). *Ideology and modern culture: Critical social theory in the era of mass communication.* Stanford, CA: Stanford University Press.

Thomson, R. G. (1997). *Extraordinary bodies: Figuring physical disability in American culture and literature.* New York: Columbia University Press.

Ware, L. (2001). Writing, identity, and the other: Dare we do disability studies? *Journal of Teacher Education 52*, 107–123.

Zola, I. K. (1982). *Missing pieces: A chronicle of living with a disability.* Philadelphia : Temple University Press.

*How Can Disability Studies in Education Contribute to
Current Issues and Debates About Language and
the Representation of Disability?*

CHAPTER 1

Teacher Education as a Site of Resistance

Nancy Rice

The purity of a concept is its danger (Porter, 1997, p. xiv).

Cultural "knowledge" and attitudes about disability are learned by young children—often indirectly but quite unmistakably. The very meanings of "ability" and "disability" are created via language, representation, and practices: metaphors, fairy tales, cultural myths, spatial organization, exclusive architecture, family stories, disability rights discourse, common parlance (e.g., "the blind leading the blind"), awkward silences, unmissed absences, and film and literature representations all convey meanings about the value of "disability" and "ability." Mitchell and Snyder (2000) observed, "[D]isabled people's marginalization has occurred in the midst of a perpetual circulation of their images. Curiously, a social erasure has been performed even as a representational repertoire has evolved" (p. 6).

Because attitudes are transmitted through ubiquitous cultural practices, they are taken to be "common sense." "Common sense has a conceptual structure that is usually unconscious" (Lakoff, 2002). The work of uncovering and unlearning "common sense" ideas—or "epistemic etchings" (Slee, 1999)—about disability is not something done all at once. For me at least, the unlearning is a continual—and frustratingly gradual—process. My most recent confrontation with my "dysconsciousness" (King, 1991) was when I neglected to schedule an ASL interpreter for a meeting with a Deaf colleague. Unlearning the idea that creating an accessible environment is not my responsibility is taking longer than I want it to.

Slee (2001) wrote:

> Traditional special educators demonstrate a remarkable resilience through linguistic dexterity. While they use a contemporary lexicon of inclusion, the cosmetic amendments to practices and procedures reflect assumptions about pathological defect and normality based upon a disposition of calibration and exclusion (p. 167)...It is this problem of language and meaning that lies at the heart of the inclusive educational project (p. 169).

Thus while language can shift, meaning and exclusionary tendencies often remain intact. Clough (1999) argued, "We have exclusive structures in our institutions because these same structures organize consciousness" (p. 63). Heshusius (2004) wrote, "Power relations in institutions and other established structures must be demystified, but the inner embodied life cannot be exempted from the process. They surely are deeply intertwined. Established structures and institutions that are separative are made by and up of separative selves."

In this chapter I explore the role that disability studies can play in teacher education, particularly in terms of disrupting the "common sense" knowledge about disability and the professional discourses that produce teachers as "subjects." I briefly present two "special" educators' accounts that describe turning points when they were introduced to counter-hegemonic discourses around disability and how these events significantly changed how they conceptualized disabled students and thus their work. Finally, I consider some ways that disability studies in (teacher) education can continue its theoretical work in shifting what is taken as "common sense" by turning the gaze back on the "unearned privileges of ability" and listening to those who have historically been on the educational and societal margins. An important aspect of such a teacher education curriculum would be informed by texts chiefly authored by individuals with disabilities and their families.

Discursive Formations

Foucault argued that knowledges are historically contingent and culturally specific. He analyzed "the shifting ways that the body and the social institutions related to it have entered into political relations" (Rabinow, 1984,

p. 10). Through his studies of the development of sexuality (1978/1990), discipline, punishment and the creation of prisons (1977/1995), the creation of mental illness (1988), and the medical examination (1994), Foucault illustrated the ways in which "discursive practices...systematically form the objects of which they speak" (1972, p. 49). The power to create "subjects" has shifted from the sovereignty and force of the state to a system in which the discourses of authorized disciplines and local forms of surveillance create and maintain those subjects. "[I]t is in discourse that power and knowledge are joined together" (1978/1990, p. 100).

Techniques of subjugation include "normalization," "surveillance," and individualizing by ordering and classifying people hierarchically. The connection to disabled students is evident: the language and practices of special education work to create and maintain the "disabled subject." Knowledge about the individual is obtained via the disciplining techniques, which in turn structure opportunities for her, including how much she can learn, what she should be taught (academics or "functional curriculum"), and, often, that some amount of exclusion from the general population is "normal." However, as Allan (1999) has shown, these subjugating practices can be transgressed.

Discourses also create teacher and teacher educator "subjects." Both those who work in K–12 schools and those of us who work in universities are also discursively created as "subjects"—surveillance and normalization are ever-present in the course of teaching. "[T]he disciplinary power...is everywhere and always alert...and constantly supervises the very individuals who are entrusted with the task of supervising" (Foucault, 1977/1995, p. 177). (While the technique of "confession"—local centers of power/knowledge—is not in play in these instances, I nonetheless argue that educators are "subject" to regulation.) For example, I am a faculty member in the Department of "Exceptional Education." Certain types of knowledges—or at least domains of knowledge—are expected of me in this role. I am "subject" to a certain "discipline." Increasingly, university curricula are driven by "standards." Discourses in the field regulate the transmission of "special education knowledge," but alternative discourses are available. Reid and Valle (2004), following Foucault, wrote, "A discourse is...the instrument through which people become *positioned*, but not determined, within that discourse" (p. 466).

Alternative Discourses

The alternative philosophical discourse on which disability studies draws is social justice, based on principles of equity and democracy. Other ways of knowing disability come from a host of other disciplines in the social sciences and humanities. These alternative ways of understanding disability, situated within a democratic framework, are crucial to the formation of a new generation of teachers if we expect the project of inclusive education to move forward.

While inclusive education is a much more widely researched topic now than it was even a decade ago, teacher education is nonetheless still often comprised of segregated special education courses taught from separate special education departments by "specialized" faculty members. Slee's assessment is uncomfortably familiar:

> The teacher training imperative revolves around the transmission of regulated chunks of traditional special education knowledge so that the professions retain their authority and classroom teachers are not so spooked when different students enter the classroom. This is conservative incrementalism writ large. Paradoxically, it is paraded as the vanguard of a progressive movement for social justice (2001, p. 173).

While many readers of this volume may be familiar with institutions that have disbanded segregated departments (e.g. Syracuse University), have instituted an inclusive teacher certification program at the elementary grades (Syracuse University, University of Wisconsin-Milwaukee), or have begun a Master's program with the express purpose of disrupting the medicalized view of disability (Teachers College Learning dis/Abilities program), the majority of institutions maintain traditional special education teacher preparation programs. Even with a focus on inclusive education, difference is often reinscribed rather than interrogated. Inclusion has become an adjective (e.g., the inclusion teacher/student/class/room).

As noted above, knowledge is historically and culturally contingent. How does power/knowledge, then, account for change? Part of the answer lies in the "regime of truth." Every society has a mechanism that establishes the criteria for determining what "counts" as truth. "Truth is to be understood as a system of ordered procedures for the production, regulation, distribution, circulation and operation of statements" (Foucault, 1984, p. 74).

Foucault eschewed the notion of a clear binary of dominant/nondominant discourses but supported the existence of "the polyvalence of discourse"—many discourses exist simultaneously. The effect of a particular group of discourses is neither "uniform nor stable" (1980, p. 100) and "can be both an instrument and an effect of power, but also a hindrance, a stumbling-block, a point of resistance and a starting point for an opposing strategy. Discourse transmits and produces power; it reinforces it, but also undermines and exposes it, renders it fragile and makes it possible to thwart it." (1980, p. 101).

Foucault provided the example of homosexuality and the legal, medical, psychological and other discourses that created this as a "perversion" during the nineteenth century; at the same time, "it also made possible a reverse discourse: homosexuality began to speak in its own behalf, to demand that its legitimacy or 'naturality' be acknowledged, often in the same vocabulary, using the same categories by which it was medically disqualified" (1980, p. 101).

The Disability Rights Movement is a recent powerful example of a "reverse discourse." That group has reclaimed language, such as "crip" and "gimp," that was once used to subjugate disabled people. Power and knowledge are inextricably woven into language and representation. This is no less true where disability is concerned. It is through a reframing of how disability is considered that traditional constructions of disability are challenged.

Identity Shifts

Identity is also formed discursively—in the "shifting space where narratives of subjectivity meet narratives of culture" (Zembylas, 2003, p. 221). A post-structuralist view of identity honors the ever-changing nature of individuals. It takes into account the experience of change and transformation—as discourses shift, so do identities (Britzman, 1993). It also takes both structure and agency into account—individuals are not shaped solely by culture nor solely by their "psychological" selves. One's class, race, ability and gender positions are not determinant of one's identity, but they do play a role. They "enable and constrain possibilities of action" (Young, 2000, p. 101). They inform one's identity but do not constitute it.

> Our experiences of cultural meaning and structural positioning occur in unique events and interactions with other individuals, and the unique events are often more important to our sense of ourselves than are these social facts. How we fashion ourselves is also a function of our attitudes toward our multiple cultural and structural group memberships. (Young, 2000, p. 101).

An essentialist view of "teacher identity," then, does not exist. Teachers choose their profession for a variety of reasons, based on their individual identities: a desire to work with youth, a passion for a subject area, a commitment to community. Once they enter teacher education, however, they are "saturated with cognitive experiences that encourage conservative, individualistic, competitive, and decontextualized tendencies....Prospective teachers encounter few experiences that challenge the status quo in schools" (Kincheloe, 1993, p. 14).

In working with pre- and in-service teachers, new ways of understanding disability must be used to counter the conservative identity into which teachers are often regulated during their professional education. Recognizing this need, Clough and Corbett (2000) have written a text for students of inclusive education. It consists of brief (3–5 page) reflections by leading authors in the field of inclusive education. The editors asked contributors to describe and trace key influences and experiences related to their thinking during the course of their lives.

Studies of teachers' lives through narratives are increasingly used in educational research to "provide reflective opportunities for the teacher" (Convery, 1999, p. 131), to compare one's views to "various other stories in order to gain new insights" (Beattie and Conle, 1996, p. 323), and to make...visible...the process of choosing among alternative perspectives and practices" (Beattie and Conle, 1996, p. 323). In a similar vein, Clough and Corbett (2000) hoped that their volume would aid the student-reader in realizing that:

- it is acceptable to change your theoretical viewpoints as you continue to learn and develop through experience
- to struggle with ambiguity and complexity is a natural process of intellectual growth, not a weakness
- our mind-maps of how we see the world will influence the type of theoretical stance we decide to select from the range available (p. 145)

In the next section, I introduce two first-person accounts that illustrate the influence of being presented with alternative discourses of "disability."

Two Accounts of Change

In this section, I offer two accounts of teachers who were discursively created as subjects in the role of "special education teacher" but who later were able to shift their identity. The first account is my own (Rice, 2001).

The second is that of a prominent figure in the field of education, disability and social justice (Slee, 2000; 2004)

In describing how I came to my dissertation project, I wrote:

> I came to this project because of my own personal development and professional education as a teacher. While growing up. . .I read and did homework with my younger sister, Lisa, who at that time (early 1970s) was said to have dyslexia. Our working together made me realize that I wanted to be a teacher. . .While I was in college. . .I came across the literature on "children with learning disabilities." Most of what I read did not describe Lisa at all. She didn't have social skill, speech or behavioral problems. She was articulate, outgoing, athletic and alternately, a buddy and an annoying-little-sister. While in college, I remember having long talks with both my mom and Lisa, asking about these "characteristics" as they related to my younger sister. We all noted the discrepancies. Nonetheless, I managed, somehow, to slowly adopt the professional construction of "learning disability," alternately using it as a lens through which I viewed my sister and then exempting her from this gaze (p. 8).

I recounted a time during my first years of teaching when I asked Lisa what had most helped her learn to read. She said it had been listening to tapes of Danielle Steele novels on her Walkman while she read the book. I remembered wanting to use tapes more in my classroom based on her experience, but the professional construction of "learning disability" and the technical rationality of how to teach "those kids" had already taken hold:

> I was impressed but not convinced. I had learned in my professional education (as   I suspected Lisa's teachers had as well) that using a tape recording for reading instruction was a "crutch." I had a listening center in my classroom that year (an area with tape recorders, head phones and packaged sets of books and tapes), and remember briefly considering using it as a central element of the reading program. But, lacking confidence in Lisa's experience, I stuck with basals and permitted use of the listening center at "free time." I continued on, charting sight word and phonetic acquisition skills of my students. (p. 9).

It wasn't until several years later that I began to question my role within the educational enterprise. I started taking courses. . .in educational sociology. In that context, I examined my role as a *haole* (Caucasian) teacher in a public school, in an area [on Oahu] that served predominately Samoan and native Hawaiian students. I realized that I had to learn much more about local culture and mores in order not to discriminate against my students (p. 9). Such a realization also meant that my "knowledge" of the neutrality of the educational system was seriously suspect. How could it be that the political nature of schooling had been obscured during my teacher education (Kincheloe, 1993)?

Slee has written about his own formation of the understanding of disability. He gives several examples, of which a few are recounted here. About his elementary school years he wrote:

> For my schoolmates and I, special kids were sent to special schools. . .because they weren't "normal." Normal became a very powerful concept established in childhood that took some time to jettison. The definition of normality for us was simple. They aren't like us (2004, p. 51).

In high school, the experience was "less dramatic, more a process of civilizing and sophistication. We gathered more sophisticated medical explanations for disability and listened to debating teams wrestling over euthanasia." (2004, p. 51).

During his early years in teaching, as with mine, his "established knowledge" was challenged. This came about when he was presented with an alternative discourse consisting of "a new sociology of education, and. . .the work of Mike Oliver, and in turn a whole chorus of disabled researchers' voices" (Slee, 2000, p. 127). "The impact...was profound" (Slee, 2004, p. 52).

Once presented with these ideas,

> [t]he work at the [behavior] unit [where I was teaching] was presenting me with deep ideological tensions. More of the kids referred to the unit came with a greater range of labels for us to sort and shelve. Yes the kids were difficult, disruptive, phobic about school, defective in academic skills; but what did this mean? I believed the immediate turn to them for individual pathological explanations let us off the hook. Why not explore the deep pathology of schooling? (Oliver, 2000, p. 127).

In both of these narratives, the exposure to an alternative discourse was the catalyst for a reconsideration of meaning and knowledge. In my case, I began to reconceptualize my work and my professional identity. I began to think of myself more as someone who worked to provide equitable arrangements for students first. A more holistic philosophy emerged—as I saw myself with a broader agenda, I saw my students as citizens, not as remedial projects. Education has the power to transform. Teacher education is well-positioned to offer interdisciplinary views on disability, education and the politics of schooling all children.

Disability Studies in Teacher Education: A Site of Resistance

In this section, I offer three ideas for a rethinking of the teacher education curriculum: *Engaging a critical pedagogy of disability*, *Educating disabled citizens and allies*, and *Redefining professional knowledge*.

Engaging a Critical Pedagogy of Disability

Centering disability. Ervelles (2000) is disapproving of critical educational theorists who address gender, race, class, sexuality and "the body" but continue to exclude "disability." She does not, however, argue that disability be added to the list of marginalized social locations to be interrogated. Instead, she suggests that disability be centered in any critical analysis of schooling, since "the category of disability [is] central in explaining how and why racial, gendered and sexual subjects are oppressively constituted within education settings and within society at large" (p. 26). This approach to critical theory rests on a historical materialist analysis—as opposed to a post-structuralist critical theory—that focuses on the actual political and social conditions of the lives of disabled people.

While analyses of oppression on the basis of identity markers such as race, gender, class, and sexuality can obscure an analysis of disabled people's oppression, a focus on disability first brings oppression of all forms into clearer view. A critical pedagogy of disability would include unpacking the norm and developing a critical consciousness.

Unpacking the norm. Similar to a pedagogy of "whiteness" advanced by critical theorists (Hytten and Adkins, 2001; Kincheloe and Steinberg, 1998), unpacking the norm of "ability" includes investigating the social forces that shape and maintain the centrality and power of "ability." Such a focus helps us to see not only how it is that ability is socially constructed, but it may also help to uncover "dysconsciousness." King (1991) defined "dysconsciousness" as

> an uncritical habit of mind (including perceptions, attitudes, assumptions, and beliefs) that justifies inequity and exploitation by accepting the existing order of things as given. . .It is not the *absence* of consciousness(that is, not unconsciousness) but an *impaired* consciousness or distorted way of thinking about race (p. 135).

In order to disrupt such naturalization, cultural products, political discourse, public policy, physical environments, everyday language (Danforth and Navarro, 1998), teacher education textbooks (Rice, 2001), K–12 curricula, and teachers' own expectations and plans for educating all their students can be investigated for the normative assumptions that underlie these products and processes. Being presented with strategies to understand how the status quo is maintained (Brantlinger, 1997) as well as being presented with alternatives we can begin to interrupt what is taken as inevitable. Such a stance is consistent with critical constructivism.

Developing critical consciousness. According to Kincheloe (1993), "critical constructivism allows teachers a critical consciousness, that is, an ability to step back from the world as we are accustomed to perceiving it and to see the ways our perception is constructed through linguistic codes, cultural signs and embedded power" (p. 109). Kincheloe provided an example of a teacher who would "explore the meaning of intelligence" and redefine the construct based on her experience. "The teacher would [consider] the concept as . . .she began to examine students who were labeled unintelligent but upon a second look exhibited characteristics that in an unconventional way seemed sophisticated. . .The old definition of intelligence would have to be negated through exposure to diverse expressions of intelligence" (p. 188). Such a stance is crucially important in rethinking what has been taken as "common-sense" around such organizing binaries as dull/smart and incompetent/competent.

Brantlinger (2004) explained that in her classes, she works with students to get them to challenge the notion of "average" and to see the consequences of the hunt for that idealized child within the education industry. She wrote, "I tell my students to add 'for what?' or 'for whom?' to any generalized claims of 'it works.'" (p. 492).

A critical consciousness allows one to view students in context and carefully observe prior to determining what lesson or skill or technique must be taught next. Such a perspective presumes that children will be treated holistically, rather than reductively (Gallagher, 2004), and that the individual is willing and able to be open to changing her mind.

Freire (1993) wrote, "It is not easy to participate in a permanent struggle against preconceived notions that are ingrained in our bodies, expecting our body to move in accordance to these preconceptions...Hence, I am convinced that one of the most important central tasks in the preparation of teachers is to invite them to think critically" (pp. 119–120). A critical consciousness makes it more likely that an individual will be able to consciously shift her identity in relation to new discourses when that becomes necessary.

Educating disabled citizens and allies

Thanks to the Disability Rights Movement, of which disability studies and disability studies in education are outgrowths, alternative discourses on disability have gained political clout and cultural currency. Teachers must be aware of the identity politics and needs for recognition of all students—including, but not limited to, disabled students.

Oliver (1996) wrote: "[T]he education system failed disabled children in that it has neither equipped them to exercise their rights as citizens nor to accept their responsibilities...the special education system has functioned to exclude disabled people not just from the education process but from mainstream social life" (p. 79).

In order to help develop their critical consciousness, it is crucial that teachers and students examine the historical and contemporary struggles between and among various groups within society.

> It is the existence of a discourse of rights that establishes the precondition of a political subject position. Individuals do not automatically occupy positions from which they can make claims on the state, but carving out a political subject position, or locating oneself within a preexisting position, is a basic condition of political agency (Jung, 2003, p. 437).

For disabled students "automatically" adopting a position of entitlement to rights is unlikely, given the systems of exclusion that necessitate their claims. A rights discourse, and the achievements that have resulted from this political movement, must become part of teacher education and K–12 curricula.

Redefining professional knowledge

Disabled people are creating new discourses—political, literary, artistic, humorous and phenomenological. Each of these should inform current understandings of disabled people. Autistic persons have provided a wealth of information to counter the professional construction that such individuals lacked empathy, perspective taking, and "cognition" (Biklen, 1993; Biklen and Cardinal, 1997; Marcus and Shevin, 1997; Rubin, 1998). First-person accounts have documented difficulties with sensory integration and stimulation, as well as with movement, communication, and compulsions (Grandin, 1996; Marcus and Shevin, 1997; Williams; 1994).

Interdisciplinary work on disability provides an alternative to the medicalized, pathological view that has been so prevalent in education. For instance, ethnographic accounts of students with Down syndrome illustrate the competence of these individuals (Kliewer, 1998). Historical accounts of deafness illustrate the ways this construction has shifted over time—and the material consequences that such shifts have engendered (Baynton, 1996).

These texts should be tapped for the various perspectives of disability they offer and for their potential to redefine "common sense" knowledge about disability. In addition, the question of inclusion/exclusion must be examined from interdisciplinary perspectives. The field that created exclusionary practices has thus far been unable to break out of that paradigm. (See Ware, 2001; 2003 for additional interdisciplinary suggestions.)

If it's true that "our struggle is to change the power relations of knowledge-authority, to consider whose voices carry weight and who never gets heard" (Slee, 2000, p. 128), then we have no choice but to introduce counter-hegemonic discourses that disrupt the reproduction of disabled cultural myths (Rice, 2001). Teacher education must be the site for challenging and resisting the negative effects of discursive and material practices where disabled students are concerned.

Two decades ago, Bogdan and Kugelmass (in Barton and Tomlinson, 1984, pp. 173–191) wrote:

> The way we think about people with alleged disabilities is filled with moral meaning. . .Disability has symbolic meaning that must be looked at in terms of what society honours—intelligence, confidence, beauty and success. Our society has traditionally been structured to bring shame to people with alleged disability. Some problems are technical—providing physical access to wheelchairs, building communication systems for non-verbal people—other problems are moral and social. They are located much deeper in the seams of our society than professionals in the field of special education touch.

Disability studies in education is beginning to locate and unravel those seams.

References

Allan, J. (1999). *Actively seeking inclusion: Pupils with special needs in mainstream schools.* Philadelphia: Falmer Press.

Baynton, D. (1996). *Forbidden signs: American culture and the campaign against sign language.* Chicago: University of Chicago Press.

Beattie, M. and Conle, C. (1996). Teacher narrative, fragile stories and change. *Asia-Pacific Journal of Teacher Education, 24*(3), 309–327.

Biklen, D. (1993). *Communication unbound.* New York: Teachers College Press.

Biklen, D. and Cardinal, D. (Eds.) (1997). *Contested words, contested science.* New York: Teachers College Press.

Bogdan, R. and Kugelmass, J. (1984). Case studies of mainstreaming: A symbolic interactionist approach to special schooling. In L. Barton and S. Tomlinson (Eds.) *Special education and social interests* (pp. 173–191). New York: Nichols.

Brantlinger, E. (1997). Using ideology: Cases of nonrecognition of the politics of research and practice in special education. *Review of Educational Research, 97*(4), 425–460.

———. (2004). Confounding the needs and confronting the norms: An extension of Reid and Valle's essay. *Journal of Learning Disabilities, 37*(6), 490–499.

Britzman, D. (1993). *Practice makes practice: A critical study of learning to teach.* Albany: State University of New York.

Clough, P. (1999). Exclusive tendencies: Concepts, consciousness and curriculum in the project of inclusion. *International Journal of Inclusive Education, 3*(1), 63–73.

Clough, P. and Corbett, J. (2000). *Theories of inclusive education: A student's guide.* Thousand Oaks: Sage Publications.

Convery, A. (1999). Listening to teachers' stories: Are we sitting too comfortably? *International Journal of Qualitative Studies in Education, 12*(2), 131–147.

Danforth, S. and Navarro, V. (1998). Speech acts: Sampling the social construction of mental retardation in everyday life. *Mental Retardation, 36*(1), 31–43.

Ervelles, N. (2000). Educating unruly bodies: Critical pedagogy, disability studies and the politics of schooling. *Educational Theory, 50*(1), 25–48.

Foucault, M. (1972). *The archaeology of knowledge & the discourse on language.* New York: Pantheon.

———. (1977/1995). *Discipline and punish: The birth of the prison.* New York: Vintage Books.

———. (1980). *The history of sexuality. Volume 1.* New York: Vintage Books.

———. (1978/1990) *Power/knowledge: Selected interviews and other writings, 1972–1977.* New York: Vintage Books.

———. (1984). *Truth and power.* In P. Rabinow (Ed.) *The Foucault reader.* (pp. 51–75) New York: Pantheon Books.

————. (1988). *Madness and civilization: A history of insanity in the age of reason.* New York: Vintage Books.

————. (1994). *The birth of the clinic: An archaeology of medical perception.* New York: Vintage Books.

Freire, P. (1993). *Pedagogy of the city.* New York: Continuum.

Gallagher, D. (2004). Entering the conversation: The debate behind the debates in special education. In Gallagher, D., Heshusius, L., Iano, R., & Skrtic, T. *Challenging orthodoxy in special education: Dissenting voices.* (pp. 3–26) Denver: Love Publishing.

Grandin, T. (1996). *Thinking in pictures.* New York: Vintage Books.

Heshusius, L. (2004). The Newtonian mechanistic paradigm, special education, and contours of alternatives: An overview. In. S. Danforth & S. Taft (Eds.) *Crucial readings in special education.* Upper Saddle River, NJ: Pearson.

Hytten, K. and Adkins, A. (2002). Thinking through a pedagogy of whiteness. *Educational Theory, (51)*4, 433–450.

Jung, C. (2003). The politics of indigenous identity: Neoliberalism, cultural rights, and the Mexican Zapatistas. *Social Research, 70,*(2), 433–462.

Kincheloe, J. L. (1993). *Toward a critical politics of teacher thinking.* Westport, CT: Bergin & Garvey.

Kincheloe, J. and Steinberg, R. (1998). Addressing the crisis of whiteness: Reconfiguring white identity in a pedagogy of whiteness. In J. Kincheloe, S. Steinberg, N. Rodriguez & R. Chennault (Eds). *White reign: Deploying whiteness in America.* New York: St. Martin's Press.

King, J. E. (1991). Dysconscious racism: Ideology, identity, and the miseducation of teachers. *Journal of Negro Education, 60*(2), 133–146.

Kliewer, C. (1998). *Schooling children with Down syndrome.* New York: Teachers College Press.

Lakoff, G. (2002). *Moral politics.* Chicago: University of Chicago Press.

Marcus, E. and Shevin, M. (1997). Sorting it out under fire: Our journey. In D. Biklen and D. Cardinal (Eds.) *Contested words, contested science.* (pp. 115—134) New York: Teachers College Press.

Mitchell, D. & Snyder, S. (2000). *Narrative prosthesis: Disability and the dependencies of discourse.* Ann Arbor: The University of Michigan Press.

Oliver, M. (1996). *Understanding disability: From theory to practice.* London: Macmillan.

Porter, J. I. (1997). Foreword, in D. Mitchell & S. Snyder (Eds.) *The Body and physical difference*. Ann Arbor: University of Michigan Press (pp. xiii–xiv).

Rabinow, P. (1984). *Introduction*. In P. Rabinow (Ed). *The Foucault reader*. (pp. 3–29) New York: Pantheon.

Reid, D. K. and Valle, J. (2004). The discursive practice of learning disability: Implications for instruction and parent-school relations. *Journal of Learning Disabilities, 37, 6,* 466–481.

Rice, N. (2001). *A "textbook" case of professional prerogative: Authority, disability and policy in introductory special education textbooks*. Unpublished doctoral dissertation, Syracuse University.

Rubin, S. (1998). Castigating assumptions about mental retardation and low functioning autism. *Facilitated Communication Digest*. http://soeweb.syr.edu/thefci/7-1rub.htm. Retrieved December 15, 2004.

Slee, R. (1999). Special education and human rights in Australia: How do we know about disablement, and what does it mean for educators? In F. Armstrong and L. Barton (Eds.) *Disability, human rights and education*. Milton Keynes: Open University Press.

————. (2000). *Reflection*. In P. Clough & J. Corbett (Eds.) *Theories of inclusive education: A student's guide*. (pp. 125–128). Thousand Oaks: Sage Publications.

————. (2001). Social justice and the changing directions in educational research: The case of inclusive education. *International Journal of Inclusive Education,* 5(2/3), 167–177.

————. (2004). Meaning in the service of power. In L. Ware (Ed.) *Ideology and the politics of (in)exclusion*. (pp. 46–60). New York: Peter Lang.

Ware, L. (2001). Writing, identity, and the other: Dare we do disability studies? *Journal of Teacher Education, 52, 2,* 107–123.

————. (2003). Working past pity: What we make of disability in schools. In J. Allen (Ed.) *Inclusion, participation and democracy: What is the purpose?* (pp. 117–137) Boston: Kluwer Academic Publishers.

————. (Ed.) (2004). *Ideology and the politics of (in)exclusion*. New York: Peter Lang.

Williams, D. (1994). *Somebody somewhere*. New York: Times Books.

Young, I. M. (2000). *Democracy and inclusion*. Oxford: Oxford University Press.

Zembylas, M. (2003). Interrogating "teacher identity": Emotion, resistance, and self-formation. *Educational Theory, 53, 1,* 107–127.

CHAPTER 2

Split------ting the ROCK of {speci [ES]al} e.ducat.ion: FLOWers of lang[ue]age in >DIS<ability studies

Phil Smith

"…the flowers of rhetoric have real power to change reality, to penetrate it through and through, to 'split rocks'." (Franke, 2000, p. 143)

i. into int(r)o[ducat]ion scion science
this is
dis is
this is a test
this is a text
      about being a text
      about being a test
      about this is
      dis is
      dis is ab[il]ity
            [ill] city   a po-em
                      a po-me
                      a pomme   filled word   tree
                                                dee
de   scribe   ing
in   scribe   ing

b(in)g
(b)e(ing)
bing   cherries ways   in w{h}I{t}   ch
                                                                           ch
┌─────────────────────────┐   ch
│ WARN   ING   │
│ WARN   ING   │ this new   th(ing)
│ [will robinson]:   │ this new disability studies   {thin}g
│ "the fallacy of   │ this new   thin{g}
│ ideational mimesis is   │   thinKING
│ that it treats ideas like│   new   study(ing
│ objects that can be   │   disability   thing
│ 'caught and held'…"   │ this new   b(rave)   thing
│ (Bernstein, 1987, p.   │   no   thing:
│ 127)   │
└─────────────────────────┘

                              what is it
                              what it is
                              how it is
                              what it can tell (talk to me now)
┌──┐   educators
│ e   **DUCAT**   ion   │ and education
│ e   money coinage filthy euchre ion   │ and educatees
│   scion   │   tease
│   science   │
└──┘

        teasing out the meaning of
        language re[present]ation
        of   another narrative
                another text
                another WORD G{u}arden
                (FLOWers)
                (WOLF)
              (talk to me now)
I am a person with a (hidden, elliptical) disability. I
                              hide it well
                    under my hide
                    under my skirts

of this otherwise **NORMATE** (bawdy) body.
My life and
existence is
l   abeled because of that
<in> some (con)texts with<in> the world I live <in> the
dis   abled

m
a
r
g
<in>
a
l
i
a

off the narrated page
of cultural texts.

So, too, does my daughter.
But for her
              her body is   marked
                                 mark[et]ed
by self-imposed   wounds
                                 gaping holes
                                 tiger stripes   to   get the red   out
                                                                get the pain   out
                                                                get the lead   out
                                                                get the world   <in>
                                                                     the word   <in>
reflecting her difference
on the mirror of her body
stigmata
{stigma}   ta
                ta ta
                bye-bye
                gotta go to the----------------------------------- edge here
                made by   this   edge here
                               this   razor ear
                                          cut it off
                                          cut it out   about

(the) scream

this is a text about being a text about describing ways in which about new disability studies thinking about can tease out about the language and representation about disability in education about what it is about how it is about you would have been instructed where about

to turn

to turn

to turn

talk to me now.

ii. notes on form. {but not ulaic} to be read in an order that is not pre(pro)scribed.

"Style and form are as ideological as content and interpretation" (Bernstein, 1987, p. 127). This is a kind of rule. The form is ideological so it must be opened up. This is a writing about writing. This writing is about writing and it is a form. We call it a form. Should we say something now about form? So I will. Is there an echo? Hello? Is someone there? Talk .	I have used this form before. In writing on the page I did it (Smith, 2001a) and in another writing on a page I did it (Smith, 2001b) but only a little. Talk to me now. Now? The talking we do is through words and we write them down. Write them down on the page. This page. Perhaps we should say something now about form. So I will. Is there an echo? Hello? Is someone there? To me.	We know one thing. Words do not mean things but they mean other words only other words and that is all. Other words and sentences sometimes. We have known it and I have said it before. We have said it before and it is a very good saying of it, to others, to be read by them, in words. It would be good to say something about form. So I will. Is there an echo? Hello? Is someone there? Now.

Like a can. Of worms. This is a disabilities studies text a new kind of a text.

All of the words that we say and we say them very much are another thing which is that they are all ideological. This is another thing that I have said before too (Smith, 1999a; Smith, 1999b). And I said it before in another way too (Smith, 2004).

Talk to me now.

Talk to me now.

Talk to me now.

Words change what we look at and describe, becoming the language itself, becoming the meaning we give it.

And in speaking I did it (Smith, 2000). I will talk about it here. About doing it. Here is where I will talk about it and I will.

This way of putting words together "…draws attention both to the non-representational capacities of language as material, and to the political power inherent in new writing… by reinventing syntax, opposing and questioning grammar… we open language and thereby society to new organizational alternatives… [It can be] transgressive: it succeeds in dismantling and rewiring the social and corporal body…" (Doris, 2001, Paragraph 2-3).

Others have said it before as I have said too (Smith, 1999a). This thing has a word it is incommensurability. And the word means that words do not mean things but only other words and sentences sometimes.

And here is a thing that another man said, he said: "Language is the first technology, the extension of the body outward toward an articulation, a *forging*, of the world, which is immediately transformed by this act, hence a *forgery*" Bernstein, 1987, p. 125).

"…we can think of the body as an ideological effect of language" (McLaren & Leonardo, 1998, p. 136)

Whatever we say changes what we say about the thing we say: "that basic truth became the Heisenberg uncertainty principle: that whatever you studied you also changed" (Crichton, 1995, p. 249).

Now here is a thing that should be said and so I will say it. In special education we number bodies (Stone, 1997) and that is an ideological effect of language. Words are always ideological (Davis, 2002). Bodies and minds that have disabilities are ideological and we make them ideological by our words. This language is a making of the world as we see it.

To make "…the modern nation-state not simply language but bodies and bodily practices also had to be standardized, homogenized, and normalized" (Davis, 2002, p. 106). And what is lost in this word practice, in this world practice, "…is the irregular, the nonquantifiable, the nonstandard or nonstandardizable, the erratic…" (Bernstein, 1993, p. 605), which is exactly and precisely what we call disability.

I will make words in a new way so that the new words will not number bodies. This way of making words will be a way of making words that talks about words and their making and what the making of them makes.

This writing that I am doing here is a writing about writing kind of doing. It is a writing about writing kind of doing which is a good kind of writing doing. It is a kind of writing doing that changes the kind of writing doing that some writers do. Other writers do not. I think it is important to do the kind of writing doing that I have been writing about doing, in order to show and to see what that kind of writing doing might be doing. This kind of writing doing is a kind of doing, it is not a done thing, it is a doing. So it is a kind of writing doing that you do, but it is not a kind of writing doing that is a done thing. It is only doing, only just doing, never done.

Words "…construct the objects which then come to populate our world" (Madill, Jordon, & Shirley, 2000, p. 12) The words of special education make the bodies that are numbered they make them and if the making of them is a thing which is not good then we need to change the way the words are which would be a good thing and so I will do it here.

A man and a woman said this and it is a very important saying, that "language is constitutive of social practices" (Wilson & Lewiecki-Wilson, 2001, p. 3).

These words will "…tap into the power of etymology. Etymological insight… involves an understanding of the origins of the construction of social, cultural, psychological, political, economic, and educational artifacts and the ways they shape our subjectivities" (Kincheloe, 2001, p. 687).

Another thing to say about this way of writing is that it is parataxic. You should look it up in a dictionary it is a good word. I'll wait while you look it up. There you're back. It is a good word and a good thing.

This new way of writing must be it certainly must be simply and irrevocably this: an "…ironic and blasphemous (re) writing of the disabled body in order to (re) invent alternative emancipatory subjectivities" (Erevelles, 2001, p. 93).

Talk to me now.

And it is ludic too this writing is which is a good thing and is another word that you should look up in a dictionary it is a good kind of word and I'll wait while you look it up. There you're back again so soon.

The awful thing that must be said is that "…nearly everything that's been written or said is wrong" (Crichton, 1995, p. 232).

This thing is a form that some will call Language Poetry and some will call Concrete Poetry and some will call it other things, but the important thing is that we can write about education and disability and special education in a new way so that we do not write about it in an old way, a way that another man has said and he called it a word he would like to "call it a *necroidiocracy*, ideas stiffened by rigor mortis wounding flesh with their rigidity and their techno-rationality…" (Bernstein, 1987, p. 124-125).

Talk to me now.

Talk to me now.

"Parataxis is crucial: the internal, autonomous meaning of a new sentence is heightened, questioned, and changed by the degree of separation or connection that the reader perceives with regard to the surrounding sentences" (Perelman, 1993, p. 313). And most of what they will mean will be a metaphor which is a thing that I will talk about later.

Talk to me now.

Talk to me now.

Talk to me now.

Talk to me now.

Talk to me now.

Talk to me now.

This writing is a bricolage, and what disability studies can bring to education is to "…study the workings of a particular discipline… such a disciplinary study would be conducted more like a Foucauldian genealogy where scholars would study the social construction of the discipline's knowledge bases, epistemologies, and knowledge production methodologies… In this genealogical context they would explore the discipline as a discursive system of regulatory power with its propensity to impound knowledge within arbitrary and exclusive boundaries" (Kincheloe, 2001, p. 683-684).

iii. pounding on a rock. (The Bobs, 1988)

pound on dis here

dis ability rock

and role

and roll

and control and control and control

dis rock abilly

hill   billy

ill   bil(ity)

dis rock please

dis please

dis ease

dis able tease

dis able tease stud

dis able tease stud ease

can de(in)scribe w{rough}t IRON[-ic] metaphor (mat)

be   **it**   **re**   **us**

   cause   **can**   **mind**   **of**

"…the referentiality of acts of language to anything but other acts of language… [It] supposes that a hermeneutics of suspicion (resisting readers) and deconstruction (texts betraying their ostensible aims) will expose… [education's] complicity in supporting and advancing middle-class ideologies of power… a hermeneutics which exposes capitalist, colonialist, racist, and sexist ideologies will help democratize a world presently closed to many marginalized groups" (Gregory, 1998, p.35-36).

he forgot to say ableist they always do

hoo ya

the   profundity

        jocularity

        homogeneity

        irony   of meta-ph(l)or (mat)

                      the irony of metal floor mats

                      is dat (a)

                                "metaphors guide our thinking and

seeing, and they pervade how we
understand the world" (Hsusu,
2001, p. 175).

    oh, and uhmm

"metaphors frame and structure meaning..." (Becker, 1994, p. 384)
which is ok, no think wrong or right, whether i'm wrong or right, whether
i'm wrong nothing wrong ring rang rung wrong with metaphors in and of
themselves (heck, Mell, I better not be sayin that there were, lawsa me no,
bein a poet and all, metaphors er my stock and trade, as it were, dontcha
know, so to speak) (easy) (heck, Mell, "it has become possible to view all
language as being metaphorical..." (Franke, 2000, p. 138) is what I'm tryin
to say here)
but (h)Our   thin (king)
not the queen but the king
down by the old....
is forced to ride in the slow lane uv

                    textual
                    processual
                    sexual
              {tr}aff®ic **{A}**
required by the metaph(l)or (mat) police of so-called
common(bourgeois)-sense, trans[parent] texts (Lather, 1996). Count(1234)er
t(w)o this is (must) be **THE** work of dis able tease stud tease,

              "exerting some control over metaphorical representation in
              language, theory, politics, and artistic practice..." (Sandahl,
              1999, p. 13),

(re)COGnizing {t}hat

              "metaphors are not innocuous artistic flourishes... but
              powerful discursive structures that can misrepresent, define,
              and confine people with disabilities" (Sandahl, 1999, p. 14).

all texts – all special texts – all species (of) all – all species awful offal
all special education texts hide behind

                    trans [parent]
                    common
                    comMAN

                               sense

                               cents

                               $ and cents

                    lan(guage)

                    gauging the size of it all

                    measuring it out

                    speci(es)al rulers and tools

                    ruling us, ruling (THEM)

disguising itself in a new   ALL HALLOWS EVE   costume

                        ALL GALLOWS EVE

      (heh, me and Freddie Kruger)

      (never even saw the movie, just heard about it)

                    "…the literal itself must be apprehended as metaphorical in its basic constitution. This ironic predicament is, in fact, written into the very term literal, itself based on the metaphor of the written character, the letter, being used to stand for a certain kind of meaning. The letter is itself nothing but a figure, a concrete image, for this kind of literal meaning that is purportedly devoid of figurativeness. And when presumably unrhetorical, fact-stating discourse itself is shown to be never given without presupposing a prior process, an originating movement, of transfer of meaning that is, in the deepest sense, metaphorical, then metaphor has become universal in scope…" (Franke, 2000, p. 140).

it's **all** metaph(l)or (mat) then

                the literal

                the limitable

           becoming, through poetic deconstruction

         (tearing it down with a wordy rotten wrecking crane)

                (talk to me now)

                a process of semiotic unparceling

semiosis
halitosis

BECOMING
the liminal
the illuminatable
the illimitable

and in   addition
         subtraction
         multiplication
         division

"Because words are part of language and
language is a communal practice, there can
be no use of language that transcends the
sociability and biases of any linguistic
community… they are therefore ideological
by definition." (Davis, 2002, p. 120).

ideo-logical = idiot logic
words log[strawberry]

jammed
jellied
jelly roll (rock and morton) into reified
                                  commodified
                                  latinate
super**{MAN}** struc   tures
                       struck   chores

filching the   homogenized
               homophobic
               enqueered
               enfreaked   bawdy
                                          badly
                                          bloody
                                          bodies and   mined
                              (moth)er {father} lode
                                                      minds
                              of the counter-normate subaltern.
                              (PHEW) SAY THAT 10 TIMES FAST

Instead, medicalized ventriloquizing "…discourses normalize modes of intelligibility and construct particular regimes of truth as legitimate" (McLaren, Leonardo, & Allen, 1999, p. 140).

In the w[h]or[le]d wor{l}d of e{ducat}ion
In the w[h]or[le]d wor{l}d of dis able tease
In the whored wired weird world
In the horrid word world of species all Ed ducat science ions

"…it is the social meaning of words that have power" (Russell, 1998, p. 16).

it is in the   **LANGUE**

tongue
lingo
patois
jargon

Ford Chrysler Chevy Toyota	Fido Rover Spot Buddy

languishing mouth bodies
the slung word (car)   (pet)
that's where the power is, jack, know what I'm sayin'?

power jack
car jack
jack knife
what we need to do is to   knife through
                           knife through the water
                                    swimming laps in the Olympic size pool of ableism
cut it all out!
Van Gogh's ear!
my daughter's skin!
Tom Dick and Harry!
The Hardy Boys! Nancy Drew! Frank Sinatra! (who?)
              knife through
                   these disability transparent commonsense bourgeois liberal
metaphor   sets
knife   sets
deconstruct and explicate the socio-cultural metaphors of modernist Western

shoot 'em up   Clint Eastwood
                 John Wayne
                 Henry Fonda
                 Henry Ford
                           disability.
(every time i go back to find something i have to stop and put something in
me and jack kerouac's crazy limber limbo dead body interrupting myself
with these birdwalks hey hey
talk to me now)
see the thing of it is we **ALL**
every golldang un a us
                 "…adopt or be adopted by perspectives which then guide
                 and limit… [our] view of the social world… metaphors
                 constitute rather than exemplify these perspectives.
                 Metaphor is not so much a word or a sentence as a
                 conceptual system or model" (Manning, 1991, p. 72).
and the   problemo
the   proBLEM{ISH}
with these metaph(l)ors these floor mats these florid images these forms
these mor(ph)s
and I ain't sayin here that metaphors are all bad, shoot no
we can't help it
honest officer, i just couldn't help myself, i just had to steal that bus
no, see, the problem that we got here dontcha know
is that there is a
d**ANGER** will robinson crusoe swiss family
d**ANGER** in the   "…mistaken conflation of words and identities…
                 The risk is that metaphor may be transformed from
                 an insightful resemblance into an all-embracing
                 world view" (Manning, 1991, p. 72).
yessir, that's it right there, dagnabit.
OK.
So.
I'll let ol' Norm say it: "Humans are always already tangled
                 up in a second-hand world of
                 meanings, and have no direct access

to reality. Reality as it is known is
lodged in narrative texts which
mediate the real" (Denzin, 1996, p.
236).
Got that?
Hey – you there –
talk to me now.

Well, ok, but then: "...discourses normalize modes of
intelligibility and construct particular
regimes of truth as legitimate" (McLaren,
Leonardo, & Allen, 1999, p. 140).

Which, as we all know, "...denies subjects their right to name the world"
(McLaren, Leonardo, & Allen, 1999, p. 140).
Well that's it right there in a nutshell.   disability
                                              dishabille stud (ebaker)
                                              disability
(I'm trying to get it out now, honest, its like some
goddam burroughsian lip-surge it won't stop)
                                              stud tease
                                              a palpitative moose base
                                              disability studies – that's it! –
                                              DISA BILK – bilking them all
                                              of   their words
                                                     their worlds
                                                     their whirled weird whored
          disability

                                              studies brings to this species of
          special
          education
it's all about the money, you know, the ducats –

                                              the opportunity for people with
                                              disabilities to take
          (no rant, thanks Utah)

                                              control of the metaphoric
                                              meta-flouric
                                              re-presentation

done over again performance
of their

too much already mined

minds and bodies, and in so doing,
to take control of their world.

These metal floor mats, these   symphonic

sympathetic

symbols   of dishabille tease

"…are inescapably inflected and entrained by the flows and circuits of capital. Slingshot into a fluctuating universe of meaning, symbols and metaphors partake of a unique semiotics that is utterly dependent upon intersecting moments of time, space, and place. We are constituted by these symbols that we are given in order to 'perform' the narratives of our lives, often in contexts not of our choosing…" (McLaren, 1999, p. xxxix).

iv. Another little note on form(ation): looting the ludic

Patti Lather   wrote

rote

root (roto)   tiller

rotilla the hun

away goes trouble down the

a great little piece back pretty near a decade ago,

talking and ranting (thanks Utah)
about her work and her rigged

rattan

writing. Given (taken) what I've just   talked about

walk(ed) about

in terms of   metaphor

meta-fluoride

toothpaste

                                          meta fluoric acid
about correspondence (strange letters sent from far away) theories of truth,
WHODUNIT   about language
GAUGING THE SIZE OF power, what she has to say makes a lot of
(DOLLARS AND) sense to me:

> "To speak so as to be understood immediately is to speak through
> the production of the transparent signifier, that which maps easily
> onto taken-for-granted regimes of meaning. This runs a risk that
> endorses, legitimates, and reinforces the very structure of symbolic
> value that must be overthrown" (1996, p. 528).

Well, duh.
instead
bedstead
she argues for   "…other practices of representation that decenter
                          traditional realistic narrative forms" (p. 527).
She calls for a way of   making texts
                          taking mex
                 that   "makes space for returns, silence,
                          interruptions, self-criticism, and
                          points to its own incapacity. Such a
                          practice ignites in writing and
                          reading what is beyond the word
                          and rationally accessible, gesturing
                          toward a textual practice that works
                          at multiple levels in sounding out an
                          audience with ears to hear" (p. 532).
She asserts (two mints in one) the importance of
                          "producing the unconscious as the
                          work of the text, working the ruins
                          of a confident social science as the
                          very ground from which new
                          practices of …representation might
                          take shape" (p. 539),
and the need   "…to construct risky practices of
                          textual innovation in order to

> perform the very tensions that this
> essay has addressed: to be of use in
> a time when the old stories will not
> do" (p. 541).

My work as a bricoleur is to work these ruins – to take some of the textual
practices I know from so called L=A=N=G=U=A=G=E and Concrete poetic
forms, understanding some of the political and cultural under/overtones
ensconced therein, and apply those tools fertile crescent wrench

> screwing the driver
> hammer   (pounding on a)

. to the growing body (literally) of work   lift that bale, tote that barge
in a humanities approach to disability studies – and using the vehicle
of disability studies, so constructed, as a way to explore education,
special or otherwise.

In doing so, I hear some critical theorist's saying: but its all just word play,
it's all   ludicity
(clearly **NOT**   lucidity, heh). And that a critical theory approach is
incommensurable with that (this) kind of ludicity.
To which I have

2

responses. First, as Ralph Waldo Emerson said,

> "A foolish
> consistency is
> the hobgoblin
> of little
> minds…"

My work, as any good bricoleur, is to
loot the ludic!
(thanks, Julia, for mishearing that word). By looting the ludic, I mean finding
what is useful in ludicity that can be productively used in creating
emancipatory rather than oppressive possibilities, and stealing it, using it for
those ends.

This writing is   hypercatalectic
                         metonymic
                         paranomatic
                         anacoluthonic

palinodic
gruic
syzygic
periphrastic
pleonasmic
echoistic
paraliptic
aposiopetic
macaronic
elliptic
caesuraic
neologistic
epizenxic
occupatiotic
asyndetonic

v. "…bodies of knowledge and knowledge of bodies." Lather, 1996, p. 541)
Species offal Ed ducat science
(special education)
is all rapped up in eu**(YOU)**genics, which we've known for a long time
now (Kliewer & Drake, 1998). It is a process   of body numbering,
of revulsion,
of disgust,
of regularity,
of the **CREATION**
of **DEVIATION**
(Davis, 1995; Sibley, 1995;
Thomson, 1996; 1997).

Where'd it all come from?   **INDUSTRIAL**   ization
MODERN   ization
MECHAN   ization
STANDARD   ization
PROFESSIONAL   ization
SECULAR   ization
(Thomson, 1996, p. 11).
and its all tied together with {numb}ers, violating
violenting

numbing integers.
Just as the eu**(YOU)**genists did (and still do), special education creates

species of difference –

a taxonomy
a tax on me
through testing processes that assign numeric values to human beings:
"In reducing learning to a test score,
policymakers seek to make the
knowledge of disparate individuals
commensurable…once knowledge is
reified in this way, it can be
manipulated and described in the
same fashion that one is accustomed
to manipulating and describing
products (commodities) of all
kinds… as complex human and
social processes are more and more
flattened into crude representations
that will conform to the logic of
commodity production and
exchange" (De Lissovoy & McLaren,
2003, p. 133).
Yeah, it's all about "…a quantification of the human body…" (Davis, 1995,
p. 11-12), a construct of "political arithmetic" (Porter, 1986, in Davis, 1995,
p. 26).
                        …a quantification of the human mind…
                        …a quantification of the human soul…
Knowledge becomes a commodity, a   thing to be
                                        bought and sold
                                        and bodies
(especially bodies of those who are   women
                                        working class

people of color
queer)

are   made different
differentiated

ENQUEERED

through the work of special educators:

"Schooling… is… a site of surveillance and the marking and reproduction of power, where working class bodies are located as inferior, quarantined within designated spaces of formal identity, dissected by the white gaze of power, masticated by the jaws of capital, made receptive to the command metaphors of formal citizenship, and transformed into semiotic battlegrounds…" (McLaren, 1999, p. xxxiii).

Some fun, huh?

Put plainly, "…the concept of disability is a function of a concept of normalcy" (Davis, 1995, p. 2). That which is   not   normal

must be ab   normal

must be   other.

And

"…the cultural other and the cultural self operate together as opposing twin figures that legitimate a system of social, economic, and political empowerment justified by physiological differences… Normate, then, is the constructed identity of those who, by way of the bodily configurations and cultural capital they assume, can step into a position of authority and wield the power it grants them" (Thomson, 1997, p. 8).

All of this happens through a process

of forgetting: "What is not worth remembering is often constructed as 'normal'" (Norquay, 1999, p. 3).

Forgetting's a funny thing: it   "…produces a form of ignorance… forgetting is the effect of an active process… forgettings work to make the boundaries and demarcations of the dominant culture invisible…" (Norquay, 1999, p. 1-2).

The question for disability studies is,

"who does 'normal' serve?"

(Russell, 1998, p. 19).

it ain't me babe, no no no

it ain't the deviations, the   (h)extremes   (Davis, 1995)

Supremes

phonemes

bulimes

Davis, he say   "…THE VERY TERM THAT PERMEATES OUR CONTEMPORARY LIFE – THE NORMAL – IS A CONFIGURATION THAT ARISES IN A PARTICULAR MOMENT. IT IS A PART OF A NOTION OF PROGRESS, OF INDUSTRIALIZATION, AND OF IDEOLOGICAL CONSOLIDATION OF THE POWER OF THE BOURGEOISE" (1995, p. 49).

And the (so-called, only temporarily and forgotten) able-bodied, looking (because "disability is a specular moment" (Davis, 1995, p. 12)) at the (so-called, permanently and always re-membered) dis-abled freak, sees

"…a hypervisible text against which the viewer's indistinguishable body fades into a seemingly neutral, tractable, and invulnerable instrument of the autonomous will, suitable to the uniform abstract citizenry democracy institutes" (Thomson, 1996, p. 11).

It's hypervisible, oh yeah

that text

those bodies

these minds.

"The act of seeing is a de facto act of violence" (McLaren, Leonardo, & Allen, 1999, p. 143).

a dismembering	violence
a dis(re)membering	violence
a forgetting	violence
a forgotten	violence

vio(la)(ess)ence
dis-membering as an act of {re}moving member-ship (mother-ship) from a community of those who would otherwise be, but never quite are, peers.

You getting' a FEEL for   who normal serves?

the maid and butler

waiting on them

subservient

SUB servant

You getting' a FEEL for   the fact that I am, with others,
"…deeply disillusioned with Western liberal
political philosophy and processes, deeming liberalism to have
corrupted itself in the pursuit of a status quo favoring middle-class
power groups. Liberalism has, furthermore, constructed an array of
ideologies to disguise social oppression and to preserve the status
quo…" (Gregory, 1998, p. 35).

What we haven't figgered out is that   DISABILITY is the rule

the norm

the mean

the median

the average

the common

All of us will spend time during our lives living with what we call disability:
"…difference is what all of us have in common" (Davis, 2002, p. 26).

We of the bourgeoisie (we have met the enemy and they is us) –

we have been   captivated

arrested

enthralled

grabbed

enamored
bewitched
enslaved
seized
ensnared

by this **STOOPID** Western
modernist positivist ventriloquizing
masquerading disguising enfleshing
"...scientific view, which depends upon the fantasy
of objectivity and sees regularity rather than
exceptionality as founding epistemology..."
(Thomson, 1996, p. 3).

Who does normal serve?   SPECIal education.
                                SPECIal educators.

Individual and SPECIfic SPECial educators
(we can't get off the hook)
as cultural representatives of liberalist ideology, unintentionally
(sorry dear, i forgot)
"...develop complex categories and
subcategories of the other, which
carry the wonderful modernist
hope... of combining the objectivity
of science with an evaluation of
ourselves as paragons of normality,
health and progress. Objective
categorization thus simultaneously
confirms the superiority of the
expert over that which is classified
away – and indeed authenticates the
identity of expert in and through
classification" (Valentine, 1998,
3.2).

vi. what to do.
1. We need new tongues – new langues of dis-ability, new speakings about
normal, new kinds of texts that can REpresent "...thinking the multiple

(im)possibilities for thought outside taken-for-granted structures of intelligibility" (Lather, 1996, p. 540). This text I am writing here is not the right best example, only merely one among many possibilities:

a new word (dis)order.

2. In addition to new ways of rePRESENTNG, we need a different kind of ideology (we won't escape that it will be ideological): "Disability studies demands a shift from the ideology of normalcy, from the rule and hegemony of normates, to a vision of the body [and mind] as changeable, unperfectable, unruly, and untidy" (Davis, 2002, p. 39). This kind of thinking will be

a thinking of difference
a thinking of freaks
a thinking of   impermanence
              margination
              promiscuity
              unkemptedness
              disorder
              anomalousness
              exceptionality
              peculiarity
              unaccustomable

3. We will need a new kind of research   (in education)
                                              (in special education)
                                              (in social sciences)
that allows for and encourages a kind of inquiry that arises from DISCiplines
                                                                    DISCourses
outside of those we're used to seeing in those lands:

research that is irregular
research that is nonlinear
research that is artistic
research that is irrational

This kind of research will be counter to typical academic exploration, where "…thought tends to be rationalized – subject to examination, paraphrase, repetition, mechanization, reduction. It is treated: contained and stabilized" (Bernstein, 1993, p. 605).
It will be counter to that; it will be   destabilizing

uncontained

untreated

Such a research will not explore traditional avenues – instead, it will look down little alleys, hidden side streets, dirty passageways, those spaces filled with crumpled newspaper, discarded boxes, bits of crumpled metal, a torn magazine cover – places overlooked and looked over and ignored by normate inquiry. It will be a research that acknowledges that the humanities and the arts has much to offer, both in form and function.

It will be a virulent research.

It will be a pissed off research (thanks, Linda).

4. And it all will be done - these researches, these languages, these ideologies – by those whose voices and signs and silences and lives have not been heard or seen or attended to by the normative educational institutions in our culture – institutions that destroy not just the lives of people with disabilities, but the lives of all of us.

References

Becker, G. (1994). Metaphors in disrupted lives: Infertility and cultural constructions of continuity. *Medical Anthropological Quarterly, 8*, 383–410.

Bernstein, C. (1987). Living tissue/Dead ideas. *Social Text, 16*, 124–135.

————. (1993). What's art got to do with it? The status of the subject of the humanities in the age of cultural studies. *American Literary History, 5,* (597–615).

Bobs, The (1988). *Songs for tomorrow morning.* (CD). Kaleidoscope Records.

Crichton, M. (1995). *The lost world.* New York: Alfred A. Knopf.

Davis, L. (1995). *Enforcing normalcy: Disability, deafness, and the body.* New York: Verso.

————. (2002). *Bending over backwards: Disability, dismodernism and other difficult positions.* New York: New York University Press.

De Lissovoy, N. & McLaren, P. (2003). Educational 'accountability' and the violence of capital: A Marxian reading. *Journal of Education Policy, 18* (2), 131–143.

Denzin, N. (1996). The facts and fictions of qualitative inquiry. *Qualitative Inquiry, 2*, 230-241.

Doris, S. (2001). After language poetry. *OEI, 7–8*.

Erevelles, N. (2001). In search of the disabled subject. In J. Wilson & C. Lewieki–Wilson (Eds.) *Embodied rhetorics: Disability in language and culture* (pp. 92–111). Carbondale, IL: Southern Illinois University Press.

Franke, W. (2000). Metaphor and the making of sense: The contemporary metaphor renaissance. *Philosophy and Rhetoric, 33*, 137–153.

Godfrey, N. & Smith, P. (June 2002). A raucous, hybrid blues: Creating an un/nerving un/holy entangled alliance between whiteness studies and disability studies. Second Annual Second City Conference on Disability Studies and Education, Chicago, IL.

Gregory, M. (1998). Fictions, facts, and the fact(s) of(in) fictions. *Modern Language Studies, 28.3, 4*, 3–40.

Hsusu, L. (2001). On metaphors on the position of women in academia and science. *NORA, 9*(3), 172–181.

Kincheloe, J. (2001). Describing the bricolage: Conceptualizing a new rigor in qualitative research. *Qualitative Inquiry, 7*, 679–692.

Kliewer, C. & Drake, S. (1998). Disability, eugenics and the current ideology of segregation: A modern moral tale. *Disability & Society, 13*, 95–111.

Lather, P. (1996). Troubling clarity: The politics of accessible language. *Harvard Educational Review, 66*, 525-45.

Madill, A., Jordan, A., & Shirley, C. (2000). Objectivity and reliability in qualitative analysis: Realist, contextualist, and radical constructionist epistemologies. *British Journal of Psychology, 91*, 1–20.

Manning, P. (1991). Drama as life: The significance of Goffman's changing use of the theatrical metaphor. *Sociological Theory, 9*, 70–86.

McLaren, P. (1999). *Schooling as a ritual performance: Toward a political economy of educational symbols and gestures* (3rd ed.). NY: Rowman & Littlefield Publishers, Inc.

McLaren, P. & Leonardo, Z. (1998). Deconstructing surveillance pedagogy: *Dead Poet's Society. Studies in the Literary Imagination, 31*(1), 127–147.

McLaren, P., Leonardo, Z., & Allen, R. (1999). The gift of si(gh)ted violence: Toward a discursive intervention into the organization of capitalism. *Discourse, 21.2*, p. 139–162.

Norquay, N. (1999). Identity and forgetting. *The Oral History Review, 26*(1), 1–12.

Perelman, B. (1993). Parataxis and narrative: The new sentence in theory and practice. *American Literature, 65*, 313–324.

Porter, T. (1986). *The rise of statistical thinking 1820–1900*. Princeton, NJ: Princeton University Press.

Russell, M. (1998). *Beyond ramps: Disability at the end of the social contract.* Monroe, ME: Common Courage Press.

Sandahl, C. (1999). Ahhhh freak out! Metaphors of disability and femaleness in performance. *Theatre Topics, 9.1*, 11-30.

Sibley, D. (1995). *Geographies of exclusion: Society and difference in the west.* New York: Routledge.

Smith, P. (1999). Ideology, politics, and science in understanding developmental disabilities. *Mental Retardation, 37*, 71–72.

———. (1999). Drawing new maps: A radical cartography of developmental disabilities. *Review of Educational Research, 69* (2), 117–144.

———. (Oct. 2000). MAN.i.f.e.s.t.o.: A Poetics of D(EVIL)op[MENTAL] Dis{ABILITY}. Desegregating Disability Studies: An Interdisciplinary Conference, Syracuse, NY.

———. (2001b). Inquiry cantos: A poetics of developmental disability. *Mental Retardation, 39*, 379–390.

———. (2001a). MAN.i.f.e.s.t.o.: Disrupting Taxonomies of D{evil}op {MENTAL} Dis{ability}. *Taboo: The Journal of Education and Culture, 5* (1), 27–36.

———. (2004). Whiteness, normal theory, and disability studies. *Disability Studies Quarterly, 24* (2).

Stone, D. (1997). *Policy paradox: The art of political decision making.* New York: W. W. Norton and Company.

Thomson, R. G. (1996). Introduction: From wonder to error – A genealogy of freak discourse in modernity. In R.G. Thomson (Ed.) *Freakery: Cultural spectacles of the extraordinary body* (pp. 1–19). New York: New York University Press.

———. (1997). *Extraordinary bodies: Figuring physical disability in American culture and literature.* New York: Columbia University Press.

Valentine, J. (1998). Naming the other: Power, politeness and the inflation of euphemisms. *Sociological Research Online, 3*(4), n.p.

Wilson, J. & Lewieki–Wilson, C. (Eds.) (2001) *Embodied rhetorics: Disability in language and culture.* Carbondale, IL: Southern Illinois University Press.

CHAPTER 3

The Natural Hierarchy Undone: Disability Studies' Contributions to Contemporary Debates in Education

Deborah J. Gallagher

At the core of disability studies lies a potentially subversive idea. Succinctly stated, the idea is that knowledge, and even reality itself, is not discovered but rather is constructed by us human beings. This idea turns on its head the most fundamental assumption about the nature of knowledge and reality of the last three centuries. For many readers, this is not new information per se, especially for those in the disability studies community. That said, I use the phrase *potentially subversive* because, from my perspective, the disability studies community has only begun to make clear just how crucial and powerful this shift in frameworks is in confronting issues of equality, social justice, and so on. In this chapter, my aim is to make apparent the pivotal contribution of disability studies, and most particularly the social model of disability, toward engaging the political debates in education/special education.

To accomplish this, I begin by discussing the widely and deeply held belief that ability is innate, biologically predicated, and normally distributed. I suspect this belief, which I refer to as the "natural hierarchy," accrues much of its illegitimate influence from its status as received knowledge. Most people buy into it, so to speak, at least some degree; yet few seem consciously aware they have done so. It is simply accepted as a matter of fact, or "the way things are." I further propose that it constitutes the central constituent that sustains conventional thinking about the schooling debates. Following this, I turn to a discussion about how I think the social model, and most particularly the conceptual framework that informs it, challenges this orthodoxy.

The Natural Hierarchy: An Idea in the Service of Power

As I suggested above, the orthodoxy of natural hierarchy shapes the main dividing line in debates over American education policy and practice. Those, for example, who support tracking and segregated special education placements view these structures as mandatory because this orthodoxy informs their beliefs. For advocates of tracking, "equal educational opportunity means equal opportunity to develop *quite fixed individual potential (intelligence and abilities)* to its limits through individual effort in school, regardless of such irrelevant background characteristics as race, class, and gender" [emphasis added] (Oakes, 1993, p. 86). Segregationists in special education simply extend this view of ability to students "falling" into lower end of the normal curve. Kauffman (1995), a prominent supporter of segregated special education programs, goes so far as to invoke principles of "sociobehavioral ecology" to suggest that special education students comprise a separate species. "A couple of things we know about ecological niches have very important implications for special education placements," he proclaims:

> We know, for example, that certain ecological niches are notoriously hospitable to some species and individuals and equally notoriously inhospitable to others. We also know that an ecosystem may be thrown out of balance or destroyed by the introduction of certain individuals or groups. And individuals or species that find a particularly hospitable niche may, if uncontrolled by others, destroy the very ecosystem that initially sustained them. Our own uncontrolled behavior as a species, for example, threatens to destroy our entire ecosphere. And all experienced teachers understand how a given individual can undermine and quickly destroy the social structure of a class. (p. 228)

If this strikes the reader as a stunning analogy, I would submit that Kauffman is merely expressing in blunter and more revealing terms what is generally believed to be the case.

Conflict theorists in the sociology of education have, since the 1970's, written extensively on the manner in which the public schools serve as sorting and selecting mechanisms (Spring, 1972; Hurn, 1993). Contrary to those holding the functionalist perspective, a framework that also recognizes that schools serve as sorting mechanisms, conflict theorists contend that rather than promoting social mobility, schools institutionalize inequality by allowing the elite to employ them as a means of passing their own advantages in wealth, status and cultural capital on to their children at the expense of other people's children (Bourdieu and Passeron, 1974; Bowles and Gintis, 1976; Gintis and Bowles, 1986). In any event, education policy and practice has been dominated consistently by the goal of establishing and maintaining a hierarchal society.

Of keen importance to this goal is the sorting out of the "good" or capable people versus the rest of what conservative political philosopher Edmund Burke famously referred to as the "great unwashed masses of humanity." For conservatives, this sorting process reflects the "natural" ordering and implies, if not outright states, that the origin of human differences in ability is biologically determined. Some people, they believe, are naturally more talented and will rise to the top. Subsequently, there is little that can be done for those not naturally gifted, and therefore no reason to invest in any except perhaps the top ten percent (those who will make wise decisions, those who are rooted in and will preserve tradition, and so on) (see: Hernnstein and Murray, 1996). For those of a more liberal bent, the natural hierarchy calls forth the requirement to invest in educational arrangements (tracking, compensatory programs, special education, and so on) aimed at providing every child, regardless of his or her "natural endowments" an equal opportunity to achieve to the "limits of their ability."

Education debates over tracking/inclusion, testing and "accountability," curriculum, pedagogy, and so on, are essentially debates over two opposing ideals of what constitutes a "good" society. On the one side are those who view social hierarchy as natural and therefore, if not good, then certainly inevitable. On the opposing side are those who not only see nothing natural about social hierarchy but also view it as inimical to the ideals of social justice and equality. From the latter perspective, the concept of the natural hierarchy has provided the crucial leverage necessary for those in powerful positions to decide through schooling who would be afforded advantages and privileges and who would not. As Brantlinger (2004) cogently points out, "in our present educational and economic ranking systems, some have to be subnormal for the seemingly desirable hierarchies to survive"(p. 491).

The concept of natural is important because it is the cornerstone of hierarchy. It offers a powerful narrative to explain the existing social order in such a way that even those at the bottom of the caste system accept its tenets.

Its power stems in large measure from the authority of science, which, in turn, derives its power from epistemic assumptions immersed so deeply into western culture that the questioning of them strikes many people as either benignly delusional or overtly inflammatory. Thus, the idea of a natural hierarchy is situated at the gravitational center of debates in education and special education, serving as an invisible hand that defends, exonerates, and affirms social/educational inequality.

In developing his concept of hegemony, Gramsci (1971) stipulated that power and social control can be accrued in two ways. The first and most obvious is through brute physical force. Far more effective, though, is a second strategy—one that achieves control through the creation of a psychic prison. By convincing some people that they deserve their lowly place in the social hierarchy, and, as importantly, that others deserve their exalted status and privilege, social control is achieved with the full, if unwitting, cooperation of the subjugated. Frank (2004) provides us a recent example of the power of hegemony in his book, *What's the Matter with Kansas*. His analysis of how political right-wing conservatives won the heart of America offers up the depressing irony of,

> sturdy blue-collar patriots reciting the Pledge while they strangle their own life chances; of small farmers proudly voting themselves off the land; of devoted family men carefully seeing to it that their children will never be able to afford college or proper health care; of working-class guys in midwestern cities cheering as they deliver up a landside for a candidate whose policies will end their way of life, will transform their region into a "rust belt," will strike people like them blows from which they will never recover. (p. 10)

Real and enduring power is invisible. Its invisibility ensures not only that those who dominant are able to consolidate their control but also that those controlled will endorse their own domination, thus absolving the former of any moral ambiguity that might twinge the conscience in a moment of weakness.

As I noted, the received ideology of the natural social order is not the purview only of cultural and political conservatives. Many, if not most, self-proclaimed liberals and progressives accept as self-evident truth that ability is naturally endowed, even if, as they also believe, environment is part of the equation. I refer here to the presumably well-meaning liberal politicians who helped sponsor the *No Child Left Behind* legislation, ordinary citizens who express the hope that schools can and should promote social and educational equality but nevertheless believe that some children are naturally superior to others, and even university academics in education who view special education as a form of unequivocal progress. Some of these individuals hold to this article of faith simply because they have had neither the occasion nor the motivation to question it. But, as Brantlinger (2003) reveals, many other self-described liberals and progressives are unapologetic about invoking naturalized distinctions among human beings when personal interests make doing so seem a necessity.

More to the point, though, the doctrine of natural inferiority/superiority dispenses with the need to reconcile the profound contradiction of social, political, and material inequalities in a nation founded on the principle of equality for all (Hayman, 1998; Irons, 2002; Kluger, 2004; Lewontin, 1991; Zinn, 2003). If human ability is arranged in a natural hierarchy, then inequality is unavoidable (Davis, 2002). Those at the top are exonerated from any blame or responsibility. Hayman (1998) captured this reasoning quite pointedly:

> The people who have made it have done so because they are smart; they, in a very clear sense, deserve their success. Conversely, the people who have not made it have failed because they are not-so-smart; they, in an equally clear sense, deserve their failure. (p. 8)

All that might remain is the moral obligation to ensure equality of opportunity. It can then be taken for granted that some people will naturally achieve, and deserve by their own merits, more success, greater material security, and higher social status. The creation and scientific justification of this framework required some highly inventive thinking.

The Making of the Natural Hierarchy: A Revealing History

At a very practical level, humans have long recognized that the physical characteristics of plants and animals show up with regularity in their offspring. This practical knowledge was used since ancient times to improve crops and domesticated animals. And the importance placed upon family bloodlines and intergenerational attributes throughout history, from ancient Greece and Rome to the expansion of western civilization, is common knowledge. But the *scientific* (i.e., supposedly neutral and objective) justification for imposing the burden of innate inferiority is a relatively recent phenomenon, achieving its ascendancy in the mid-nineteenth century beginning with Herbert Spencer's concept of the "survival of the fittest," Gregor Mendel's pea experiments, and Charles Darwin's theory of natural selection (Black, 2003). My purpose here is not to recount an exhaustive history of this era, fascinating though it is but rather to center on a particular aspect with direct bearing on educational inequality. I would also direct interested readers to disability studies scholars Lennard Davis (1997) and Ruth Hubbard (1997), both of whom have done a marvelous job of bringing this history to the fore. Here I would like to review and extend their analyses because it is so important and central to my contention that disability studies is situated at the center of the pivotal issues in the overall picture of debates over schooling.

As the disability studies community is (painfully) aware, the mental testing movement made dramatic inroads toward convincing most of the western world that intelligence is an inherited and measurable trait (Braddock and Parish, 2001; Chappell, 1998; Parmenter, 2001; Simpson, 1999). And, as is well documented, Binet, who published the first IQ test, never believed his test measured innate and unchangeable mental attribute (Gould, 1981). That view, of course, changed decisively when the IQ test fell into the hands of the legatees of Galtonian eugenicists in England and the United States (Lewontin et al., 1984). This could have been anticipated, since it was Galton and his protégés who actually invented the normal curve and statistical methods still used in standardized testing. While Galton's role as the "father" of the eugenics movement is widely known, he and his protégés' role in the scientific naturalization of ability/disability is somewhat less well known. Because the legacy of their work figures so prominently into the collective (un)consciousness of most people, it deserves more widespread public scrutiny than it has thus far received.

MacKenzie's (1981) meticulous documentation of the seamless nexus between the early British eugenicists and the development of the modern theory of statistics demonstrates rather conclusively the extent to which these seemingly neutral scientific procedures are permeated with eugenicist ideology. Galton's development of the normal curve provides a very telling case in point. The now familiar normal curve, MacKenzie explains, traces its origins to eighteenth and nineteenth century physicists and astronomers' work on error theory as a means for accounting for measurement error in physical phenomena. In particular, Galton was enticed by the work of Belgian astronomer, Quetelet, who had demonstrated that, "several human physical measurements followed the law of frequency of error" (p. 57). This observation held intriguing possibilities for Galton, but it also presented a problem of some consequence in that measurements both below and above the mean constituted errors—something requiring elimination since they were, after all, errors. "Most basically," MacKenzie poses, "was it really useful [for Galton] to think of an exceptionally able person as a large *error* by nature?" (p. 58). Clearly not. His solution was simply to replace error theory's inconvenient notion of absolute value for the more amiable concept of relative rank. That way, the human traits he measured would fall neatly into a continuous, rank-ordered, distribution with the desirable ones falling above the mean.

Once Galton had solved his problem with the error curve, he went on to develop the bivariate normal distribution and delve into the concepts of regression and correlation. These concepts, too, were useful in affirming his convictions concerning human inheritance. And, as MacKenzie demonstrates in detail too extensive to recount here, Galton found it necessary to perform various manipulations of the statistical formulas to accommodate his political aims. "The closeness of the connection [between Galton's statistics and eugenics] is sufficient," MacKenzie concludes, "to suggest that it is reasonable to see Galton's eugenics not merely as providing the motive for his statistical work, *but also as conditioning the content of it*" [emphasis added] (p. 68). This work was carried on by Galton's protégés and members of the eugenics movement, Karl Pearson (who further developed statistical correlation procedures) and R. A. Fisher (who developed the theory of, and formulas for, statistical inference).

As the eugenics movement spread across Europe and the United States (see: Black, 2003; Duster, 2003; Kuhl, 1994), the tenet that all human traits, including moral, social, and intellectual ones, are determined by genetic inheritance became firmly adopted by everyday people. Henry Goddard (1919), author of the now infamous, *The Kallikak Family: A Study in the Heredity of Feeblemindedness*, expropriated and distorted Binet's I.Q. test as an instrument in his eugenicist campaign to eradicate the impending threat of inherited inferiority. His work was furthered by Robert Yerkes, Lewis Terman and a contingent of other ardent eugenicists. In March of the same year that Goddard published his book on the Kallikak family, Edward L. Thorndike lectured an audience at the University of California, Los Angeles on the urgency of implementing eugenic policies (see: Aldrich, et al, 1914). Thorndike, founding editor of the *Journal of Educational Psychology,* is

most well known for his influential work in psychometrics. His active involvement in the eugenics movement is perhaps less well known.

As I earlier indicated, the overarching purpose of this brief review is to
connect some important historical "dots" on the ideological and technological map. More to the point, this review illustrates the collusion of positivist
science, biological determinism, and politics of educational/social entitlement. To the modern ear, the term "eugenics" has a rather eerie, somewhat
antiquated ring; yet, the taken-for-granted belief that genetics accounts for
differences in intellectual ability, personal dispositions, and so on, remains
culturally ubiquitous. Evidence of this is fairly conspicuous. For example, a
television advertisement for Swiffer mops opens with a middle-aged woman
dancing around the house enthusiastically cleaning every surface floor to
ceiling. The camera pans to her teenage daughter who remarks with embarrassment to her girlfriend, "I hope it's not genetic." In another television
advertisement, a preschool boy is seen soundly defeating a grown man on the
tennis court. A car pulls up and his parents summon the boy. It turns out that
he is the son of famous tennis players, Andre Agassi and Stephi Graff. The
voice-over states, "It's the jeans (genes) that count."

More recently, the animated adventure film for children *The Incredibles*
was reviewed in the *New York Times* (Tierney, 2004) as a forum for discussion on educational excellence versus egalitarianism and competition versus
cooperation. The main character of the film, a third grade boy named Dash,
is forbidden from racing on the track team because his "supersonic" running
ability gives him an unfair advantage over others. The film's villain, "Syndrome" seems bent on trying to make everybody super so that nobody will
be. The author of the review poses the question, "Is Syndrome, the geek
villain trying to kill superheroes, an angry Marxist determined to quash
individuality? Or is his plan to give everyone artificial superpowers an
uplifting version of 'cooperative learning' in an 'inclusion classroom?'"
(section 4, p. 1). The article goes on to quote Christina Hoff Sommers (2000)
of the American Enterprise Institute who, in her book, *The War Against
Boys*, states that "males are wired for competition, and if you take it away
there's little to interest them in school."

Although the appalling denouement of Nazi Germany's eugenics, in addition to the forced sterilizations of tens of thousands of American citizens,
tarnished the political usefulness of the term "eugenics," the movement was
nevertheless a resounding cultural success in lending powerful epistemologi-

cal authority to the philosophy of biological determinism which, in turn, supports the social hierarchy as a political philosophy. Disputes over the effects of nature versus nurture notwithstanding, it is fairly obvious that we are living in an era of dramatically renewed interest in genetic explanations for virtually all realms of human functioning. As Lewontin (1991) observes, "Living beings are seen as being determined by internal factors, the genes. Our genes and the DNA molecules that make them up are the modern form of grace, and in this view we will understand what we are when we know what our genes are made of" (p. 13). Clearly, this is an idea that is not going away until its epistemological authority, and hence its unquestioned acceptance, is thoroughly undermined.

Disability as a naturalized, or scientifically objective, condition signaling "subnormality" is an artifact of this framework. Disability must "exist" as the defining antithesis of "normality" or "normalcy" (see Davis, 2002). Moreover, "superiority" has no meaning without the defining concept of "inferiority" embodied in the concept of disability. These distinctions provide an indispensable form of exoneration for a unequal society predicated on the ideal of equality for all. The field of disability studies, as I see it, is uniquely situated to dislodge this framework, to reveal its status as political and ideological rather than neutral knowledge.

Disability Studies' Contribution to Contemporary Education Debates

The social model of disability centers on a seemingly simple question: what is a disability? In casting aside the view of disability as an objective, or what Slee (1997) refers to as an "essentialist" condition, disability activists and disability studies scholars fundamentally recast disability as a cultural construction, the consequence of which is social restriction and oppression (Barnes, 1996; Corker and Shakespeare, 2002; Finkelstein, 1980; Oliver, 1990; Thomas, 1999). Much more than calling attention to the pervasive oppression imposed on those disabled by their fellow human beings, the social model calls for a shifting of the very metaphors through which people see the world. In so doing, this model subverts the underlying conceptual framework that sustains the medical model of disability. By extension, and in no uncertain terms, it also undermines the orthodoxy of ability as innate, biologically predicated, and normally distributed.

In the world of education, as well as in the broader society, nothing seems to be quite as "real" as disability. Even people who can concede race as a social construct continue to buy into disability as an objective condition.

As well, many who view educational segregation on the basis of race gender, social class and ethnicity as fundamentally unjust find separate educational placements for those with disabilities to be entirely unproblematic if not warranted. My argument here is that because disability holds the strongest purchase on philosophical realism or objectivism, to make the case for disability as a cultural construct strikes a powerful blow to traditional education ideology. By undermining the medical model of disability, the social model "undoes" the very substantiation for inequality, educational or otherwise, because it derails that most important stronghold of human ability as naturalized. Once disability as an objective condition evaporates, once it is reframed as a social construct embedded in educational/social arrangements, research, pedagogy, policies, and practices of schools, the failures experienced by some children, both those labeled as "special needs" and those who are not, must be reexamined as social and institutional problems.

Disability studies in education, in other words, engages the longstanding debates over education purposes, practices and policies in ways that other schools of thought or movements have not and cannot. For one thing, as both an intellectual and political movement, it transcends the classic liberalism that has long stood as the only counter to conservatism. The degree to which either of the conservative or liberal/progressive schools of thought dominate schooling in the US or the UK ebbs and flows. Neither ever banishes the other from the field altogether. One might also argue that neo-Marxian and conflict theory perspectives, as on the mark as they have been, have had their run at promoting change.

On the other hand, disability studies in education emerges from a position that recognizes the moral and political nature of all knowledge. Its unique contribution centers on acknowledging the constructed rather than the presumed objective nature of ability/disability. This stands in contrast to the literature in education as a whole that has raised this distinction tangentially, if at all. And so the question can be raised, what and who is going to challenge conventional education orthodoxy. I would suggest that disability studies in education should be moved to the front and center as a forum for vibrant debate. From my vantage point, this new and growing field challenges more deeply and hits the mark more squarely than those that preceded it. In the end, the issue of disability is not just about disability, it's about all of us in a just society.

References

Aldrich, M. A.; Carruth, W. H.; Davenport, C. B.(Eds.) (1914). *Eugenics: Twelve university lectures*. New York: Dodd, Mead, and Company.

Barnes, C. (1996). Theories of disability and the origins of the oppression of disabled people in western society. In L. Barton (Ed.) *Disability and society: Emerging issues and insights*. London: Longman.

Black, E. (2003). *The war against the weak: Eugenics and America's campaign to create a master race*. New York: Four Walls Eight Windows.

Bourdieu, P., and Passeron, J. (1974). *Reproduction in education, society and culture*. Thousand Oaks, CA: Sage.

Bowles, S., and Gintis, H. (1976). *Schooling in capitalist America*. New York: Basic Books.

Braddock, D. L., and Parish, S. L. (2001). An institutional history of disability. In G. L. Albrecht, K. D. Seelman, and M. Bury (Eds.), *Handbook of disability studies* (pp. 11–68). Thousand Oaks, CA: Sage Publications.

Brantlinger, E.(2003). *Dividing classes: How the middle class negotiates and rationalizes school advantage*. New York: RoutledgeFalmer.

———. (2004). Confounding the needs and confronting the norms: An extension of Reid and Valle's essay. *Journal of Learning Disabilities, 37*(6), 490–499.

Chappell, A. L. (1998). Still out in the cold: People with learning difficulties and the social model of disability. In T. Shakespeare (Ed.), *The disability reader: Social science perspectives* (pp. 211–219). London: Cassell.

Corker, M., and Shakespeare, T. (2002). Mapping the terrain. In M. Corker and T. Shakespeare (Eds.) *Disability/postmodernity: Embodying disability theory*. (pp. 1–17). London: Continuum.

Davis, L. J. (1997). Constructing normalcy: The bell curve, the novel and the invention of the disabled body in the nineteenth century. In L. J. Davis (Ed.), *The Disability Studies Reader* (pp. 9–28). New York: Routledge.

———. (2002). *Bending over backwards: Disability, dismodernism and other difficult positions*. New York: New York University Press.

Duster, T. (2003) *Backdoor to eugenics*. New York: Routledge.

Finkelstein, V. (1980). *Attitudes and disabled people: Issues for discussion*. New York: World Rehabilitation Fund.

Frank, T. (2004). *What's the matter with Kansas? How conservatives won the heart of America*. New York: Metropolitan Books.

Gintis, H., and Bowles, S. (1986). *Capitalism and democracy*. New York: Basic Books.

Goddard, H. H. (1919) *The Kallikak family: A study in the heredity of fee-blemindedness.* New York: Macmillan.

Gould, S. J. (1981) *The mismeasure of man.* New York: Norton.

Gramsci, A. (1971). *Selections from the prison notebooks* (Q. Hoare and G. N. Smith, Eds.). New York: International Publishers. (Original work published 1929–1935)

Hayman, R. L. (1998). *The smart culture: Society, intelligence, and law.* New York: New York University Press.

Hernnstein, R., and Murray, C. (1996). *The bell curve: Intelligence and class structure in American life.* New York: Free Press.

Hubbard, R. (1997) Abortion and disability: Who should and who should not inhabit the world? In L. J. Davis (Ed.) *The disability studies reader* (pp. 187–200). New York: Routledge.

Hurn, C. J. (1993). *The limits and possibilities of schooling: An introduction to the sociology of education* [3rd ed.]. Boston: Allyn and Bacon.

Irons, P. (2002). *Jim Crow's children: The broken promise of the Brown decision.* New York: Viking Penguin.

Kauffman, J. M. (1995). Why we must celebrate a diversity of restrictive environments. *Learning Disabilities Research and Practice, 10*(4), 225–232.

Kluger, R. (2004). *Simple justice: The history of Brown v. Board of Education and Black America's struggle for equality.* New York: Vintage.

Kuhl, S. (1994) *The Nazi connection: Eugenics, American racism, German national socialism.* New York: Oxford University Press.

Lewontin, R. (1991). *Biology as ideology: The doctrine of DNA.* New York: HarperCollins.

Lewontin, R. C., Rose, S., and Kamin, L. J. (1984). *Not in our genes: Biology, ideology, and human nature.* New York: Pantheon Books.

MacKenzie, D. (1981). *Statistics in Great Britian, 1865–1930: The social construction of scientific knowledge.* Edinburgh: Edinburgh University Press.

Oakes, J. (1993). Tracking, inequality, and the rhetoric of reform: Why schools don't change. In H. S. Shapiro and D. E. Purpel (Eds.), *Critical social issues in American education: Toward the 21st century* (pp. 85–102). New York: Longman.

Oliver, M. (1990). *The politics of disablement.* Basingstoke, UK: Macmillan.

Parmenter, T. R. (2001). Intellectual disabilities–Quo Vadis? In G. L. Albrecht, K. D. Seelman, and M. Bury (Eds.), *Handbook of disability studies* (pp. 267–296). Thousand Oaks, CA: Sage Publications.

Simpson, M. (1999). Bodies, brains, behaviour: The return of the three stooges in learning disability. In M. Corker and S. French (Eds.), *Disability discourse* (pp. 148–156). Buckingham, UK: Open University Press.

Slee, R. (1997). Imported or important theory? Sociology interrogations of disablement and special education. *British Journal of Sociology of Education*, 18(3), 407–419.

Sommers, C. H. (2000). *The war against boys: How misguided feminism is harming our young men.* New York: Simon and Schuster.

Spring, J. (1972). *Education and the rise of the corporate state.* Boston: Beacon Press.

Thomas, C. (1999). *Female forms: Experiencing and understanding disability.* Buckingham, UK: Open University Press.

Tierney, J. (November 21, 2004). When every child is good enough. *New York Times*, Section 4, p. 1, 3.

Zinn, H. (2003). *A people's history of the United States: 1492–present.* New York: HarperCollins.

CHAPTER 4

Learning from Our Historical Evasions: Disability Studies and Schooling in a Liberal Democracy

Scot Danforth

The contemporary educational debates that deserve our greatest energy and effort involve the ways that our public schools are not advancing the goals of liberal democracy; generally speaking, that public schools are not adequately helping us embrace and include a wider and more varied plurality of people under the social umbrella of support, sensitivity, and economic stability that the United States has to offer. In this essay, I will address the question of how disability studies can help us address those serious issues. Rather than coming head on, I will travel a somewhat inside-out or backwards route by asking the reverse question: *Why have educational disability researchers in the United States so far failed to contribute to the resolution of these educational issues?*

This inside-out question springs from an awareness that research and practice geared toward education and disability in the United States have been primarily constituted by the field of special education for many decades. That is, until recently, very little scholarship or energy has been devoted to disability concerns in the public schools from outside of the professional group and ideological boundaries of special education. Since inception during the first decades of the twentieth century, special education practice and research have served mainly as obstacles to the pursuit of democratic goals within public schools. This has occurred through a series of contingent historical turns that have bypassed a more constructive confrontation with serious issues of diversity and equality. A critical narrative of failed special education research and practice will provide glimpses of opportunities missed, social issues and democratic purposes evaded, diluted, and reconstituted via the knowledge and practices of the young profession. In these evasions, we will catch counter-glimpses of more useful and hopeful—given democratic purposes—ways of framing issues of diversity and schooling that will inform the work of disability studies scholars. In the conclusion, I will describe the possibilities inherent in disability studies in education as a host of intellectual practices that pry open the very doors that special education has unfortunately closed so many times.

Contemporary Educational Issues

At first glance, the most prominent educational issues today are accountability and persistent patterns of low achievement (e.g. low standardized test scores, low high school graduation rates) among specific groups of students or specific schools where those students predominantly attend. Efforts initiated by the No Child Left Behind legislation and carried on by the various state educational agencies draw our eyes first to concerns about low levels of achievement among African-Americans, working class and poor students of all races or ethnicities, and also the urban schools that often educate these students (Bainbridge and Lasley, 2002; Hunter and Bartee, 2003).

Behind this public discussion about achievement scores and educational policies linger enduring issues about social injustices based on race and class and the unequal schooling of American children (Bowles and Gintis, 1976; Brantlinger, 2003; Kozol, 1991; McLaren, 1986). Social class hierarchies, racial discrimination, varied educational opportunities, and disparate educational outcomes intertwine in a continuing historical narrative of an American democracy that has not yet included, valued, and supported all individuals and groups. This narrative includes successful changes of the cultural terrain that have created greater respect and fairness toward persons of color, women, gays, and disabled persons. This on-going narrative also involves many starts, stops, and painful regressions as the economic split between rich and poor widens in the United States and civil rights gains of past eras seem to stall or backpedal in the current moment (West, 1993; Rorty, 1998, 1999).

I view issues of social inequality and cultural difference involving race/ethnicity, class, gender, sexual orientation, and disability in terms of the political and social utilization of the uncertain boundaries of these categories within a broader social background of economic competition and social cruelty. My focus attends to how these categorical identities are socially constituted and positioned within public schools toward either ends of greater equality, respect, and fraternity or greater hierarchy, cruelty, and suffering.

I begin from the premise that a central goal of liberal democracy in the United States is to broaden the general sense of who "we Americans" *are* to include more interesting and diverse variations, including the provision of satisfactory levels of economic and social support for the many proletarian or marginalized groups (Dewey, 1939/1993; Rorty, 1998, 1999; Westbrook, 1991). With this broad democratic goal in mind, respect for cultural or biological diversity, egalitarian forms of participation, sensitivity to the perspectives and needs of others, and social solidarity refusing exclusion are the most important goals within public education. Disability concerns make up one vital, ever-shifting thread within that complex, contested social fabric (Barnes et al., 2002).

Two Unfortunate Turns in Special Education History

Why have educational disability researchers in the United States failed to contribute to the resolution of these educational issues? More pointedly, why has American special education research not only failed to work toward the resolution of conditions of social and economic inequality but has actually served as an obstacle or deterrent to that democratic effort?

Two specific turns in the historical path of the field of special education carried that profession away from democratic, egalitarian purposes:

1. *Building the individual deficit disability construct as the cornerstone of special education ideology, research, legislation, and practice.* Arising in conjunction with a range of social science-based professions during the Progressive Era, the creation of the deficit notion of disability reduced a broad array of complicated social and educational issues involving race/ethnicity, social class, nationality, language, gender, and schooling practices into a single problem target requiring professional treatment. That conceptual and practical re-

duction evaded issues of cultural difference and social inequality, effectively repoliticizing American public schooling behind an ostensibly apolitical ideology of positivistic science (Brantlinger, 1997; Danforth, 1997; Skrtic, 1991, 1995).

2. *Limiting professional language, thought, and practice to a discourse of positivistic social science.* This move rendered human social and political problems, issues about how diverse peoples can cooperatively live together under democratic values of equality and freedom, as technical problems to be resolved through measurement and techniques of professional precision (e.g. Schön, 1983). The question here isn't whether some kinds of social progress might be made through technical metaphors such as engineering and bio-medicine. More pointedly, the question is what happens when a profession limits itself to *only* a medicalized discourse of research and practice, thereby failing to develop the wide array of conceptual and practical tools necessary for collaboration, creativity, contextual flexibility, and the pursuit of a democratic community.

In order to gain a greater understanding of each of these turns in the history of special education, I will provide specific narratives about how and when the turns occurred. These narratives necessarily will be provisional snapshots, less than comprehensive from the historian's point of view. But they will allow us to envision the historical context and contingency of the two unfortunate turns and thereby begin to broaden our imagination about the possibilities for more expansive and hopeful forms of scholarship that disability studies in education scholars might pursue today.

Building the Individual Deficit Disability Construct

In the first three decades of the 1900's, American special education grew at the intersection of the expansion of cultural diversity and the development of an incipient professional ideology of positivistic social science. Urban public schools were confronted with a dramatic influx of working class and poor immigrants, and their response depended on the new psychological science that formed the ideological cornerstone of the nascent fields such as social work, special education, and educational administration (Danforth et al., 2005; Lazerson, 1983; Platt, 1969; Tyack and Hansot, 1982).

In 1909, 57.8% of all students in urban public schools were the offspring of foreign-born parents, primarily immigrants from southern and eastern Europe (Cremin, 1961). School enrollment in New York City rose 57% between 1900 and 1910. Three-fourths of the city population were first or second generation immigrants (Chapman, 1988). Similar immigration patterns and enrollment growth occurred in other large cities.

One of the primary ways that public schools coped with the enormous number of immigrant students was through the creation of special classes. The first special education class specifically for "mental defectives" was founded in Providence, Rhode Island in 1896. By 1922, at least 133 school systems provided special education classes for over 23,000 students considered "mentally deficient" (Lazerson, 1983; Osgood, 2002).

Notions of individual deficit—of an organic or functional limitation inhering to an individual—were nothing new. Concepts of mental deficiency had been around for many decades. Talk of moral or intellectual weakness was common in nineteenth and twentieth century American life, especially due to the popularity of eugenics at the turn of the century (Davis, 1997). The key question for our purposes is, how did a construct of individual deficit become viewed as both central and necessary to professional ideology during the early 1900s? How did this become the beginning point and foundational assumption in professional fields like special education?

An exploration of the political terrain of the Progressive Era birth of a series of "helping" professions locates special education as just one of an interlocked group of new practical disciplines. Social work, psychology, educational administration, and medical psychiatry all rode the new social and human sciences to political legitimacy in the first three decades of the twentieth century. A brief telling of the creation and victory of the "juvenile delinquency" construct will provide a good example of how the early social sciences provided a professional rhetoric that framed social issues in ways that called for professional intervention upon individuals with deficits.

Turn-of-the-century urban problems were built of immigration, industrialization, and poverty. Urban ghettos filled with poor immigrant working families surrounded the many factories and foundries. A frequent complaint of civic leaders and politicians focused on the rowdy and even illegal behavior of the immigrant families, most specifically the unruly activities of teenaged boys.

By 1915, when physician William Healy published the landmark volume entitled *The Individual Delinquent*, the widespread apprehension over unseemly youth behavior had already been congealed within the term "juvenile delinquency." Healy's work served to further define and hypostatize this individual deficit construct as the basis of both research and professional activity. In his studies of delinquent youth in Chicago, Healy (1915) searched for the root factors that caused individual delinquency. He combined environmental factors and individual biology to define delinquency as a complex phenomenon with many causes but only one location: the defective character of the individual (Horn, 1989; Jones, 1999).

A 1921 conference of leaders in the new field of juvenile delinquency in Lakewood, New Jersey provides insight into the victory of the individual deficit construct over the possible development of a social or political explanation of deviant and defiant youth behavior. A prominent social worker named Edith Abbott claimed that the Illinois Child Labor Law of 1917 had done more to decrease juvenile delinquency than all the mental health treatment offered by a well-known Chicago child guidance clinic. She proposed a version of what disability studies scholars today would call a "social model" of delinquency, focusing on how the difficult social, environmental, and economic conditions that immigrant families confronted in their lives served as obstacles to stability, well-being, and success. She contended that an approach based on social activism and the improvement of social conditions in urban neighborhoods would do more to assist so-called juvenile delinquents than individual psychological treatment. She was alone in her contention. The final report of the conference described "poverty, variations in employment, migration to cities with consequent exposure to bad housing and other similar conditions" (as quoted in Jones, 1999, p. 59) as irrelevant topics and therefore beyond the scope of meaningful discussion.

Following Healy's lead, the conference participants concluded that juvenile delinquency was not a social and political problem. It was a medical and psychological problem of poor adjustment requiring professionals to help youth effectively adjust to the conditions of their lives. A social understanding of individual struggle occurring within social conditions of inequality had been defeated by a medicalized construct of personal limitation (Horn, 1989; Jones, 1999; Richardson, 1989).

This tale of juvenile delinquency only provides insight into the birth of one individual deficit construct. Similar historical stories about the social and political development of other deficit conditions have been written by prominent researchers. Sleeter (1986) and Carrier (1986) tell of the social class and racial politics behind the creation of the learning disability in the Cold War Era. Conrad (1975) provides a rich narrative about how Attention Deficit Hyperactivity Disorder grew at the intersection of parental concern, aggressive pharmaceutical marketing, and acritical medical practice. Conrad and Schneider (1992) have articulated social explanations for the historical shift of heavy alcohol and narcotics use from concepts of moral failure to constructs of medical illness.

The importance of these narratives outlining the social processes and events contributing to the initiation, development, and victorious dominance of specific deficit disorder constructs lies in the way that they direct our attention to the historical contingency and political positioning of the disorders themselves. Although many deficit constructs are viewed by special educators and other professionals as unavoidably and undeniably "real" in the sense that this page and these words are "real," these critical sociological narratives display the human activities and turns of events that first built these disorders, thereby alerting us to the contingent, constructed nature of what often seems to be baldly self-evident. From this appreciation of contingency grows the possibility for creativity, for redescribing and retheorizing disability concerns in public schools through an opportunistic, flexible language of social and political hope, shifting from a metaphor of schooling as treatment for disease to schooling as everyday crucible for democratic living in a diverse society.

Limiting Professional Discourse to Positivistic Social Science

Skrtic (1991, 1995) identifies two specific continuations of nineteenth century positivism as the ideological underpinnings of the technical way that special education has framed disability and schooling: psychological measurement and behavioral science. The former, particularly the intelligence test, provided the scientific language of educational diagnosis. The latter became the preeminent science and practice of professional treatment, a way to bring the actions of disabled persons into conformity with so-called nondisabled social norms. Together, these two social sciences have granted the profession of special education political legitimacy through a stance of political neutrality and epistemic privilege.

These two social sciences have been unified under a medicalized language of educational treatment. The field has used these positivistic sciences to formulate a clinical discourse that casts perceived biological or cultural difference as educational illness requiring proper diagnosis, quarantine, and treatment by scientific professionals. This disease metaphor not only proscribes the individual deficit and social conformity foci that comprise the special education construal of disability. More broadly, it provides the conceptual tools utilized by the profession to constitute disability itself within the subjective judgments and appraisals of human value that fill the educational processes of referral, diagnosis, and intervention (Harry et al., 2002; Kugelmass, 1987; Mercer, 1973; Mehan et al., 1986).

How did this positivistic, medicalized discourse—this way of speaking about, thinking about, acting upon—become the *only* driving engine that both propels and limits special education? Again, we look to the initiation of the profession in the Progressive Era to ask, how did early special education adopt a disease metaphor of disability and the incumbent medical language of professional practice instead of including a social and political discourse about human physical and cultural differences?

Historian Barry Franklin (1986) has hypothesized that the new helping professions of the Progressive Era were driven by a nostalgic desire to recreate rural forms of community within the booming industrial, urban neighborhoods. Most helping professionals had been raised in small, rural towns where cultural homogeneity formed the basis for social alliance. Their understanding of how a safe and orderly community should operate was based in an experience of regularity based on ethnic and religious commonalities.

> If growing up in a small town taught these Americans anything, it taught them that stability, order, and progress ultimately depended on the degree to which beliefs and attitudes were shared. It taught them that if American society was to be both orderly and progressive, a homogeneous culture and spirit of like-mindedness and cooperation had to exist within its population. It was the effort of this emerging group of American intellectuals to construct a homogeneous culture which they came to talk about as their search for community (Franklin, 1986, p. 6).

Social order itself, within the experiences and the minds of these helping professionals, depended on cooperation flowing from cultural conformity and sameness. To be alike was to be unified and stable.

The helping efforts of the new professionals generally targeted urban neighborhoods teaming with working poor families transplanted from rural

areas or from foreign countries. The overwhelming challenge was to cultivate homogeneity of values, attitudes, and actions among the ostensibly
problematic peoples who did not share a single religion, language, cultural
background, or pastoral experience. Though the cultural diversity, harshly
class-based economics, and squalid living conditions of the industrialized
cities bore little resemblance to rural towns of agrarian days, the new special
educators, social workers, and psychologists attempted to cultivate a bucolic
culture of homogeneity.

While professional practice in the Progressive Era relied on a nostalgic
form of community, the modus operandi relied on the power of science.
Specifically, the helping professions adopted the language and reasoning of
the most attractive and seemingly powerful human science–medicine. Complex, often daunting social issues involving industrial conditions, social class
politics, cross-cultural conflict, racial/ethnic discrimination, capitalist exploitation, and more were distilled by professions like special education into
digestible units of understanding and focus through a medical rhetoric of
diagnosis and treatment. This positivistic language united the new development of psychological measurement with a convincing clinical framework
that cast "deviant" persons as educational patients, thereby achieving three
social results:

1. Seemingly problematic (non-conforming) populations were posi-
    tioned as bearers of illness rather than bearers of immorality. Al-
    though the case can be made that professionals viewed themselves as
    bringing morality to the immoral, the professional scientific dis-
    course depended on the practical conversion of moral judgements
    into clinical diagnoses.
2. Special education sought and gained legitimacy as a profession
    through the language of medical and social science. Becoming a pro-
    fession meant becoming authoritative, gaining a discourse deemed
    superior to other modes of talking and acting. Science, in particular
    the new science of psychological measurement, provided the basis
    for that authority.
3. Special education was framed within a politically tame purpose of
    adapting individuals rather than changing society. In addition to the
    authority of science, a stance of neutrality rendered special education
    politically conservative, standing for the preservation of the domi-

nant order. This allowed the profession to avoid conflict with powerful groups within society.

Rather than working to achieve communities of social justice, greater equality, and deeper respect, the new professions adopted the task of helping deviant individuals adapt to the existing social conditions. Special education took on the professional role of working at the margins of society with groups and individuals who were somehow failing to fit in and succeed within the dominant order, providing diagnosis and treatment for the ailments that "cause" widespread economic and social failures in individuals.

By framing itself through a medicalized language and clinical purpose, the profession has generally avoided a substantial critique of the broader social conditions and political arrangements that create and maintain the kinds of economic and social marginalization that ensnare and oppress "disabled" students and their families (Ware, 2001). By focusing on concerns of individual dysfunction and goals of increasing functionality, the field has rarely raised its eyes to question the pervasive social structures and processes that capture specific forms of biological and cultural difference within social conditions of economic poverty and community exclusion. The field has had tremendous difficulty even beginning to envision and imagine professional goals and activities that do not involve psychological measurement of individual deficits leading to individualized treatment of those deficits. The social and ethical purposes of liberal democracy fail to gain credence when the professional language circumscribes action within tasks of individual measurement and modification.

Conclusion

By forsaking the disease metaphor of disability and a solitary allegiance to positivistic discourse in favor of a social approach to disability, disability studies in education holds the democratic promise that special education research has evaded.

By theorizing disability as one of many roving identity markers such as race/ethnicity, class, gender, and sexual orientation—while avoiding an essentialist view of these categories as distinct, universal, and constant— disability studies in education holds the democratic promise of critically examining the social structures and processes that perpetuate injustice and cruelty. By refusing to enfranchise a limited and limiting discourse of human difference, thereby opening educational research about disability to the widest range of work from the humanities, the arts, the social sciences, and the many professions, disability studies in education holds the promise of an expansive, creative democratic dialogue. By opening imaginative minds and sensitive hearts to the experiential accounts of disabled persons as legitimate contributions to scholarship, disability studies in education holds the promise of an inclusive, anti-hierarchical democratic dialogue.

As a field seeking dramatic social change, this inchoate enterprise must champion democracy over science, experimentation over tradition, fraternity over hierarchy, solidarity over professionalization, individuality over homogeneity, creativity over conformity, and hope over authority. It must be a field of scholarship that tumbles out from all sides, creates untried languages for unmet challenges, pulls off the unexpected when no one is looking, upends the perennial victors when everyone is looking, allies with the political losers whenever losing means suffering, exposes the politics behind the social games that create winners and losers, and reinvents itself whenever it gains comfortable standing. It must be a scholarship transpiring *with* the disability community and disabled persons rather than a paternal regime operating *for* disabled persons. It must be the inventive opposite to what special education has made, a multi-dimensional, multi-voiced arena of opportunity, a continuous source of innovation and hope for those who embrace the challenge of schooling in this liberal democracy.

References

Bainbridge, W. L. and Lasley, T. J. (2002) Demographics, diversity, and K–12 accountability: The challenge of closing the achievement gap. *Education and Urban Society, 34*, 422–37.

Barnes, C., Oliver, M. and Barton, L. (2002) *Disability studies today.* Cambridge, England: Polity Press.

Bowles, S. and Gintis, H. (1976) *Schooling in capitalist America: Educational reform and the contradictions of economic life.* New York: Basic Books.

Brantlinger, E. (1997) Using ideology: Cases of nonrecognition of the politics of research and practice in special education. *Review of Educational Research, 67, 4*, 425–59.

———. (2003) *Dividing classes: How the middle class negotiates and rationalizes school advantage.* New York: RoutledgeFalmer.

Carrier, J. G. (1986) *Learning disability: Social class and the construction of inequality in American education.* New York: Greenwood Press.

Chapman, P. D. (1988) *Schools as sorters: Lewis M. Terman, applied psychology, and the intelligence testing movement, 1890–1930.* New York: New York University Press.

Conrad, P. (1975) The discovery of hyperkinesis: Notes on the medicalization of deviant behavior. *Social Problems, 23,* 12–21.

Conrad, P. and Schneider, J. W. (1992) *Deviance and medicalization: From badness to sickness.* Columbus, Ohio: Merrill.

Cremin, L. A. (1961) *The transformation of the school: Progressivism in American education, 1876–1957.* New York: Vintage Books.

Danforth, S. (1997). On what basis hope? Modern progress and postmodern possibilities. *Mental Retardation, 35, 2,* 93–106.

Danforth, S., Ferguson, P., and Taff, S. (2005) Place, profession and program in the history of special education curriculum. In Brantlinger, E. (Ed.) *Who benefits from special education? Remediating (fixing) other people's children* (pp 1– 25). Mahwah, NJ: Lawrence Erlbaum.

Davis, L. J. (1997) Constructing normalcy: The bell curve, the novel, and the disabled body in the nineteenth century. (pp. 9–28) In L. J. Davis, *The disability studies reader.* New York: Routledge.

Dewey, J. (1939/1993) Creative democracy–the task before us. In D. Morris and Ian Shapiro (Eds). *The political writings.* Indianapolis: Hackett Publishing Co.

Franklin, B. M. (1986) *Building the American community: The school curriculum and the search for social control.* Philadelphia: Falmer Press.

Harry, B., Klingner, J. K., Sturges, K. M., Moore, R. F. (2002) Of rocks and soft places: Using qualitative methods to investigate disproportionality. (pp. 71–92) In D. J. Losen and G. Orfield (Eds.) *Racial inequity in special education.*

Healey, W. (1915) *The individual delinquent; a text–book of diagnosis and prognosis for all concerned in understanding offenders.* Boston: Little, Brown.

Horn, M. (1989) Before it's too late: The child guidance movement in the United States, 1922–1945. Philadelphia: Temple University Press.

Hunter, R. C. and Bartee, R. (2003) The achievement gap: Issues of competition, class, and race. *Education and Urban Society, 35,* 151–60.

Jones, K. W. (1999) *Taming the troublesome child: American families, child guidance, and the limits of psychiatric authority*. Cambridge, MA: Harvard University Press.

Kozol, J. (1991) *Savage inequalities: Children in America's schools*. New York: Crown.

Kugelmass, J. W. (1987) *Behavior, bias, and handicaps: Labeling the emotionally disturbed child*. New Brunswick, N.J.: Transaction Books.

Lazerson, M. (1983) The origins of special education. (pp. 15–47) In J. G. Chambers and W. T. Hartman (eds), *Special education policies: Their history, implementation, and finance*. Philadelphia: Temple University Press.

McLaren, P. (1986) *Schooling as a ritual performance: Towards a political economy of educational symbols and gestures*. Boston: Routledge and Kegan Paul.

Mehan, H., Hertweck, A., and Meihls, J. L. (1986) *Handicapping the handicapped: Decision making in students' educational careers*. Stanford, CA: Stanford University Press.

Mercer, J. R. (1973) *Labeling the mentally retarded:Clinical and social system perspectives on mental retardation*. Berkeley: University of California Press.

Osgood, R. L. (2002) From 'public liabilities' to 'public assets': Special education for children with mental retardation in Indiana public schools, 1908–1931. *Indiana Magazine of History, 98,* 203–225.

Platt, A. M. (1969) *The child savers; the invention of delinquency*. Chicago: University of Chicago.

Richardson, T. R. (1989) *The century of the child: The mental hygiene movement and social policy in the United States and Canada*. Albany, NY: State University of New York Press.

Rorty, R. (1998) *Achieving our country: Leftist thought in twentieth century America* Cambridge, MA: Harvard University Press.

———. (1999) *Philosophy and social hope*. New York: Penguin Books.

Schön, D. A. (1983) *The reflective practitioner: How professionals think in action*. New York: Basic Books.

Skrtic, T. M. (1991) *Behind special education: A critical analysis of professional culture and school organization*. Denver: Love.

———. (1995) *Disability and democracy: Reconstructing (special) education for postmodernity*. New York: Teachers College Press.

Sleeter, C. E. (1986) Learning disabilities: The social construction of a special education category. *Exceptional Children, 53, 1*, 46–54.

Tyack, D. and Hansot, E. (1982) *Managers of virtue: Public school leadership in America, 1820–1980.* New York: Basic Books.

Ware, L. (2001) Writing, identity, and the other: Dare we do disability studies? *Journal of Teacher Education, 52, 2*, 107–123.

West, C. (1993) *Keeping faith: Philosophy and race in America.* New York: Routledge.

Westbrook, R. B. (1991) *John Dewey and American democracy.* Ithaca, N.Y.: Cornell University Press.

*How is Disability Studies in Education (Ir)Relevant to the
Practical Interests, Experiences, and Goals of
Disabled People in Schools?*

CHAPTER 5

Disability Studies and Young Children: Finding Relevance

Chris Kliewer

Disability studies is the wonderfully convoluted convergence of autobiography, political advocacy and activism, social critique, the humanities, arts, theater and film, phenomenology, critical sociology, anthropology, cultural studies, economics, and modes of qualitative inquiry. It is an infinitely situated complex effort toward holistic realizations of disability experience that displace traditional, reductionistic psychological and medical orientations with their emphases on defect, impairment, and abnormality.

Disability studies emerged from various efforts to rewrite the text of disability, reorienting cultural meanings and challenging traditional power arrangements. As a rubric of critical human cultivation and democratization, however, disability studies has unfortunately had little influence on the experiences of young children with disabilities, their families, or the course of early childhood education. In this chapter I will respond to the initiating question: *How is disability studies in education (ir)relevant to the practical interests, experiences, and goals of disabled people in schools?* To do so I will explore what may be referred to as the gap of relevance between disability studies scholars and the lived experience of young children with disabilities. I describe the origins and history of this gap and present strategies for overcoming this separation.

Resisting a New Values Hierarchy

Famously or infamously, the arena of disability and education is rife with perceived gaps that when made visible reflect hierarchies of value. For instance, behaviorist researchers encased at universities have for many years dominated the general discourse of what they name to be *best practices* in special education. When concern is expressed that *best practices* appear to have extremely limited, restrictive, or even detrimental results, researchers have commonly responded that the fault lies not with the laboratory-crafted practices, but with the practitioners in classrooms who fail to correctly implement the practices. For instance, Heward (2003), described what he sees as a *"distressing gap* between what research has discovered about effective instruction and what is practiced in many classrooms" (p. 189, emphasis added).

In addition to the hierarchal gap set up by researchers between what is presented as the sage scholar and the incompetent practitioner is a second common gap articulated by school-based professionals between the reasoned practitioner and the seemingly unhinged parent of a child with disabilities. Parents in this hierarchy are commonly cast as crazed and destructive. If only, the logic goes, they would heed the sound professional advice of the sensible educator. For instance, Chesley and Calaluce (1997), both public school administrators in Connecticut, described parents who supported inclusive schooling as "unrealistic and absurd" (p. 489). They complained that parents were placing their children with disabilities in danger of a life-threatening nature "on purely philosophical grounds" (p. 489), meaning in inclusive rather than segregated educational environments.

A pattern is evident in these hierarchal gaps: Reason and reflectiveness are associated with forms of knowing that originate with those who are most distant from the lived experience of disability. Conventional researchers place themselves above practitioners who place themselves above families. It is just this type of stratification that was challenged at the genesis of disability studies. This occurred precisely because it was those most close to disability, people so labeled and their families, who saw past the societal machinery of dehumanization into a new text of valorization and full humanity. This initial effort was one of advocacy and political struggle for the creation and recognition of civil rights including access to education. But as disability studies has followed Black studies and women's studies from the streets, so to speak, into academia, a danger emerges that the element of action and advocacy may be deemphasized in favor of a distant intellectualization that has little relevance to the actual experience of people with disabilities, their family and friends, and their teachers. A new gap emerges but one that is not dissimilar to that which preceded it: conventional researchers (change now to disability studies scholars) valuing their psychology (change now to critical paradigms) over the deep understanding of disability in daily experience.

The Troubled History of Young Children with Disabilities and Critical Consideration in Academia

Understanding the role early childhood has played in fostering the disability studies movement is necessary if disability studies is to become useful to early childhood education and vice versa. The *genesis myth* of early childhood special education has taken on such canonical proportions that perhaps it is difficult for disability studies scholars to see beyond the shroud of psychological benevolence into more accurate interpretations of the original separation of young children labeled with disabilities from their peers who carried no such label.

The canon-of-benevolence decrees that early in the twentieth century concerned and caring advocates realized that thoughtful schooling might enrich the lives of America's youngest citizens (for a more complete description (see Kliewer and Raschke, 2002). These educational pioneers crafted a new arm of psychology referred to as child development and opened classrooms for children who had not yet reached school age. In these classes, certain children struggled to fit. Because professionals designed the curricula based on the new science of normal development, the children who stumbled were, according to this science, logically defined as abnormal, impaired, or as having special needs. Hence, a new field emerged, that of early childhood special education, focused on creating specialized classrooms considered to be more clinically conducive and scientifically responsive to the impaired developmental needs of children with disabilities.

The canon continued that as the years of the twentieth century passed, the two distinct fields of early childhood education (ECE) and early childhood special education (ECSE) evolved separately from one another, with their distinct teaching technologies conscientiously grounded in the separate scientific knowledge bases of either normal or abnormal development. In the latter half of the century, however, the workings of the educational sciences, perceived as neutral and objective, could no longer ignore societal changes occurring apart from science on the cultural and moral plain of America.

Strict and automatic educational segregation of students with disabilities, though often perceived to be a scientific endeavor, was challenged from a values standpoint. Certain educators, the story suggests, began to ponder the possibility of a less stratified and stigmatizing system for early schooling: "Perhaps a way exists to merge, in part, the two distinct pedagogues of ECE and ECSE to lessen the segregation experienced by certain students." The merger might occur by actually bridging the technologies when possible; or, at the least, by enacting each separately within the same classroom and at the same time. Thus, in the canonical tale, we arrive at some semblance of inclusive early childhood education when the distinctions in technologies are in a sense slight enough.

Disability studies scholars should recognize that this description of events, locked as it is in the myths of psychology with no reference to families, has no resemblance to the actual origins of childcare for young children presumed to fall outside normality. This realization is exceedingly important because it is in a more accurate representation of the genesis of early childhood special education that we find a vital part of the story of segregation enacted on devalued groups and ultimately a movement in response to this segregation that was galvanized as new texts of disability forming the basis of what we eventually call disability studies.

Early Childcare

Early childhood special education originated neither out of benevolence nor as a legitimate scientific response to so-called detached notions of non-normality, but as a direct result of the destructive eugenics movement that swept America beginning in the late 1800s. In the apparent cultural turmoil brought on by industrialization and new immigration patterns, eugenic science staked a firm foothold in the social psyche of America's privileged classes. According to the eugenicists, the mass emergence of social problems at the end of the 1800s, from poverty to moral decay, was directly attributable to *feeblemindedness*, an early label describing intellectual impairment and moral vacuity (Winship, 1900). Eugenicists believed immigration to be the primary source of what was perceived to be the moral decline of America (Goddard, 1914). Immigrants tended to be, after all, poor, and poverty was assumed to be a symptom of feeblemindedness.

One specific eugenic concern was the increased numbers of mothers of young children working outside the home. Between 1890 and 1910, the proportion of mothers in the paid labor force rose from 16% to 26% (Polakow, 1993). The fear-induced question was asked, "Who will socialize (i.e., Americanize) the young children?" In response emerged a new charity movement, the day nurseries (now called daycare), begun by middle and upper class women as a solution to the *problem* of poor children *and* their mothers.

By 1898, nearly 200 day nurseries existed in America's urban centers (Clarke-Stewart, 1993). The underlying rationale for these programs was a compensatory and curative one: "Day nursery founders generally defined the consumers of their services as 'pathological' and viewed such families as threatening or 'at risk'" (Swadener, 1995, p. 411). Care provided the children was of a custodial nature. Instructional programming focused on obedience and cleanliness. Organizers of the day nurseries also demanded that the working mothers of enrolled children participate in parenting classes designed to "overcome family deficiencies" (Swadener, 1995, p. 411). Individual by individual, the day nurseries sought to cure the social problem of poor children through forced conformity to upper class values without questioning such a framework's inherent devaluation of the family's experiences, the societal structure of poverty, or, indeed, the delimiting notion of normality imposed from positions of privilege. It is here, in the day nurseries, that we find the origins of early childhood special education as a segregated, charitable response to a child and family's pathological impairments. Soon, the new science of child development would further solidify and objectify community standards denoting the boundary between family normality and abnormality.

In the 1920s, well after the rise of day nurseries or day care as a response to the perceived pathology of the poor, child development departments at universities around the country began to organize nursery schools for the children of middle and upper class families. The curricula of the nursery school differed dramatically from the parallel system of day nurseries (Bloch 1992): the nursery school was not a compensatory model of schooling, but one of enrichment and actualization. The affluent children in attendance were in essence thought to define normality, so there was no general need to fix them. Instead, the nursery school functioned as a community extension of the care provided by stay-at-home mothers.

Thus the canonical story of early childhood special education is fundamentally flawed. The dual system of early childcare originated not with general preschool, but with the perceived pathology of immigrant and poor children and their families. Only later did so-called normal early childhood education develop for middle and upper class children. As such, segregation was not a scientifically deduced response to children who struggled in a thoughtful curriculum, but was a cultural first response born of eugenics.

Importantly, young children with significant disabilities did not attend day nurseries or nursery schools. In the early twentieth century, they either remained at home under the family's care, or they were institutionalized. Popular acceptance of eugenic science increased the number and size of institutions, and institution superintendents sought to procure more funds by opening their doors to even the youngest children (Kliewer, 1998).

Following World War II, however, families largely apart from professionals instigated a profound revolution in services available to their children with disabilities. The professions associated with disability had basically ignored children with moderate to severe disabilities other than to incarcerate them into institutions. In contrast, parents recognized their children as human beings and worked to treat them accordingly. Newly formed parent groups such as the United Cerebral Palsy Association (founded 1948), the Muscular Dystrophy Association (founded 1950), and the National Association of Parents and Friends of Mentally Retarded Children (renamed The Arc, founded 1950) organized the first educational programs for children with moderate to severe disabilities. By 1955, The Arc operated nation-wide over a thousand educational services for children. The schools and classes represented what parents described as "a need to challenge the validity of the finality in the words, 'Nothing can be done for your child'" (Hay, 1952, p. 1).

Research, policy, and professional interest in the education of students with significant disabilities emerged *only after* parents initiated such schooling. Parents led the way in recasting and altering the text of disability in a direction of humanization and a limited sense of democratic participation. Facing deep, societal-wide intolerance toward their children, parents were forced to create schools quite separate from the general public school spaces provided to children in general. Here again, segregation had nothing to do with science, but was rather the result of profound community antagonism toward children who were considered to be different from the norm.

Over the subsequent decades, segregated school programs were professionally misapprehended according to the canonical tale recounted earlier: as benevolent and scientific responses to children who had failed to fit sound curricular experiences. In response to the growing entrenchment of segrega-

tion, parents were again required to spark change in the professions associated with disability and education. Parents demanded access to public
schools and eventually to nonsegregated settings. These parents were galvanized by the accumulating victories of the Civil Rights Movement. They
began to take note of the power of the courts when confronted by abject
community and scientific intolerance aimed directly at the spirit of their
children.

In 1964, the internationally recognized special educator, Gunnar Dybwad
asked, point-blank, "Are we retarding the retarded?" through the *treatment* of
segregation forced on those so labeled. Four years later, in 1968, the parent
group *Pennsylvania Association for Retarded Children* ended an investigation into the decrepit services available for children with disabilities across
the Commonwealth of Pennsylvania. In the face of staunch opposition from
institution personnel and school districts alike, the parents concluded that the
reduction and eventual elimination of state institutions required legal intervention. The law suit filed ended in a 1972 consent decree. The central issue
of the decree for which parents fought was that children labeled mentally
retarded require the benefit of the presumption of educability; hence, each
child is guaranteed a free and appropriate education in the least restrictive
environment. At the time, Pennsylvania offered not a single community-
based educational program for children of school age "adjudged uneducable
and untrainable by the public schools" (*PARC v. Commonwealth* 1972, 22).
Overcrowded state institutions forced large numbers of youths with disabilities into makeshift asylums. Remarkably, one such location was set up on the
prison grounds of the Dallas State Correction facility.

In its decree, the Court mandated the development of educational programs for Pennsylvania's children with disabilities, stating,

> It is the Commonwealth's obligation to place each mentally retarded child in a free,
> public program of education and training appropriate to the child's capacity, within
> the context of the presumption that, among the alternative programs of education
> and training required by statute to be available, placement in a regular public school
> class is preferable to placement in a special public school class and placement in a
> special public school class is preferable to placement in any other type of program of
> education and training. (3)

In the two years that followed the *PARC* decision, 46 right-to-education
cases in 28 states wove their way through the courts, filed generally as class-
actions by parents on behalf of their children with disabilities. The outcomes

of these cases were consistent with the *PARC* decree and moved Congress to action in 1975 with the passage of what has come to be called *The Individuals with Disabilities Education Act* which guarantees children with disabilities a right to education in the least restrictive environment (Yell, 1998). The legislation ignored preschool children and it was largely parent efforts that led to amendments in 1986 guaranteeing educational rights to America's youngest citizens who happened to have disabilities.

Advocacy at the Heart of Disability Studies

Knowing an accurate depiction of the struggle parents initiated to challenge cultural representations of disability is not enough. Action in the continuing struggle is vital. At each juncture in the history of disability and education, professionals and researchers largely resisted the active shift toward progressive realizations of civil rights and access to the wider school community on the part of students with disabilities including in early childhood. Generally this resistance was shrouded in the language of science and care while parents, pushing forward as advocates, recognized their cause as one of the creation and realization of political and moral rights for their young children. Only after the rights were established and enacted did professionals and researchers move in to more thoroughly understand the new contexts of disability. Advocacy, however, established the parameters by radically revolutionizing the very text of disability. Thus the moral shift precedes what we might term the science.

A striking example of advocacy and action in rewriting the text of disability is the Jowonio School, an early childhood education center serving children from birth through age six in Syracuse, New York. In 1969, at the height of the Viet Nam war and the Civil Rights Movement, a small group of concerned parents met one evening to discuss the possibility of starting a school for their children that would exist as a free school outside the rigidity of the public system. The curriculum would be integrally linked to issues of economic and social justice. The result of those initial discussions was Jowonio (an English transliteration of the Onondagan phrase meaning *to set free*). Over the next several years, Jowonio grew in size, stature, and reputation as more families joined the community. From a church basement to abandoned army barracks to an old house owned by the local university to excess rooms at the community playhouse, the growing numbers of Jowonio families followed the transient location of their program, eventually landing in a closed down public school building on the verge of being condemned. Here Jowonio would remain for the next three decades until moving in 2001 to a modernized building.

In 1975, six years after Jowonio began, a member of the now-reputable faculty, on personal business, toured the local mental retardation institution, Syracuse Developmental Center. On the children's ward of the institution she met Mikey Logan who was four years old and the unit's only ambulatory inmate. Mikey was nonverbal and labeled severely mentally retarded and autistic. The Jowonio teacher encountered Mikey strapped to his bed which is how he spent the majority of his life because staff on the institution ward did not want to chase after him. When released from his bed for meals he generally was strapped to a chair. He was offered no educational programming at all. This was the reality of disability for countless children across America at the time.

The Jowonio teacher left the institution and Mikey that afternoon, but could not forget the abuse she had witnessed. The teacher approached the parent committee that oversaw Jowonio and on which sat Ellen Barnes and Peter Knoblock. In addition to her work at Jowonio, Barnes was a part of the Center on Human Policy at Syracuse University, a pioneering institute for the rights of individuals with disabilities. Knoblock was on faculty at Syracuse University's School of Education, and father to three Jowonio children. Along with Barnes he was a founding member of the Jowonio community and the school's first director. Knoblock was recognized nationally for his psychoeducational, therapeutic interventions in the lives of children labeled with emotional disorders and autism. "Could Mikey come to Jowonio?" the teacher asked.

At about the same time in 1975, parents of two other preschool-aged children labeled with severe disabilities including autism and mental retardation approached the public schools requesting that their children have access to an educational program. Congress had just passed what would become the *Individuals with Disabilities Education Act* guaranteeing access to education, but implementation had not yet begun and, as noted earlier, the initial version of the bill ignored preschool children. The parents' request was rejected. They then turned to Jowonio: "Might your school have space?"

Jowonio had from its inception served children of wide ranging abilities and interests, but never before had anyone requested that a student with diagnosed severe disabilities be allowed to enroll let alone three such students! Still, Jowonio faculty and families recognized the school's mission of a more just community, so opened up a separate "special education" class-room for the three, each assigned a graduate student from Syracuse University who acted as an aid.

"It took us maybe a week to realize we needed to get rid of the wall we had put up between our children," recalled Ellen Barnes in an interview many years later, "Inclusion started simply, naturally. The children shared lunches, field trips, and pretty soon the whole day." The three children, two of whom had weeks earlier been rejected from public preschool and one who had lived in an institution, immediately became integral members of the Jowonio learning community. Mikey would be adopted by the teacher who freed him from the institution. The faculty, in awe of the children's unheard of progress, quickly organized the Committee for the Development of a Therapeutic Nursery which brought together prominent members of the education, research, and psychological establishment in Syracuse. The group began planning for the systematic inclusion into Jowonio of children with severe disabilities, work that continues to this day.

Under the thoughtful eye of the Committee for the Development of a Therapeutic Nursery, inclusion became a planful, reflective process, but it is vital to recognize that inclusion would not have happened at all without initial advocacy and a vision of social justice. It was the teacher on the ward of the institution and two sets of parents who initiated the rewriting of the text of disability. They saw in their children's eyes a humanness that was lost on the wider culture. Jowonio, however, as a community, was responsive toward this new vision and quickly created valued space for the children. This moment in combination with other instances of struggle and advocacy on the part of people with disabilities and their families would eventually come together to form the rubric of disability studies. The rewriting of the text of disability was an intellectual, emotional, and spiritual endeavor, but it was as importantly *action* in the form of a personal and communal commitment to struggle, advocacy, political and cultural change, and democratic participation in the daily experience of individuals labeled disabled. Absent *action*, there would be no disability studies.

Finding Relevancy in Action

Disability studies has much to offer to discussions of early childhood education, particularly in fostering full democratic participation on the part of people with disabilities. Such participation must start early in the child's life, in preschool, and disability studies holds the key to theorizing and pushing the paradigm of full participation for all citizens. However, for disability studies to impact the texts of disability in early childhood, scholars must extend theory into action. Jowonio would not be if conversations had simply ended with conversations. Instead, there was movement that visibly altered the very nature of disability. Distant intellectualization may be sport to some, but we are in danger of allowing it to craft a new values gap between those who matter in actual everyday experience and those who provide commentary from afar.

I suggest three strategies for building relevancy between disability studies and early childhood education. First, certain disability scholarship should focus on wrenching the story of early childhood education from the tight grasp of psychology which has to date largely protected the myths of young children's schooling from critical and sociological inquiry. In this way we may begin to uncover the influences families and young children have had on disability studies. Second, scholarship from the perspectives of disability studies must increasingly be directed at affecting the lived experience of young children and their families in directions of democratic participation. This means that at some level scholarship must arise out of actual experience and/or be directly applicable to actual experience. Third, scholars must then expend energy on *enacting* (i.e., putting into action) paradigmatic challenges to the conventional text of disability. This might mean supporting the development of an inclusive preschool where none existed, starting a movement to shut down a segregated preschool, opening a playgroup welcoming to families of children with disabilities, starting a teacher preparation licensure program focused on inclusive education, or producing a video that teaches effective strategies for democratic participation at the early childhood level. The list is, of course, endless. The focus is on action and democracy.

References

Bloch, M. N., (1992). Critical perspectives on the historical relationship between child development and early childhood education research. In S. Kessler and B. B. Swadener, Eds. *Reconceptualizing the early childhood curriculum: Beginning the dialogue*: 3–20. New York: Teachers College Press.

Chesley, G. M. and Calaluce, P. D. (1997). The deception of inclusion. *Mental Retardation, 35*, 488–490.

Clarke–Stewart, A. (1993). *Daycare.* rev. ed. Cambridge, MA: Harvard University Press.

Dybwad, G. (1964). Are we retarding the retarded? In Gunnar Dybwad, ed. *Challenges in Mental Retardation* (pp. 19–25). New York: Columbia University Press.

Goddard, H. H. (1914). *Feeble–mindedness: Its causes and consequences.* New York: Macmillan.

Hay, W. (1952). *Association for parents of mental retardates.* Arlington, TX: National Association for Retarded Citizens.

Heward, W. L. (2003). Ten faulty notions about teaching and learning that hinder the effectiveness of special education. *The Journal of Special Education, 36,* 186–205.

Kliewer, C. (1998). *Schooling children with Down Syndrome: Toward an understanding of possibility.* New York: Teachers College Press.

Kliewer, C. and Raschke, D. (2002). Beyond the metaphor of merger: Confronting the moral quagmire of segregation in early childhood special education. *Disability, Culture, and Education, 1,* 41–62.

Pennsylvania Association for Retarded Children v. Commonwealth of Pennsylvania 343 F. Supp. 279 E.D. Penn., 1972.

Polakow, V. (1993). *Lives on the edge: Single mothers and their children in the other America.* Chicago: University of Chicago Press.

Swadener, B. B. (1995). Stratification in early childhood social policy and programs in the United States: Historical and contemporary Manifestations. *Educational Policy* 9, 422–424

Winship, A. E. (1900). *Jukes-Edwards: A study in education and heredity.* Harrisburg, PA: R.L. Myers.

Yell, M. L. (1998). *The law and special education.* Upper Saddle River, NJ: Merrill.

*How is Disability Studies in Education (Ir)Relevant to the
Practical Interests, Experiences, and Goals of
Disabled People in Schools?*

CHAPTER 6

Theory Meets Practice: Disability Studies and Personal Narratives in School

Santiago Solis and David J. Connor

Scholarship in disability studies has developed into an "academic" discourse, not unlike other fields of inquiry. Such growth may be a phase in the emergence and institutionalization of a new discipline. However, as a whole, disability studies in the United States has been criticized for its lack of relevance to the lives of disabled people—including, most pertinently, by disabled people themselves. It is fair to ask questions, then, such as: how much influence does disability studies exert in tangible, qualitative changes that improve the lives of people with whom it claims a central concern? How does disability studies positively impact upon general living conditions of people with disabilities? How much does disability studies (re)shape conceptualizations of disability within social and cultural frameworks, offering more empowering alternatives to dominant deficit-based medical, psychological, and legal discourses? What *actions* and *results* can be seen from the influence exerted by disability studies? In short, does disability studies in education actually exist—or is it mere rhetoric? Finally, is it confined to the ivory tower, or does it circulate through the grass roots level of the "real" world?

One important aspect of this discussion is the language used in academic discourse. In disability studies, as often happens in any area of inquiry, the language used by scholars is not accessible to non-academics, including many disabled people. Thus, it is with a substantial degree of irony that many discussions within the current field of disability studies are *inaccessible* to people outside academe. In writing this chapter, therefore, we were forced to ask ourselves: who are we writing it for—academics or teachers? Our intended audience, we have decided, should be *both*.

Academics with and without disabilities have access to theoretical language and therefore can discuss disability in terms of their own experience and/or in the abstract. However, instead of being a medium for social change, disability studies can appear to settle within a circumscribed arena, often falling short of practical applications. A concern of ours is the potential for disability studies in education to remain in a realm of theorizing that does not lend itself to the everyday experiences of people with disabilities—both children and adults—in schools. While we assert that the relevance of practical theorizing over disability studies in education is underdeveloped, we also interpret this gap with a large degree of optimism. The field of disability studies in education is ripe to cultivate ways of thinking that challenge social attitudes and mores (including schooling structures and practices) that currently marginalize people with disabilities.

In this chapter, we therefore continue furthering the tentative conversation between disability studies and practical application to the lives of individuals with disabilities. This is done with the purpose of raising many issues for which we, as people interested in disability studies in education, have not yet fully developed answers. Because of length limitations, we have confined ourselves to contemplating two broad areas: first, the practical interests, experiences, and goals of students/children with disabilities; second, the practical interests, experiences, and goals of educators/adults with disabilities.

It is important to note that we are currently working full time in public school systems as, respectively, a resource room teacher and as a teacher coach. In addition, we are doctoral students using disability studies as part of the theoretical framework in our dissertations as well as teaching disability studies based classes in education at the university level. Furthermore, one of us has a disability. Thus, navigating academia and public education simultaneously—as disabled and non-disabled—has allowed us to weigh the possibilities of utilizing disability studies in the "real" world. In addition, our previous research uses a theoretical framework with a disability studies grounding, including the use of narratives to show how teachers and students understand what it means to have a disability in school settings (Connor, 2005; Ferri, Connor et al., 2005; Solis, 2006).

Students/Children

Practical Interests

It is difficult, for a number of reasons, to pinpoint practical interests of students with disabilities in schools. The *types* of disability vary enormously, including thirteen federally defined categories and a plethora of conditions included in section 504 of the Rehabilitation Act of 1973. In addition, kindergarten through twelfth grade exemplifies a breadth of ages and developments (including physical, psychological, emotional, and academic), with each age and stage of development possibly meriting different interests of students with disabilities. Furthermore, the experience of disability is also mediated by other factors such as race, ethnicity, social class, and sexual orientation. It is simply not feasible to assume that all students with disabilities share practical interests, as if they constituted a homogenized, self-recognizing, and self-defined group.

There are, however, some commonalities that deserve to be brought to light. For example, many students who have experienced school in segregated placements state their dissatisfaction in having been separated from their non-disabled counterparts. In a study by Reid and Button (1995), the authors reported stigmatization of students with disabilities and name calling by non-disabled peers. Gibb et al. (1999) noted that the majority of students labeled as having a behavior disorder (BD) or emotional disturbance (ED) preferred being educated in general education classes. Walsh (1994) found that some students with disabilities saw placement in general education as the defining moment in their lives in terms of career path, self-esteem, intellectual functioning, and social relationships.

In a recent study by Connor, youth who graduated from high school critiqued their experience in special education in very powerful ways—alluding to the social, psychological, and academic consequences of segregated placements. One person, Chanell,[1] describes her experience in special education thus; "It was like jail." Another participant, Michael, reveals, "When I was in there, I really wanted to kill myself, because that's the most embarrassing thing to a kid." In terms of academics, Precious shares, "The classes that they put me in was baby work all the time. I don't think I got a fair education coz we didn't do as much work that we should have been doing." Another participant, Vanessa, laments the difficulty of academic improvement, saying "Of course you're going to have a fourth grade reading level coz that's what they teach you. It's kind of hard for the RCTs".[2] Similarly, in a class project led by Solis, middle school students expressed their dissatisfaction with their placement in special education classrooms. Gustavo indicates, "I do not like being in special education because people make fun of me. They do not try to get to know me first; instead, they just start calling me names." Another student, Adrian, states, "I feel bad being in special education because the kids in general education make fun of me. They call me names such as stupid and retarded." Based on our own work with students of various ages, it is clear that many students do not like to be in segregated settings, believing them to disadvantage their academic progress and social growth.

However, in Connor's study there were also people who liked the support services offered through special education, for example, W.G. claims, "I'd say I prefer special ed., even though I don't want to say that. Coz in special ed. they give you individual attention." Another participant, Jarrel simply states, "I thought I learned more in special ed." In a similar vein, Solis found that some of his students preferred to be educated in special education classrooms. For instance, Jeremy indicates, "I like being in special education because the other kids are nice to me. All my friends are in the classroom with me. I like everything about special education." One of the other students, Joel, states, "I feel good being in special education because kids in my class treat me well. I help the students who sometimes misspell words and those who cannot read well." These comments suggest that, while integration is of great practical interest to many students with disabilities, others prefer separate placements and services. Such contrasting sentiments highlight the difficulty in claiming a practical interest shared by *all* students with disabilities.

What is interesting about the above studies is their concern with *student point of view*. One mantra of the disability movement is "nothing about us without us," yet the overwhelming amount of research in special education is done without consulting with people labeled disabled. There is insufficient information about what students with disability labels want, feel, think, and understand, both in and out of school. As decisions are made for them, the "practical interests" of students are eclipsed and subjected to determination by teacher(s) and/or parent(s). Managing the disability of others in this manner is highly problematic, because the practical interests of students are at best obscured and at worst ignored. Arguably, the practical interest of a child with a disability is to get the best education he or she can in preparation for a highly competitive world. However, the disunited system of general and special education, while on the surface designed to provide support services to those who most need them, serves to remove students from the general education classroom. Special education, therefore, *creates* and *defines* general education as a place for the student "normate" (Thomson, 1997, p. 8).

Experiences

The experiences of students with disabilities in schools can be seen in terms of both the academic and social realm. For students, schools are primarily social spaces in which they learn to interact with others, particularly their peers (Garnett, 1996). It is in schools that students are influenced by conceptualizations of normalcy. The experiences of students who have been positioned *outside* the realm of the normal—by implication the non-normates, or abnormates—are largely assigned to the auspices of special education. Yet it is also important to remember that there are many students with disabilities who spend the overwhelming majority of their time in general education; their perceptions of disability and their qualitative experiences differ enormously from those in segregated classes. For example, as a rule, those labeled mildly learning disabled who receive resource room services may not consider themselves "special ed." (i.e., "disabled"). In addition, students labeled disabled with a variety of psychological, physical, emotional, and cognitive conditions often do not need segregated services, yet their options are still far more circumscribed than their non-disabled counterparts. For example, despite laws such as the Americans with Disabilities Act (ADA), when students who use wheelchairs articulate from middle school to high school their academic and/or placement choices may be reduced by up to 90% or more.

What all students with disabilities do have in common, regardless of placement in general or special education, is their negotiation of stigma associated with disability. Unlike other markers of identity such as race and gender, disability has not engendered a comparable sense of pride. This, of course, is problematic, and countered by Linton (1998) through her celebratory "claiming [of] disability." In schools, however, taunting, teasing, and general "put downs" are rife toward students with disabilities (Reid and Button, 1995; Rodis et al., 2001). Indeed, the word "retard" and phrase "that's retarded" echo shamelessly along many school hallways, used by both students and teachers alike, without forethought. Solis observed that his students often encounter derogatory language associated with their labels and special education placements. For instance, Dwayne states "I hate special education because the students in other classes call me names such as stupid, dumb, retarded, and slow. I hate the names that they call me." Correspondingly, another student, Misael, indicates "One thing that makes special education bad is when the kids say mean names to me. They yell at me like I am retarded. They do this because I am in special education."

Students with disabilities, therefore, attempt to downplay or actively hide their status of disability. They avoid being associated with special education by arriving to class late, leaving early, and sitting out of view of students who pass the door. For teenagers, social relations are severely influenced by the disability label. In Connor's study Chanel explains that when she was a student she vigilantly hid the fact that she was in special education, admitting that she actually began developing "this phobia about what people are thinking about me." Another participant, Michael, remembers his high school experience in terms of the kiss-of-death stigma associated with special education whenever he attempted to make romantic connections, stating, "Once they find out, girls don't want to date you, no one wants to talk to you."

Another point we must make to dispel the notion of a homogenized group of disabled students is the hierarchy based on *type* of disability evident in both formal school structures and informal social interactions. For example, "visible" and "invisible" disabilities differ in that students with self-evident disabilities do not need to disclose, whereas students without discernable disabilities have an option. Many students, who have been deemed disabled, are defined as such by trained professionals whose sole purpose is to detect "abnormal" academic progress and behavior in order to assign labels and determine placements. Thus, "soft" labels—those highly subjective and contextual—such as learning disabled, emotionally disturbed, speech and language impaired, and arguably, mentally retarded,[3] constitute approximately 85% of all students with disability labels. Students with these labels overwhelmingly opt not to disclose their disability status if given the chance for fear of experiencing discrimination. And while some disabilities are decidedly taboo (such as being developmentally delayed, or "retarded"), others are viewed as relatively harmless, such as Attention Deficit Disorder (ADD), while still others are occasionally viewed by their "owners" as a badge of honor such as having a Behavior Disorder (BD).

Despite negative connotations, there is also a positive side to being labeled disabled while in school. One such benefit is the receipt of modifications and accommodations that benefit students. Students talk about the relief of having extra time to complete tests, or the options of taking exit examinations (in New York State, students with disabilities are currently allowed to take different examinations than their non-disabled counterparts[4]) in order to obtain a local high school diploma, as evidenced by several of the participants in Connor's study. In this particular research, working class youth labeled disabled discuss the difficulties of participating in a high school Regents-level curriculum culminating in passing final examinations that are required to graduate, indicating the struggles and pressures they experience on a daily basis. Furthermore, in our own professional experience, we have noticed that the advantages of being disabled also intersect with social class; middle-class parents often mobilize to capitalize on accommodations, requesting (and at times demanding) that their children receive extended time on highly competitive college entrance examinations, thereby ensuring an even greater chance to succeed when compared to working class or poor students. In addition, affluent, savvy parents can manipulate the system to obtain private schooling at public expense by having attorneys argue that the local education authority cannot provide highly specific services needed for their child.

Goals

The goals of students with disabilities in school are often spelled out *for them* by teachers and/or parents in their Individual Educational Plans (IEPs). Goals are clinical in nature, quantifiable in terms of evidence, and, ultimately appear to primarily serve the function of accountability in institution rather than work for real "live" students. Often, IEP meetings are held without students or parents, including the generation and documentation of student goals. Here, it is important to note that student and/or parental participation also depends on social class—as middle-class students and parents are more likely to reference their rights according to the law. Nevertheless, while the law requires that students have input in generating goals for themselves in their transition plan from the age of fourteen, the process is often severely curtailed by pre-generated computerized check off lists from which to choose "appropriate" goals.

However, what about the students' *actual* personal goals? What do students with disabilities hope to gain from a high school education? Perhaps debatably, and definitely controversially, the majority of students with disabilities—as demonstrated by their desire to be out of special education and in general education—want to "fit in" as documented by Solis. The concepts of "fitting in" and "belonging" are perhaps almost universal desires. Yet, how much does the "fitting in" rely upon conforming to physical, social, psychological, and cognitive norms? In other words, how much do students with disabilities want to be "normal"?[5] And how much of this desire to be "normal" stems from parental expectations and pressure?

An assumed, but often unspoken premise of the system of schooling is its expectation that students will perform academically and behaviorally at a certain rate in a certain way by a certain age. Failure to comply with this developmental model leads to a series of tests, interviews and examinations that often result in a label of disability. However, since the deficit-based model of disability that pervades schools is synonymous with special education, labels are often rejected by those to whom they have been assigned. Instead, labels become something students seek to shed. As indicated by Connor, one young woman, W.G. explains, "[with a local diploma] I can go to college and put the special ed. business behind me."

In many respects, it appears that the goals of disabled students are very similar to those of non-disabled students: to graduate from school, attend college, and obtain a satisfying job. Solis found that his students have many goals and aspirations as evidenced by Johnetta, who states, "When I grow up, I want to be a teacher. I want to teach kindergarten." However, as can be seen in the comments of W.G. in Connor's study, unlike markers of identity such as race and gender, students seek to "lose" their disability label or at least conceal it. Others contend to be proud of who they are but still prefer not to disclose unless they specifically trust people. What strikes us here, among other things, is the centripetal gravitation of "the disabled" toward normalcy and how disability is seen as a centrifugal force, limiting possibilities of attaining status as a normate student.

While a generalized and admittedly sweeping comment, the rush to normalcy is a disturbing idea to us. Specifically, we feel that the unquestioned acceptance of normalcy reinforces a powerful hold on the imagination of how cultures and societies at large conceptualize variation among humans, how they view corporeal difference. Stated bluntly, the disabled are positioned as abnormal, defective, and "not quite right," as deviants who are, by definition, strange creatures—as evidenced by one of Joel's statements in the study conducted by Solis, "They [general education kids] think that kids in special education look like aliens." Differences that are labeled "disability" are not acknowledged as a natural or desirable part of the human spectrum. Thus, the goal to conform and pass as normal is born from the pressure to self-inscribe into the template of what it means to be a standardized human being. Consequently, to be disabled continues to signal a devaluation of individual worth in our society.

Educators/Adults

Practical Interests

The practical interests of teachers with disabilities in some ways parallel that of students: they want maximized access to jobs, and when necessary, accommodation in their employment. In many ways, administrators with disabilities probably share similar interests as they have faced challenging hurdles, but their experiences are less researched as a group than those of teachers with disabilities. Furthermore, school administrators in general are often gatekeepers as to whether teachers are employed in the first place and crucial in their support to guarantee survival. These points were stressed over two decades ago by Shapero and Dupper (1982) who urged school administrators to develop an informed and balanced attitude toward educators with disabilities. Thus, to reiterate, the practical aspect of gaining and maintaining employment appears to be of primary concern to teachers with disabilities.

In contemplating this section of the chapter, we recalled seeing a small excerpt in the newspaper of the teachers union about a group calling themselves "The Capably Disabled" (United Federation of Teachers, 2004). Searching the teachers union webpage, we found more information about this group in a section titled, "Working with a Disability." On this site, a succinct history of the organization reveals that the group was founded in 1990 "to focus on the concerns of members seeking certain accommodations to continue as educators" (2004, ¶2). Here, the implication is that teachers with disabilities required intervention and assistance to ensure that they carried on with their job. The group mobilized and pressured the New York City Board of Education to employ a Disability Rights Coordinator with the express purpose of having an advocate to ensure necessary accommodations. While this group represents educators with disabilities who have mobilized and organized for fifteen years, they also have no apparent knowledge of disability studies. We assume this based on multiple e-mail conversations with a representative, during which he informed us that he and other members of the group did not understand what we meant by "disability studies." We found it ironic that educators who have become politicized by their disability, in particular, through the *contexts* in which they have to work, are not familiar with disability studies. What this encounter highlighted for us is that the field of disability studies has not sufficiently reached a critical mass of educators.

Experiences

Similar to students, the breadth of disability experienced by teachers and administrators is wide ranging. As a result, a national coalition of educators with disabilities does not exist in the same way as other national minority organizations.[6] In addition, inhospitable conditions and ableist attitudes often make schools places in which teachers and administrators with disabilities feel unwelcome and unsafe. This can be seen in our own research where educators with "invisible" disabilities evaluated the risks and benefits of "coming out" (Valle et al., 2004). One teacher with a learning disability, Robert, describes his fearfulness in disclosing his status to the school community, speculating, "…what kind of reaction am I going to get from everybody? I think I'm going to be, like, scorned, burned at the stake…I don't think I would have as much credibility…I should have more credibility" (p. 8). It appears that the stigma of disability can weigh heavily in favor of individuals not directly sharing their status. For example, teachers with a learning disability fear they will be characterized as inefficient.

Recently, disability studies scholar Tom Shakespeare (2004) compared disability not only to markers of identity such as race or gender but rather to the social class of poverty, implying that the *pride* felt for the former is counterbalanced by the *shame* of the latter (¶3). Because disability is often widely perceived as emanating from something that is "missing," the celebration of disability to those who view it through a deficit lens is incomprehensible. However, to counter this thinking, the recognition—and acceptance—of "disability" simply as another way of being, allows the concept to be one in which the whole person can feel proud of him or herself.

Yet, the experiences of teachers with disabilities have included negotiating inaccessible buildings or multi-floor assignments, utilizing inadequate teaching materials, and facing hardship in traveling to assigned sites. All of these merit requests for assistance, and as such, could be perceived by ableist peers or unsympathetic administrators as a nuisance. Disabled educators can be accused of having "special needs wanting special deals." Thus, a real fear of resentment and reprisal serves to contain many teachers and administrators working in schools from being openly disabled (Solis, 2006). These factors probably contribute to the fact that studies about teachers and administrators with disabilities—particularly from their own perspectives—are very rare.

Once again, it is ironic that the dominant source of knowledge about disability and education in schools is through the auspices of "special education"—a field in which research is done largely by non-disabled people under the premise of social justice and equity for all. However, such "help" like stigmatizing labels, segregated placements, and overreliance on medication must lead us to question the motives of those who seek to maintain the current special education system. Teachers with disabilities are, like all members of society, immersed in understandings of disability that are largely framed within scientific, medical, and legal discourses. Hence, it is easy to self-inscribe into these limiting (and silencing) discourses if other options are not apparent or available.

In contrast to the deficit-driven, scientific/medical/legal discourse, the field of disability studies consciously strives to work *with* "disabled" people *for* disabled people. The common refrain of, "nothing about us without us," holds true in research as it does elsewhere. Personal experience and professional interchange with students and staff members with disabilities also shape knowledge about disability for teachers with disabilities. Nonetheless, experiences of teachers with diverse disabilities, validating their own knowledge and ways of thinking have yet to be adequately documented in the field of disability studies in education.

Goals

By all accounts, the goals of teachers and administrators appear to overlap with their practical interests. Using the ADA to ensure "reasonable accommodations" is a major step in exerting their rights. Each individual deserves a safe, accessible workplace. However, beyond the basic accommodations required to gain and maintain a job, the goals of teachers who have a disability are largely unexplored. It can be argued that African-American educators, gay and lesbian teachers, and pedagogues from poor backgrounds, hypothetically share a desire to improve society, albeit in different ways: in terms of equality among the races, a broader and more tolerant understanding of sexuality, and efforts to promote economic fairness. However, can we just as readily argue that teachers with disabilities want a more socially just world in terms of corporeal differences? And if this is in fact true, then what have they done as a group to accomplish that goal? Do all disabled teachers have a responsibility toward creating improved understanding about the concept of disability in schools? What about disabled teachers who prefer to assimilate and blend into the mainstream?

In many respects, we are left continuing to raise questions for which there are no fully developed answers. For example, in what ways can teachers with and without disabilities who are familiar with disability studies be advocates for people with disabilities? How can disability be taught in schools within a disability studies context, primarily focusing on the social implications of disability and their repercussions throughout society? How can special education as it is currently configured shift to embrace disability studies without co-opting and metamorphosizing it for its own ends? Should special education and disability studies be taught alongside each other?[7] How do students come to understand disability through the structures of schooling? How do students come to understand disability through the curriculum in schools? Can traditionally dominant conceptualizations of disability be challenged by more humane understandings of human variation? Can disability, like race, be reborn as a pertinent topic, analyzed and discussed in more multi-faceted terms, including the incorporation of perspectives of and by "the disabled"? If so, how might that change syllabi in English, history, and biology classes?[8] We raise these questions to argue that one of the goals of disability studies in education should be to transform existing ableist school practices in the hopes of creating new ways of thinking, doing, and being in school, and ultimately, the world.

Conclusion

The realm of academia and the world of schooling should always be interconnected. However, they continue to remain, by and large, virtually separate entities. For this reason, the question that we chose to examine— How is disability studies in education (ir)relevant to the practical interests, experiences, and goals of disabled people in schools?—is highly personal in that we remain hopeful about the relationship between disability studies and education. While we anticipate much growth, we also acknowledge that this growth can only come about if strategic work is ongoing, resources are developed, and derogatory discourses continue to be challenged. As a symbol of commitment to practical needs, the academic community needs to mobilize in order to ensure that "ableism" becomes as common an expression as "racism" and "sexism" both in the academy and in daily interchanges, including those in schools. One way to achieve this goal would be to append the term "ableism" into dictionaries. For as Weise (2004) points out, "If ableist has been adopted by the disabled, and scholars in the field of disability studies, but it has not been adopted by dictionaries, what does this say about the public consciousness of the word ableist?" (p. 32).

Furthermore, in order for disability studies to be recognized and respected as a field of inquiry such as African-American Studies, Women's Studies, and Gay and Lesbian Studies and contribute toward the shaping of teacher education, we must continue introducing it through interdisciplinary research, journals in and out of "special" education, education texts, and K through 12 classes, as well as college seminars. Inclusive education appears to be an ideal arena in which to center usually marginalized voices of students with disabilities. In addition, interdisciplinary approaches to education can be enhanced by developments within the field of disability studies, such as the recent vibrant growth within the humanities (Davis, 1997; Longmore and Umansky, 2001; Longmore, 2003; Snyder et al., 2002). Finally, we must continue taking risks, and we must continue supporting each other—in weaving the powerful perspectives embedded throughout disability studies into existing educational structures and school curricula. The infusion of disability studies into learning environments has already occurred in middle school classrooms (Solis, 2006), high school classrooms (Ware, 2001), and at district-wide professional development for school administrators (Connor, 2004).

We have found that disability studies—whether in K through 12 class-rooms or college seminars—is a powerful tool that can potentially transform thinking about disability in terms of respect, support, dignity, and equality. In this way, its relevance to all people is undeniable. As ideological theory, disability studies has already begun to challenge the notion of disability as corporeal deviance; as a practical concept; however, disability studies is still nascent and only beginning to flourish in the field of education. Conse-quently, we *must* continue to cultivate new and innovative ways to help bridge the gap between disability studies and education. One important and effective way to accomplish this objective is by inviting students and teach-ers with disabilities to share their personal experiences and by asking them many questions: what are your practical interests? What are your experi-ences? What are your goals? From our own research we have discovered that disability studies is relevant to the daily experiences of disabled students and teachers in schools. As a result, we continue to strive in making connections between theory and practice, understanding that these junctions need to be made before actual change can be forged. Hence, we urge a maintenance and deepening of the dialogue, a persistence in asking further—often difficult—questions, for as Grumet (1995) contends, "the path to what we should teach to children originates in what we are willing to know about our own lives" (p. x).

References

"A and F Rising Stars," (2004, November 14) [advertisement] *The New York Times Magazine*, p. 10.

Connor, D. J. (2004). Infusing disability studies into "mainstream" educa-tional thought: One person's story. *Review of Disability Studies, 1*, 1, 100–120.

————. (2005). *Labeled "learning disabled": Life in and out of school for urban black and/or latino(a) youth from working class backgrounds.* Unpublished doctoral dissertation, Teachers College, Columbia Univer-sity, New York.

Davis, L. J. (Ed.). (1997). *The disability studies reader.* New York: Routledge.

Ferri, B. A., Connor, D., Solis, S., Valle, J., and Volpitta, D. (2005). Mediat-ing discourses of disability: Teachers with LD revising the script. *Jour-nal of Learning Disabilities* (in press).

Garnett, K. (1996). *Thinking about inclusion and learning disabilities: A teacher's guide.* Reston, VA: Council for Exceptional Children.

Gibb, S. A., Allred, K., Ingram, G. F., Young, J. R., and Egan, W. M. (1999). Lessons learned from the inclusion of students with emotional and behavioral disorders in one junior high school. *Behavioral Disorders, 24, 2,* 122–136.

Grumet, M. R. (1995). Foreword in J. G. Silin, *Sex, death, and the education of children: Our passion for ignorance in the age of AIDS.* New York: Teachers College Press, Columbia University.

Linton, S. (1998). *Claiming disability.* New York: New York University Press.

Longmore, P. K. (2003). *Why I burned my book and other essays on disability.* Philadelphia: Temple University Press.

Longmore, P. K., and Umansky, L. (Ed.). (2001). *The new disability history: American perspectives.* New York: New York University Press.

Losen, D. J., and Orfield, G. (Eds.). (2002). *Racial inequality in special education.* Cambridge, MA: Harvard Education Press.

Parrish, T. (2002). Racial disparities in the identification, funding, and provision of special education. In D. J. Losen and G. Orfield (Eds.), *Racial inequality in special education* (pp. 15–37). Cambridge, MA: Harvard Education Press.

Reid, D. K., and Button, L. J. (1995). Anna's story: Narratives of personal experience about being labeled learning disabled. *Journal of Learning Disabilities, 28,* 10, 602–614.

Rodis, P., Garrod, A., and Boscardin, M. L. (Eds.). (2001). *Learning disabilities and life stories.* Needham Heights, MA: Allyn and Bacon.

Shakespeare, T. (November 4, 2004). The economics of metaphysics. Message posted to DISABILITY–RESEARCH@JISCMAIL.AC.UK.

Shapero, S., and Dupper, M. (1982). Balancing the scales: Attitudes toward handicapped educators. *Journal for Employment and Training Professionals, 4* (2), 79–82.

Snyder, S. L., Brueggemann, B. J., and Thomson, R. G. (Eds.). (2002). *Disability studies: Enabling the humanities.* New York: Modern Language Association.

Solis, S. (2006) I'm 'coming out' as disabled, but I'm "staying in" to rest: Reflecting on elected and imposed segregation. *Equity and Excellence in Education, 39, 2,* 146–153.

Thomson, R. G. (1997). *Extraordinary bodies*. New York: Columbia University Press.

United Federation of Teachers (2004). Working with a disability. Retrieved October 10, 2004, from http://www.org/?fid=218andtf+1174.

Valle, J., Solis, S., Volpitta, D., and Connor, D. (2004). The disability closet: Teachers with learning disabilities evaluate the risks and benefits of "coming out." *Equity and Excellence in Education, 31*, 1, 4–17.

Walsh, R. (1994). Making the journey to communication with assistive technology. *Exceptional Parent, 24,* 11, 37–41.

Ware, L. (2001). Writing, identity, and the other: Dare we do disabilities studies? *Journal of Teacher Education, 52*, 2, , 107–123.

Weise, J. (2004). "I'll pick you up by your back brace and throw you like a suitcase": On naming discrimination against disability. *Review of Disability Studies, 1*, 1, 29–33.

Notes

[1] We have included real people's names, unless individuals have indicated otherwise. Using an individual's real name is an effort to counteract anonymity used in much "clinical" research, thereby centering actual people with disabilities in the research.

[2] The Regents Competency Exam (RCT) was replaced by Regents Examinations during the late 1990s. However, only students with disabilities may still take the RCT, a far less demanding academic examination, and still be eligible to receive a local diploma.

[3] The label of MR has a history of misuse that is still with us today. See Losen and Orfield (2002) for statistics on the overrepresentation of African-American males in this category. In some states the label is over five times as likely to be given to an African-American as to a European-American (Parrish, 2002).

[4] See footnote 2.

[5] The phenomenon of desiring normalcy is a commonplace trope in disability-related stories and features in the public eye. For example, in an advertisement of Abercrombie and Fitch, soliciting donations from customers for the Juvenile Diabetes Research Foundation, able-bodied Cyler Sanderson gives a "piggy back" to Kyle Maynard, a person born with congenital amputation. The first line of text is spoken by Kyle and reads, "My whole life has been a pursuit of normalcy." "A and F Rising Stars" (2004, November 14) [advertisement] *The New York Times Magazine*, p. 10.

[6] National organizations to support individuals with disabilities such as the Council for Exceptional Children are largely operated by non-disabled people who subscribe to traditional forms of conceiving "disability," locating their understanding in medical, scientific, and legal discourses that people with disabilities often cite as oppressive.

[7] See, for example, the Department of Special Education and Disability Studies at the University of Newcastle, Australia.

[8] Note, for instance, that Syracuse University has initiated a new on-line resource for teachers (http://www.disabilitystudiesforteachers.org/), which offers lesson plans, essays, and other materials that teachers can utilize in their classrooms to help infuse disability studies into subjects such as social studies and English at the secondary (6–12) level.

CHAPTER 7

Disrupting Normalcy and the Practical Concerns of Classroom Teachers

Kagendo Mutua and Robin M. Smith

This chapter examines the relevance of disability studies to the practical concerns of teachers. To explore those concerns and disability studies' response to them, we begin the chapter by providing a brief overview of the key special education and disability studies perspectives that we use to discuss current practices. In the section subtitled mapping the terrain, we highlight the contrast between the medical/deficit oriented model of disability that undergirds special education research and practice and the social model of disability that underscores disability studies in which disability is socially constructed and therefore seen as a category of an oppressed minority. Next we discuss the concerns of teachers, with an emphasis on special education teachers, and disability studies' response to those concerns. Further, we discuss how research has and could be reframed using the principles of disability studies to empower researchers and teachers in special education on issues that affect disabled students. Finally, we end with a summary of our thoughts on what we propose as the possibilities for a re-theorization of special education from the standpoint of disability studies. Our proposal for a marriage of disability studies and special education focuses on how transforming what we see as the critical issues in research and practice in teacher education might have a catalytic and transformative effect on prevailing ideas about student disability.

In this chapter, we speak from the perspective of teacher educators. Both authors teach pre-service teachers, mainly those going into careers in special education and allied professions and occasionally with prospective general education teachers. Our analysis here is therefore based on common threads that we have observed and experienced while preparing pre-service teachers for those professions. We find that pre-service teachers express concerns (or more precisely, fears) ranging from who and how to include students with disabilities in the general educational contexts, behavior management of such students and their perception of a prevailing inadequacy of supports for students with various impairments placed within general education classrooms, accessing general educational curriculum and participating in state-/school-wide assessment of progress, testing versus teaching and other curriculum issues.

Additionally, we frame the issues in this chapter from the perspective of researchers in special education and our research attempts to understand and re/address disability issues from the standpoint of disability studies whilst being mindful of the majority of our readers in special education who may not be knowledgeable of disability. As researchers in special education, we problematize special education research as deficit-oriented, reductive—as positivist research tends to be—and implicated in the creation of oppressive structures in the education of students with disabilities in public school settings. We contrast those approaches with the competence-based student-centered research in which disability is seen as socially constructed rather than inherent deficits resident in the individual student.

Mapping the Terrain: Drawing the Lines
Between Special Education and Disability Studies

Special education and disability studies concern themselves with representing disability in research and praxis. However, as Davis (1995) points out, "the term 'disability,'…is at the base one that has been used to create rigid categories of existence: it is necessary to remember that the term serves at least two masters"(p. xv). It appears that among the masters that the concept of disability serves as the "disability expert." Historically, disability experts have wielded enormous power over disability from the assignation of names of disability, to disability research, and to the definition of disability practice. As Linton (1998) observes, disabled people (and their non-disabled allies) in the western/industrialized world historically have neither been in a position to even control the referent "disability" nor any terminology that has been used to linguistically represent the various human differences referred to as "disabilities." Yet the terms used to refer to disability, as Davis and Linton suggest, are more than just terms. They have the power to script interactions and relationships in everyday lives of disabled and non-disabled people alike. While the disability 'expert' fields and disciplines are many, special education is one whose influence and power on student disability is direct and well-documented. For instance, in public school, the assignation of a disability label to a student is more than just a denotation of a physiological, sensory or emotional attribute, indeed it is an assignation of identity. Rather appending the label of disability to a student in the public school in the United States encrypts his/her interactions (or opportunities for interactions with non-disabled peers) and relationships (or opportunities to develop relationships with non-disabled peers) not only in school but out of school as well. Further, the assignation of the disabled identity also sets in place compulsory limits that are temporal-spatial in nature, that designate spaces in the schools that such students can occupy (or from which they are barred) and further define the lengths of time that they can occupy those spaces. Such demarcations of time and space are enforced and adhered to through the Individualized Education Plan (IEPs) that typically state the Least Restrictive Environments (LRE) and also often include a statement of the frequency and percentage of time the disabled student is to interact or not interact with non-disabled peers and the spaces where such interactions can take place. Built into this temporal-spatial governance of disabled students through special education is a compulsory surveillance to which the disabled student is subjected. The continuation or increase in the time that such students spend with non-disabled peers is usually contingent upon their ability to meet and/or exceed the heteronormative expectations that such interactions and environments typically demand. Disability studies implicates special education, among other "expert disciplines," in the production and maintenance of such oppressive structures in which disabled peoples' lives are daily ensnared and views with suspicion those "standard practices" of special education, for instance, that intentionally segregate students merely on basis of disability, ostensibly for their own good.

Further, special education relies solely on the medical/deficit model in its dispensing of disability identities to children in school and has been impervious to disability studies' argument that society plays a key role in the construction and production of disability. Additionally, special education has not succeeded in casting the gaze inwards to itself to examine the way in which it has successfully coupled disability with other un/under-valued human differences, specifically racial differences, in its construction of student Otherness. For instance, tracing the process of the disabling of children from minority and poor backgrounds in school, Mutua (2001) argues that the process begins long before a child ever gets into the public school system, thereby challenging the idea that special education steadfastly holds on to that disability bears its origin from bodily impairment and is resident in the individual person.

Critics of the practice of special education do not necessarily object to all the elements that constitute special education practice. However, in this chapter we highlight some of them because they are so frequently used to legitimize and exacerbate the Othering of disabled students in the public school. For instance, for disabled students, participation in the general education curricula and activities is predicated upon meeting specified pre-set eligibility criteria. Such criteria, for example, the ability to speak clearly or read fluently regardless of intellect, are assumed to be a natural pre-qualifying index or property that nondisabled students possess that assures them the right to participate unfettered in all public school activities. When brought to bear upon disabled students in the public school setting, the unquestioned assumptions about innate precursors to learning script disabled students as lacking in the capabilities necessary for success in school, thereby justifying their seclusion in specially designed environments, ostensibly for their own good. Dis/abilities encrypted in that manner further legitimate their constant surveillance, oftentimes named behavior monitoring/managing, ongoing evaluation, and ultimately denial of access to the same curriculum as same age peers. Instead disabled students in public school receive "specially designed instruction" under IEPs. Disability studies scholars (e.g. Abberley, 1987) view such social arrangements as those employed by public schools to exclude disabled students from fully participating in the activities at school as oppressive social arrangements cartographically demarcating the lines of valued/under-/un-valued student differences.

Embodied Practices: Teacher Concerns
and the Construction of Disability

With special education being what it is, what kind of teachers does it produce? In order to respond to this question, one must engage with the discourses that construct bodies and how such discourses embody practices. The discussion of disability is in a sense a discussion of society's construction of degrees of "fitness" of particular bodies, the disciplinary practices that serve to legitimate society's hierarchical ordering of bodies by degrees of "fitness," and the state apparatuses, to use Althusser's (2001) concept, that perpetuate society's ideology of the body. As a state apparatus, school practices are caught up in the construction, consumption and the enactment of discourses around which bodies are woven. Those discourses make certain bodies, for example, the disabled body, unwelcome, and therefore special spaces (e.g., special classrooms) are created for them to keep them separate from bodies that are deemed fit. This tradition continues to reflect the influences of the eugenics movement in the use of now discredited science, and current testing and diagnostic traditions to segregate those who might sully the gene pool (Selden, 1999; Kliewer and Drake, 1997).

The socialization of a teacher into the special education profession begins with the introduction to, induction into and acquisition of the special education language. In colleges of education across the country, pre-service teachers often begin by taking a special education introductory course, often a 'disability-a-week' type course. In such a course, among other things, pre-service teachers learn the language and terminology that are appropriate for describing different disabilities; in essence therefore, they learn the labels with which to describe disabled students they will later encounter in their own classrooms. Clearly, those "labels are not value-free, but rather they mark physical or sensory differences and are charged with meaning" (Russell, 1997, p. 14). However, many pre-service teachers in special education courses are neither critical of underlying messages with which the labels are inscribed, nor are they conscious of the nuanced ways in which those labels function to create regimes of fitness among students in schools. The average special education pre-service teacher is oblivious of the power inherent in the social and political meanings of the labels they use for children in the classrooms and how those labels reify, reinforce and reproduce the hierarchical social arrangements of the larger society. The ability to see disability as oppression, to see disability as the missing discourse in the gender, race and class triad (Davis, 1995) is minimal at best and non-existent for many special educators. Socialized under deficit models of disability, special educators, like medics, see their role as that of correcting or remediating the effects of student disability on student learning. This reflects the deficit based special education traditions of diagnosing, ranking, and sorting.

In addition, many special education teachers are socialized to view the special educational intervention on the disabled student as the best option for disabled students. Indeed many such teachers do not see as problematic the inability of many disabled students, particularly those whose disabilities are more severe, to participate in the full educational experience that is available without pre-qualifications to non-disabled students. Perhaps, this is so because of the normal-disabled binary that often underlies the deficit models of disability. Russell (1997) argues that the primacy accorded normality makes disabled people all too easily disposable. She argues that normalcy is all too often equated with humanness and therefore disabled people, seen as "less than fully human; [makes] it easy to justify continuing inhumane policy towards us, to cut us out of the social contract even to eliminate us at political will. We become all too easily disposable" (p.17).One can argue that equity and access in education is a critical index of the extent to which one is partaking of the social contract that Russell speaks to. However, many disabled students' participation in many aspects of public school educational experience is predicated upon meeting pre-set criteria that are usually based on demonstrating certain abilities/skills (e.g., articulateness, physical prowess, etc.) that many disabled students do not possess. But abilities/skills, under the normal-disabled binary, are taken as a given for their non-disabled peers. This therefore leaves the special education classroom and its variations as the default placement option for a large number of students with disabilities. In this way, then special education is effectively transformed to a place rather than a service which many even in special education would argue to be the spirit of special education law.

The average special education teacher is apolitical insofar as disability is concerned. Indeed, many special educators, like the students in our classes, following the diagnose-and-treat process of the medical model, believe that appending a label to students is a necessary first step to providing appropriate services to those students. While a number of our students often make very well pre-packaged/textbook arguments about the ills of labeling, the majority of them embrace the idea that labeling students is necessary if not essential for service delivery. Therefore, a major concern shared by pre-service teachers is whether or not their students will have the "correct" diagnosis and therefore whether they will be correctly labeled. The belief that having the correct label makes for effective teaching and learning is sustained by research that provides detailed menu-like or cook-book-like treatments and interventions of particular disabilities. Such details give pre-service and practicing teachers the impression that what they know about students with particular disabilities or behaviors is concrete and irrefutable, and therefore they have sufficient knowledge to prescribe the 'right' educational interventions. However, such research does not help teachers inquire about what is actually going on with real students in their classrooms, nor does it help them acquire the attitudes and approaches that will allow them to really understand and support the students in their classes. For example, medicalized details about learning disability or a particular developmental disability do not inform thinking about what school might actually be like for the student whose thoughts, feelings, and actions—particularly academic and social engagement—are a reaction to the environment rather than a manifestation of disability. Furthermore, this research has not proven capable of making teachers politically savvy in ways that they are able to question underlying issues such as minority over/under-presentation. The success of the special education research tradition is today clearly self-evident in the way that it has produced practitioners who do not question its authority over student disability and practitioners who do not consider or take seriously alternative conceptualization of student disability.

The school has been implicated in the construction and production of identities of disability among students (Mutua, 2001; Slee, 1996). The special education teacher's role is not only one of providing appropriate educational services to students who may be deemed unfit for the general educational classroom but also one of executing surveillance of the disabled student by participating in the writing of the Individualized Educational Plan (IEP). The IEP, meant to elaborate the supports and services the student needs, is also a vehicle by which the school can marginalize and segregate the student by defining a restrictive environment as "least restrictive." Framed within the legal framework of LRE, the school is thus able to avoid charges of discrimination and segregation that would otherwise be leveled against it if the student thus segregated were of another minority category (e.g., gender, race).

This brings us to another major concern of our pre-service teachers: how to write a good IEP. Their concern here may be stated as one of how to understand student needs so as to meet them in a way that assures them social justice, yet teachers are comfortable with the resulting increase in their power over students as the holders of professional knowledge. The power that the IEP team wields over what disabled students can learn is clearly self-evident. As an IEP team member, the teacher as the expert is placed in an unchallenged position that allows them to regulate what and where students can learn and participate in while in school. Disability, constructed as an individual deficit, precludes teachers and the school from noticing socially constructed causes and other factors that inform how the student experiences the challenges of disability. Schools are generally charged with the role of socializing the citizenry in ways that prepares them to function as citizens in a particular country. Schools and teachers participate in universalizing/enforcing marginality of the student with the disability. This is done by labeling, separate placements, and student participation in an educational curriculum that is assured to lead the student to low educational outcomes. Special educators participate in the construction of students as deficient and therefore slot them for an inferior social position well into their future, thereby reproducing the larger social order in which disabled persons are cast as consumers rather than producers of goods and services. Indeed research (e.g., Apple, 1981; Sleeter, 1986; Ysseldyke and Algozzine, 1982) has documented the relationship between special education and the social competition for and access to power, wealth, and prestige. As consumers, they are often expected to either be compliant recipients of lifelong supports for daily living in relation to institutions or to use these supports and educational opportunities to become invisible as disabled people and pass as "normal." Thus the disabled person either experiences being treated as less than human or invisible with a difference (disability) that does not make a difference in society (Michalko, 2002).

Disability Studies' Response to Teacher Concerns

The concerns raised by our students, many of whom are practicing teachers, reflect the paradigm of "lack" in their students. Our students often talk about the disabled students' inability to "keep up" with their non-disabled peers and their having to deal with behavioral differences/disorders. Analogous to Audre Lorde's assertion that the master's tools will never be used to dismantle the master's house, these problems that face the disabled students in the public school setting cannot be solved in an environment that creates them unless radical changes are instituted in the environment. Slee (1996), on the subject of creating enabling schools, suggests a number of strategies that not only address the theoretical framework that undergirds special education knowledge and practice but also the need for instituting structural changes related to the intricate interplay between identities and social structure.

Agreeing with Slee's suggestions vis-à-vis addressing/responding to teacher concerns, we argue that a necessary first step is a re-theorization of the disability from a social model standpoint. Teacher candidates need to be exposed to the social model of disability which shifts the view of disability away from an individual deficit orientation. The reductionism inherent in special education research's view of disability is well documented. To empower pre-service teachers getting into careers in education of disabled students is to expose them to the range of poststructural theoretical tools that recognize the political primacy of embodied subjectivities and agency in the theorization and understanding of disability.

In order to have pre-service teachers thinking about student disability in empowering ways that increase rather than decrease the educational opportunities for disabled students we might also require a dismantling of "the special education expert" who currently produces and controls the knowledge. This is by no means an easy task in that the control of knowledge is powerfully seductive and well historicized. Today, there are few "experts" who are themselves disabled and therefore the knowledge that permeates, informs and regulates special education practice is based upon etic or outsider conceptions of what is best for disabled students. Tied to this also, is the fact that the current arrangement in special education serves to maintain social and political subjugation of the disabled student in the school, thereby assuring that schools continue to function in ways that keep intact the hierarchical arrangement of students by degrees of "fitness." In addition, the status quo also assures that the normal-disabled binary is adhered to in ways that maintain the epistemological divide between special education/general education knowledge.

Marrying Disability Studies and Special Education:
A Proposal for Transforming the Status Quo

The current theoretical orientation to disability that special education teachers bring to the classroom places the problems that disabled students have in accessing classroom learning solely and squarely on the student. Teachers see the student (or his/her disability) as the cause of learning difficulties. The difference that disability makes in teaching and learning is a problem of or within the disabled individual and not of/within the non-disabled majority, much less the teacher. The hegemony of the dominant/ableist society dictates that the disabled person fits into the non-disabled world which provides accommodations. Thus, if a student cannot "keep up" with the class in spite of accommodations (Braille, readers, technology, etc.), then the student is likely to be excluded. Universal design that fits all is rarely presented as an option so that students who may be able to learn and show learning through diverse media are excluded. Such an attitude obscures and precludes the valuing of different types of participation. Similar to the view that cultural differences are the problem of recent immigrants and not of the society that excludes, an argument that renders material the propinquity of their advent into the United States, the disabled person is penalized for his/her disability in an ablest culture although, as Davis (1995) asserts, disability is an unavoidable outcome of living. Thus while we advocate that special education teachers understand this disability studies perspective, they are still employed as agents of an oppressive system of institutionalized ableism where even the laws intended to support their disabled students mire them in non-supportive classifications and labels. To effect such a shift, more and more teachers and policy makers must be willing and able to subvert (as opposed to reform) the system.

Examples are those who understand the lived experiences of students with disabilities in the context of a social model of disability where the social factors are acknowledged and changed without losing sight of the real strengths and dilemmas a student may have living with disability (see Thomas, 1999). This plays out in issues that arise among advocates and teachers. For instance, a typical issue in inclusion is advocacy of reciprocal relationships among disabled and non-disabled people, yet one needs to be creative about what such reciprocity might look like. For instance, on the one hand, the student might be the tutee or the receiver of support. Typically the result includes increase in self-esteem for the helper, learning for the helpee, but stasis in the typical power relationships society furthers between able-bodied and disabled students. On the other hand the helper can facilitate the student's making a contribution such as in a service project or cooperative learning project contribution in a way to benefit both parties and disrupt the typical power relationships with reciprocal value added for both.

Another key issue, behavior, is coping with the similarity to prison inherent in the point/level system and finding ways to subvert it and actually relate with students as human beings without losing one's job (see Danforth, 2005). In these and other issues such as "keeping up," teachers are finding ways to teach outside rigid paradigms and ally with special and general education professionals to merge disability studies perspectives into society at large. Worth looking into are the tools teachers use to shift paradigms such as from surveillance that disempowers both teacher and student to collaborative advocacy and empowerment of both. Such tools might follow in the manner of a Foucauldian toolbox where an understanding of the concept of surveillance, originally developed for prisons, enables one to understand the predicament of the special education students. Such students live under a microscopic gaze more than their non-disabled peers with the consequence of having to deal with their teachers' attempts to regulate not only their social and academic lives but their inner lives as well. Such tools that teachers may use can arise out of definitions of disability we accept such as one offered by Linton (1998) which focuses on disability utilizing a minority group model; the model neither signifies a denial of the presence of impairments, nor a rejection of the utility of intervention and treatment, but rather disentangles impairments from the negative attributions to which disability has been socially and politically attributed. Thus, while instances of subversion are few and far between, a proposal for marrying special education and disability studies, while an uneasy one, cannot follow a predictable path, but rather, it calls for an elopement, a disruption of well-known and well-adhered to procedures and traditions.

References

Abberley, P. (1987). The concept of oppression and the development of a social theory of disability. *Disability, Handicap and Society 2*, 1, 5–19.

Allan, J. (1999). Actively seeking inclusion: Pupils with special needs in mainstream schools. London: Falmer Press.

Althusser, L. (2001). *Lenin and philosophy and other essays*. New York: Monthly Review Press.

Apple, M. W. (Ed.). 1981. *Cultural and economic reproduction in education*. Boston: Routledge and Kegan Paul.

Brantlinger, E. (1997). Using ideology: Cases of nonrecognition of the politics of research and practice in special education. *Review of Educational Research 67*, 4, 425–459.

Danforth, S. (2005). Compliance as alienated labor: A critical analysis of public school programs for students considered to have emotional/behavioral disorders. (pp. 85–102) In S. Gabel (Ed.) *Disability studies in education: Readings in theory and method*. New York, Peter Lang Publishing.

Davis, L. J. (1995). *Enforcing normalcy: Disability, deafness, and the body*. London: Verso.

Erevelles, N. and Mutua, N. K. (2005). "I am a woman now!" Rewriting cartographies of girlhood from the critical standpoint of disability. In P. Bettis and N.Adams (Eds.) *Geographies of girlhood: Identity in-between*. (pp. 255–269) Mahwah, NJ: Lawrence Erlbaum.

Kliewer, C. and S. Drake (1997). Disability, eugenics, and the current ideology of segregation: A modern moral tale. *Disability and Society, 13, 1,* 95-111.

Linton, S. (1998). *Claiming disability: Knowledge and identity*. New York: New York University Press.

Michalko, R. (2002). *The difference that disability makes*. Philadephia: Temple University Press.

Mutua, N. K. (2001). Policed identities: Children with disabilities. *Educational Studies, 32*, 3, 289–300

Russell, M. (1997). *Beyond ramps: Disability at the end of the social contract, a warning from an Uppity Crip*. Monroe, ME: Common Courage Press

Selden, S. (1999). *Inheriting shame: The story of eugenics and racism in America. New York,* Teachers College Press.

Skrtic, T. J. (1995). *Disability and democracy: Reconstructing (special) education for postmodernity.* New York: Teachers College Press.

Slee, R. (1996). Disability, class and poverty: school structures and policing identities. In C. Christensen and F. Rizvi (Eds.), *Disability and the dilemmas of education and justice* (pp. 98-113). Philadelphia, PA: Open University Press.

Sleeter, C. (1986). Learning disabilities: The social construction of a special education category. *Exceptional Children, 53, 1,* 46–54.

―――. (1991). *Behind special education: A critical analysis of professional culture and school organization.* Denver: Love Publishing Company.

Smith, R. M. (2000). View from the ivory tower: How academics construct disability. (pp. 55–73) In B. B. Swadner and L. Rogers. *Semiotics and disability: Interrogating the categories of difference.* New York: SUNY Press.

Thomas, C. (1999). *Female forms: Experiencing and understanding disability.* Philadelphia: Open University Press.

Ysseldyke, J., and Algozzine, B. (1982). *Critical issues in special education and remedial education.* Boston: Houghton Mifflin.

CHAPTER 8

Disability Studies in Education and the Practical Concerns of Teachers

Alicia A. Broderick, D. Kim Reid, and Jan Weatherly Valle

Although most educators, be they "general" or "special," ascribe to the constructivist and democratic values associated with the best ideals of American schooling, classroom practices continue to be steeped in traditional models and discourses of technical rationality (Taylor, 1911/1967; Schön, 1983), particularly when the students in the classes carry disability labels. Thus, a pressing question for many teachers beginning to engage with alternative discourses—of concern here, of course, is a disability studies (DS) discourse—is how the discourse might inform their everyday practice.

We elected to reframe the question, "How can DS in education be relevant to the practical concerns of teachers?" Rather than asking how DS *can be* relevant, we ask rather how it *is* relevant. To this end, we circulated a questionnaire inviting both current and former teachers in preschool, elementary school, middle school, high school, and higher education who identify as espousing a DS perspective to share their thoughts on how this perspective has supported their practical, pedagogical concerns. Consequently, in addition to presenting our own conceptual exploration and analysis of this question, we interweave the ideas and voices of teachers at all levels throughout our essay.

In an attempt to target a group of respondents who would likely identify as "teaching from a Disability Studies perspective," we distributed our questionnaire electronically through the Disability Studies in Education listserv, the Columbia University Seminar in Disability Studies listserv, and the Disability Studies in the Humanities listserv, asking the professionals who participate on those listservs to respond and, at their discretion, to send the questionnaire to their students who are inservice or preservice teachers and ask them to respond as well. We also sent the questionnaire to present and former students studying learning dis/abilities, special education, and DS in Education at our respective universities.

We invited feedback from respondents on what we identified as three central themes of this essay: (a) we cannot essentialize teachers and teaching, (b) theory and practice are necessarily dialectically related, and (c) teachers, when necessary, engage in resistance. We arrived at these themes through our own critical conceptual analysis of the central question posed (not through inductive analysis of data gathered through open-ended queries to our respondents) and asked respondents to comment upon these three themes. In addition to asking for background information on respondents' identity and positionality, the three questions we asked people to address in the questionnaire were: (1) How does who you are (i.e., factors such as your age, ability, race/ethnicity, social class, etc.) affect your teaching? (2) How does your commitment to disability studies affect how you think about your students, interact with them and plan for and teach them? (3) Have you experienced any dissonance or mismatch between your disability studies perspective and the dominant ideological perspectives of the educational system in which you teach? If so, please (a) describe that dissonance or mismatch, (b) describe what its meaning or significance has been to you as a teacher, and (c) describe any way(s) in which you have negotiated this disso-nance in your own practice.

We did not attempt to define in our questionnaire what we meant by "teaching from a Disability Studies perspective," and this circumstance, as may be expected, yielded a diversity of responses reflecting a wide variety of assumptions about what it means to people to hold a "disability studies perspective." This has been both instructive and problematic, and we turn a critical eye on this aspect of our data in our analysis throughout.

Resisting the Essentializing of Teachers and Teaching

Reflecting on how DS might be relevant to the practical concerns of teachers, we first considered whom we mean when we refer to "teachers" and what bearing our definition of "teachers" might have upon our under-standing of their practical concerns. If we resist conceptualizing teachers as a monolithic group and instead acknowledge their diverse and intersecting positions in the world (e.g., race, class, gender, ability, age, teaching contexts, teaching experience), we are able to consider how positionality might impact the practical concerns of teachers who implement a DS approach. For example, how does a teacher's life experience influence receptivity to DS and its subsequent application to the classroom? How important is it for teacher educators who teach DS to consider the positionality of teacher candidates? In short, with respect to DS, how might a teacher's identity matter?

Each of us teaches in graduate programs grounded in a DS orientation— Kim and Alicia at Teachers College, Columbia University and Jan at The City College of New York (CCNY), City University of New York. Jan, while a doctoral student at Teachers College, also taught for four years in the masters' program in learning dis/abilities. Thus, together we have contrasting experiences of presenting a DS perspective to graduate students who predominantly, although not exclusively, represent privilege and mainstream culture as well as graduate students attending one of the most racially-ethnically diverse universities in the country and who, predominantly but not exclusively, grew up under less privileged circumstances, attended New York City public schools, and currently live and teach within these same communities.

In reflecting upon her experiences teaching in both settings, Jan recognizes that, in general, CCNY teacher candidates more readily grasp the relevancy of DS and its relationship to issues of social justice than do, at least initially, more privileged and culturally mainstream teacher candidates. This observation is not meant to reinscribe any essentializing of particular groups, but rather to suggest that such noticings warrant our consideration. In a similar vein, Andersen and Collins (2004), in the fifth edition of their noted anthology *Race, Class, and Gender*, comment upon the significance of student positionality in accepting, resisting, or embracing alternative educational discourses:

> We realize that the context in which you teach matters. If you teach in an institution where students are more likely to be working class, perhaps how the class system works will be more obvious to them than it is for students in a more privileged college environment (p. xvii).

Thus, it is somewhat unsurprising that less privileged and racially-ethnically diverse teacher candidates engage with DS by drawing upon their lived experiences within a culture where race, class, gender, and ability intersect in ways that privilege some groups over others. Given their positionality in the world, these teacher candidates understand all too well the themes undergirding such issues as the overrepresentation of minority students in special education (specifically "soft" disabilities, such as learning dis/abilities and behavior disorders), low academic expectations for special education students, and persisting assumptions about minority students and their families. For them, DS puts new language around familiar truths. On the other hand, she observed that teacher candidates who negotiate the world as privileged and culturally mainstream may need first to understand and acknowledge White privilege in order to fully grasp the relevancy of DS, particularly in regard to issues of social justice. We do not imply enhanced capability or desirability of one graduate student over another but rather suggest that positionality of teacher candidates seems to matter.

As an illustration, we offer the following account of a class discussion among CCNY teacher candidates in one of Jan's graduate classes. Recently, she presented a political cartoon by Ted Rall that appeared in the *Washington Post* (as well as 140 other publications) on November 10, 2004, in which he compares the election of George W. Bush as president as "something akin to putting the special needs kids in charge of the class" (Rall, 2004). Rall represents the "special needs kid" as a grotesque figure in a wheelchair, drooling and wild-eyed. In the midst of a lively discussion about their multiple readings of this political (and offensive) cartoon, an African American student drew attention to the similarity between the exaggerated and grotesque physical representation of disability and historical representations of exaggerated and grotesque physical features of "Blackness" (e.g., Jim Crow imagery of "Negro as buffoon"). This observation led to deeper conversation regarding the parallels and intersections between race and disability. Moreover, students wrestled with the implications of Rall, a privileged White male and, ironically, a graduate of Columbia University, who appropriates disability to make a political statement, then responds to public criticism by clarifying via a listserv his opposition to including "special needs" children in "ordinary" classes because they "sacrifice the needs of the other children...I remember sitting in classes where one slow kid would plunge the rest of us into fits of boredom, I also favor 'tracking' students by ability" (Rall, 2004).

The superior stance and sense of entitlement possessed by this privileged White male indeed seemed familiar to them. We do not mean to imply that teacher candidates who are privileged and culturally mainstream could not grasp similar meanings, but rather that teacher candidates of less privilege and greater racial diversity may be more likely to draw upon lived experiences of marginalization in their meaning-making.

In addition to factors such as race, class, gender, and ability, Jan also noted the relevancy of DS to teacher candidates whose second language is English. Such students often find that DS helps them to clarify their own educational and cultural exclusions. In the following excerpt from a reflective journal entry, Ivette, whose native language is Spanish, comments upon the connections between her own experiences and those that Roseman (2001) describes in his autobiography about negotiating life with dyslexia and attention deficits.

> As a young monolingual Spanish-speaking student in the United States I experienced a lot of the fears, feelings of inadequacy and self-doubt Bruce [Roseman] did. I too recall "The Look" on a lot of my teachers' faces when it came to my English. It was, as Bruce put it, difficult to understand and to react to, but clearly there was something wrong with the way the teachers made me feel. I can now put it into words; it was very intimidating, cruel and traumatic.

Given the multiple points of entry into DS, it appears relevant for teacher educators not only to consider teacher candidates' positionality, but also the resulting potential for a recursive understanding of diversity. As Crenshaw (1993) argues, it is counterproductive to conceive of multiple systems of subordination (e.g. gender, race, class) as separate entities. DS is, of course, not just about disability, but rather about the intersections of disability with such factors as race, class, and gender as well as issues of social justice. Andersen and Collins (2004), from their viewpoint as scholars concerned with the intersectionality of race, class, and gender, likewise advocate for relational thinking in regard to diversity:

> The movement to "understand diversity" has made people more sensitive and aware of the intersections of race, class, and gender. Thinking about diversity has also encouraged students and activists to see linkages to other categories of analysis, including sexuality, age, religion, physical disability, national identity, and ethnicity (p. 3).

We supplement Jan's experiences and observations *about* teachers with responses to the questionnaire described earlier. We first asked teachers to reflect upon ways in which their positionality might influence both their understanding and implementation of DS. Their responses point to myriad ways in which positionality may inform and orient teachers toward new ways of thinking and practicing.

In the following response, an Asian American special education teacher reflects upon the relationship between her positionality and her understanding and application of DS in the classroom.

> My race (Asian-American, stereotypically considered to be acceptable in current American culture), my enculturation as a middle-class, English speaking American, and my success in the traditional method of schooling underlies my experience in the world and certainly affects my teaching in many ways…Certainly I believe that my position as a "minority" and "female" might impact my belief in social justice and recognition of institutionalized racism in schools and education, but I can't say that I feel as though I have adopted these criticisms or stances through my own experience of marginalization. Rather, I think they have developed through my development of critical awareness through my formal education.

Thus, despite "minority status" as an Asian American female, this teacher recognizes that her positionality as an English-speaking, middle class, academically successful "model minority" negates the usual marginalization afforded to groups outside mainstream culture. She credits her enhanced awareness and understanding of DS to her formal education rather than to any lived experiences of marginalization.

Another special education teacher speaks about the impact her positionality as a culturally mainstream and upper middle class woman had upon her teaching practice.

> I started teaching as a 22 year old, Jewish, White, upper middle class, fresh from college female…Because of my background, I came to teaching with a preconceived notion regarding education and the role of schools…I placed blame on my students and their families for doing nothing to advocate for themselves thereby perpetuating the inequities and negative social circumstances from which they suffer. I viewed education as an opportunity, equally distributed, that is taken or left based on one's motivation to improve their lot in life…Within months of working in the public school system of NYC, I began to recognize the unfairness and inaccuracy of these perceptions and beliefs. In coming to understand that education is a political, social, and economic institution inherently designed to serve the dominant, privileged component of our society, my focus changed from blaming the victims to recognizing

the crisis within our public school system. This realization fueled an evolution, or perhaps revolution is more apt, in my teaching practices.

For this culturally mainstream, upper middle class teacher, it is her lived experiences within the New York City public school system that she credits for informing and challenging her belief, constructed largely from within her positionality in the world, that public education is equitable to all. Thus, it is her teaching experience that provides the framework upon which to understand and implement DS in the classroom.

In the following reflection, a teacher locates her entry point to DS within her lived experiences as a child and teacher.

> I would have to say that my experiences growing up a poor white child in rural Pennsylvania made me hungry for knowledge and instilled a sense of determination, fairness and faith in others. As I became a teacher, I worked with many students with many disabilities over the years...My introduction to Disability Studies formulated many of the thoughts I'd had and observations I made.

Crediting her lived experience as a "poor white child in rural Pennsylvania" as the basis for her "sense of determination, fairness, and faith in others," this teacher notes, like many CCNY students, that DS provides new language for familiar truths and a framework for "thoughts I'd had and observations I made."

A special education teacher and adjunct professor identifies a point of connection to DS within his position in the world as a gay White man.

> I think being gay makes an enormous difference, too. I have always identified with the concept of W.B. DuBois' of double-consciousness—understanding the world (heterosexual) in terms of how I am supposed to be while simultaneously understanding the world from an outsider's point of view. I can be in situations and interpret them differently than heterosexual people—little, everyday situations in classrooms... e.g. when all activities are geared toward defining, describing, reinforcing (straight) role expectations, whether in writing activities (describe your ideal boyfriend/girlfriend), or analyses of plots (boy gets girl), rigid role-types, e.g. cheerleaders and football players... So, when a teenager, I transferred this concept of "other" ways of knowing to Black people and women, and felt "they" would know and understand, intuit, certain things that would be lost on whites or men—things that are taken for granted, that usually aren't seen. This, of course, I have come to learn is true of people with disabilities—they can recognize situations, language, expectations, stereotypes, etc. when non-disabled do not or seemingly cannot.

In making meaning of DS, this teacher largely draws upon his experiences of marginalization as a gay man. He recognizes that his own experience of negotiating the heterosexual world with a "double consciousness" informs his understanding of how disabled people negotiate an "abled" world.

It appears, then, that as researchers and scholars in the field of DS, we must pursue more deeply the ways in which positionality impacts teachers' receptivity to and implementation of DS in the classroom. Furthermore, teacher positionality appears not only to be relevant but also essential to achieving the vision of social justice for disabled students. As Andersen and Collins (2004) remind us, "Resistance to oppression on behalf of one's own group is not enough. Achieving social justice can only take place when people and groups build coalitions with others" (p. 11).

Theory, Practice, and Praxis

A second issue that the query, "How is DS relevant to the practical concerns of teachers?" raises in our minds regards the nature of the relationship between theory and practice and the need for an ongoing interrogation of the assumptions underlying any conceptualization of that relationship.

Susan Gabel (2005) offers a simple working definition of DS as "the use and application of disability studies assumptions and methods to educational issues and problems" (p. 10). Referencing the Society for Disability Studies (SDS) Guidelines for Disability Studies programs, Gabel offers a "sense of the landscape" of a DS perspective:

> (1) it is multi-/inter-disciplinary, (2) it "challenges the view of disability as an individual deficit that can be remediated" and explores the external factors (e.g., culture, society, economics, politics) that define people and "determine responses to difference," (3) it studies disability from national and international perspectives, (4) it encourages participation by disabled people and "ensures physical and intellectual access," and (5) [it] prioritizes leadership by disabled people while also welcoming the contributions of those who share the above goals. (pp. 10–11)

Save the first descriptor of DS as "[being] multi-/inter-disciplinary," each of the remaining characterizations of a DS perspective employs action verbs and active voice (i.e., challenges, studies, encourages, ensures, prioritizes, and welcom[es]). Thus, it would seem that action or praxis may be an integral, even defining, aspect of DS.

Attempting to elicit reflections upon the relationship between taking a DS perspective and one's own daily practice, we asked respondents: "How does your commitment to disability studies affect how you think about your students, interact with them, and plan for and teach them?" Because our respondents teach a variety of students in a variety of settings, in this section we roughly organize their responses into two broad categories: a) responses from university teacher educators and b) responses from present and former public and private school K–12 teachers, many of whom are teachers of students with labeled disabilities.

Relevance of DS Perspective to University Teacher Educators

Responses from teacher educators teaching in institutes of higher education indicate that the "lens" or "perspective" of DS informs their current practice in a number of ways, most notably in (a) the ways that they critically frame (both in their scholarly writing and in instructing their students) the very structures within which they work (i.e., working as professor of special education within programs that train K–12 special educators), and (b) the choices of epistemological and pedagogical models and instructional strategies that they draw upon in their instructional decision-making.

DS as a critical lens framing institutional practices
A professor with a significant disability reports:

> My commitment to disability studies has caused me to repudiate much of the framework underlying Special Education as a discipline even though it is the intellectual arena and medium in which I operate. The result is that students are so challenged by the information they are presented that they are not quite sure how to proceed. The one thing that is certain is that students are questioning everything they are presented and they are being given license to assume a role not only as educational advocates for the youth they serve but as advocates for the preservation of their own intellectual integrity—that is to say, that they are beginning to understand that the disability world is not flat as many academics in Special Education would have them believe. Thus, they have begun to understand how they have been enculturated in a belief system that at least one professor challenges them to question.

This professor of special education goes on to contend that

> …most Special Educators have had minimal or no exposure to cultural understandings of disability. As a result, while we MAY be good at training teachers how to teach youth with disabilities, they are generally clueless about the shared, collective

and cultural elements of disability that emerge from having and living with a disability. In short, I am convinced that Special Education is culturally destructive with respect to disability as indicated by the emphasis placed on acquisition and master[y] of skills that promote assimilation into the dominant nondisabled world. The code words for this assimilation are "independence", "integration", "productivity", "inclusion", and "self-determination" as defined by the professional community.

A retired professor of education with nine years' public school and agency teaching experience and twenty five years' university teaching experience says,

> I have openly confronted the problems caused by labeling, segregation, and competitive schooling ever since I began teaching (my mother did as a second grade inclusive teacher—who was opposed to pull-out programs from the get-go—so she was a good model).... Students were fairly receptive because I was quite different than—hence somewhat refreshing in comparison to—my positivist, conservative colleagues. At first my support for inclusion made special education students worry about their ability to find jobs—after a semester with me, they knew it meant thinking differently about kids and arranging schools and classrooms differently—this meant they would have work.

We can see illustrated in these two respondents' reflections some of the ways in which a DS perspective critically frames their perspectives on institutional practices, with one reporting that she has taken this critical stance (of "openly confronting" problems with schooling) "ever since [she] began teaching," and the other reporting that her commitment to a DS perspective "has caused [her] to repudiate much of the framework underlying Special Education as a discipline," even asserting that she is "convinced that Special Education is culturally destructive with respect to disability."

These respondents are also cognizant of the intellectual challenges that their own critical DS lens or perspective poses, not only for their own work, but also for their students'. One reports that her "students are so challenged by the information they are presented that they are not quite sure how to proceed," while the other reports that at first, "my support for inclusion made special education students worry about their ability to find jobs." However, in addition to its challenges, this perspective appears also to have afforded students an opportunity to engage in a discourse not only of critique ("they have begun to understand how they have been enculturated in a belief system that at least one professor challenges them to question") but also of possibility ("after a semester with me, they knew it meant thinking differently about kids and arranging schools and classrooms differently—this meant they would have work"). These respondents' accounts also reflect a sense of these individuals working in relative isolation, with one reporting that "I was quite different than—hence somewhat refreshing in comparison to—my positivist, conservative colleagues," and with the other reporting that "at least one professor" challenges her students to question the dominant belief systems. While the latter remark could be read to mean "at least [i.e., potentially more than] one" professor challenges students in this way, it could also be read to mean, "at [the very] least[,] there is one professor" doing this work, which is, after all, better than no one doing this work. While a more optimistic reader may infer the former meaning, we are somewhat inclined to read the latter.

DS lens informing pedagogical decision-making

Several respondents working in higher education offered a number of practical examples of the ways that their pedagogical decisions are informed by their DS perspective. For example, a Caucasian professor of higher education with five years' experience notes that:

> One lesson I have learned, that I think is especially pertinent to DS, is the importance of making a course as accessible as possible and accommodating to a variety of learning styles. I present course materials in a variety of formats: interdisciplinary nonfiction, autobiography, fiction, film, cartoons, TV series, and websites. I also grade so as to capture student effort in a variety of different ways. Instead of focusing entirely on formal written work (such as exams or papers), I diversify to allow students to present information orally, through class discussion and formal presentations. I expect students to submit written discussion questions and "real world" examples that link the readings to "real world" data. I require them to submit journals of their subjective and analytical reactions to the readings and films. I pay attention to class participation. I know who completes and truly understands the assignments. I know who consistently participates in class discussions. I have moved away from grading 50% midterm 50% final paper after a few experiences where slackers, who happened to be good paper-writers, did better than earnest students, who did not write well, but who completed and understood all the readings, films, site visits, and led class discussions throughout the semester....I have also offered special credit worth 5–10% of the grade to avoid routinely penalizing people whose disabilities or cultural backgrounds result in their being especially quiet in class.

Similarly, a Caucasian teacher who teaches students with identified disabilities full-time at the high school level and who also teaches traditional reading and special education courses as an adjunct in higher education has

…made an effort to include awareness of disability issues in the college courses I teach. I teach graduate and undergraduate reading and special Ed courses so I am directly teaching teachers of students with disabilities. I hope to expand their horizons throughout the weeks we have together. Specific examples of activities and assignments include (in no specific order):
(a) I have a large collection of children's books that positively feature a character with a disability. Each week, I begin class by reading one of these short stories and then we discuss the story. I also share my collection with my students so they are aware of these great books to use with their students; (b) when I teach "Intro to Special Ed" I begin each class by reading a short children's story that has a positive character with the disability that corresponds to our studies; (c) we discuss the importance of having quality children's lit that has characters with disabilities to promote acceptance and diversity; (c) discussion of social vs. medical model; (d) we talk about the historical context of disability and negative social associations. We take a walk through American disability images as portrayed in books, movies, media, education. This is often eye opening; (e) we brainstorm the many "special ed" terms that exist (ex: blind as a bat) and compare them to racial/gender slurs; (f) assignment to analyze a children's book that features a main character with a disability; (g) assignment to create an annotated bibliography with children's books featuring characters with disabilities.

Thus, while none of these university educators explicitly illustrates *how* a DS perspective informs their pedagogical decision-making, they nevertheless assert that it does, and cite a variety of instructional decisions that they identify as being informed by their DS perspective (i.e., "making a course as accessible as possible," "accommodating to a variety of learning styles," "present[ing] course materials in a variety of formats," "diversify[ing]" "grad[ing] so as to capture student effort in a variety of different ways," and "ma[king] an effort to include awareness of disability issues" in the courses that the respondent teaches).

Relevance of DS Perspective to K–12 Teachers

Responses from present and former K–12 public and private school teachers similarly indicate that the "lens" or "perspective" of DS informs their current practice in a number of ways, most notably in (a) the ways that they "frame" or understand their students, and (b) the choices of epistemological and pedagogical models that they draw upon in their instructional decision-making.

DS as a lens for understanding students

Several teachers noted that a DS perspective has informed the ways that they frame and approach their own students in their teaching. A former teacher with two years' experience in "special schools and special class-rooms" who identifies as a thirty year old, middle class, nondisabled Korean male notes that

> ...Disability studies make me think about my students. I have continuously changed my perception of ability/disability. I know and understand normalcy is constructed by society and hegemony. My educational plan and goals have changed as the establishment of equality and social justice of all people.

A young Caucasian teacher with two years' teaching experience across resource, self-contained, and inclusive classroom settings who him/herself identifies as learning disabled similarly reports that his/her perceptions of ability and disability, and hence his/her perceptions of his/her students with labeled disabilities, have changed during the course of his/her work as a graduate student with a DS concentration:

> My definition of learning disability is the result of my personal experience growing up with a visual perceptual learning disability. Through the medical model lens, I learned to associate disability within myself and I worked hard to rid myself of the ugliness I associated with disability. Through my time at TC, I began to see disability as a label rather than an innate condition. As a teacher, I hope to use my sensitivity towards LD in order to foster a classroom of inclusion.... I believe that in order to foster self-efficacy and self-esteem in our students, we must have and moreover, communicate to our students high expectations for them, which stems from our "belief and attitude that all students are worth the effort" (Nieto, 1999, p. 18).

Other teachers report that a DS perspective has had a similar impact on the ways that they view and approach their own students. A White male teacher with fifteen years' experience including K–12, undergraduate, and graduate education notes that first and foremost, he *presume[s] that all of my students are individuals, with individual needs, dreams, and desires.* Likewise, a White middle-class teacher with five years' experience in self-contained special education settings notes that

> ...disability studies has helped me to separate the conventional (or socially constructed) idea of disability from who my students are as human beings. I do not identify my students by the label on their IEP. I see them as complex individuals with different needs and talents.

An Asian-American teacher with six years' experience teaching students with labeled disabilities at the secondary level reports that

> ...DS allows me to view my students as positioned. This view of them impacts every aspect of my work with them. When I plan and teach I am constantly aware of my need to create situations that can re-construct their position as powerful and centered. I do much direct talking about power and the school institution to help them realize their positionality toward the goal of working against their negative self-perceptions as failures.

We can see illustrated in these teachers' reflections the many ways in which their DS perspectives shape the ways in which they frame and understand their own students, enabling them to "think about" not only their students but also their "perception of ability/disability" and ideas about "normalcy," "equality," and "social justice." In addition, these authors attribute to their DS perspectives their "high expectations" of their students, their "presump[tion] that all...students are [not only] individuals" but are "complex individuals with different needs and desires," and their "separat[ion]" of "the conventional (or socially constructed) idea of disability from who [their] students are as human beings." Additionally, as the final teacher reports, not only does a DS perspective frame the ways that she views and understands her own students, it also has a significant impact on the ways that she shapes and supports a particular framing of her students' self-perceptions as well.

DS as a lens informing pedagogical decision-making. As noted by the Asian-American secondary teacher above, the perspective that frames one's perceptions of one's students will also have a significant impact on other aspects of one's teaching (or, as this teacher asserts, "on every aspect of my work with them"). A second common theme among K–12 teachers in response to the question, "How does your commitment to disability studies affect how you think about your students, interact with them, and plan for and teach them?" regards the relationship between a DS perspective and the choices of epistemological and pedagogical models and particular instructional strategies that teachers draw upon in their daily decision-making.

A Chinese-American teacher with six years' experience teaching in a private, self-contained elementary school for students with learning disabilities notes:

> Although I teach at a private school where teachers have considerable freedom to design their own curriculum, there is still a heavy emphasis (from administration

and teachers themselves) on using tests to show knowledge. In interacting with students and teachers, I try to convey my belief in various ways of demonstrating knowledge as well as broadening the idea of what constitutes as legitimate knowledge.

A Jewish, White, former public school special educator with nine years' teaching experience notes:

> Fueled by the recognition that my students were not their disabilities, it became abundantly clear that the construction of curriculum and teaching practices must begin with the individuals for whom it is meant. Although the structure of schools may appear the same on the surface, learning takes place within a context of culture, family, past and present experiences. Packaged curriculum and traditional methodologies that render students' voices obsolete reflect the belief that there is only one way of knowing, and that only certain realms of knowledge and experiences are valuable. How could anyone be successful in an environment that makes someone feel so disregarded and worthless? As a result, community building and differentiating instruction drove the core of my teaching philosophy. These goals became the foundation of my planning—identifying strengths to build on; seeking opportunities for every student to feel significant and an essential component to our learning community; fostering mutual respect and a sense of interdependence; celebrating achievements, regardless of how small; learning from and with one another; and ensuring every student felt successful and capable.

A former elementary educator who currently teaches in higher education reports that

> I use the social constructivist model as an epistemological tool in all of my courses. It is very important, I believe to understand the social context of disability, and so I think about my students and interact and plan for them using a similar ecological, or social context perspective. I try to be sensitive to what might be going on in their lives outside of class. I try to build on their own experiences in developing course content and projects. I try to understand their thinking from multiple-perspectives, and I encourage them to challenge and debate issues from multiple perspectives, taking into account multiple contexts.

The young Caucasian teacher who identifies as learning disabled describes her pedagogical decisions in similar ways:

> Taking from the idea of Dewey, teachers must incorporate interest, personal experiences, and input into activity planning so that learning is active and purposeful for students....In my self contained classroom, I give students several different types of

assessment (different students I assess in different ways contingent on their learning style), always use multisensory instruction, scaffold students' writing and reading comprehension slowly moving them towards doing tasks independently, and I have students do an enormous amount of self-reflection involving thinking about themselves as learners and how our classroom learning relates to their lives.

Other teachers also identify particular pedagogical practices that are informed by their DS perspective, but these teachers seem to problematize the relationship between theory and practice somewhat more than those teachers quoted in prior paragraphs. For example, a teacher who identifies as White, male, "able-bodied," of working-class origins, who currently works in public high schools full time as a teacher coach offers several examples of the ways that a DS perspective shapes particular pedagogical decisions that he makes:

In schools, I always discuss the theme of disability with teachers when they plan to teach novels, plays, films—seeing it as a lens, a perspective (along with other possible readings/lenses, like race and class). I [also] have encouraged teachers to do disability awareness issues, but find even (whom I consider) the best teachers inadvertently slide into simulations that become trite and fun. I counter this by sharing information from the Disability Rag web page on authentic simulations—but not going to the cinema (because of inaccessibility issues) is less fun that being strapped, bandaged, and roaming the hallways like a mummy. I feel this is tantamount to a white being in blackface and claiming to know what it's like or "getting a taste." The entire SOCIAL positioning is not examined in such activities, and this makes me frustrated.

Likewise, the Asian-American secondary teacher contends that

When I worked in self-contained classrooms where students were not expected to be held to the norms of standardized tests, I felt that I could work with them in inquiry experiences where they could develop their own learning at the pace and in the areas where they could develop real understanding of concepts. In the wake of standardization, however, I feel a greater need to be complicit with the measures that will define their success and I become much more aware of how I need to consider my "privileged" view of education with the needs of the students to become demarginalized through the very standards that marginalize them in the first place....I walk a tenuous balance between helping them mitigate against their positions and also enabling them to be successful within the structures that marginalize them. Many times, particularly in inclusive settings, I am compelled to reproduce marginalization by modifying tests, intervening on their particular behalf in assigning grades, and generally using the "power" of special education and the IEP to construct them as successful (in opposition to how I'd rather create situations where they ARE successful).

In problematizing the relationship between their espoused DS perspective and their daily pedagogical practice, these latter two teachers point to the powerful, ineluctable, complex, and dynamic nature of the relationship between pedagogical theory and pedagogical practice. The Asian-American secondary teacher goes on to lament, *Despite my views, I constantly feel as though I am compelled to act against my DS beliefs in order to maintain a working relationship with the teachers who I work with.* Thus, due to the entrenched nature of institutionalized non-DS discourses around disability, it would seem that some teachers are acutely aware of the disjuncture between their espoused beliefs and the practices and actions they are "compelled" to engage in over the course of a day's work.

The respondent who identifies as a Jewish, White, former public school special educator with nine years' teaching experience reflects:

> In coming to understand that education is a political, social, and economic institution inherently designed to serve the dominant, privileged component of our society, my focus changed from blaming the victims to recognizing the crisis within our public school system. This realization fueled an evolution, or perhaps revolution is more apt, in my teaching practices.

For others, perhaps the metaphor of evolution would be more appropriate after all: An Austrian teacher with six years' experience teaching students with labeled disabilities notes that

> As their teacher and a member of the society I have to design and develop ideas [about] how these needs can be best met so that the students are able to participate as full members of the society...I am far away from doing it in every class and every day but maybe one day I [will] get to a point where my lesson plans and my teaching style reflects my belie[f]s 100%...I hope that my actions and conversations reflect my belie[f]s. I am still in the process of negotiating this dissonance. I want to figure out for myself how I can put into practice what I believe. Sometimes I feel overwhelmed and frustrated that theory and reality are so far apart at the moment. I do not have a comprehensive solution to bridge that gap. Little by little, in very small steps I try to (a) change routines in my classroom, (b) listen differently to parents, (c) write the next IEP the way it is supposed to be written, (d) very, very rarely question my administration's requests or try to explain my point of view.

While this teacher wades through the process of "negotiating [the] dissonance" between her "beliefs" and her "lesson plans and…teaching style," another teacher, the respondent with two years' experience who identifies as learning disabled writes, *I think that disabilities studies gave me the theories to back up my teaching practices.* It seems evident that teachers' perceptions of the relationship between their theoretical perspectives and their own pedagogical practices are varied, complex, and shifting.

Susan Gabel (2005) points to the methodological dilemma that these and other teachers who espouse a DS perspective may face, particularly when they are working as "special educators" within the dual system of educational bureaucracies in the United States:

> One methodological dilemma for educators is the problem of deciding how to balance the need for the improvement of function (often the school's concern) with the refusal to pathologize and the reticence to "cure" difference (two concerns of social interpretations.) (p. 9)

This methodological dilemma is often indicative of broader and deeper dilemmas—namely, the recognition that such dilemmas are not merely about methodological decisions, but rather are fundamentally about shifting epistemological, and even paradigmatic, beliefs and assumptions. Indeed, Heshusius and Ballard (1996) place such epistemological shifts squarely in the context of broader shifts in intellectual paradigms. While these authors began their collective inquiry as an exploration of experiences with shifting and alternative epistemologies, they report that contributing authors nearly always reported these epistemological shifts as preceding an accompanying shift in broader intellectual paradigm, specifically, the shift from "a quantitative, positivist epistemological framework to a qualitative, interpretive one," a shift that involves a "fundamental deconstruction and reconstruction of agreements about what counts as real and how we allow each other to claim knowledge" (p. 2). For Heshusuis and Ballard both, this shift in paradigmatic assumptions was not consciously embarked upon, nor was it brought about by any "systematically carried out intellectual pursuit" (p. 2). Rather:

> When we started to consciously reflect on how we had changed our most basic beliefs, we had to acknowledge that we knew, before we could account for it intellectually, that we no longer believed in what we were doing or in what we were being taught. (p. 2)

While many of the teachers whose voices we hear in these pages have consciously pursued these shifts in epistemological and paradigmatic grounding through their decisions to pursue graduate education at institutions that espouse and identify with "disability studies" perspectives, they nevertheless describe a process of "coming to understand" (special) education differently than they had before. Thus, a common experience among many of the teachers we hear from in these pages seems to be that experience of a rupture, or disjuncture, between their current, emerging beliefs and their daily, institutionalized practices. The recognition of that rupture, whether it be experienced as a revolution or an evolution, would seem to inform and embody many teachers' experiences of "walk[ing] a tenuous balance" in hopes of "put[ting] into practice what [they] believe."

Teachers thus become positioned and operate, in complex ways, within multiple, often conflicting discourses. Reid and Valle (2004) note that this positioning, although powerful, need not be deterministic: "As Foucault (1972) explained, we are not determined because we, as individuals and groups, have the agency to resist any particular discourse, thereby expanding, challenging, or otherwise reformulating it" (p. 466). Once teachers have experienced the disjuncture between theory and practice described above and begin to engage in alternative discourse communities (i.e., DS), the stage is set for resistance work to begin. We turn our attention now to the third theme we wish to explore in this essay: the notion that teachers can effectively engage in resistance.

Teachers Resist

Today teachers are faced with unprecedented constraints. Thirty years ago, the legislation antecedent to IDEA (i.e., PL 94–142) revolutionized (special) education by requiring that schools provide education to all disabled students. It was the first of what has become a rather lengthy list of mandates that impact, both positively and negatively, what (special education) teachers may do. On the positive side, subsequent reauthorizations of IDEA have continued to press for greater integration of students with disabilities through an emphasis on delivering instruction successfully in the least restrictive environment (LRE) (Fisher and Frey, 2001; Lipsky, 2003). Similarly, the nation came to recognize the discriminatory stance of the "culturally disadvantaged" label (Carrier, 1986) and the need to support, but not segregate, immigrant students whose first language is not English (Artiles, 2003). In short, there has been genuine progress toward educating all students in the mainstream (Kluth et al., 2003)—although we still have a long way to go to convert successful geographic integration into social, emotional, and academic integration (Gourley, 2002; Smith, 1999), that is, to assure genuine acceptance and participation of all students.

On the other hand, since the more recent passage of the No Child Left Behind Act of 2001, the legal mandates even more intrusively permeate nearly every act of teaching—more tightly controlling curriculum and the testing of student progress, which of course translates into teacher, school, and district responsibilities, restrictions, and accountability. The Council for Exceptional Children (CEC), the certifying body for teacher education programs in special education, has consistently supported the implementation of most mandates. Nevertheless, regulations as they are written and stated, are not necessarily isomorphic with their implementation (Barton, 2004).

Consequently, we would like to begin this section of our chapter by reiterating that, although the number of degrees of freedom is smaller, there remains a good deal of diversity among teachers at all levels and that the ways teachers enact curriculum and social justice in the "fuzzy spaces" still available depends on both their personal positioning and personal theorizing as they interact with these more formal demands of schooling. Nevertheless, the problem of providing a free and appropriate education for *all* students is complex, and there are no answers about how we could or should accomplish the kind of significant change that would bring special education more closely in line with the perspective of DS. Here, then, in no particular order, are but a sampling of moves/solutions/forms of resistance reported by teachers that illustrate their negotiation of a DS perspective in schools that embrace traditional special education practices and assumptions about disability. After we hear their voices, we will present a critical commentary.

A former teacher and current graduate student from South Korea reports:

> The educational system in my country is a medical model. I struggled how to challenge the medical model because I might [have] be[en] a person marginalized in special education. But, I published two articles in South Korea last summer…using the concept of disability studies. I now believe I can challenge [the] current special education system in South Korea…to make disabled people and nondisabled people get the concept of equal human beings.

A second year teacher who works in a private school in inclusive and resource-rooms settings explains that she experiences no dissonance.

I teach in a school that is very much in sync with disability studies. We put the individual before the curriculum....Students are grouped by learning style and not ability, so I have students of all ages in my class. The curriculum is decided upon once we meet the students and have them tell us about their interests. For instance, my high school biology class is studying diseases and viruses as the year long curriculum since that is what students...wanted to study. I am building the curriculum around strengthening their skills and a curriculum that will tie into their lives and interests.

A teacher who works in high school special education and also teaches courses in traditional reading and special education as an adjunct in higher education identifies one of her/his greatest challenges as the "students who will not consider the views I am sharing. I cannot ask them to agree or accept, just listen and it is most frustrating when they will not allow perspective[s] other than their own deeply engrained beliefs."

A teacher coach in a large metropolitan school district notes,

...in terms of professional development for administrators, teachers, and special education 'industry' people...I have infused a DS lens over the last few years. This gave me a great deal of satisfaction as it calls everything into question—existing structures, labels, humans pigeon-holing of others, medicalization of the teaching profession, disability-as-deficit, etc. It makes people sit up, debate, challenge me back regarding the information I present. I think we have to continue to infuse DS where it is useful and can open up some new doors where people didn't formerly have the knowledge to conceptualize.

He continues:

The dissonance is so great that it can be disheartening. Bureaucratization of special education has reinforced damaging associations with the concept of disability. It's as if alternative modes of thinking are incomprehensible. We know that alternative conceptualizations are discouraged, but feel they're imperative. In a simple example, some people have enormous difficulty conceptualizing how inclusive classes may look and keep harping of the need for special ed. as it is...unwilling to see high drop out rates, overrepresentation of students of color, etc.

A Chinese-American high school teacher rues the predisposition of teachers in her school to teach

to the disability. If students are having problems with complete sentences, then the entire attention is focused on identifying fragments, run-on sentences, etc. What is problematic for me is that there seems to be very little room for creative inquiry and some students respond to this type of instruction by shutting down. However, their shutting down is perceived as a result of their 'disability.' One of the ways I have found to be effective in negotiating this tension is through discussions and collaborations.

A White high school teacher describes the private school where she works as

an exclusive setting for this population of students. She notes that she is the only one who ever brings up positive change or progress in my students....I have a very difficult time with this and it is very exhausting to be the only voice of positivity after a while. To counter this situation, I use my time with my students...as wisely as possible. And, I have been told...that the issues I have raised regarding practices of the administration (i.e., the focus of staff training on restraining children as opposed to teaching how to set up a proactive environment) have altered the way training sessions were subsequently handled. By speaking out, I have also elicited a lot more support, which I needed, for my students/classroom.

An Asian-American high school teacher with six years' experience regrets that:

Schools are designed to be standardized and the student with 'difference' can only secure her/his place in the school by 'passing' as a 'normal' student. For my students in inclusive settings, they very much are expected to 'earn' their placement with the set arrangements. Although my job is to make modifications to assist their success, their success is still defined in accordance with how well they 'approximate the norm.' I daily encounter great resistance to the idea that we can create whole classrooms that are simultaneously responsive to diverse students. The 'need' for standardization, the idea that school is for the 'normal' student, and moving at a pace to 'cover' curriculum are three themes that are constantly at odds with a DS perspective.

She adds:

I can't (yet) seem to create the type of DS education I envision within the settings that I have to work with....At times, it's too draining to constantly engage in the debates that surround the conflict of DS with school ideology and the power struggles over whether or not my ideas can be enacted in the inclusive classroom....I constantly feel as though I am compelled to act against my DS beliefs in order to maintain a working relationship with the teacher...I'd say that there is a pervading attitude that wants students in special education to fail in order to support initiatives to phase them out of the community. Helping them to be successful through challeng-ing the status quo is not on the agenda.

And finally,

My position as a 'lowly' special education teacher in the school does not allow me the position to change as much as I think needs to be changed and I am getting very weary of being what I feel is the 'lone voice' of dissent....I increasingly feel 'over-come' by the lack of support and failure of the school to sustain any kind of change. For example, when I worked as self-contained teacher in the school, one of my goals was to get most of my students into at least one 'mainstream' class for the following year. We did it, with the support of parents and the special ed. faculty. This year, without me, as the recommending teacher who invoked the power of LRE during IEP meetings, pushing for it, the student and parents stopped pushing for 'main-streaming' when they were told that the schedule of classes could not accommodate so many students from special ed. I don't believe that it's not that they don't want it, they were told...that it simply can't be done. It is very discouraging to have former students explaining that the reason they can't take Mainstream History is because they couldn't fit into the schedule.

An elementary school special education teacher believes that

the dominant ideological perspectives of the public school system... have marginal-ized my students both physically and emotionally....I have tried to negotiate this dissonance by being open and honest with my students about the place and position that they're in....We have open discussions about what special education is and what it means to them: I teach them about their IEPs, we talk about self-advocacy skills; we talk about being teased and called 'different.' The idea of embracing dif-ference has become a central theme in my teaching, one that I hope is carried with my students beyond their time in the classroom.

A professor of graduate and undergraduate students who identifies as

a person with a (mostly) hidden, highly stigmatized disability finds [h]uge disso-nance, huge differences. I walk a sharp razor between the need of the university to teach what CEC tells them are best practices, and what I know about the sociocul-tural implications of those practices and disability in general.

Citing issues related to promotion and tenure, he acknowledges that

[n]egotiating this dissonance is a troubling and difficult enterprise...it is VERY dif-ficult to need to critique a set of standards and approaches that is also what is pro-viding me my (current) living.

A professor with a severe disability says,

My colleagues of 17 years really don't know what to do with me. I'm called on to teach all sorts of...courses, but never asked to collaborate in research projects...I don't think any faculty member in my special ed program has ever read anything I've published. I am also rather a thorn in their side, because as they are trying to maintain the autonomy of the special ed program, I am constantly working at assimilating the program into teacher education....These events have led me to seek collegiality elsewhere—in other countries and in other institutions where disability studies scholars have positions....But I feel that my work in integrating disability studies issues and content in teacher education has made progress, and that faculty in teacher education are receptive to these ideas. This is what has kept me going.

An elementary special education teacher argues that

The need for systemic educational reform has become critical. Schools must seek to teach students the value of diversity by breaking down the barriers of judgment that predetermine one's potential. Through no fault of students and their families, the narrow definitions of teaching, learning, and success result in the systemic maintenance of inequity produced by our public education system. In this context, education as the great equalizer can never be realized. It was an awesome privilege to witness the courage, determination, and resilience of students who have been labeled, segregated, and repeatedly marginalized. They have much to teach the world if only the doors could be opened wider so that they could walk through, rather than be kept peering through the cracks.

These open and often poignant responses reveal how teachers come to understand that they have the power to resist and to encourage others to resist the debilitating positioning of disabled students and their families by traditional assumptions and practices of special education. Some do it through challenging students and their families to re-think their own or others' positioning. Some find the power to challenge in research, workshops and other presentations, and publications (e.g., Johnson, 2004). Some operate on a person-to-person basis; others call for systemic change, although none suggests how this should be accomplished. In addition, these responses run the full gamet of approaches Ware (2004) elucidates as characteristic of inclusive educators—those who see the necessary changes as educating stakeholders to implement a new skills set, those who critique the foundational knowledge of special education, and those who view the transition to a disability studies perspective as a "complex and transformative social project" (p. 191).

What is somewhat dismaying about this set of responses from people who identify as grounded in a DS perspective is that few examine the contours of *exclusion,* and some still rely on arguments based on negative images of disability, those associated with remnants of the deficit model, but also the social model (Baker, 2002). Some seem to imply that they are glad that they are not disabled, calling on the binaries of abled/disabled, successful/failing. Others focus on the disabled *individual,* helping such students become hardened to othering and to self-advocate when negotiating IEPs. Still others stress the need to help students fit into traditional models of success and often imply that students must earn entrance into inclusive settings. As one of the better-informed respondents lamented, school success continues to depend on "passing as normal," as "approximating normal" (See also Watts and Erevelles, 2004 on the topic of school violence). It seems that even among those who consider themselves as operating within a DS perspective ableism is still lingering (See also Hehir, 2002). As Scot Danforth and Terry Jo Smith (2005) put it, teachers "often internalize the dominant norms and believe, consciously or unconsciously, that students must do the same in order to succeed" (p. 135). A number of these teachers at all levels have not yet realized that a DS perspective "calls everything into question—existing structures, labels, humans pigeon-holing of others, medicalization of the teaching profession, disability-as-deficit, etc."

These responses also indicate, however, how difficult and painful/isolating/ exhausting/draining/discouraging /disheartening resistance can be. There is a subtext of disempowerment and sadness underlying the reactions we report here. Several teachers note that they are of low status and nearly impotent in the face of the increasingly federalized educational bureaucracy. These respondents discuss the frustration of trying to enlighten people—students, teachers, administrators, etc.—who simply will not see, who will not consider other views, who will not—or cannot—entertain alternative visions. These brief commentaries speak to how deeply entrenched, how absolutely transparent, how widespread throughout virtually all public institutions dominant ideologies about sorting and hierarchicalizing humans have become (Brantlinger, 2004).

The professors particularly speak to the sense of neutrality with which research and schooling are viewed and how this acceptance by the wider professional community and the public threatens their positions in a variety of ways—with respect to promotion and tenure, with respect to licensing of their teacher-education students, and with respect to their everyday relationships with colleagues. It is clear from all teachers, however, how wearing it is to be discounted, to be the 'lone voice,' the only one speaking out, the outsider. Nevertheless, there seems to be little else we can do. We *must* speak out.

Susan Gabel and Susan Peters (2004) argue that resistance is central to the disability rights movement and to theorizing disability at both societal and individual levels. They consider resistance the cornerstone of understanding "the complex relationships and negotiations between divergent ideas like discourse, the material body, sociopolitical systems and processes, power relations, cultural contexts of disability, impairment, and so on" (p. 586). As Foucault (1972, 1979) notes, power is not limited to the sovereign. Power circulates throughout the social nexus and comes into being when exercised. Consequently, if we do not speak out, however difficult or costly, we lose not only our integrity, but also our power to refuse to be complicit with practices we do not consider positive, healthy, or ethical.

We all have power. We need to bring it into existence—individually and collectively, consciously and deliberately—because once we know, we cannot retreat into ignorance. The diverse moves/solutions/forms of resistance we report here suggest that cautious hope is warranted, given that we are willing to do the work. Although different teachers have chosen different avenues of resistance for different sets of students, a number of respondents report that they have achieved *some* modicum of satisfaction, seen *some* progress. Knowing others are struggling too, we may find that small gains may be just enough to keep us going.

References

Andersen, M. L., and Collins, P. H. (Eds.). (2004). *Race, class, and gender: An anthology*. Belmont, CA: Thomson Wadsworth.

Artiles, A. J. (2003). Special education's changing identity: Paradoxes and dilemmas in views of culture and space. *Harvard Educational Review, 75(2),* 164-202.

Baker, B. (2002). The hunt for disability: The new eugenics and the normalization of school children. *Teachers College Record, 104,* 663-703.

Barton, L. (2004). The politics of special education: A necessary or irrelevant approach? In L. Ware (Ed)., *Ideology and the politics of (in)exclusion* (pp. 63–75). New York: Peter Lang.

Brantlinger, E. (2004). Ideologies discerned, values determined: Getting past the hierarchies of special education. In L. Ware (Ed)., *Ideology and the politics of (in)exclusion* (pp. 11–31). New York: Peter Lang.

Carrier, G. (1986). *Learning disability: Social class and the construction of inequality in American education.* New York: Greenwood Press.

Crenshaw, K. W. (1993). Beyond racism and misogyny: Black feminism and 2 Live Crew. In M. J. Matsuda, C. R. Lawrence, R. Delgado, and K.W. Crenshaw (Eds.), *Words that wound: Critical race theory, assaultivespeech, and the First Amendment* (pp. 111-132). Boulder, CO: Westview Press.

Danforth, S., and Smith, T. J. (2005). *Engaging troubling students: A constructivist approach.* Thousand Oaks, CA: Corwin Press.

Fisher, D., and Frey, N. (2001). Access to the core curriculum: Critical ingredients for student success. *Remedial and Special Education, 22(3),*148—157.

Foucault, M. (1972). *The archeology of knowledge and the discourse on language.*New York: Pantheon Books.

———. (1979). *Discipline and punish: The birth of the prison.* New York: Vintage Books.

Gabel, S. (Ed.) (2005) *Disability studies in education: Readings in theory and method.* New York: Peter Lang.

Gabel, S., and Peters, S. (2004). Presage of a paradigm shift? Beyond the social model of disability toward resistance theories of disability. *Disability and Society, 19,* 585—600.

Gourley, J. J. (2002) Curriculum reform for inclusion: Infusing issues of social justie and caring. Annual National Conference Proceedings of the American Council on Rural Special Education, Reno, Nevada. March.

Hehir, T. (2002). Eliminating ableism in education. *Harvard Educational Review, 72 (1),* 1–32.

Heshusius, L. and Ballard, K. (1996). *From positivism to interpretivism and beyond: Tales of transformation in educational and social research (the mind-body connection).* New York: Teachers College Press.

Johnson, J. R. (2004). Validation and affirmation of disability culture and deaf culture: A content analysis of introductory textbooks to special education and exceptionality. *Disability Studies Quarterly, 24,* n.p.

Kluth, P., Biklen, D. P., and Straut, D. M. (Eds.) (2003). *Access to academics for all students: Critical approaches in inclusive curriculum, instruction, and policy.* Mahwah, NJ: Lawrence Erlbaum Associates.

Lipsky, D. K. (2003). The coexistence of high standards and inclusion. *School Administrator, 60(3),* 32–35.

Nieto, S. (1999). *A light in their eyes.* New York: Teachers College Press.

Rall, T. (November 10, 2004). Editorial cartoon. *Washington Post.* Retrieved November 11, 2004 from http://www.uclick.com/client/wpc/tr/.

———. (November 12, 2004) http://www.tedrall.com/rants.html.

Reid, K. & Valle, J. W. (2004) The discursive practice of learning disability: Implications for instruction and parent-school relations. *Journal of Learning Disabilities, 37, 6,* 466–481.

Roseman, B. (2001). *A kid just like me: A father, a family, and an exceptional child.* NY: A Perigee Book..

Schön, D. (1983). *The reflective practitioner: How professionals think in action.* Basic Books.

Smith, P. (1999). Drawing new maps: A radical cartography of developmental disabilities. *Review of Educational Research, 69(2),* 117–145.

———. (in press). Off the map: A critical geography of intellectual disabilities. *Health and Place.*

Taylor, F. (1911/1967). *Principles of scientific management.* New York: Norton and Company.

Ware, L. (2004). The politics of ideology: A pedagogy of critical hope. In L. Ware (Ed)., *Ideology and the politics of (in)exclusion (pp. 183–204).* New York: Peter Lang.

Watts, I. E., and Erevelles, N. (2004). These deadly times: Reconceptualizing school violence by using critical race theory and disability studies. *American Educational Research Journal, 41,* 271–299.

CHAPTER 9

Misconceptions and Misunderstandings: Twin Fallacies That Influence Disability Policies

Ron Ferguson

Orientation and Mobility (O and M) is the process used by blind persons to travel in the environment. The primary tool used in travel by blind persons is the long white cane. A formalized pedagogy for teaching these skills was developed in the late 1940s. How to teach O and M and who is qualified to teach O and M has been contested from its beginnings, and the conflict between professionals in the blindness field and blind persons with regard to those two questions is the context for this essay. The purpose of this essay is to discuss how disability studies could be relevant in examining this and other policies that impact persons with disabilities. This essay will begin by discussing the advantages of disability studies as a theoretical framework and advocacy model that promotes social justice and provides historically marginalized groups a voice in critiquing policies that impact their lives. Next, the policy to exclude blind persons from the O and M profession will be examined through a disability studies framework to demonstrate its usefulness in policy studies and to serve as one model for analyzing local, state or national policy.

Disability Studies
Disability studies is a relatively new academic discipline. Longmore and Umansky (2001) cite the 1980s as its genesis. Some of the early disciplines

associated with disability studies included policy studies, political science and sociology with the goal of "providing an analytical base for reform of public policies and professional practices, seeking ultimately to reconstruct society" (p.12). Many scholars from a wide range of disciplines have since identified themselves with disability studies. As a relatively new, growing and diverse field of study it may be helpful to identify some common characteristics of disability studies as opposed to trying to provide a single definition that encompasses this multifaceted and complex field.

One of the prominent characteristics of disability studies scholars is that they are also activists. A commitment to social justice often compels them to challenge the fabled and pietistic notions of "detached objectivity." It is not unusual for disability scholar-activists to participate in organizations of persons with disabilities and to support disability rights efforts on societal and individual levels. Scholar-activists who are disabled draw on first-person perspectives and experiences in their work. In addition, by utilizing critical methodologies they are able to challenge much of the "taken-for-granted," that is, the unquestioned assumptions that guide traditional policy studies. Consequently, their work regularly confronts misconceptions and misunderstandings of disability that are embraced by the public, justifying inequities and reinforcing discriminatory practices and attitudes. Challenging established social and educational policies in the rehabilitation and education fields has created conflicts between disability scholar-activists and persons with disabilities on one side and professionals and policy makers on the other.

The professionalization of the special education and rehabilitation fields is closely associated with the progressive era (c. 1880–1920). During this time there was a rapid growth of professional organizations which often required undergraduate or graduate education for membership. Linked to this was an optimism and confidence in the ability of these well educated professionals to organize, manage, and—if need be—fix society (Haskell, 1984 and Bledstein, 1978 examine these ideas in detail). Professionals working in agencies and organizations "for" the blind and other disability groups controlled and managed their "patients." With the rise of consumer movements and the emergence of disability studies scholar-activists, who themselves, may be persons with disabilities and consumers of services administered by professionals, the power relationships and oppressive polices governing the special education and rehabilitation systems were confronted. Those who were once governed were now demanding that their voices be heard.

The challenge by disability scholar-activists of the policies was more sophisticated than the assembling of a group of wild-eyed radicals to picket offices in protest against paternalistic treatment and invasion of one's privacy. The desire to confront and resist the widely held misconceptions and misunderstandings of disability by professionals in the disability field was grounded in and informed by a variety of theoretical methodologies. Disability studies not only drew on new and more complex theoretical methodologies but they also critiqued traditional methods of policy studies.

The relevance of disability studies in examining local, state, and national policy may be seen more clearly by contrasting it to traditional policy studies. In the traditional approach to policy studies there is an assumption that certain social problems just do exist. These social problems can be described from this view, metaphorically, as a disease. Researchers attempt to diagnose the disease by trying to isolate one or two conditions which caused the disease and then prescribe a treatment—the creation of a policy to solve the problem. The manifestations of social problems, although seen as unfortunate, are considered to be a natural occurrence in society. Given this sort of conception about social problems, traditional policy studies have given attention to four arenas of study: (1) descriptions of social problems, (2) discussion of competing policy solutions, (3) consideration of general implementation problems, and (4) evaluation of particular policy implementations (Scheurich, 1994).

These four arenas of traditional policy studies are evident in educational and social issues related to the blind. From the time of the early researchers and policy makers, and extending to the present, there has been an extensive compilation of data that describes social problems related to blindness and probable causes of these problems. Policy researchers, might, for example, investigate attitudinal characteristics of blind students who have been unsuccessful in securing employment after graduation from university, for the purpose of isolating some of the attitudes that may have contributed to the problem of unemployment. In these types of studies the solution typically focuses on some deficiency—physical, mental, emotional—of the blind person.

Policy researchers in the second arena, the discussion of competing policy solutions, may compare the merits of different policy solutions but without ever questioning the assumptions the policy solutions embrace. For instance, the list of requirements for the certification of orientation and mobility instructors (see Blasch et al., 1997, pp. 718–730) by the Association for Education and Rehabilitation of the Blind and Visually Impaired (AER) seems reasonable to ensure that only well qualified persons will teach blind persons cane travel. For many years one of those requirements has been that the instructor must have good vision. The assumption was that vision was the only way that an instructor can ensure proper monitoring of the student. This requirement privileges sight and in doing so does not question the assumptions about vision that the policy embraces.

In the third arena policy researchers evaluate "policies that have already been implemented in order to consider possible problems in implementation" (Scheurich, 1994, p. 298). There are numerous examples of educational and social policies that have been created on behalf of the blind that are within the boundaries constructed by the grid of social regularities; for instance, separating the blind from society in the seventeenth and eighteenth centuries by placing them in asylums, adding vocational education and workshops to residential schools due to the low expectations of the students' abilities as well as a means of reducing the economic liability of the blind students, the creation of agencies to provide custodial care for the blind because the assumption is that they are incapable of functioning independently, and minimizing the need for blind persons to be literate. Each of these examples reflects an educational or social policy that was created by humanitarians or social reformers or professionals that seemed reasonable to sighted people and clearly fell within the range of acceptable policy solutions.

Finally, in the fourth arena policy researchers examine the social functions of the policies that were implemented; in other words, how do the policies influence the general public to reinforce and maintain misunderstandings and misconceptions of blindness. Examples include: blind persons being denied access to cruise ships, weight rooms, tanning beds, leasing apartments that are on the second floor or a building, as well as teaching jobs and a host of other jobs that are deemed unsuitable for blind persons. In both of these arenas (three and four) the key is that policy analysts do not question the policy itself, they are only interested in possible ways the policy could be better implemented.

Disability Studies and Policy

Disability scholar-activists use a variety of critical methodologies to examine social and educational policies impacting persons with disabilities. I will draw on Foucault's archeology as one example of how disability studies can be relevant to local, state, and national policy. The French historian, Michel Foucault (1961; 1966; 1969) developed a historiographical methodology he called archaeology, which is a very useful tool to critically examine the assumptions that researchers and policy makers take for granted. Foucault's archaeology provides the analytical framework for policy archaeology. Policy archaeology is a development in policy studies that provides a historiographical methodology for analyzing educational and social policy. This methodology goes beyond traditional policy study's framework, which is restrictive since it accepts or presumes a commitment to the larger liberal worldview in which it exists and does not consider the policy in a historical context. In contrast, this methodology argues for a different approach to policy studies, one that opens up new territory, one that establishes a new problematic and, thus, one that serves to alter and broaden policy studies. Policy archaeology is useful because it expands the analysis of policy studies by asking questions that promote the investigation of groups and issues that have traditionally been ignored or taken for granted by policy researchers. Scheurich (1994) develops policy archaeology, and Ferguson (2001) expands on Scheurich's work by providing a description of Foucault's archaeology. In addition to its value in policy studies I believe it is a useful tool to critically examine the practice and application of research and policy making.

This theoretical model includes four arenas of investigation and is briefly summarized as follows. Arena I studies the social construction of specific education and social problems. The basic assumption that a certain social problem is an empirical given or is a natural occurrence is questioned. Arena II focuses on the identification of the network or grids of social regularities across educational and social problems. The regularities: 1) constitute both categories of thought and ways of thinking, 2) constitute the set of conditions in accordance with which a practice is exercised or the conditions that make it possible for a social problem to emerge, and 3) can change and new ones can emerge. Four social regularities that I use are vision, disability, governmentality, and professionalization. Arena III concentrates on the study of the social construction of the range of acceptable policy solutions. The focus is on the study of how the range of possible policy choices is shaped by the grid

of social regularities. Without this type of analysis it is easy for policy researchers to believe that the policies they create are based on objective
methods of investigation. In arena IV the concern is with the study of the
social functions of policy studies itself.

For the purposes of this essay, arenas I and II are particularly relevant.
An important assumption of policy archaeology is that problems on which
researchers focus with regard to education, rehabilitation, or society are
socially constructed—they are not innate. In other words, policy archaeology
questions the basic premise that social problems are an empirical given or are
a natural occurrence, and in so doing is able to examine more closely and
skeptically the emergence of educational and social problems. Consequently,
some of the critical questions that arise include: How did a particular problem come to be seen as a problem? Why do some problems come to be seen
as problems while other problems are overlooked or explained away? What
factors influenced researchers to focus their "gaze" on certain problems?
Why did a certain problem appear when it did as opposed to at a different
time? The pursuit of such questions assumes that social problems are social
constructions, and they allow for a critical examination of the social construction process (Scheurich, 1994, p. 300). Exploration in this arena concentrates on the "numerous, complex strands and traces of social problems prior
to their naming as social problems" (p. 300). In so doing, "[i]t critically
probes why and how these strands and traces congeal (become visible) into
what is thereafter labeled as a particular social problem" (p. 300).

Arena II of this methodology focuses on the identification of the
network or grids of social regularities across educational and social
problems. Foucault's desire to eliminate the fundamental role of the human
subject and to examine "the space in which various objects emerge and are
transformed" (Foucault, 1969, p. 32) is a very important part of analysis in
this arena. Policy archaeology's concern with the grids of social regularities
reflects Foucault's belief that historical research is more complex than merely
connecting one event in the past to the next in a linear fashion. Archaeology
(and specifically policy archaeology) is an attempt to show this complexity
by identifying the grids which will reveal "several pasts, several forms of
connexion, several hierarchies of importance, several networks of
determination..." (Foucault, 1969, p. 5). The importance of identifying and
analyzing these grids is that social problems are constructed, and it is the
"regularities that constitute what is labeled as a problem and what is not

labeled as a problem" (Scheurich, 1994, p. 301). Furthermore these grids define the parameters from which acceptable policy choices are drawn.

Application to Blindness Studies

I believe there are four regularities that are indispensable for studying the construction or emergence of the social and educational policies associated with the blind. The social regularities in the case of the blind are vision, disability, governmentality and professionalization. I have separated my discussion of vision as a regularity from disability even though lack of vision (i.e., blindness) has been classified as a disability. The reason for this is because historically vision has also represented a fundamental component of western culture. It is what vision represents within the development of western civilization that I will focus on when I discuss vision as a social regularity. Vision has been associated with being able to see, know, measure, sort into categories, and process information, and this ability has been and still is privileged over other senses in the pursuit of knowledge. The second regularity, disability, has long been a detectable social regularity which has been used as justification, in and of itself, to separate and classify people. The next regularity is governmentality. Foucault uses the category of governmentality to "denote the emergence of a kind of governance mentality that expands its reach into all aspects of the lives of its citizens; it is the kind of governance that counts, describes, defines, that brings everything under its gaze..." (Foucault 1991, pp. 87–104).

It is clear that the role of the government in the lives of the blind, as well as within the general population, has steadily increased over the past century. A marked escalation can be seen during the progressive era (1880–1920) with the rise of administrative rationality (and professionalization) which made it possible for the government, through the coordination of "appropriate" forms of expertise and assessment, to be able to identify "all those individual members of a society who can be deemed, by manifesting some combination of a specified range of 'factors,' to present a significant, albeit involuntary, risk to themselves or to the community" (Gordon, 1991, p. 45).

Professionalization is the fourth social regularity and, like governmentality, is closely associated with the Progressive Era. As noted earlier, this was a time of unprecedented growth of professional organizations with membership reserved for those who possessed the proper credential—a university degree. There was great optimism in the potential of these "professionals" to solve the economic, educational, and social problems of that day and the future. These regularities form a complex, interconnected grid that make it possible for particular problems/issues that are linked to blindness to emerge as problems. In addition, this grid of social regularities influences how the problems are to be interpreted. Certain features of these particular regularities are readily detectable. However, there are other aspects which are not easily discernible; thus their influence in shaping thought often goes unnoticed and unquestioned (Scheurich, 1994, pp. 304-305). These regularities are seen as common sense or natural or the best or are just assumed. When considering a social problem the regularities restrict how the problem is viewed and what solutions emerge as being reasonable. With respect to policy making, the regularities form the boundaries in terms of how a policy is identified, conceptualized, and drafted.

Using the theoretical model I have outlined I will examine the assumptions that underpinned the establishment of policies in the blindness field as it relates to the O and M profession. The most influential person associated with the genesis of the orientation and mobility (O and M) profession, especially the formulation of the policies which shaped its development and guided its course for five decades, is C. Warren Bledsoe (Bledsoe, 1969; 1997). Bledsoe, along with several other prominent members of the blindness field, outlined a set of criteria that would ensure that only well-qualified men (and later women) would be able to be orientation and mobility instructors (see National Conference on Mobility and Orientation, 1960). One of the assumptions underpinning this curriculum and the subsequent professionalization of the orientation and mobility (O and M) field, including certification, was that an O and M instructor must have 20/20 vision with no field loss in either eye. Later the visual standard was broadened to 20/40. That restriction has subsequently been dropped (Wiener and Siffermann, 1997).

The policy decision to exclude blind persons from teaching cane travel corresponded with the establishment of the training center for the blind at the Veterans Administration Hospital located in Hines, Illinois. Bledsoe exerted considerable influence in his role as the chief architect of the blind rehabilitation program in the Physical Medicine Rehabilitation of the Blind section at Hines. This included the hiring of its first Chief, Russell Williams, and the selection and training of instructors at Hines (Bledsoe, 1969, 1997).

Others in positions of influence also supported the policy to have only sighted O and M instructors (National Conference on Mobility and Orientation, 1960). Without such support the policy could not have become one of the pillars on which the graduate programs in O and M and certification of O and M instructors rested. A series of conferences were held in the 1950s to discuss how best to meet the growing demand for O and M instructors and the general development of the O and M profession. The most prominent meeting (June 1959) was funded by the U.S. Office of Vocational Rehabilitation and held at the American Foundation for the Blind in New York City. A noted occurrence at the conference was an infamous declaration by William Debetaz, of The Seeing Eye, Inc., to the question: "What can a sighted mobility instructor do better than a blind one at fifty paces from the trainee?" The answer given was: "The sighted instructor can see danger and say 'Stop'" (Voorhees, 1962, p. 18). This ejaculation seemed to be sufficient evidence that the policy requiring sight in order to teach O and M was just.

For nearly half a century this policy was supported by professionals in the blindness field. It seemed reasonable, and efforts by blind persons to challenge this policy were dismissed. The establishment of policies by able-bodied professionals for the benefit of persons with disabilities has been and continues to be common practice. As mentioned earlier, the single most influential person associated with the O and M profession is arguably Bledsoe (1969, 1997). One of his many "contributions" to the field was the reading lists he compiled to be read by mobility instructors (Bledsoe, 1947, 1965). His belief was that the books and articles on the lists gave valuable insights into the blind and blindness; thus reading them would better prepare O and M instructors to understand and teach blind students. These works are still relevant in that the basic beliefs about blindness and the rehabilitation of the blind that they discuss underpin current teaching and practice. Therefore, these are still the foundational works for policy and remain unquestioned by professionals and policy makers in the blindness field.

I will focus on three authors from his list: Thomas Cutsforth, Louis Cholen, and Thomas Carroll. Bledsoe (1965) exhorts students to know and examine an edited work by Zahl (1950) in which Cutsforth's "Personality and Social Adjustment Among the Blind" appears. Bledsoe credits Cholden (1958) as providing an objective view point (Bledsoe, 1965, p. 7). He praises Carroll's *Blindness* (1961) as brilliant and a "most serious, intelligent and creative application to the subject" of blindness (Bledsoe, 1965, p. 8).

In "Personality and Social Adjustment Among the Blind," Cutsforth (1950) maintains, "The blind person...has both a personality problem and a social problem" (p. 174). In order to cope with this the blind person manifests either one of two defense mechanisms. Either the person will compensate, in which she or he attempts to prove to "himself and the group that the inadequacy does not exist" (p. 176) or retreat, which is when "the individual accepts his feelings of inadequacy as a valid evaluation of his ego-importance and establishes a false security by failing to meet life aggressively" (p. 176). Cutsforth notes that the blind person can shift back and forth between these coping strategies based on the group or person he or she is involved with at the time.

Furthermore, Cutsforth labels as neurotic the responses of the blind as they manifest one of these two defense mechanisms. He notes four factors that are found in any neurotic condition.

> First, the individual fails to establish himself in his social relationships at his own self-evaluation. Second, he meets the situation with inadequate emotional response; that is, he fails to feel the natural, normal irritations, resentments, and furies produced by failure of accomplishment. Third, he makes an unconscious attempt to resolve the tensions from anger by withdrawing from the objective world and concentrating attention, interest, and concern upon the subjective realm. Fourth, he employs a substitute problem which gives a false feeling of assurance and importance (Cutsforth, 1950, p. 178).

On a closer examination of the four neurotic manifestations it becomes obvious that it promotes a destructive and hopeless situation for the blind. One of the symptoms of neurosis among the blind is the reaction pattern produced by their inadequate emotional response to blindness (p. 178). This response, according to Cutsforth (1950), is evident in animals and human beings and is "an attempt to establish ego-importance, approval, and security, docility and compliance..." (p. 178). He then gives a concrete illustration of this by referring to his family pet. He writes:

> Many of the blind live in the same social world as does my spaniel. If you must be a dog, at least you can be a nice dog. He is. His ego demands my affection and approval. And he sacrifices his aggressiveness, his normal temper and pugnacity to attain it. With strangers, he is not neurotic. He is a healthy, aggressive, self-assured dog (Cutsforth, 1950, p. 178).

What is the inevitable conclusion? Be suspect of blind people who appear to be psychologically healthy and well adjusted.

According to Cutsforth, the blind person, or the dog, is building up unresolved tensions which become egocentrically directed. Clear examples of these unresolved tensions for the blind are "daydreaming, fidgeting habits, and automatisms" (p. 178) which, along with rocking, pressing thumbs into the eyes, and head drooping, are referred to as "blindisms." Cutsforth asserts that these are not just socially objectionable habits but are attempts "to resolve the tension and gain the satisfaction denied by his non-aggressiveness...Likewise, daydreams and fantasies are an expression of the heightened emotionality resulting from conflict" (p. 181). These are evidence of "an inevitable and inescapable phase of a neurosis" (p. 178).

Cholden's (1958) research provides insights into blindness, particularly as it relates to adventitiously (someone who goes blind in childhood or later) blinded adults. He believes that the "concept of blindness as death, while overly grim is not altogether inappropriate, for the patient must indeed 'die'" (p. 18). This "death" includes the need for the "internal reorganization to the fact that he is now a different person." All aspects of his personality are affected, "if not completely changed. And it is important to know that until he accepts the fact that he is this different person—a blind person—rehabilitation or the relearning necessary for adjustment to blindness, cannot proceed" (p. 73). In other words, if the blind person does not accept the "tragedy model" of blindness, then he or she is assumed to be in denial and therefore in need of therapy. Cholden describes clearly this model when he states,

> During the first stages of blindness, the person is almost totally dependent upon others for even his smallest requirements. This even extends to the need to be fed. In many ways, after the loss of sight the patient becomes an infant again....He must learn to walk, hear, talk and eat (Cholden, 1958, p. 82).

The psychiatrist is indispensable in the rehabilitation process as it is his or her role to help the newly blinded individual come to "realize with his whole being that he has lost something of himself and is now a new person with different capacities and potentialities from the person he was" (p. 76). Group therapy, according to Cholden, is one of the essential ingredients in this process.

The work of Carroll (1961) is probably the best known of the three among persons in the blindness field. Carroll ranks vision as the most valuable sense. He asserts that "sight is *real*; sight is concrete....This severing of a major bond with the reality world is a kind of dying to the things around us—and one of the most frightening aspects of the multiple trauma of blindness" (p. 25). Mobility is one area that is severely impacted. Carroll believes blind persons have neurotic fears and describes fears of trying to get around his or her own home. Even "without any inclusion of the neurotic whatsoever—the blind person has many things to fear if he intends to walk or travel" (p. 39). There will, according to Carroll, "be danger—real danger—of minor physical injury, or major injury, of death itself, or only of embarrassment" (p. 39). With regard to "Loss of Basic Skills" Carroll believes that the blind person has become a blank slate—losing all experiences and the ability to problem solve (see p. 41ff).

A careful examination of these works and much of the body of writing in the blindness field through the theoretical framework of policy archaeology reveals that researchers and policy makers are influenced by many of the misconceptions about blindness. Furthermore, their writings perpetuate the myths and misconceptions which influence practice and are in turn referenced by other researchers and policy makers. The pioneers of the O and M profession were influenced by these writings as they developed curricula, rehabilitation programs, and policies. The requirement that an O and M instructor must be sighted is one example of a policy that seemed "reasonable" to the policy makers. However, examining it though a disability studies lens helped expose the misconceptions about blindness that were a basis for the policy. It also helped to secure an Experimental and Innovative grant from the United States Department of Education (1996) to create an alternative graduate program at Louisiana Tech University to prepare blind persons to become O and M instructors (Ferguson, 2003).

This program is unique in several ways, (1) it is based on input from blind consumers of O and M services, (2) the curriculum is based on non-visual techniques for teaching and monitoring O and M and thus does not discriminate against blind O and M instructors, (3) and all students go through immersion into blindness training where they are taught by blind instructors. This reverses the traditional role of sighted instructors teaching blind students.

Disability Studies (Ir)relevant

The question to be addressed in this essay was, "In what ways is disability studies (ir)relevant to local, state, and national policy?" The description of policy archaeology and the examples given in this essay hopefully demonstrate that disability studies provides a useful theoretical methodology for examining policy. It provides a framework to expose the socially constructed assumptions that have influenced the policy and to examine the policy from the perspective of the ones for whom the policy was implemented. In other words, the potential exists for disability studies to be relevant in evaluating current policy and as a resource for creating non-discriminatory, non-patronizing and non-oppressive policies that impact persons with disabilities.

Even though disability studies has a significant potential for policy makers to consider issues of equality, inclusion and social justice, the challenge, as I see it, is for professionals and policy makers to recognize and take seriously the relevance of disability studies. A challenge in this regard is that the policy makers may be influenced by the work of disability scholar-activists and thus attempt to appease them by making policy changes that appear to reflect their influence but in reality are only cosmetic in that they do not confront the socially constructed attitudes which continue to shape attitudes and practice. The debate over the policy to have only sighted O and M instructors illustrates this challenge (see Ferguson, 2004, pp. 57–59).

The policy was established in the 1940s, reaffirmed through the 1950s, and formalized in the "Standards for Orientation and Mobility Services" (Standard 1.4.1, p. 226) of the *COMSTOC Report* (Koestler, 1966). This report established standards for accreditation of agencies in work with the blind. A year later a report from an ad hoc committee at a National Conference on Mobility Instruction for the Blind confirmed the need for sight for O and M instructors (Report, 1966, p. 7). In 1971 the sight mandate remained entrenched, however the vision acuity and visual field requirements were modified to 20/40 and 120 degrees, which are the standards used by many state for issuing drivers' licenses. When the certification requirements were revised in 1977, with the development of the Functional Abilities Checklist (examples provided in the following paragraph), vision was still essential in order to qualify for certification (Wiener and Siffermann, 1997, p. 557).

It was not until the early 1980s that the exclusionary policy mandating sight was challenged. At that time the American Association of Workers for the Blind (AAWB) (the body responsible for the certification of O and M instructors) denied the certification of Fredric Schroeder, a blind graduate of an approved university O and M program. Justification for this action was that Schroeder's supervisor was not able to answer "yes" to several items on the Functional Abilities Checklist including the following: (1) "Can the applicant describe in detail the posture, gait and techniques of a student within the distances of 5 to 125 feet as required for indoor training?" (2) "Can the applicant describe actions and gross techniques of a student from a distance of 250 feet (1/2 block)?" and (3) "Can the applicant, moving in an unfamiliar area, assess collision paths of a student and construction equipment, traffic control boxes, and other large stationary objects at a distance of 375 feet (3/4 block)?" These functional abilities reflect the belief that sight is essential for teaching O and M.

Under pressure from the organized blind and the threat of a lawsuit as a result of the Americans with Disability Act (1991) the O and M profession recognized the need to modify its policy of excluding blind persons from the profession. Thus in 1996 AER Division Nine officially recognized that a blind person could be a qualified O and M instructor (Wiener and Siffermann, 1997, p. 559). However, an assumed accommodation for the blind O and M instructor would be a sighted assistant. To be more precise, the official AER policy states:

> The certification policy now requires that when an otherwise qualified person with a disability is unable to perform the monitoring tasks, the universities must explore the use of alternative strategies, accommodations, and auxiliary aids (Wiener and Siffermann, 1997, p. 558).

In common practice in the field many O and M instructors, agency administrators and blind persons themselves interpret this list of accommodations to mean sighted assistance. This presumption, whether accurate or not, tends to inflame the sensibilities of blind instructors who reject the notion that any accommodations are necessary. This misperception of the abilities of blind instructors may also result in lost job opportunities because agency directors fear greater costs and hassles by hiring blind instructors. Therefore, AER's support for blind O and M instructors is only a recent development and is by no means universally accepted within the O and M profession.

I believe that disability studies is clearly relevant for examining local, state and national policy. This is because of the growing influence of disability scholar-activists whose work exposes and challenges current polices which are influenced by socially constructed beliefs about disability. For the sake of social justice disability studies is relevant, and to give voice to injustice makes it worth while.

References

Blasch, B.B., Welsh, R. L., and Weiner, W. R. (Eds.) (1997) *Foundations of orientation and mobility* (2nd edition). New York: AFB Press.

Bledsoe, C. (1947). Manual for orientors. *Outlook for the Blind* 41:10, 271–279.

————. (1965). Selected readings concerning blindness, for graduate students. *Faculty Contributions, School of Graduate Studies, WMU,* 7:2, 5–12.

————. (1969). From Valley Forge to Hines: Truth old enough to tell. *Blindness,* 97–142.

————. (1997). Originators of orientation and mobility training. In Blasch, B.B., Welsh, R. L., and Weiner, W. R. (Eds.) *Foundations of Orientation and Mobility* (2nd ed). New York: AFB Press, 580–621.

Bledstein, B. (1978). *The culture of professionalism: The middle class and the development of higher education in America.* New York: W. W. Norton and Company.

Carroll, T. (1961). *Blindness: What it is, what it does, and how to live with it.* Boston: Little, Brown and Company.

Cholden, L. (1958), *A psychiatrist works with blindness.* New York: American Foundation for the Blind.

Cutsforth, T. (1950). Personality and social adjustment among the blind. In P. Zahl (Ed.). *Blindness: Modern approaches to the unseen environment.* Princeton, N.J.: Princeton University Press.

Ferguson, R. (2001). *We know who we are: A history of the blind in challenging educational and socially constructed policies. A study in policy archaeology.* San Francisco: Caddo Gap Press.

————. (2003) Blind mobility instructors: A graduate program designed with blind people in mind. *Proceedings 11th International Mobility Conference,* Stellenbosch, South Africa.

————. (2004). The impact of socially constructed beliefs about blindness on the O and M profession . In D. W. Dew and G. M. Alan (Eds.). *Contemporary Issues in Orientation and Mobility, 29.* Washington, DC: The

George Washington University, Center for Rehabilitation Counseling Research and Education, 51–64.

Foucault, M. (1961/1988). *Madness and civilization: A history of insanity in the age of reason.* New York: Vintage Books.

———. (1966/1970). *The order of things: An archaeology of the human sciences.* New York: Pantheon.

———. (1969/1972). *The archaeology of knowledge.* (A. M. Sheridan, Trans.). New York: Pantheon Books.

———. (1991). Governmentality. In *The Foucault effect: Studies in Governmentality.* Burchell, G., Gordon, C, and.Miller, P. (Eds.). Chicago: University of Chicago Press, 87–104.

Gordon, C. (1991). Governmentality rationality: An introduction. In *The Foucault effect: Studies in governmentality.* Burchell, G., Gordon, C, and.Miller, P. (Eds.). Chicago: University of Chicago Press, pp. 1–51.

Haskell, T. (Ed.) (1984). *The authority of experts: Studies in history and theory.* Bloomington: Indiana University Press.

Koestler, Frances A., (Ed.). (1966). *The COMSTAC report: Standards for strengthened services.* New York: Commission on Standards and Accreditation of Services for the Blind.

Longmore, P. K. and Umansky, L. (2001). Introduction: Disability history: From the margins to the mainstream. In Longmore, P. K. and Umansky, L. (Eds.) *The new disability history: American perspectives.* New York: New York University Press, 1–29.

National Conference on Mobility and Orientation (1960) Mobility and orientation—A symposium. *New outlook for the blind, 54,* 77–94.

Report of the National Conference Vocational Rehabilitation Administration. (1966). Washington, DC: Vocational Rehabilitation Association.

Scheurich, J. (1994). Policy archaeology: A new policy studies methodology. *Journal of Educational Policy,* 9:4, 297–316.

Voorhees, A. (1962). Professional trends in mobility training, *Standards for Mobility Instructors.* New York: American Foundation for the Blind, 11–23.

Wiener, W. and Siffermann, E. (1997). The Development of the profession of orientation and mobility. In Blasch, B.B., Welsh, R. L., and Weiner, W. R. (Eds.) *Foundations of Orientation and Mobility* (2nd ed). New York: AFB Press, 553–579.

Zahl, P. A. (Ed.) (1950) *Blindness: Modern approaches to an unseen environment.* Princeton University Press.

CHAPTER 10

Applying Disability Theory in Educational Policy: NIDRR's "New Paradigm of Disability" as a Cautionary Tale

Susan L. Gabel

Disability studies in education faces some interesting challenges in the next few years, many of which are addressed in this book, including finding new ways of thinking and talking about practice, figuring out how to use disability studies in policy analysis, and incorporating international perspectives. Perhaps one of the most difficult tasks ahead is the challenge of evolving from a basic theoretical agenda to an applied one that poses and studies solutions to practical educational problems and that persuasively argues for solutions in the public sphere. The problem of application, I argue, is a conversational one in which theory, policy, and practice must be mutually informative. Conversations between disability theory and pedagogy, for example, have the potential for dramatically shifting the ways in which teachers understand learning and could have consequences for how teachers make decisions about whether they refer students for special education assessments or, contrastingly, figure out how to teach inclusively without the need for referrals and labels. Likewise, understanding or being reminded of the complexities of classroom teaching by immersion in classrooms and schools can inform theoretical arguments, and help academicians in disability studies in education construct arguments and pose solutions more and more persuasive and useful to teachers and principals. Applying disability theory to policy, as another example, could influence whether or not a district constructs inclusive education policy and whether or not policy results in the creation of inclusive school communities. On the other hand, deep understanding of the policy milieu could provide a disability theorist the perspective needed to analyze disconnects between policy and theory and recommend policy solutions more consistent with a disability rights perspective, while simultaneously being more useful to policy makers.

Of course, to markedly transform policy and its related practices, new ideas and ways of doing things that are diametrically opposed to tradition are usually required. Disability studies in education has many new ideas, and my attempt in this chapter is to illustrate the degree to which disability theory alters the foundations of policy work to the extent that radical changes are necessary if disability theory is to be effective at all. To offer a contemporary example directly related to and drawn from the intersections of theory and policy, I explore a cautionary tale from the rehabilitation field in the United States in which the players and consequences are similar and directly related to those in education (particularly special education), the stakes are as high, and the conundrums and paradoxes are as complex and confusing. I conclude this chapter with a discussion of what we can learn from the cautionary tale and proposals for what could be some next steps.

Why Choose an Example from Rehabilitation?
In several ways, the field of rehabilitation in the United States is disabled people's adult parallel to school-age special education. Historically, both institutions operate under distributive policies, or policies that provide services based on categorical eligibility, measurable need, and carefully restricted access; and their eligibility and need determination policies are based on a medical model of disability. Both institutions aim to intervene when a person's functional limitations are such that s/he cannot benefit from established institutional opportunities without such intervention. Special education is intended to provide support needed to benefit from education while rehabilitation support is intended to help one benefit from work opportunities or to gain access to work. Finally, based on tradition and resulting from their adherence to a medical model, practitioners in both institutions are required by policy to utilize what Vic Finkelstein (2003) describes as the cure/care intervention model. In cure and care interventions, it is assumed that the disabled individual needs to be fixed or cured and that once the impairment is stable and "there is no cure then *care* must be prescribed to cure the as-

sumed social consequences of impairment and disability" (p. 4). In special education, the *care* component of intervention might be considered to be the self-contained classroom, from which it is nearly impossible to escape. In rehabilitation, the *care* component could be viewed as the pressure to "prepare" people for sheltered workshops or other menial labor rather than competitive employment that meets their interests and abilities. Given the historical similarities between these two applied fields, and even though this is not a perfect analogy, I argue that the use of an example from the rehabilitation field can illuminate the problems facing disability studies in education as we attempt to influence policy.

The Cautionary Tale

> NIDRR has led the way in the research for a new conceptual foundation to organize and interpret the phenomenon of disability—a new paradigm of disability (NIDRR *Five Year Plan*, 1999).

With pronouncements such as the one above, the US National Institute on Disability and Rehabilitation Research (NIDRR) announced its *Five Year Plan* and a "new paradigm of disability," an ostensible move toward what NIDRR refers to, in other sections of the *Plan*, as the social model of disability. The announcement was met with a flurry of listserv and chat room activity among disability activists, rehabilitation researchers, and scholars in disability studies, in part because of NIDRR's bold claim that it has led the way even though the international Disabled People's Movement and Disability Studies have sought the acceptance of a new paradigm for decades.

The announcement also generated significant attention in professional and scholarly conferences including, to name a very few, NIDRR's own conference in 2000, "New Paradigm on Disability: Research Issues and Approaches"; the American Psychological Association's Annual Conference theme "Fundamental Changes in Disability and Rehabilitation"; and the 2000 annual conference of the Rehabilitation Engineering and Assistive Technology Society of North America with the theme "Public Policy as Related to Disability and Rehabilitation: Is It Time for a New Paradigm?" Publications ensued, as well. An *American Psychologist* special issue included several articles by NIDRR staff extolling the virtues of the new paradigm, claiming it to be an "important conceptual advancement in the rehabilitation research and health-related disciplines"(Tate and Pledger, 2003, ¶4), while also claiming allegiance to disability studies as the foundation for the new paradigm (Pledger, 2003a, 2003b; Olkin and Pledger, 2003; Tate and Pledger, 2003). A detailed list of the post-*Plan* activity can be found on the National Rehabilitation Information Center's (NRIC), NIDRR Project Information Management System (n.d.) website by conducting a simple document search for "new paradigm of disability" within the NRIC/NIDRR webpages.

To top off the excitement, the then-Commissioner of NIDRR, Kate Seelman, along with Gary Albrecht and Michael Bury (2001), published the *Handbook of Disability Studies*, the first handbook of its kind. Interestingly, the *Handbook* itself is full of work largely antithetical to NIDRR's new paradigm, as *Handbook* readers will come to realize from my analysis, but rather than denigrating the *Handbook* and its editors and authors, this points to the practical problem of influencing policy by applying novel theory. Judging by its contents, the *Handbook's* editors and authors adhere to the social model or, more generally, social interpretations of disability. The disconnect between the *Handbook's* contents and the *Five Year Plan* reveal the unpredictability of policy work (Kingdon, 2002) and the difficulties of applied research. Later, I return to this problem of disconnect by comparing a paradox in the NIDRR case to the challenges facing disability studies in education.

Amidst the fanfare associated with the *Five Year Plan* and the new paradigm, a critic of the new paradigm alleged that there was nothing new about it. In his article in the *American Psychologist*, "Old Wine in a Slightly Cracked New Bottle" (Thomas, 2003), he writes that similar emphases "in disability and rehabilitation date back, at least, to…1958" (¶1). Thomas continues by citing works from 1946 through the 1960s as evidence for his assertion. While other claims made by Thomas have less punch—for example, his claim that disability studies actually stigmatizes disabled people by emphasizing disability in its title—his arguments against the new paradigm are, for the most part, quite apt, as my analysis will illustrate.

The *Five Year Plan*

Originally announced in the *Federal Register* (1999, hereafter referred to as *Register*) and available in less detail online (NIDRR, 1999), the new paradigm is detailed in NIDRR's *Long Range Plan for Fiscal Years 1999– 2003* (found in both the *Register* and the NIDRR website but with more detail in the *Register*) in which disability is defined, a continuum of enable-ment-disablement is described, etiologies and demographics of disability are explored, and the "emerging universe of disability" (NIDRR, Chapter 2, Section 6) is discussed in which the

> emerging universe is identified with new disabling conditions; new causes for impairments; differential distributions within the population; increased frequency of some impairments; and different consequences of disability (¶2).

The *Plan* continues by outlining NIDRR's research agenda and funding priorities, which look quite similar to those priorities found in previous years. Many aspects of the *Plan* could be submitted to an analysis but for brevity, I concentrate here on the *Plan's* definition of disability, which I take to be the core issue at stake in NIDRR's claims of a new paradigm and which NIDRR emphasizes as the transformative feature of the *Plan*.

Old paradigm

In the old paradigm, NIDRR defined disability as "an *individual* [who] is limited by his/her impairment or condition" (*Register*, 1999, Table 1, emphasis added). The *Register's* report indicates that "the definition of disability is critical to building a conceptual model that identifies relevant components of disablement and their relationships to each other, and the dynamic mechanisms by which they change" (*Register*, 1999, page 45751, ¶5). The report continues by reminding that

> [t]he majority of Federal definitions of disability, including those in the Rehabilitation Act, the ADA, and the National Health Interview Survey (NHIS), derive from the old paradigm. These definitions all attribute the cause of limitations in daily activities or social roles to characteristics of the individual (2001, ¶6).

Furthermore, notes the report, "even the ADA, which promotes accessibility and accommodations, locates the disability with the individual" (2001, ¶7). The old paradigm, then, is clearly the medical model paradigm which is also found in other federal legislation related to disability, including Section 504 of the Rehabilitation Act (1973), the Individuals with Disabilities Education Act (IDEA, 2005), and as mentioned previously, the Americans with Disabilities Act (ADA, 1990).

What kind of intervention strategies are used to address disability in the old paradigm? According to the *Five Year Plan*, intervention strategies in the old paradigm are cure/care oriented (Finkelstein, 2003) and are intended to "correct the deficit," and "fix the individual," and are used by professional clinicians and other rehabilitation service providers, while the role of the disabled individual is to be the "object of intervention," the "beneficiary" or "research subject" (*Register*, Part V, Table 1). Within the old paradigm, welfare entitlements, or those federal resources available to qualified disabled individuals (e.g., adult home help or chore services such as housekeeping, food stamps, Medicaid, SSI, etc.), become benefits "based on severity of impairment" (*Register*, Part V, Table 1) and require verification by experts in rehabilitation, medicine, and/or psychology. Of necessity, then, the focus on the need to qualify for entitlements in the old paradigm requires practitioners to rely upon distributive policies and funding streams which can lead people who care about social justice to operate unwittingly under the assumption that their work will create equitable social relations (Armstrong, 2003; Mutua, 2001; Slee and Allan, 2001; Stone, 1984). This is the paradox of many manifestations of the old paradigm: to provide resources to disabled people, one becomes complicit with the system.

New paradigm

What of the new paradigm? Is it also paradoxical in the same sense? As in special education, rehabilitation funding hinges on categorical definition and eligibility. Naturally, then, NIDRR's new paradigm focuses on redefining disability and holds that disability is "an individual with an impairment [who] requires an accommodation to perform functions required to carry out life activities" (*Register*, 1999, Table 1). Throughout the *Register* (1999), the *Five Year Plan* (1999), and the *American Psychologist* publications by NIDRR staff (Tate and Pledger, 2003; Pledger, 2003a, 2003b), the new paradigm is described as a holistic framework focusing on whole person functioning (Tate and Pledger, 2003) where functioning is understood within a socioecological context (Pledger, 2003b) involving the interplay between the person and the built or natural environment. "Invariably, when disability is defined," notes Pledger (2003b), "the individual is at the core. However, contemporary (new paradigm) definitions presuppose that the environment is a major determinant of individual functioning" (Section 6, ¶1).

It would seem that NIDRR's new paradigm has, indeed, broken from the medical model; however, a closer look is warranted, particularly in how NIDRR compares its new definition to other definitions. The *Register* (US, 1999) and online *Plan* (NIDRR, 1999) texts differ slightly in their sections on the "Definitions and Concepts of Disability and Disablement." The *Register's* comments regarding the conflict between public law and the new paradigm are revealing and quite surprising, given the federal policy milieu during the time of the *Plan*.

> Prevailing definitions, based on statute and supporting program authorities, clearly do not reflect new paradigm concepts of disability. Nearly all definitions identify an individual as disabled based on a physical or mental impairment that limits the person's ability to perform an important activity. Note that the complementary possibility—that the individual is limited by a barrier in society or the environment—is never considered. This Plan suggests that it is useful to regard an individual with a disability as a person with an impairment who requires an accommodation or intervention rather than as a person limited solely by a condition (Part V, 45753, ¶4).

The differentiation between disability and impairment, a distinction borrowed from the strong social model in disability studies (Shakepeare and Watson, 2001), emerges as central to NIDRR's definition. Since NIDRR's references to the social model are actually references to what Shakespeare and Watson (2001) call the strong social model (evidence of this is in NIDRR's attempts at clear distinction between disability and impairment), I will use NIDRR's point of reference in my discussions in this section and I will avoid a critique of the strong social model, which can be found in Shakespeare and Watson (2001) and Corker (2000), is criticized in Light (2000), and is summarized in historical context in Gabel and Peters (2004).

The various conversations about NIDRR's new paradigm also include references to other concepts from disability studies. Pledger (2003b) refers to disablement, or what she calls the "disability process," which she defines as "those personal, societal, and environmental factors that interact with biological and behavioral factors to influence individual functioning" (Section 9, ¶1). The *Register* (1999) and the *Plan* online (NIDRR, 1999) also refer to disablement, implying that it hinges on a continuum of disability based on the severity of consequences of impairments, as in the excerpt below.

> In keeping with the new paradigm, NIDRR emphasizes the importance of explicating the connection between the person and the environment, and interface that de-

termines the disabling consequences of impairments and conditions (*Register*, 1999, 45754, ¶2).

The *Plan's* criticism of the old paradigm holds that the role of the individual with an impairment is a passive one of receiving cure or care. The new *Plan* is less clear about the role of the individual under the new paradigm but inferences can be made. Even under the new paradigm, emphasis is placed on impairment and what is wrong with the body of the individual. Therefore, one can surmise that the emphasis in intervention will be placed there, as well. That leaves one with a focus, again, on cure and care. If the argument is made that the new paradigm does, in fact, recognize environmental factors, then it must be observed that the *Plan's* concept of the environment is a depoliticized one; similar to the ecological theory of the 1970s (Bronfenbrenner, 1979a, 1979b; Rhodes and Paul, 1978; Swap, 1972).

Analysis

The *Five Year Plan's* title, "New Paradigm of Disability," and its references to Thomas Kuhn's (1962) book The *Structure of Scientific Revolutions* together indicate that NIDRR believes that the new paradigm is a significant enough departure from the old paradigm to constitute a revolution, or a dramatic change in the way rehabilitation policy and practice will be considered and enacted. Discussions of paradigm shifts have become somewhat passé but NIDRR's reference to Kuhn's work requires a brief review at this point. Kuhn's sense of paradigm shifts is that they are revolutionary, "*noncumulative* developmental episodes in which an older paradigm is replaced in whole or in part by an *incompatible* one" (Kuhn, 1962, IX., ¶ 1, emphases added). Real paradigm shifts, according to Kuhn, result in the replacement of all or part of a previous paradigm such that theory is radically transformed, as in the Newtonian to Einsteinian shift or, more recently, Planck's discovery of quantum mechanics and the resulting shift in scientific understanding of the cosmos.

I next demonstrate that NIDRR's new paradigm has not replaced all or part of the old paradigm with an incompatible one, per Kuhn's criterion for a paradigm shift and I do so by focusing on NIDRR's definition of disability and its consequences for intervention practices. To demonstrate the problems with NIDRR's claims about a new paradigm, I first examine it's attempts to differentiate between disability and impairment. After that, I focus on NIDRR's claim that the new paradigm does not position disability within the individual.

Impairment and disability

The *Plan* attempts to disentangle impairment and disability by borrowing from the strong social model but actually ends up conjoining the concepts. On one hand, the *Plan* refers to the importance of the interplay between the individual with an impairment and the environment that, together, result in disability. On the other hand, the *Plan* refers to the "disabling consequences of impairments and *conditions*" (*Register*, 1999, 45754, ¶2, emphasis added), implying that impairments are what cause disabling consequences and avoiding clarification about whether or not the term "conditions" refers to individual conditions (this usually refers to diagnosed impairments under the medical model) or environmental conditions. Using the term conditions to refer to environmental factors would move the discourse closer to a social model but it does not appear that NIDRR has done this. Under the medical model the term "conditions" refers to diagnoses without explicit reference to the contrary; therefore one would reliably guess that when NIDRR uses the word "condition(s)," it is referring to a characteristic of the individual usually considered disability or impairment in everyday thought. NIDRR gives no such reference and, in fact, uses the term "conditions" as it has in the past and consistent with the medical model. NIDRR also uses "conditions" to refer to medical diagnoses, as in "[the] emerging universe is identified with new disabling conditions" (¶2). In other words, for most people and for NIDRR, saying "She has *a disability*" is nearly the same thing as saying "She has cerebral palsy" because *a disability* refers, in this case, to cerebral palsy and in other cases, to whatever medical diagnosis one might be assigned. Therefore, using the phrase "disabling consequences of impairments and conditions" (45754, ¶2) does not change the meaning of disability at all. Instead, it seems to instantiate disability even more strongly within the individual. Even the *Plan's* most basic definition, that a person with a disability "is a *person with an impairment* who requires an accommodation or intervention rather than as a person limited solely by a condition" (45753, ¶4, emphasis added) still positions disability as an individualistic rather than a collective social phenomenon, which is where social modelists would position it (Barnes et al., 2002; Finkelstein, 2003; Abberley, 1987; Oliver, 1990; Shakespeare and Watson, 2001; Titchkosky, 2001)

Intervention and accommodation

One could argue that although NIDRR's *Plan* pairs impairments and conditions and locates them within the individual, its new definition remains, nevertheless, transformative because it changes the ways in which intervention is understood. Finkelstein (2003) would argue that this is not possible; that of necessity, models of disability are directly associated with models of intervention. A side-by-side comparison of old and new paradigm definitions may help here.

Table 1

Old Paradigm Definition of Disability	New Paradigm Definition of Disability
An individual [who] is limited by his/her impairment or condition	*An individual with an impairment* [who] requires accommodation to perform functions required to carry out life activities

(source: NIDRR, 1999, Table 1, emphases added)

While both definitions locate disability within the individual there is a shift from old to new in that the new paradigm indicates that interventions are accommodations (rather than cures or fixes). However, the "normal" conditions of society (i.e., built environments or social institutions that deny access and thereby disable people with impairments) remain privileged while the disabled individual must seek accommodations or interventions in order to gain access and/or perform functions required for everyday life.

Rather than taking a universal design for living (UDL) approach, in which efforts are made to make all physical and social environments fully accessible to the greatest number of people regardless of functional ability, and which would be much more consistent with the strong social model, NIDRR has perpetuated a retrofit mentality, common in architecture, but also in any environment built without the application of universal design principles. Educational environments (e.g., opportunities to learn) can apply universal design for learning (also UDL) or instruction (UDI), although the idea has primarily been advocated in literature related to higher education (Hackman and Rauscher, 2004; Mino, 2004; Pliner and Johnson, 2004; Scott, et. al., 2003). Other references to UDL/I can be found (e.g., Bremer et al., 2002; King-Sears, 2001; Rose and Meyer, 2002), but as with any idea, there appear to be conflicting assumptions about the purposes of UDL/I at play in the literature. Regardless of one's assumptions, one problem with retrofitting, rather than applying principles of universal design, is that retrofitting rarely is as successful as is the universal design approach because it solves access problems one at a time and requires disabled people to ask for access

rather than expecting access as a natural course of things. Such attempts at access suggest that, as in prior iterations of the medical model, disability is the negation of ability. Unfortunately, retrofitting and other depoliticized interventions avoid the kind of social overhaul needed to prevent disablement on a broader scale.

Strong social modelists in disability studies would argue that being disabled is not a negation of ability; rather, it is a status imposed upon the individual by the external world (Abberley, 1987; Finkelstein, 1998, 2003; UPIAS, 1974/75, 1980; Titchkosky, 2001). The not-so-subtle difference between this standpoint and the one taken by the new paradigm is key here: disablement is a social process of denying access to a whole group of people—not just particular individuals—and it is not a clinical or medical or scientific process, nor does it involve a continuum of severity of impairment. In contrast, even though the *Plan* seems to be attempting to place disability within a socioecological context, the new paradigm still views disability as an individual characteristic and the negation of ability. Furthermore, it fails to recognize the intractability of the medical model, as well as the inextricability of meaning (disability) from function (intervention). This failure is a common one in positivist paradigms

Meaning and concept

One of the errors in the new paradigm is a conflation of the meaning and relative importance of definitions and concepts. A definition is a "concise explanation of the meaning of a word" (hyperdictionary). At first glance, one might argue that the two definitions are different in meaning and in one way they are: the old emphasizes limitations, the new emphasizes accommodations. In another way, however, the definitions are similar because both emphasize disability as located within an individual and as dependent on impairments or conditions defined within a medical model.

While a definition denotes the meaning given to a word, a concept is a more powerful tool: an idea behind the word; a thing imagined when one says the word. A concept is an abstraction, a mental picture, a construct (Pitha, 1996; hyperdictionary) formed through social relations (Vygotsky, 1978, 1985). Regardless of the definition of a word, when the word is used, the user conjures up a mental image of the idea behind the word that is constructed by the assumptions the user holds in relation to that idea or image. This conjured image is the concept or idea to which a word has been assigned. While NIDRR has shifted part of the *definition* of disability (the type of meaning), it has not altered the *concept* of disability (the idea), which, if truly altered, would represent a more fundamental shift and one more consistent with the notion of shifting paradigms. Unfortunately, conceptual shifts are more difficult to accomplish but they are, according to Kuhn (1962), the foundation of paradigm shifts.

If the *Plan* were to define or conceptualize disability as does the strong social model, it would not associate disability with innate individual characteristics. Instead, disability would be viewed as a socio-cultural phenomenon, a macro-concept, or an idea that expresses itself within and between the threads of the broad fabric of society. In disability studies, there are not many different disabilities (as in conditions that are diagnosed); there is a single phenomenon—disability—that is variously manifested, experienced, lived and studied. A real paradigm shift with a transformative reconceptualization of disability would lead to novel responses to disability and new ways of talking about disability. Since NIDRR's definition of disability does not shift paradigms at all, it follows that the *Plan* continues to associate rehabilitation with stem cell research, clinical treatments, and severity of condition, and it is inevitable that to obtain funding from NIDRR one must propose to investigate within the confines of the medical model.

Paradox and Problem

One of the paradoxes facing NIDRR is similar to those uncovered by Roger Slee and Julie Allan (2001) in their analysis of inclusive education policy in Australia and England: policy can say one thing but mean another. One way in which Slee and Allan illustrate this is with the name-change tendency of some university special education departments that start using the title "inclusive education" rather than "special education." This seems to be about the same degree of change as in the *Five Year Plan*. Words may change and be redefined but if ideas or concepts do not change, there is no epistemological shift. As I have done here in relation to NIDRR's definition of disability, Slee and Allan argue that inclusive education policy requires a "fundamental paradigm shift and needs to be presented and recognized as such" (177). In their deconstruction of inclusive education policy, they uncover the paradox of attempting inclusion within policy contexts that pathologize disability. As in the United States, "so-called inclusion policy," they argue, has "collapsed...into a crude model of distributive justice" (179) with many of the same effects identified by Stone (1984) in her critique of distributive policies related to disability and Mutua (2001) in her study of the ways in which welfare policy constructs a disability identity. The mere act of using experts (psychologists, special education teachers, etc.) to make special education eligibility decisions and to subsequently "allow" students to be "included" reproduces exclusion. This process of identifying students eligible for inclusion is like the problem of retrofitting for accommodations discussed earlier. It assumes that the general education context is acceptable as is and that it merely needs slight adjustments to accommodate particular special education students with specific needs. Paradoxically, and reminiscent of the rehabilitation field, even those educators who wish to participate in the project of inclusion easily become complicit in exclusion because of institutional assumptions about the nature of disability and the policies derived from such assumptions.

Given the policy context within which this cautionary tale is told, one must remember the nature of the policy process and the ways in which it takes on a life of its own. Although NIDRR's Commissioner Seelman, a long-time member, past President and current Treasurer of the Society for Disability Studies (SDS, n.d.), surely hoped that the social model of disability would prevail, she must have known that once policy leaves the cocoon of its originator(s), it becomes entangled in the politics of all participants of the policy process (Kingdon, 2002). I have not investigated what transpired prior to the publication of the *Five Year Plan*, but one can guess, if this official document evolved in ways similar to most, that politicians were engaged in considering the consequences of a paradigm shift, the legal offices of NIDRR authorized what could and could not be written into the record, and any NIDRR staff member or nationally renowned rehabilitation expert resistant to a paradigm shift attempted to block it. Thus, what is left is what remains in many (if not most) attempts at radical policy reform—a watered-down version of the original idea that, in the end, will have little lasting impact but that might shift the conversation ever so slightly toward conceptual and practice change (Tyack and Cuban, 1984).

Implications for Disability Studies in Education

These examples and the cautionary tale in general point to the problem of whether or not it is possible and if possible, how, to use the social model or more nuanced social interpretations of disability in policy in an applied field; in education, for example. In effect, the problems boil down to those facing any applied field in the midst of a paradigm shift or even during less dramatic epistemological changes:

(1) Are we tackling the most important applied issues or problems that emerge from basic knowledge in disability studies and if not, what are those central issues or problems?

(2) How can we communicate basic knowledge or theory and its relevance for applied issues and problems in ways that are understandable to people working in applied fields?

(3) How can we influence resources and resource allocation?

(4) How can we persuade practitioners or policy makers that new ideas are useful and beneficial?

(5) How can we allow practitioners to inform our own theoretical work so that continued dialog between theory and practice exists and, by extension, our policy work is influenced?

(6) Finally, how can we avoid the pitfalls in the NIDRR example?

The responses to the above six points could fill several volumes. I concentrate on three of them (1, 3, 6) because they seem to be at the heart of the cautionary tale.

Issues and Problems to Tackle

As mentioned early in this chapter, those working in disability studies in education are already addressing a wide variety of issues and problems. I propose that more work is needed on the policy problems contributing to disablement in education. As in the NIDRR case, regardless of how much good NIDRR does for disabled people in spite of the medical model, it remains significantly constrained by the medical model under which it operates. The same could be said for education in which IDEA drives most of the work related to disabled students. Yet with the exception of Gregg Beratan's (2005) paper at AERA, I have seen no other studies aiming significant criticism at the IDEA. In fact, the IDEA still seems to be a sacred cow in the United States. In my conversations with disability studies colleagues who are not educators, the IDEA remains an example of civil rights legislation that continues to hold promise. Is this what a disability studies in education analysis would yield, or would arguments be made that IDEA is a historical artifact that might have outlived its usefulness, or would some other analysis suggest alternatives? If there are alternatives, what might they be? What might policy look like under the social model or social interpretations of disability? How might these alternatives influence practice at the school and classroom levels? Are there international examples of national civil rights policy in education working for disabled people?

Resources and Resource Allocation

This question is closely connected to the first since resource allocation hinges on policy decisions, and policy decisions hinge on epistemological assumptions, among other things. Currently, resources allocation for disabled students in US schools is directly connected to the categorical imperatives of the IDEA. Therefore, resources are available if a district opts into the medical model bureaucracy which, of course, all districts must do if they want to receive federal funding. We need to generate research that proposes creative options within the current system, but we also need to study and write about ways in which the protections of the IDEA—particularly equal access—can be maintained while its drawbacks, dangers, and expenses—particularly those associated with medical model thinking—are minimized or extinguished. International educational studies can be helpful in this regard since the limited resources of the developing world have caused those educators and policy makers to think differently about resource allocation. Pertinent to the question of alternatives, above, what would the funding streams and regulatory demands look like, and what consequences would be faced in a revolutionized policy environment?

Pitfalls of Cautionary Tale

The pitfalls are many and are not limited to this cautionary tale. Here, I address three. First, NIDRR's boast that it "led the way" to a "new paradigm of disability" is untrue and was quite offensive to the international Disability Rights community that has trudged on for decades pressing for a new paradigm. As disability studies in education grows, we will need to avoid over-promoting ourselves and our accomplishments. Most of us currently work within the same conflicted policy milieu that faced NIDRR during its *Five Year Plan*. Our influence is constrained by that milieu, as was NIDRR's influence on the ultimate published record. Second, NIDRR's tale indicates our need to be politically active and savvy. Considering the outcome of NIDRR's attempts, imagine the pressure faced by anyone attempting to radically overhaul the IDEA's definition of disability, for example. If we are to have any influence in the seat of power, and I argue that we need to attempt to influence those in power as well as practitioners and teacher educators working in the trenches, we need to figure out how to be persuasive and "speak truth to power" (AFSC, 1955), an idea originating among Quakers during the Cold War and more recently used by Kerry Kennedy Cuomo (Kennedy, 2000) in relation to international human rights. This is not referenced to suggest that the IDEA is a human rights violation, but to recall the importance of standing in the halls of power and making one's voice heard, particularly when one has an ethical or moral agenda with which policy is in conflict. (Deborah Gallagher, 2005, makes an excellent argument that the agenda of disability studies in education is an ethical one.) Political savvy, on the other hand, requires us to understand the processes behind large-scale policy moves and to figure out how to influence those processes when possible. The third pitfall to avoid is the lack of self-critique. The *Five Year Plan*, for example, is not self-critical. It purports to offer up a radically different definition of disability and notions about intervention when, in fact, there is no radical change. Instead, NIDRR could have recognized that its *Plan* was transitional and incremental, and NIDRR staff (Olkin and Pledger, 2003; Pledger, 2003a, 2003b; Tate and Pledger, 2003) who subsequently published articles about the plan in the *American Psychologist* could have critically realized that they were presenting "old wine in a slightly cracked new bottle" (Thomas, 2003). Disability studies in education needs to be self critical, too. We need to interrogate our own work and be open to diverse ways of thinking and approaching educational issues and problems, even when those are critical of the dominant ideology of our field. Often, critiques of dominant ideology yield important discoveries. Criticism, I maintain, can make our arguments, proposals, and ideas stronger, more useful, and more persuasive.

Conclusion

Disability studies in education faces challenges similar to the ones facing NIDRR. In this chapter, I have focused on NIDRR's claim of a "new conceptual foundation" for rehabilitation grounded in what I have interpreted as the strong social model of disability. My analysis of NIDRR's new paradigm has primarily emphasized NIDRR's definition of disability and, secondarily, its consequences for intervention. I have argued that, contrary to NIDRR's claims, its new paradigm does little to shift the definition of disability closer to the social model or any social interpretation of disability within disability studies. Under the old paradigm, intervention consisted of the cure/care model identified by Finkelstein (2003) as an inevitable consequence of the medical model (or what Finkelstein calls the social death model of disability) of disability. Under the new paradigm, intervention is less well fleshed out but is stated as consisting of accommodations or interventions. I have indicated the problems of the inevitability of a retrofit mentality in accommodations.

A remaining question is whether or not NIDRR's slight shift toward accommodations as interventions is significant enough to avoid the cure/care model of intervention. Given this analysis, I suspect not. NIDRR's continued use of disability categories certainly demonstrates its adherence to the medical model in spite of its attempts at a paradigm shift. As stated in the *Plan*, all federal disability legislation in the United States uses similar categorical imperatives. They are believed to be measurable and make for ease of distribution. This is an important lesson to learn from the cautionary tale and one that Christopher Donoghue (2003) pointed out in the recent past: the resistance to the social model is strong, particularly in US regulatory systems.

Reflecting on this cautionary tale, I have considered its direct implications for disability studies in education beginning with the paradoxes of the cautionary tale, particularly the incompatibility of striving toward justice— inclusion, for example—without radical epistemological shifts. The cautionary tale suggests that without radical epistemological change—perhaps as basic as a definitional change with consequences substantive enough to create conceptual change—policy and practice cannot radically change. This leaves those advocating a disability studies perspective struggling in the same way the proponents of NIDRR's new paradigm have struggled. We profess radical epistemologies but we do so within traditional policy contexts and in relation to funding streams and practices entangled with those policy contexts. We slog on, writing and talking differently about disability; all the while the old paradigm continues, holding the purse strings and keeping radical reform at bay.

What can be done to ring in a new era? Are we tackling the central issues and targeting all the right audiences? More and more I am in agreement with Gregg Beratan (2005) who argues that the IDEA perpetuates institutionalized ableism. Slee and Allan (2005) imply something similar in their deconstruction of inclusion policy, as does Finkelstein (2003) in his work on modeling disability. I propose that as long as we are operating within a distributive system that depends upon the medical model to allocate resources we will not see radical social or educational change on a broad scale.

References

Abberley, P. (1987). The concept of oppression and the development of a social theory of disability. *Disability and Society* 2(1), 5–20.Retrieved October 15, 2004 from http://www.medanthro.net/research/disability/index.html.

Albrecht, G. L., Seelman, K. D., Bury, M., Eds. (2001). *Handbook of Disability Studies.* Thousand Oaks, CA: Sage Publications.

American Friends Service Committee (AFSC) (1955). Speak truth to power: A Quaker search for an alternative to violence. Retrieved July 10, 2005, from http://www.quaker.org/sttp.html.

Armstrong, F. (2003). Difference, discourse and democracy: The making and breaking of policy in the market place. *International Journal of Inclusive Education 7(3)*: 241–257.

Barnes, C. M., Oliver, M., and Barton, L. (2002). *Disability studies today.* Oxford: Blackwell Publishing Company.

Beratan, G. D. (2005). *Institutional ableism and IDEA: Undermining inclusive education for 30 years (and still going strong).* Paper presented at the American Educational Research Association, Montreal, Canada. April 14.

Bremer, C. D., Clapper, A. T., Hitchcock, C., Hall, T., and Kachgal, M. (2002). Universal design: A strategy to support students' access to the general education curriculum. *National Center on Secondary Education and Transition Information Brief 1,3,* pp. 3–5..

Bronfenbrenner, U. (1979a). Beyond the deficit model in child and family policy. *Teachers College Record 81*, 95–104.

———. (1979b). The *ecology of human development: Experiments by nature and design.* Cambridge: Harvard University Press.

Corker, M. (2000). Disability politics, language planning, and inclusive social policy. *Disability and Society 15(3)*, 445–461.

Council for Exceptional Children (1999). Universal design, ensuring access to the general education curriculum. *Research Connections in Special Education, No. 5.* Washington, DC: US Department of Education (ERIC–OSEP document).

Donoghue, C. (2003). Challenging the authority of the medical definition of disability: An analysis of the resistance to the social constructionist paradigm. *Disability and Society 18, 2,* 199–208.

Finkelstein, V. (1998). Emancipating disability studies. In T. Shakespeare (Ed.), *The disability reader* (28–52). New York: Cassell and Co.

Finkelstein, V. (2003). *The social model of disability repossessed.* Retrieved September 15, 2004 from http://www.leeds.ac.uk/disabilitystudies/archiveuk/finkelstein/soc%20mod%20repossessed.pdf.

Gabel, S., and Peters, S. (2004). Presage of a paradigm shift? Beyond the social model of disability toward resistance theories of disability. *Disability and Society 19, 6,* 585–600.

Gallagher, D. (2005*). Disability versus impairment: Conceptual entanglements in disability studies discourse.* Paper presented at the American Educational Research Association, Montreal, Canada, April 14.

Hackman, H., and Rauscher, L. (2004). A pathway to access for all: Exploring the connections between universal instructional design and social justice education. *Equity and Excellence in Education 37(2),* 114–123.

Hyperdictionary. Retrieved November 17, 2004 from http://www.hyperdictionary.com/search.aspx?define=definition.

Kennedy, K. C. (2000). Introduction and interviews in N. Richardson, Ed., *Speak truth to power: Human rights defenders who are changing our world.* New York: Random House.

King–Sears, M. (2001). Three steps for gaining access to the general education curriculum for learners with learning disabilities. *Intervention in School and Clinic 37, 2,* 67–76.

Kingdon, J. W. (2002). *Agendas, alternatives, and public policies.* New York, NY: Harper Collins.

Kuhn, T. (1962). *The structure of scientific revolutions.* Chicago: University of Chicago Press.

Light, R. (2000). Disability theory: Social model or unsociable muddle? *Disability Tribune.* December 1999/January 2000, 10–13.

Mino, J. (2004). Planning for inclusion: Using universal instructional design to create a learner–centered community college classroom. *Equity and Excellence in Education 37, 2,* 154–160.

Mutua, N. K. (2001). Policed identities: Children with disabilities. *Educational Studies 32,3,* 289–300.

National Institute on Disability Research and Rehabilitation (NIDRR) (1999). *Long Range Plan for Fiscal Years 1999–2003*. Retrieved April 20, 2005, from http://www.ncddr.org/new/announcements/nidrr_lrp/lrp_ bg.html#1di.

National Rehabilitation Information Center (NRIC) (n.d.). NIDRR Project Information Management System. Retrieved June 20, 2005, from http://www.naric.com/.

Olkin, R., and Pledger, C. (2003). Can disability studies and psychology join hands? *American Psychologist 58, 4*. Retrieved October 26, 2004 fromhttp://80web15.epnet.com.proxy.nl.edu/citation.asp?tb=1and_ug=si d+7B29C2B8%2DC88.

Oliver, M. (1990). *The politics of disablement*. Basingstoke: Macmillan.

Pitha, E. W. (1996). *Bartlett's Roget's thesaurus*. New York: Little, Brown and Company.

Pledger, C. (2003a). Disability paradigm shift. *American Psychologist 59(4)*, 275–277.

Pledger, C. (2003b). Discourse on disability and rehabilitation issues: Opportunities for psychology. *American Psychologist 58(4)*. Retrieved October 26, 2004 from http://80web15.epnet.com.proxy.nl.edu/citation.asp ?tb=1and_ug =sid+7B29C2B8%2DC88.

Pliner, S., and Johnson, J. (2004). Historical, theoretical, and foundations principles of universal instructional design in higher education. *Equity and Excellence in Education 37, 2*, 105–113.

Pope, A. M., and Tarlov, A. R. (1991). *Disability in America: Toward a national agenda for prevention*. Washington, DC: National Academy Press.

Rhodes, W., and Paul, J. (1978). *Emotionally disturbed and deviant children: new views and approaches*. Englewood Cliffs: Prentice Hall.

Rose, D. H., and Meyer, A. (2002). *Teaching every student in the digital age, universal design for learning*. Alexandria: Association for Supervision and Curriculum Development.

Scott, S. S., McGuire, J. M., and Foley, T. E. (2003). Universal design for instruction: A framework for anticipating and responding to disability and other diverse learning needs in the college classroom. *Equity and Excellence in Education 36, 1*, 40–49.

Shakespeare, T., and Watson, N. (2001). The social model of disability: An outdated ideology? In Barnartt, S., and Altman, B. (Eds.), *Exploring* theories and expanding methodologies: *Where we are and where we need to go*, 9–28. Oxford, UK: Elsevier Science Ltd.

Slee, R., and Allan, J. (2001). Excluding the included: A reconsideration of inclusive education. *International Studies in Sociology of Education 11, 2,* 173–191.

Society for Disability Studies (SDS) (n.d.). Retrieved July 10, 2005, from http://www.uic.edu/orgs/sds/board.html#2.

Stone, D. (1984). *The disabled state.* Philadelphia, PA: Temple University Press.

Swap, S. W. M. (1972). *An ecological study of disruptive encounters between pupils and teachers.* Ann Arbor: Doctoral Dissertation.

Tate, D. G., and Pledger, C. (2003). An integrative conceptual framework of disability: New directions for research. *American Psychologist 58(4),* 289–295. Retrieved October 25, 2004 from http://80–web15.epnet.com.proxy.nl.edu/citation.asp?tb=1and_ug=sid+7B29C2B8%2DC88.

tenBroek, J. (1971). The character and function of sheltered workshops. Retrieved July 10, 2005, from http://www.nfb.org/books/books1/wam13.

Thomas, K. R. (2003). Old wine in a slightly cracked new bottle. *American Psychologist 58(4).* Retrieved October 26, 2004 from http://80–web15.epnet.com.proxy.nl.edu/citation.asp?tb=1and_ug=sid+7B29C2B8%2DC88.

Titchkosky, T. (2001). Disbility: A rose by any other name? "People–first" language in Canadian society. *CRSA/RCSA 38, 2,* 125–140.

Tyack, D.B., and Cuban, L. (1984). *Tinkering toward utopia: A century of public school reform.* Cambridge, MA: Harvard University Press.

Union of the Physically Impaired Against Segregation (UPIAS) (1980). *Fundamental principles of disability.* Retrieved July 5, 2004 from http://www.leeds.ac.uk/disabilitystudies/archiveuk/upias/fundamentalprinciples.pdf.

———. (1974/75). *Policy statement.* Retrieved July 5, 2004 from http://www.leeds.ac.uk/disabilitystudies/archiveuk/UPIAS/UPIAS.pdf.

US Congress (1990). Americans with Disabilities Act. Retrieved July 13, 2005, from http://www.usdoj.gov/crt/ada/pubs/ada.txt.

US Department of Education (2005). IDEA Reauthorization. (Federal Register). Retrieved July 13, 2005, from http://a257.g.akamaitech.net/7/257/2422/01jan20051800/edocket.access.gpo.gov/2005/pdf/05–11804.pdf.

US Department of Education (1999). *Final Long Range Plan for Fiscal Years 1999-2004*. (Federal Register). Retrieved October 26, 2004 from http://www.ed.gov/legislation/FedRegister/other/1999–3/082099a.html.

Vygotsky, L. (1985). *Thought and language*. Cambridge, MA: MIT Press.

———. (1978). *Mind in society: The development of higher psychological processes*. Cambridge, MA: Harvard University Press.

CHAPTER 11

Developing Inclusive Practice Through Connections Between Home, Community and School

Claire Tregaskis

The social model of disability has been a demonstrably emancipatory force in the lives of many disabled people in Western capitalist societies (Campbell and Oliver, 1996; Sutherland, 1981). Yet, nearly thirty years on from the Union of the Physically Impaired Against Segregation (UPIAS) (1976) declaration that it is society that disables people with impairments through its failure to take account of their needs, disability studies as an academic discipline arguably remains something of a specialist field, of interest primarily to disabled people and their allies. Recently, some academics have begun to attempt to bridge the gap between disability studies and other disciplines (see Barnes et al.,1999); and others (e.g. Swain et al., 1998; Swain et al., 2003) are developing dialogic teaching materials that aim to disseminate social model ideas to wider audiences, principally those in health and social care. However, it is perhaps questionable to what extent social model ideas and practices have been successfully promoted by academic disability studies to mainstream audiences in schools and the wider community, whose individual and collective attitudes, behaviors, policies and practices will also need to change if full social inclusion for disabled people is to be achieved (Tregaskis, 2004a).

Where We Are Now

The fact that disabled people and their allies are finally achieving positions of influence across a range of social and work-based organizations (Campbell and Oliver, 1996) may now increase the potential for utilizing social model ideas to help develop more inclusive mainstream settings. Also noteworthy in the United Kingdom is the work already being undertaken by activist groups such as Disability Equality in Education (Mason and Rieser, 1990, 1999) and Parents for Inclusion. They are working alongside education providers to develop the delivery of inclusive education in mainstream schools and thereby challenging the supremacy of medicalized rationales that had previously sustained the principle of educating disabled children separately from non-disabled ones. Such practice-based educational initiatives are being further supported by the development of materials for educators and administrators like the Index for Inclusion (Booth and Ainscow, 2002), that show schools how they can develop inclusive cultures in which difference is viewed as a positive contribution to diversity in education. These are all highly positive developments that suggest that disability studies is beginning to meet the challenge of engaging with mainstream audiences in ways that lead to the development of more inclusive practice.

And yet, right now I suspect we still cannot claim that most educators today will automatically welcome disabled children into their classrooms. There are some encouraging signs, as illustrated by new work that shows how participation in mainstream education has enabled some disabled young people to go on to enjoy ordinary lives of regular achievement (Mason, 2004). For too many others, however, such inclusion remains a far-off goal (Murray and Penman, 1996). So, where are the remaining gaps that are preventing wholesale inclusion from becoming a reality?

Clearly, organizational and resource issues play a big part in affecting how far schools are able and prepared to go in promoting and enacting inclusion (Clough, 1998). However, I suspect that behind many of these particular issues of time, money and the need for appropriate teaching skills lies the fact that historically we are still at a stage where most of the teachers and policy-makers with whom we seek to engage are from those generations when disabled and non-disabled children did not generally go to school together. As a result, it is possible that some of these educationalists may be resistant to, or actively fearful of, moves to include disabled people in settings that lie within their own non-disabled 'comfort zones'; and that psychological factors like these may also be playing a large (though relatively unacknowledged) role in delaying or preventing inclusion.

In itself, such an observation speaks volumes of the need for truly inclusive education systems, so that future generations learn to grow up seeing difference in all its forms—be it in terms of gender, race, family background, class, impairment status or sexuality—as ordinary and accepted (Phillips, 1999; Taylor, 1992). As things stand, however, in pushing for greater inclusion for disabled children in schools I suspect that we may first need to acknowledge many non-disabled people's ongoing fear of difference, and then find ways of supporting them through that fear so that they can begin to deliver more inclusive practice. This is partly about supporting them to explore and challenge their fear of difference 'head-on' and partly about offering them practical inclusive solutions to issues and situations that they may previously have pathologized and individualized, simply because alternative ways of dealing with these matters had not been suggested to them.

Accordingly, in this chapter I will look at both attitude and structural barriers to educational inclusion and will suggest that, in order to maximize the potential for change now available to us, we may need to more systematically elaborate the links between those elements of social life that, between them, influence children's life experiences across all sectors of activity. As a starting point in generating debate on this, I now present extracts from my past educational history that have shaped my own approach to advocating for inclusion and reflect on what such personal investigations have taught me about the importance of recognizing the links that connect children's experiences across school, family, and community.

Inclusion and Me: From Skeptic to Convert

As a disabled person growing up in the 1960s in rural England, my personal experience of mainstream schooling at secondary level was so awful, and the daily bullying in particular so intense, that at the time—and indeed for many years afterwards—I wished fervently that someone in authority would have recognized that I was not coping, and whisked me off to the safety of a 'special school', where I would be protected from such dangers. In this respect, then, my family was no different from many disabled families today, whose concerns for their disabled children's safety may initially take priority over their need for educational achievement (Murray and Penman,

2000). For me, being in mainstream meant that I certainly got a good education, but as much as anything it was a time when I received my first introduction to the harsh way that I, as a disabled person, could expect to be treated throughout my life. So I had to get tough quick in order to survive and only realized later, as I progressed into adulthood, how emotionally stunted this strategy had left me.

Given these childhood experiences, it may at first appear surprising that I now see educational inclusion for disabled children as a central strand amongst our strategies to develop more inclusive societies. Three things happened to me as an adult, however, that made me revisit my original position. The first was hearing of the experiences of disabled friends from my generation who had gone to special schools as boarders, and who had experienced a loneliness and isolation resulting from the separation from their families that, even now as middle-aged adults, they were still struggling to overcome. Having grown up within a strong family unit myself I suddenly realized that actually, however bad my own school experience had been, at least I had had the sanctuary of my family to return to at night, whereas many of my disabled peers had not been that lucky. This was the first time I began to properly understand the importance of the relationship between school and family and of the need for both to be equal but different partners in how children are brought up.

The second thing that happened was that one of these special school survivors, having listened to my tale of woe about what a hard time I had in mainstream, turned round and asked me what made me think I would have had it any easier within the special school system. This remark gave me even greater cause for reflection, challenging as it did my previous assumption that special schools were automatically places of sanctuary for disabled children. From what she and my other disabled friends told me, I now learnt that this was by no means always the case. My pre-conceptions shattered, I came to realize that I had actually been relatively lucky in experiencing what was then called 'integrated education' at a mainstream school, because in doing so I had at least remained present and active within the life of my family, and within that of the equally close-knit rural community in which we lived. Thus gradually over time I began to recognize and to actively value the links between school, home and the wider community that I had taken for granted while I was growing up.

The third key contribution towards the development of my thinking was an educational colleague's casual observation that, in the United Kingdom, disabled people and the mainstream schools that took them in back in the 1960s and 1970s were all guinea pigs, because this was before the Warnock Report (1978) had made concrete recommendations about how disabled children's integration could be achieved. Being made to recognize that actually everyone at my school had been doing their best at the time, within a system based overall on a presumption that disabled children were not present in mainstream schools, and that as such we could have been regarded as pioneers, was an important step in enabling me to forgive both teachers and pupils for not being able to make things perfect.

And so finally, as a result of these basic but crucial insights, I was able to revisit my educational experience, and accept that it was the best I could have hoped for at that time and in that political and social climate. This process also forced me to recognize how many of the elements that I had taken for granted during my childhood might have been absent, or at least less influential on my development, had I spent most of each year at a residential boarding school away from my family and my home community, as some of my disabled friends had done. I now began to ponder on many aspects of the key relationships that have helped to make me who I am today. Would my bond with my sister, which is the most important one in my life, have been able to develop as strongly as it did had I lived mainly away from home, or would we instead have grown up as polite strangers to each other? Would I have such a strong sense of local identity as I still do now, twenty years after I grew up and left our close-knit town, where even today when I return and walk down the main street, everyone hails me by my first name? Would where I come from be of such central importance to my sense of who I am had I only spent two weeks per year there when I was growing up? In short, would I still have that certainty of belonging, within my family, my town and my county, if I had not gone to my local mainstream school, which kept me within those local places and spaces? And perhaps it is worth reinforcing the point here that whilst school, family and the community all have their part to play in fostering the development of our children, the act of segregation by one of these partners — here, the school — can also damage those children's potential for inclusion across the related settings as well. This is why I believe we must advocate for inclusive education for all our children, so that they all have the opportunity to grow up as citizens who are secure in the knowledge of who they are and where they come from.

So, that is my position at present. Yet in working towards making inclusion a reality, I also recognize that there are real problems to be overcome, especially in advocating for change with people to whom disability issues represent new territory. In the next section I continue to analyze my own educational experience, since this too involved engaging with people who had had no previous contact with disabled people. My aim here is to explore whether, with the benefit of hindsight, there were things that might have made my own time at school any better, and what this might in turn have to tell us about ways of promoting inclusion now. Although in doing so I am going back 40 years, I suspect the issues are still pertinent, since subsequent discussion around some of the issues with my current education colleagues, combined with contemporary evidence from families who have reported the ongoing lack of universal educational inclusion for all disabled children (Murray and Penman, 1996, 2000), suggests that many of the barriers we faced back then still remain today. My tentative conclusions are therefore presented below, and are offered as suggestions for some of the ways in which we might continue to work towards centralising disability studies within debates around the intersection of school, family and community life.

Centralizing Disability Studies in Education

Analyzing my own experience with the benefit of hindsight led me to conclude that several related factors would have improved life across family, school and community settings, for me and for everyone else around me. Firstly, I now realize that as a disabled child I needed, but was never offered, a safe space in which to explore a range of issues around my self-image and self-esteem and where I could also identify and discuss any external barriers that might be preventing me from achieving full inclusion. That such a space for reflection was not provided is unsurprising, given that in those days there was no such thing as a social model of disability, and so any failure to achieve social or educational parity with non-disabled peers was viewed by disabled and non-disabled people alike as being due to the presence of impairment. In my own case, class and related family values were also an issue, in that as children my sister and I were brought up to 'keep our heads down and our noses clean'—in other words, to do nothing that would attract undue attention to ourselves. In that family setting it was impossible to openly discuss my impairment, because that would have meant acknowledging that I was different in ways that could not guarantee such social invisibility. Instead we all learned to pretend that my impairment either was not there, or that it was not relevant to our family relationships or to my acceptance within the wider community. As a result, I felt that I grew up having to deny a key part of my identity, even though secretly I yearned to explore the whole of who I was.

Having latterly spoken about this experience to those non-disabled women who had been my friends at school, I then discovered that they too had felt completely constrained, by a combination of social stigma and the violence of my own over-reaction if they did inadvertently mention my impairment, from talking openly at the time about how they felt about impairment and disability issues. Thus it emerged that actually we had all spent our childhoods ignoring 'the elephant in the room', as if by not talking about impairment we could truly pretend either that it did not exist, or at least that it had no effect on our relationships, nor on those with others around us. Yet since one of my friends was regularly threatened with violence by other pupils, just because she was my friend, this was clearly not true. As a result of these revelations I finally began to realize that in part we had both been open targets for bullying precisely because of my obvious inability to accept the whole of who I was, a fact that the bullies had found it all too easy to pick up on. A further contributory factor was the failure to provide my non-disabled classmates with the safe spaces they had needed in order to explore and understand difference, which could have avoided their fear turning into violence. Only now that I have the social model to help me make sense of my experience do I recognize what a tragic waste of our lives this was and how much as children we all needed adults in our lives who could have calmly facilitated the discussions we needed to have about who we were.

I know that it is too much to expect of schools that they should take on complete responsibility for offering and managing such essential debates, because that is to deny the equal responsibility of families to discuss issues of concern with their children. However, in a social climate where even today not all families may feel able to discuss disability issues with their children, I believe that schools offer one sort of safe space where these discussions can begin to happen. Before that can take place, however, given that many of today's teachers are themselves from the educationally segregated generations there is an initial need for more disability equality training in schools, so that all teachers and administrators can learn why disability pride is important, and how by fostering it they can help to nurture a stronger self-image amongst their disabled students. Further, since good quality disability equality training includes discussion of other aspects of diversity, such as issues around race and gender (e.g. Mason and Rieser, 1999), there should be a high degree of transferability between strategies for inclusion for disabled children, and those that work for other minority groups. Highlighting this level of transferability is one way of persuading hard-pressed and resource-poor educators that it is worth spending time learning about disability issues, and beginning to challenge the disabling barriers that may be preventing some of their students from having full access to the curriculum. Adding to teachers' skills in this way should in turn give them more tools than at present to support all their students to openly explore their own complex mix of identities, and those of their peers, and to develop strong and confident voices that do not need to oppress others in order to make themselves heard.

Advocating for more disability equality training links into the second key factor that would have improved my own educational experience, which is that actually we need not only short courses for in-service teachers, but also a wholesale revision of teacher training, so that new teachers are prepared to work with and nurture diversity from day one. At present, in the United Kingdom at least, it is still too often the case that trainee teachers get only half a day's training in the whole of their course on diversity issues. This cannot be anywhere near adequate to prepare teachers for the reality of managing diversity in the classroom. Further, by separating off diversity issues from the rest of the curriculum in this way, we are reinforcing an individualised approach to difference that is antithetical to the goal of inclusion. Some educators are recognising the dangers of this approach and are seeking to include Disability Studies modules within more general masters and PhD level education courses, but it is questionable how far this move has been replicated across initial teacher education.

In my view, Disability Studies needs to be systematically lobbying governments and academic teaching institutions to show them how and why embedding social model principles within the wider curriculum makes sense as a means of helping to ensure universal access to learning that will in turn produce better educated and more grounded citizens. As an access advisor friend never tires of saying, if all lessons were taught on the assumption that the audience contained students with dyslexia, visual impairment, hearing impairment, mobility impairment and communication impairment, then it is likely that what was being taught would be more accessible to all students. Encouraging teachers to work one-to-one with disabled students to identify physical and program barriers to their learning needs to be part of this process, and including overt reference to disabled people within teaching materials and curriculum content would also help develop a culture in which impairment is seen as ordinary. In this respect it would be helpful to introduce more reading books that include positive images of disabled characters rather than reinforcing the devaluing of difference as in many 'classic' texts (Keith, 2001). It may also be necessary to remind teachers that not all children learn in the same way and that they may need to go with teaching methods that would not have helped them as individuals to learn in order to get the best out of all their students (Sainsbury, 2000). Encouraging more disabled adults to become teachers, with the added outcome that disabled children would then have more adult role models to follow, would be another practical step toward achieving inclusion.

A third factor that could improve disabled children's opportunities for inclusion would be more effective dialogue between schools and families that acknowledges the relative expertise of each party in their respective area of knowledge. After all, the children's families will be the people with the most experience of supporting their child both to manage the effects of their impairment, and in overcoming the disabling barriers they are likely to routinely face across a whole range of social settings. Asking families for advice on a range of practical issues, from finding out how best to communicate with children who do not use speech, through learning how a child may express the need to go to the toilet or to be fed, to understanding that not all disabled children are like fragile toys that must be treated with kid gloves and extreme caution, are all ways in which vital knowledge about how to include each child at school can be shared.

This is not about families telling teachers how to do their jobs but is rather about providing them with the baseline information that they may need in order to deliver the curriculum in an accessible way to all their students. For example, there may be little point in a teacher dictating a whole lesson's worth of notes to the class if not all of the children can write quickly for sustained periods of time, and in that instance a compromise might be for copies of the teacher's notes to be offered as handouts. Such an approach might actually benefit all students, as it would allow for more time in the classroom to be spent in discussion of the topic in question. Teachers could also take their lead from families in assessing what sports activities disabled children can safely be included in, and engage in a two-way information exchange about alternatives to inclusive sporting events where this is deemed the more suitable option. In such ways may all children be given equal access to the curriculum.

Some teachers may find it hard to engage with families in this manner, either from sheer embarrassment at having to acknowledge and talk about a child's impairment (in which case they really do need disability equality training to get them over this barrier), or because they are worried that displaying any gap in their knowledge to a parent might be interpreted as weakness or as symptomatic of a wider lack of ability to teach the child. For some, concerns about maintaining their own professional status and relative power over the families they are dealing with may also be a barrier to open communication. Yet I suspect that most parents of disabled children expect to have to educate most of the people with whom their child comes into contact so that their needs are understood, and that they would probably only infer weakness on a teacher's part if they had had to repeatedly give them the same information because it had not previously been acted upon. Further, listening to families' knowledge about their children and respecting their expertise in this area offers the potential for both parties to meet and communicate as equals, each having different but complementary skills that can be combined to give children access to the best possible education. In my view, therefore, teachers have nothing to lose, and a lot to gain, from meeting families halfway on the issue of 'who knows best' about the practicalities of how children should be educated.

Toward Inclusion Through Valuing Difference

To come full circle, perhaps it is the case that in order to bring about this sort of systemic change we need to acknowledge that as a first step we have to convince educators that disability issues are important to education as a whole, rather than being a separate specialist area of interest only to disabled people and their allies. While disabled people as a group remain socially marginalized with, for example, only 12% of disabled adults in Britain being in paid employment (www.drc–gb.org), we continue to face an uphill battle in this respect. Yet we face a catch-22 situation here. Unless disabled people are visible at some level as active citizens within society, it may be difficult to persuade schools and the wider community of the need for more inclusion. Yet without at least some initial moves in the direction of inclusion, many disabled people will remain isolated and unable to press for further change. This is one battle that disabled people cannot fight alone—nor should they have to.

Perhaps one key to moving things forward is to learn from the limitations of other approaches. For example, in discussing the effectiveness of normalization/SRV techniques in training health and social care staff to deliver training to people with learning difficulties, Brown (1992, p. 188) has commented that one of the problems with the approach is that the staff who are expected to deliver these programs are taught about the concept of normalization/SRV '*as if it were something outside of themselves*'. In other words, they are not encouraged to see any similarity between their clients' experiences and their own. In particular, they are not asked to make connections by recognizing the ways in which they themselves have previously had to try to make sense of their own differences from ideals of behavior and performance in making their way in the world, in the way that they are now encouraging the disabled people they work with to do. Seeing this personal growth process as being somehow different for people with learning difficulties may then make it harder for these staff to properly support them as they too work towards making sense of their differences from the ideal. This critique suggests a serious gap in organization and practice that may make it difficult for these staff to deliver effective training, because in not being encouraged to identify with the people to whom they are delivering the training, they may well fail to convince the audience that they should take on board what they are being told. In other words, a failure to empathize may mean the message being lost.

I suggest, therefore, that if we want disabled children to be fully included in mainstream schools, and to have their experiences reflected in and through what they are taught, then we need to show educators where the similarities lie between the children's experiences and their own. That way it is more likely that they will begin to understand that their commonality is as important as their differences from each other. To achieve this, we need to stress that, yes, impairment is an important factor in developing relationships between teachers and students, because unless disabled children have their access and support needs met to start with, they will not be competing on a level playing field. But once those practical issues have been addressed (and revisited on an ongoing basis to ensure the child's needs are still being met), I would argue that the school community needs to move on and view impairment as just one aspect of an individual's identity rather than representing the whole of who they are (Tregaskis, 2004a, b).

Admittedly, this process is not being helped at present in the United Kingdom by moves such as the increased citing of health and safety reasons to 'justify' the exclusion of some disabled children from school field trips, solely on the basis of their impairments. Yet disabled children and their families are increasingly refusing to accept these individualizing negative value judgments and, supported in some instances by the Disability Rights Commission, they are beginning to win court battles against local authorities to overturn these exclusions (www.drc–gb.org). We need to build further on this work, using a combination of legal and training approaches that reveal to educators how many of these exclusionary practices unconsciously derive from the irrational fear of difference.

Yet because this fear pervades most Western societies, it is seen as acceptable, and as a result it is difference itself that becomes objectified, rather than the people who are perpetrating that differentiation. If we are to achieve inclusion in schools, then, I believe that we need to support educators to revisit their position on difference. In this respect we have much to learn from work on race equality (e.g. hooks, 2000), and debates around acknowledging difference in social policy and practice (Phillips, 1999; Taylor, 1992). Making connections between disability and other forms of oppression in this way is, in my view, a key means of challenging the state's 'divide and rule' tactics that currently keep us all under, by institutionalizing the fear of difference to the extent that too many of us have learnt to systematically internalize our own oppression as a means of survival. In the long term, a strategy of internalization will be of no use to us, especially not in day-to-day situations in classrooms and in the wider community when we have to engage with people who are not 'like us'. In this real world we cannot avoid engaging with difference, and so we need to learn to manage these encounters in ways that draw the best out of the people with whom we are dealing. That is the surest way I know of moving beyond the prevailing mood of confusion, fear and objectification of difference in which academics and practitioners too often find themselves mired.

Conclusion

In this chapter I have advocated for inclusive education as one of the cornerstones of establishing disabled children's right to belong within their schools, families and local communities. Drawing on my own educational experience, I have explored some barriers to disabled children's educational inclusion and have looked at some of the ways that Disability Studies might support educators develop more inclusive practice. In so doing, I have highlighted three key factors that I believe would further assist moves towards inclusion. These are: the need to provide safe spaces at school and elsewhere for disabled and non-disabled children to explore their own feelings around difference, impairment and identity; the need to embed social model theory and practice within teacher education, as a means of properly supporting educators to teach classrooms of children where diversity is valued instead of feared; and the need to build more equitable relationships with the families of disabled children so that their impairment-related skills and knowledge can be utilized in giving the children equal access to the curriculum and to the wider social environment of the school.

I believe that Disability Studies can and should have a central role in making these changes happen. One way of achieving this is by working alongside and supporting those activists who are already engaging with educators to help them to develop more inclusive practice and developing greater symbiosis between disability theory and practice in education. Another way is by demonstrating to governments and teacher training agencies why and how incorporating an understanding of disability issues within the mainstream teacher training curriculum makes social and economic sense, in terms of maximizing the potential for all children to learn in the ways that they find easiest. Finally, I suggest that disability studies needs to engage more directly with other disciplines that have an interest in developing social policy that is inclusive of all minority groups, as a means of sharing good practice and identifying ways of further generating the potential for inclusion. Through a combination of these approaches, I believe that we can begin to make wholesale inclusion a reality.

References

Barnes, C., Mercer, G., and Shakespeare, T. (1999) *Exploring disability: A sociological introduction.* Cambridge: Polity Press.

Booth, T., and Ainscow, M. (2002) *Index for inclusion: Developing learning and participation in schools*. Bristol: Centre for Studies in Inclusive Education.

Brown, H. (1992) Working with staff around sexuality and power, in A. Waitman and S. Conboy-Hill (eds.) *Psychotherapy and mental handicap*. London: Sage, 185–201.

Campbell, J. and Oliver, M. (1996) *Disability politics: Understanding our past, changing our future*. London: Routledge.

Clough, P. (ed) (1998) *Managing inclusive education: From policy to experience*. London: Sage.

hooks, bell. (2000) *Feminist theory: From margin to center*. London: Pluto Press.

Keith, L. (2001) *Take up thy bed and walk: Death, disability and cure in classic fiction for girls*. London: The Women's Press.

Mason, M. (ed) (2004) *Where are they now? Travelling the road to inclusion*. London: Alliance for Inclusive Education.

Mason, M. and Rieser, R. (1990) *Disability equality in the classroom: A human rights issue*. London: Disability Equality in Education.

Mason, M. and Rieser, R. (1999) *Altogether better (from 'special needs' to equality in education)*. London: Charity Projects/Comic Relief.

Murray, P. and Penman, J. (1996) *Let our children be...a collection of stories*. Sheffield: Parents with Attitude.

Murray, P. and Penman, J. (eds) (2000) *Telling our own stories: Reflections on family life in a disabling world*. Sheffield: Parents with Attitude.

Phillips, A. (1999) *Which equalities matter?* Oxford: Blackwell.

Sainsbury, C. (2000) *A Martian in the playground: Understanding the child with Asperger's Syndrome*. Bristol: Lucky Duck Publishing.

Sutherland, A. (1981) *Disabled we stand,* London, Souvenir Press.

Swain, J. Gillman, M. and French, S. (1998) *Confronting disabling barriers: Towards making organizations accessible*. Birmingham: Venture Press.

Swain, J. French, S. and Cameron, C. (2003) *Controversial issues in a disabling society*. Buckingham: Open University Press.

Taylor, C. (1992) *Multiculturalism and "the politics of recognition"*. Princeton: Princeton University Press.

Tregaskis C. (2004a) *Constructions of disability: Researching the interface between disabled and non–disabled people*. London: Routledge.

————. (2004b) 'Social model theories and non–disabled people: some possibilities for connection', in C. Barnes and G. Mercer (eds.) *Implementing the social model of disability: Theory and research.* Leeds: The Disability Press.

UPIAS (1976) *Fundamental principles of disability.* London: Union of the Physically Impaired Against Segregation.

Warnock Report (1978) *Special educational needs.* London: HMSO. www.drc–gb.org.

CHAPTER 12

Finding the "Proper Attitude": The Potential of Disability Studies to Reframe Family/School Linkages

Philip M. Ferguson and Dianne L. Ferguson

As with many developments in the evolution of public education throughout American history, the Boston public school system was one of the first to implement a system of separate classes for 'defective' children. The effort was not without its problems. One of these was a perceived resistance from families to the efforts of educators to label their children as 'feeble-minded' and move them to these new "ungraded" classes. A doctor used by the Boston schools to give medical examinations to such children, Arthur Jelly, lamented the resulting misplacement (Jelly, 1905). Dr. Jelly bemoaned the jam of feeble-minded children into the city's reform schools, attributing the situation to a lack of parental cooperation with the schools' best judgment about the nature of the defect involved:

> I feel sure that many children who should be taught in the public schools, in special classes for mentally deficient children, are now constantly placed in truant and reform schools at the suggestion of parents because they find it easier to admit that their children are stubborn or wayward or even criminal, rather than feeble-minded. I have encountered this attitude on the part of parents so often in the last three years in Boston, that I have no hesitation in making this statement very positively. (p. 160)

However, only 4 years later, a dramatically different description of parent/school relationships was offered by someone involved in a similar effort in another city. In 1909, a newly appointed supervisor, Kate Cunningham, reported to the Board of Education of the St. Louis Public Schools that the district's effort to start its first six 'special schools' for 'mentally defective' pupils was going well (Cunningham, 1909). Among the positive results described in her account, Cunningham claimed to be especially pleased with the support the teachers had received from the families of the students transferred to these early examples of public school special education:

> We have been much gratified by the kindly co-operation of parents. In no instance has a child been forced into our Special Schools. As a result parents and children have come to us in *the proper attitude toward our work*, and, at the close of the term, the kind comments and expressions of thanks have been an encouragement and inspiration to our teachers to make greater effort, if possible, in the future. (p. 83, emphasis added)[1]

From the earliest days of special education, then, educators have portrayed their relationships with the families of the students viewed as needing 'special' programs or support as both full of mutual cooperation and riven with conflict and resistance. However, even today, whether portrayed as a success or a failure, the goal of such parent involvement is consistently framed as one of helping teachers and administrators do their job. Whether we use the special education rhetoric from 1905 or 2005, the importance of working with parents and other family members is persistently framed as, at a minimum, to acquire the families' quiet acquiescence (exhibiting the "*proper attitude toward [teachers'] work*"), or at best, their active endorsement. From their earliest days, educators and families have approached each other in a "cyclical historical pattern of love and hate" (Valle and Reid, 2001, p. 23). From their position of professional expertise, teachers, administrators and associated specialists have all too often viewed "parent involvement," as, at best a necessary inconvenience, and at worst a mandated burden to be carried out with a grudging resentment.[2]

For their part, parents also show a tension between rhetoric and practice in their relationships with educators and other professionals that has persisted over time. They, too, have sought to identify and preserve that "proper attitude," although definitions of propriety often differed from those of the educators. While many parents eagerly sought to have their children admitted to the special schools and classes that were rapidly growing in school districts across the country in the early decades of the twentieth century, others resisted the recommendations of the educators. The superintendent of St. Louis Public Schools anticipated such resistance in his recommendation for what to call the new separate buildings for "defective" students:

> It is suggested that these schools shall be known by the name of "Special Schools for Individual Training." This name indicates their purpose and avoids the stigma which the name "Schools for Defectives" would carry." (Soldan, 1906, p. 208)

In the 1930s, a mother from Pennsylvania wrote to the Children's Bureau in Washington, DC, to complain that the special education classes were simply dumping grounds for children the schools did not want to teach.

> [The] special class was a disgrace to a township as rich as Montgomery Co. A dismal room with colored boys and girls, 3 feeble minded from 1 family, a place to send a child in order to be relieved from their care. (cited in Abel, 2000, pp. 215–216).

In our experience, the same ambivalence (either with or without the racial undertones) can emerge quickly in conversations with parents of today's children. In one recent national survey, some 87% of the parents of children in special education said that the schools were doing a fair to excellent job of providing their children the support they needed (Johnson and Duffett, 2002). Yet, the very same survey found that almost one third (31%) of the parents of children with severe disabilities had at least considered or threatened to sue their school districts over an issue with the special education services.

We are left, then, with a special education system governed by legislation that mandates superficial evidence of family involvement in the planning and implementation of a child's special education program while simultaneously enmeshed in a parent/professional culture marked as much by distrust and stereotypes as by collaboration and engagement. Moreover, as experience of inclusive placements grows, so does the awareness—or, at least the relevance of what was already known—that family-school linkages within general education are just as problematic (Cutler, 2000; Hiatt-Michael, 2001; Lareau, 2000; 2003). Sarah Lawrence-Lightfoot, in a recent study of parent/teacher conferences talks about parents and teachers as "natural enemies" (Lawrence-Lightfoot, 2003) because of the different roles each plays with students and the ways in which, all too often, each views the other's role with suspicion and distrust. In the face of dysfunctional parent/educator relationships of such persistence and pervasiveness, it is often difficult to remain optimistic that the newest reform initiative or template for home/school collaboration will be successful where so many past efforts have failed or faded.

Nonetheless, with perhaps more than a touch of naiveté, we believe that the infusion of disability studies' assumptions and perspectives into the educational context generally, and specifically into the dialogue between school and family, can gradually forge a more constructive foundation on which to build something that is a qualitative improvement over the current policies and practices. In the remainder of this chapter we will review three dimensions in which we think that a disability studies orientation can fundamentally change the conversation between families and schools.

Reframing Research on Families

The anti-essentialist, socially embedded perspective that disability studies endorses in various manifestations is important not only—or even most importantly—for what it teaches us about disability. Perhaps the true value of such a perspective is what it can teach us about the social construction of human differences generally. As the historian Douglas Baynton has persuasively argued (2001), debates over citizenship and equality for this or that group throughout our country's history have repeatedly used the frame of disability to argue either side of the issue. Whether in its attribution by the powerful or its denial by the oppressed, the disability label served as the signifier for justifiable exclusion and pathology. "Thus, while disabled people can be considered one of the minority groups historically assigned inferior status and subjected to discrimination, disability has functioned for all such groups as a sign of and justification for inferiority" (Baynton, 2001, p. 35). In an analogous way, we believe that disability studies can also shed new light on how social institutions such as our public schools employ a "deficit model" to shape interactions with the families of the children served by those institutions, whether or not a "real" disability is involved.

For years, researchers have studied the effects of disability upon the family by assuming that the underlying process was one of responding to an unarguably negative event. Disability was at least an unwanted challenge if not an undeniable tragedy for both the child and the family. The research challenge was to understand how families succeeded or failed in their response to the tragedy (Ferguson, 2001). Failure, then, was interpreted as a situation where the disability spread from child to family like an uncontained virus, disrupting "normal" operations in ever-widening circles of kinship and care. Indeed, the disability was metaphorically portrayed as tantamount to death in terms of the reaction of the family to a disability diagnosis. Even today, perhaps the single most common "script" (the latest 'proper attitude') that professionals impose on parents of disabled children is the Kübler-Ross (1969) five-stage theory of reactions to death and dying. With the growing infusion of disability studies into research and practice in education, the 'deficit' equation for calculating family reactions should more and more often just not add up for those involved in the family-school interactions.

By the same process, disability studies perspectives can help us use techniques of literary analysis to interpret more critically the various imagery, metaphors and symbolic messages embedded in the very language of "parent involvement." The sensitivity to the 'deficit' model of disability can extend, then, not only to our assumptions about families of children with disabilities, but to characterizations of families from other groups that are often pathologized by our language and expectations. In the words of one researcher, such research would reveal the different uses of the term "parent involvement" depending on the race and class of the parents themselves:

> Even relatively positive, or sympathetic, accounts of the lives of such families [i.e., "low-income, linguistically, ethnically, or culturally diverse"] tend to center on the idea that such parents are empty, or lacking, as expressed in the use of words such as *don't* or *can't*. Rather, then, than considering what lower income, language minority, or so-called *diverse*, families can contribute to their children's upbringing, or to their children's schools, most accounts of *parental involvement* among low-income parents focus either on what the families lack or on what the schools can do to teach them exemplifying the common metaphor framing lower income parents as empty. (Lawrence-Lightfoot, 2004, p. 99)

Another way in which the research and practices of schools and families need to change involves the very meaning of *family*. Just as we have made a dramatic shift in understanding the meaning of disability, so have we "discovered" that families come in different shapes and sizes as well. The adaptive shift from a normative to a contextual understanding of response to disability has allowed recognition of family structure and life course. As often happens in social science research, once a finding is pronounced, it becomes strikingly obvious: families have a structure and history of their own, in addition to that of each family member. Researchers are recognizing the importance of identifying families' shape and location in their "life course." Particularly important today is to understand how a particular family may depart from what used to be seen as the normative family model (e.g., grandparents as primary caregivers, blended families, gay and lesbian couples as parents, multi-generational families, and, of course, single parents). Researchers are only beginning to explore how the variation in these critical elements of family structure can affect patterns of response to disability (Banks and McGee, 2001; Ferguson, 2001; Fewell and Vadasy, 1986; Turnbull et al., 1986).

Emergence of a life-course perspective toward families has encouraged researchers to "discover" older parents, which is especially relevant for secondary and transition support programs for students with disabilities and families. Until recently, almost all research on family response to a child with a disability focused on families with young children. Studies that follow families across a life span or that specifically seek out older parents of young adults with disabilities provide fascinating information about why some families are more resilient than others and how extended coping with disability and chronic illness affects families over time (Ferguson et al., 2000; Hayden and Heller, 1997). Recent attention to the role of families in the education of adolescents also bring a life span perspective to trying to redefine both families' roles and experiences (e.g., Epstein et al, 2002; Ramirez, 2002; Sanders et al., 1999; Xu, 2002). Again, the emergence of this broader definition of what families look like and how they think about schools and education has been especially pronounced in urban schools.

Finally, disability studies should help researchers not only expand their understanding of the meaning and structure of "family," it should also help expand what researchers count as evidence about that family experience. If disability studies stands for anything, it is an explicit endorsement of a multi-disciplinary approach to understanding the meaning of disability in people's lives. For research in applied fields such as special education, this opens up broad vistas of information and perspective previously off-limits for serious consideration. Essays, memoirs, and other forms of personal artistic expression become legitimate sources of narrative knowledge within disability studies. The long tradition of personal and family narratives about the experience of disability become, within the orientation of disability studies, strikingly neglected sources of information and perspective. At the same time, the validation of such narrative strategies for collecting information should open up new, culturally varied ways of interacting with families: oral traditions of story-telling; family journals; digital diaries and video exchanges; and drawings and other visual communication with families. Research into the effectiveness of such strategies becomes available only when the right questions are asked. Disability studies makes those questions newly available for educational research.

Thus, disability studies can provide alternative scripts for characterizing families who seem unresponsive to the entreaties of educators for greater involvement in the schools. As with the earlier debates of marginal groups as disabled (or not), families seen as 'uninvolved' in their children's education are now located somewhere on the disability spectrum: dysfunctional, disengaged, disturbed, or disbelieving. A disability studies approach should encourage us to contextualize those definitions of what should and should not be seen as "normal" for families to do.

Restructuring the Policies on Family/School Linkages

A disability studies lens through which to view the relationships among all school personnel and family members of students can lead to interpretations of current policy and new policy that forges a more effective partnership. Current NCLB policies regarding families require schools to involve *family members* in (1) policy development, (2) sharing responsibility for increased student achievement, (3) building capacity for involvement of all families, and (4) ensuring accessibility to all families. The newly reauthorized IDEA continues to require family participation in decisions about referral to special education, assessment and evaluation, and IEP planning.

But the persistent divide between families and school personnel that is grounded in traditional perspectives of "parent involvement" does not provide opportunities for teachers and parents to address the cultural divide between a predominately white teacher work force and a culturally and linguistically diverse student population. Nor does it assist schools to discover what a reconceptualization from "involvement" to "linkage" actually means.

Problems with traditional models of home-school interactions are already clear (Banks and McGee, 2001; Lopez et al., 2001; Shumow and Harris, 2000). As we already argued, there is an increasing awareness of the systemic cultural bias embedded within some core assumptions in both the rhetoric and regulations of general and special education.

> Special education in the United States is a product of American culture. There are certain core American values that have contributed to the way in which the field of special education has developed over the years, and they continue to be the underpinnings for current policy and practice. For instance...the principle of parent participation is based on the value of equality and the expectation that parents and service providers should develop partnerships in the education decision-making process of students with disabilities...Conversely, when families believe in social hierarchies rather than in social equality and consider professionals to be the experts and the holders of authority, the expectation that the family should partner with professionals can be bewildering. When families do not value individual rights because they believe that society is more important than the individual, the expectation that they will advocate for their children and assert their rights can make them quite uncomfortable. If they do not have someone to explain what is happening and make them feel a little less out of place, then they can end up becoming alienated from the process. (Harry et al., 1999, p. 3)

Acknowledging such cultural diversity does not abandon the core beliefs of our own dominant culture (equality, self-determination, due process, etc.). Rather, it acts on the discovery that they are not universal truths by designing strategies for family collaboration that respect the subtlety of different interpretations. In the face of such diversity in beliefs and values, it is unfeasible and undesirable to replace one recipe for parent involvement with another. The key to true family/school linkages will likely lie in the avoidance of such prescriptive checklists.

For example, the perspective of parental agency[3] is one that is beginning to challenge schools' traditional understandings of family "involvement" and one that could lead to implementing current federal policies in new ways. Parental agency is concerned with documenting the ways in which parents are proactive protagonists who act and respond to concerns with their children's education (Auerbach, 2002, p. 1385; Vincent, 2001). The notion of parental agency also includes the attitudes, values, and beliefs that guide, for example, Latino parents' interventions and advocacy on behalf of their children (Civil et al., 2000; Friedel, 1999; Hammond, 2001; Samaras and

Wilson, 1999). Examples of these ideational components of agency are found in parental "counterstories" that commented on the barriers faced by Latino parents within the education system such as institutional racism (Auerbach 2002). These counterstories illustrate that Latino parental agency may also be exercised through insightful critique of the educational system as well as participation in educational activities. In the case of Latino parents, parental agency is linked to the dual mission of supporting their children's education and reaffirming the value and contributions of Latino culture to the educational careers of their children (e.g. Auerbach, 2002; Villenas and Deyhle, 1999; Villanueva, 1996). But more importantly, the idea of parental agency can lead to discovering the "counterstories" of other families.

Dominant research and policy on parent involvement then, first limits consideration to *parents* (Villenas and Deyhle, 1999) and then creates understandings of involvement that limit roles to participation in formal school-initiated activities. (e.g., Epstein et al., 2002; Shumow and Harris, 2000). However, such a focus overlooks the involvement of parents in out-of-school contexts such as church-sponsored activities (Baquedano-Lopez, 2000). As Barton, et al., (2004) point out most parent involvement literature focuses on what parents do and how that fits with school defined needs, what they term a deficit mode of understanding, especially for families in high poverty urban communities (e.g. Gutman and McLoyd, 2000; Moll and Greenberg, 1990).

Examinations of Latino parental agency, for example, need to also address parents' understandings of the educational process as expressed in the term "la educación" which refers to both formal study and the moral upbringing of the child (Reese et al., 1995). It is critical to differentiate the English term "education" from culturally specific notions of "la educación" since the latter term encompasses much of what drives Latino parents' effort to educate their children and teacher-parent interactions can be supported through knowledge of what the term represents (Galindo and Olguin, 1996).

As Barton et al. (2004) point out, traditional understandings and research conclude that "either parents participate in school-sanctioned ways (i.e., Family Science Night) or their children's educational growth may suffer" (p. 4). Instead, they argue for focusing not just on what parents *do* but also how and why they engage and participate in their children's education and how that engagement relates to their history and experience in and outside of the school community. Family involvement or engagement, then, must be viewed in more complex terms of relationships, agency, and an ongoing dynamic of mediation of all stakeholders' knowledge and cultural capital (Abrams and Gibbs, 2002; Lareau and Horvat, 1999).

For family members to truly gain the entrée to become partners in the ongoing improvement of schools and the education and achievement of their children, schools need a model of family/school linkages that (1) challenges traditional assumptions and practices, (2) is grounded in the knowledge, experience, and culture of all members of the educational community, and (3) if flexible and dynamic, encouraging the community to develop, question, and change as they build relationships and an authentic learning community.

Redirecting the Practice

Trying to define disability studies runs the risk of violating the constructivist spirit that seems to drive much of the work that we might cite as examples of what we are trying to define. Such efforts seem too often to end up chasing their own tail with statements about how disability studies is essentially anti-essentialist. The smooth abstractions of general definitions quickly become the slippery semantics of exclusion: who is in and who is out. As Wittgenstein put it, we may be better off returning to the "rough ground of practice" where usage may cover some truly varied terrain, but at least we have real examples with which to gain some traction in our arguments with the powers that be. In that spirit, we will conclude with some thoughts about how all of this reframed research and restructured policy might play out in terms of the things families and educators actually do together. Without pinning down a specific definition for disability studies, how might such an orientation push educational practice to redirect its efforts to partner with families in support of children?

One reason many schools struggle to get parents to come to meetings and events or engage school initiated activities of other kinds is that for many family members schools can be unwelcoming and/or intimidating, especially to those whose primary language is other than English, are working hard to raise their income level out of poverty, or who may feel shy about developing relationships with teachers for some reason (Gutman and McLoyd, 2000; Rao, 2000). Yet these reasons may not be very obvious to school personnel and get interpreted as lack of interest, disengagement, lack of caring, and even the labeling of families as "not acting in the best interest of children."

Definitions of family "involvement" or engagement in their children's education vary a good deal between school personnel and family members, especially some groups of family members, like those who have less cultural capital (Bourdieu, 1984), are culturally and linguistically different from the teachers in the school or who operate at a quite different economic level (e.g., Lareau and Horvat, 1999; Lopez et al., 2001). For example, teachers typically focus on ways family members can support teachers' efforts through such things as helping with homework or doing special learning activities at home along with attending parent/teacher conferences and other school meetings and events focused on helping families teach their sons and daughters more effectively at home.

Family members, on the other hand, might have other notions of what "being involved" in their children's education might entail that never involves going to school at all and might not involve doing school activities at home, including homework (Lopez et al., 2001). Of course, these interpretations vary from family to family. Some families do share teachers' most common interpretations and definitions of involvement. But many more do not. Schools that make their decisions about family relationships based on the perspectives shared with only some families all too often leave out large populations of families.

A growing number of family support specialists and educators are moving away from the terminology of "parent involvement" altogether because they feel it symbolizes the limitations of unsuccessful past attempts to bolster relationships between home and school (Banks and McGee, 2001; Barton, Drake, Perez, St. Louis, and George, 2004; Dunst, 2002; Ferguson and Asch, 1989; Ferguson and Ferguson, 1987; Harry et al., 1999; Lopez et al. , 2001; Rao, 2000; Turnbull and Summers, 1987). Instead, there must be a mutuality of interaction and collaboration that commits both home and school to each other. Parents must not only be involved with schools, but schools must be involved with families. Especially in our cities, the linkage between families and schools must be strong enough to hold in these most challenging settings. Finally, even this move from involvement to linkage is not enough. The reciprocity required by the notion of linkages must also be played out in a process of cultural awareness and critical reflection (Abrams and Gibbs, 2002; Harry et al., 1999; Kalyanpur et al., 2000). It is just this shift that the perspective of disability studies fosters.

A current research project working with schools in Colorado and Louisiana—The Family/School Linkages Project (FSL) —is trying to help educators and families become comfortable with the inquiry tools offered by disability studies and action research. The Project is beginning to show encouraging results.[4] The main goal for each of the 13 participating school teams of both teachers and family members was to improve the relationships between school personnel and students' families. Most of the schools framed this initially as increasing family involvement in the traditional sense discussed here, but each school developed its own inquiry focus from which other ideas and activities emerged. Sometimes teams wanted to know why some families did some things, but others did not. Other schools initially wanted to know what parents thought about the school and teaching, and some wondered what teachers thought of parents and their involvement or perceived lack of involvement. Still others had a wide range of family oriented events and activities already happening and just wanted to improve and expand the number of family members and teachers that participated.

Some of the specific activities and areas of inquiry focus across the inquiry teams have included:

- *Systematically asking parents and teachers what they thought* about the school, about the relations between school personnel and families, about how those relationships could be improved to better support families and student learning. Often this entailed learning some of the counterstories about what families were doing that teachers simply didn't know about. In most cases teams learned that what they *thought* families thought about school and education didn't match up to what they *said* when asked.

- *Creating a welcoming environment for family members* in schools that had reputations among families for not being very welcoming. Many teachers had not realized the distancing effect, for example, of counters in school offices, or the fact that no one greeted people who entered quickly, and often didn't greet them in their own language. Other school personnel learned that while many families were learning English, they felt unwelcome by the fact that so few of the schools' communications were in their native language.

- *Providing more opportunities for family participation in school activities* by moving some activities off campus into familiar places in families' neighborhoods, translating materials and announcements into Spanish, or trying novel strategies for getting information to families about events (like putting up flyers in the families' neighborhoods or handing out flyers as families dropped off or picked up their children from school).

- *Increasing attendance and participation of families who had not typically participated.* Several schools targeted African American or Asian family members who did not typically attend events or meetings by taking events to their neighborhoods or by planning events that drew upon their culture and interests.
- *Increasing participation of all family members in classrooms and PTA functions* by creating a larger menu of choices for participation.
- *Providing support and ideas to family members so they could help their child learn* by offering more specific information about what was going on in school, or explaining how to help students prepare for state tests, or just making it easier for families to reinforce things their children and youth were learning during typical family activities and routines.
- *Supporting school staff to get to know the community in which the school is located* by systemically exploring the community, by talking to families about the community, and by getting out into the community for some school activities.
- *Increasing the presence of family volunteers,* especially in secondary schools, and helping the school develop new activities for volunteers to ensure they had successful, meaningful, and interesting experiences that go beyond the usual offerings of making copies, doing bulletin boards, and reading to students.

What Next?

The schools in the FSL Project example, as well as many more schools around our nation are using the perspectives about difference, deficit, and disability surfaced and challenged by disabilities studies to turn their thinking about families on its head. Challenging their own assumptions, seeking others' perspectives, and asking questions about what could be different are all ways that school personnel are finding new attitudes about the possibilities of family/school relationships and linkages.

They are also discovering that for far too long, the "proper attitude" they sought from families was limiting and shortsighted. Like Moll (Gonzalez and Moll, 2002; Moll, 1992) and his colleagues, they are discovering that family members possess "funds of knowledge," skills, and values that, better understood, foster ways to tailor curriculum and learning in ways that result in improved student achievement and satisfaction with school. Expecting families to follow educators prescription for being "involved" in homework, IEPs, conferences and assemblies is the "improper attitude" that is slowly beginning to change into the ongoing efforts to question, listen, learn, and change that will help all involved build not only the attitudes but the relationships of trust, respect, and cooperation that will really lead to the kind of family/schools linkages we all seek.

References

Abel, E. K. (2000). *Hearts of wisdom: American women caring for kin, 1850–1940*. Cambridge, MA: Harvard University Press.

Abrams, L.S. and Gibbs, J.T. (2002). Disrupting the logic of home–school relations: Parent involvement strategies and practices of inclusion and exclusion. *Urban Education*, 37(3), 384–407.

Auerbach, Susan (2002). "Why do they give the good classes to some and not to others?" Latino parent narratives of struggle in a college access program. *Teachers College Record, 104*, 1369–1392.

Banks, J. A.. and McGee, C.A. (2001). Families and teachers working together for school improvement. In J.A. Banks and C.A. McGee Banks (Eds.), *Multicultural education: Issues and perspectives*. 4th edition (pp. 402–420). New York: John Wiley and Sons, Inc.

Baquedano-Lopez, P. (2000). Narrating community in *Doctrina* classes. *Narrative Inquiry, 10*(2): 1–24.

Barton, A.C., Drake, C. Perez, G., St. Louis, K. and George, M. (2004). Ecologies of parental engagement in urban education. *Educational Researcher, 33*(4), 3–12.

Baynton, D. (2001). Disability and the justification of inequality in American history. In P. K. Longmore, and L. Umansky (Eds.), *The new disability history: American perspectives* (pp. 33–57). New York: New York University.

Bourdieu, P. (1984). *Distinction: A social critique of the judgment of taste* (translated by R. Nice). Cambridge, MA: Harvard University Press.

Civil, M., Andrade, R., and Anhalt, C. (2000). Parents as learners of mathematics: A different look at parental involvement. In M.L. Fernández (Ed.), *Proceedings of the Twenty Second Annual Meeting of the North American Chapter of the International Group for the Psychology of Mathematics Education* (Vol. 2, 421–426). Columbus, OH: ERIC Clearinghouse.

Cunningham, K. L. (1909). *54th Annual report of Board of Education to the City of St. Louis*. St. Louis, MO: St. Louis Public Schools.

Cutler, W. (2000). *Parents and schools: The 150–year struggle for control in American education*. Chicago: University of Chicago Press.

Dunst, C. J. (2002). Family-centered practices: Birth through high school. *Journal of Special Education, 36:* 139–147.

Epstein, J. L., Sanders, M. G., Simon, B. S., Salinas, K. C., Jansorn, N. R., and Van Voorhis, F. L. (2002). *School, family, and community partnerships: Your handbook for action (2nd Ed.)* Thousand Oaks, CA: Corwin Press.

Ferguson, P. M. (2001). Mapping the family: Disability studies and the exploration of parental response to disability. In G. Albrecht, K. D. Seelman, and M. Bury (Eds.), *Handbook of disability studies* (pp. 373–395). Thousand Oaks, CA: Sage Publications.

Ferguson, P.M. and Asch, A. (1989). Lessons from life: Personal and parental perspectives on school, childhood, and disability. In D.P. Biklen, D.L. Ferguson, and A. Ford (Eds.), *Schooling and disability: 88th yearbook of the National Society for the Study of Education, Part II* (pp. 108–140). Chicago: NSSE and University of Chicago Press.

Ferguson, P.M. and Ferguson, D.L. (1987). Parents and professionals. In P. Knoblock (Ed.), *Introduction to special education* (pp. 346–391). Boston: Little, Brown.

Ferguson, P. M., Gartner, A., and Lipsky, D. G. (2000). The experience of disability in families: A synthesis of research and parent narratives. In E. Parens and A. Asch (eds.), *Prenatal testing and disability rights* (pp. 72–94). Washington, DC.: Georgetown University Press.

Fewell, R. R., and Vadasy, P. F. (Eds.) (1986). *Families of handicapped children: Needs and supports across the life span*. Austin, TX: Pro Ed.

Friedel, T.L. (1999). The role of Aboriginal parents in public education: Barriers to change in an urban setting. *Canadian Journal of Native Education, 23(2),* 139–158.

Galindo, R. and Olguin, M. (1996). Reclaiming bilingual educators cultural resources: An autobiographical approach. *Urban Education, 31,* 29–56.

González, N. and Moll, L. C. (2002). *Cruzando el Puente:* Building bridges to funds of knowledge. *Educational Policy, 16,* 623–641.

Gutman, L.M. and McLoyd, V.C. (2000). Parents' management of their children's education within the home, at school and in the community: An examination of African-American families living in poverty. *The Urban Review, 32,* 1–24.

Hammond, L. (2001). Notes from California: An anthropological approach to urban science education for language minority families. *Journal of Research in Science Teaching, 38*(9), 983–999.

Harry, B., Kalyanpur, M. and Day, M. (1999). *Building cultural reciprocity with families: Case studies in special education.* Baltimore: Paul H. Brookes Publishing Co.

Hayden, M. F., and Heller, T. (1997). Support, problem-solving/coping ability and personal burden of younger and older caregivers of adults with mental retardation. *Mental Retardation, 35,* 364–72.

Hiatt–Michael, D. (2001). Parent involvement in American public schools: A historical perspective 1642–2000. In S. Redding and L. G. Thomas (Eds.), *The community of the school* (pp. 247–258). Lincoln, IL: Academic Development Institute.

Jelly, A. C. (1905). Special classes for defectives in reform achools. *Journal of Psycho-Asthenics, 9,* 158–164.

Johnson, J., and Duffett, A. (2002). *When it's your own child. A report on special education from the families who use it.* New York: Public Agenda (available from website: http://www.publicagenda.org)

Kalyanpur, M., Harry, B., and Skrtic, T. (2000). Equity and advocacy expectations of culturally diverse families' participation in special education. *International Journal of Disability, Development and Education, 47,* 119–136.

Kübler-Ross, E. (1969). *On death and dying.* New York: Macmillan.

Lareau, A. (2000). *Home advantage* (2nd ed.). Lanham, MD: Rowman and Littlefield.

———. (2003). *Unequal childhoods: Class, race, and family life.* Berkeley: University of California Press.

Lareau, A. and Horvat, E.M. (1999). Moments of social inclusion and exclusion: Race, class, and cultural capital in family–school relationships. *Sociology of Education, 72* (1), 37–53.

Lawrence-Lightfoot, S. (2003). *The essential conversations: What parents and teachers can learn from each other.* New York: Random House

Lightfoot, D. (2004). "Some parents just don't care": Decoding the meanings of parental involvement in urban schools. *Urban Education, 39,* 91–107.

Lopez, G.R., Scribner, J.D., and Mahitivanichcha, K. (2001). Redefining parental involvement: Lessons from high performing migrant impacted schools. *American Educational Research Journal, 38* (2), 253–288.

Moll, L. C. (1992). Bilingual classroom studies and community analysis: some recent trends. *Educational Researcher, 21*(2), 20–24.

Moll, L and Greenberg, J. (1990). Creating zones of possibility: Combining social contexts for instruction. In L. Moll (Ed.), *Vygotsky and education* (pp–319–348). Cambridge: Cambridge University Press.

Osgood, R. L. (2000) *For "children who vary from the normal type": special education in Boston, 1838-1930.* Washington, DC: Gallaudet University Press.

Ramirez, A.Y. (2002). Follow–up study: High school students' comments regarding parents. *The School Community Journal, 12*(1) , 29–51.

Rao, S.S. (2000). Perspectives of an African American mother on parent–professional relationships in special education. *Mental Retardation, 38,* 475–488.

Reese, L., Gallimore, R., Goldenberg, C., and Balzano, S. (1995). Immigrant Latino parents' future orientations for their children. In R. Macias and R. Ramos (Eds.), *Changing schools for changing students: An anthology of research on minorities, schools and society.*

Samaras, A.P. and Wilson, J.C. (1999). Am I invited? Perspectives of family involvement with technology in inner–city schools. *Urban Education, 34, 4*, pp. 499–530.

Sanders, M. G., Epstein, J. L., and Connors-Tadros, L. (1999). *Family partnerships with high-schools: The parents perspective.* Baltimore: Center for Research on the Education of Students Placed at Risk, Johns Hopkins University and Howard University.

Shumow, L. and Harris, W. (2000). Teachers' thinking about home–school relations in low income urban communities. *School Community Journal, 10*(1), 9–24.

Soldan, F. L. (1906). 52nd Annual Report of Board of Education to the City of St. Louis. St. Louis, MO: St. Louis Public Schools.

Turnbull, A.P. and Summers, J.A. (1987). From parent involvement to family support: Evolution to revolution. In S.M. Pueschel, A.C. Crocker, and D.M. Crutcher (Eds.), *New perspectives on Down syndrome* (pp. 289–306). Baltimore: Paul H. Brookes.

Turnbull, A. P., Summers, and Brotherson, M. (1986). Family life cycle: Theoretical and empirical implications and future directions for families with mentally retarded members. In J. J. Gallagher and P. M. Vietze (eds.), *Families of handicapped persons: Research, programs, and policy issues* (pp. 58–90). Baltimore: Paul Brookes.

Valle, J., and Reid, D. K. (2001). Parent–educator partnerships: A critical history of the search for authentic and respectful home—school relationships. *School Public Relations Journal, 22* (1), 23–36.

Villanueva, I. (1996). Change in the educational life of Chicano families across three generations. *Education and Urban Society, 29*, pp.13–34.

Villenas, S. and Deyhle, D. (1999) Critical race theory and ethnographies challenging the stereotypes: Latino families, schooling, resilience and resistance. *Curriculum Inquiry, 29*, 413–436.

Vincent, C. (2001). Social class and parental agency. *Journal of Educational Policy, 16*, 347–364.

Wald, L. D. (1934). W*indows on Henry Street.* Boston: Little, Brown and Co.

Xu, J. (2002). Do early adolescents want family involvement in their education? Hearing voices from those who matter most. *The School Community Journal, 12, 1*, 53– 72.

Notes

[1] In Boston as well, there were opinions about parental cooperation that countered those of Dr. Jelly. In his valuable history of special education in Boston, Robert Osgood (2000) refers to some accounts from the same era that found "friendly support" from families (p. 133).

[2] Of course, even in the earliest days there are reports of interesting exceptions to this generalization. In her account of Elizabeth Farrell's early work in starting the first special education classes in New York City, Lillian Wald recounts Farrell's early efforts to make immigrant parents feel welcome and involved in her classroom. "When an Italian mother was asked [by Farrell] to prepare spaghetti for the children 'like the old country,' it dignified Italian parentage and custom in the eyes of these on-coming American citizens. We often overlook how important it is for children to hold to their traditions. Sometimes their loyalty and respect are

greatly imperiled by the appeals to be 'one hundred per cent Americans'." (Wald, 1934, p. 136).

[3] This discussion of parental agency is drawn from work and personal conversation with Dr. Rene Galindo, Associate Professor, University of Colorado at Denver.

[4] The Family/School Linkages research project operates under the auspices of the National Institute for Urban School Improvement and works with elementary and secondary schools in both the Denver area and in 2 parishes of Louisiana. Case accounts of the work in these schools along with other project products are available on the National Institute's website:www.inclusiveschools.org.

CHAPTER 13

Informing Instructional Technologies: Re-readings of Policy, Practice, and Design

Alan Foley

In general, the field of instructional technology has not incorporated a developed critical and sociocultural language into its discourse. There have been isolated attempts to bring issues of culture and production of knowledge to the forefront, but they have been sparse and infrequent (DeVaney, 1998; Hlynka and Belland, 1991; Streibel, 1986; Streibel, 1998). Most standard views of instructional technology are grounded in some form of "scientific" practice: behaviorism (e.g. Burton et al., 1996), cognitivism (e.g. Wynn and Snyder, 1996), systems theories (e.g. Banathy, 1996), or constructivism (e.g. Jonassen, 1990) Traditional approaches to instructional technology (qua instructional design) are typically predicated on the principles of systematicity, replicability, and predictability (Smith and Ragan, 1999). Unfortunately, many of these models fail to consider the social and cultural aspects of technology, and thus instructional technologists do not consider the broader role of technology within society

This results in a good deal of instructional technology work and research that considers technology as "immune" from ideology, and which takes up identity as a static construct, not considering the fluid and socially constructed aspects of identity so mediated by information technology. Subsequently, educational technologists often do not consider how the ways in which they use technology or the assumptions they make about individuals and technology position people within particular and often inflexible subject positions. Similarly, conceptualizations of disability are not static. What is considered a disability changes in different social and historical contexts (Foucault, 1988). These views of technology and identity as static and ideology-free impact the instructional tools that instructional designers construct for diverse populations including considerations for acculturation, ethnicity, educational media design, proficiency, or culturally specific learning strategies. For example, "objective" statements about ability and disability position people within particular and often inflexible subject positions that are neither value neutral nor often accurate (Charlton, 1998).

Because of the close historical linkages that educational technology research maintains with industrial and military training (Saettler, 1968) and its co-evolution with Educational Psychology and the Cognitive Sciences (Anglin, 1995), many existing research discourses that address technology and education complement the scientific language perpetuated by deficit models of disability, contemporary legislation such as No Child Left Behind (NCLB), and policies mandating access to web-based content for individuals with disabilities. These initiatives often do not take into consideration the complexity of issues related to social and cultural difference or the continuation and reproduction of inequality vis-à-vis the integration of technology. For example, in K–16 education, they tend to focus on narrowly defined concepts of computer literacy; quantifiable goals of computer adoption (i.e., access); integration in a standards-based curriculum; and the use of technology to improve performance (e.g. standardized test scores). These initiatives are typically predicated on the assumption that technology is a value-neutral phenomenon and that its integration into diverse environments can create consistent and replicable results. Striving for consistent and replicable results has the potential to reify the privilege and normalization of "ability" while rendering difference in the form of disability as deficient (Warren, 2001). In these contexts, technology is often viewed by educators in terms of what it can add or how it can supplement current educational practices rather than as a material change in the pedagogical dynamics of educational practice. Consequently, the research and policy on issues around disability tend to be interventionist and often do not attend to the complex extant material and social realities of the individuals they purport to address. These projects consistently neglect the broader role of technology within society, instead relying on narrowly defined constructions of technology as a pedagogically and culturally neutral "tool" (Bowers, 1988; Postman, 1992)

The theoretic foundations of this chapter are grounded in understandings of power and discourse that make use of linguistics and textual models of social understandings in which subjectivities and agency are co-constructed by cultural and historical dynamics. In this framework, individual choices, desires, and learning arise from and are regulated by discursive formations (in this case the discursive formations of disability, technology, and learning). According to Foucault (1972) a discursive formation is defined by how intuitions regulate truth and contribute to the formation of subject positions, concepts, and strategic choices. An important component of this framework is the way in which power is theorized through the techniques of discursive regulation and subject construction and how power flows back and forth, often in unpredictable ways (i.e., agency), between official discourses like institutional, state, and national accessibility standards, and local discourses including local and classroom culture, individuals, pedagogy, community attitudes, individual subjectivities, and learning.

Working within these theoretical foundations, symptomatic reading offers a useful tool for thinking about the construction of disability in instructional technology research and development. Symptomatic reading—reading a text for what is neither visible nor knowable and considering how that absence structures and enables what is visible/knowable. Ellen Rooney (1989) uses the practice of symptomatic reading to establish a relationship between two discourses, the discourse being analyzed and the researcher's discourse. Symptomatic reading, then, looks for "a necessary silence" (Rooney, 1989, p. 15). It is this silence that enables a particular practice, theory, research methodology, construction of difference, discourse of performance standards, or ideology (and the texts, images, policies, and effects they foster) to persist and develop. Attention to this silence, even the recognition of it, is to begin to trace the limits of what has silenced it. In this chapter, symptomatic reading offers re-readings of instructional technology policy, practice, and design with attention to the silence(s)—in this case disability—that structures them.

While the predominant discourses of instructional technology can serve political and ideological agendas and help to justify a field of study as a "science," their structured absences often fail those who need the greatest assistance to learn about and with technology. These understandings of technology limit the possibilities for the development of educational technologies that do not marginalize users on the basis of ability.

There have been significant strides in theorizing the conceptualization of disability that move beyond highly medicalized, deficit-based understanding of persons with disabilities toward a "social model" of disability that contends that disability is a social status resulting from cultural values and practices that stigmatize, marginalize, and oppress disabled people (e.g. Erevelles, 2000; Linton, 1998; Peters, 1995; Pugach and Seidl, 1998; Ware, 2001). Unfortunately, the vast majority of instructional technologists still conceptualize disability according to dated deficit models (if they consider it at all) (Pfeiffer, 2002). These perspectives can be limiting because they focus primarily on how to teach with technology, not on how those technologies shape the world in which we live, the ways in which we work, learn, are entertained, communicate, and form relationships. My hope is to continue the facilitation of placing theories of instructional technology within larger social contexts than generally considered.

As a practical device for this essay, I will discuss Internet technologies, specifically web-based instruction and the related issue of web-accessibility; however, it is important to note that the notion of technology is much broader than just the Internet and its related technologies. Central to this discussion is an understanding of the constructions of disability and ability within the educational context, and the definition/use of technology as well. An entry point for this discussion is the politics and practice of web accessibility within higher education; a brief analysis of the web courseware WebCT[1] will also be presented to illustrate the exclusions and silences with web-based instruction; and excerpts from a technology discussion LISTSERV will be analyzed. I specify higher education at this point because the technology is so pervasive in this environment, although there are currently several movements to make computing in primary and secondary school environments ubiquitous as well. Within in this discussion are a host of issues including the legal, rhetorical, and technical strategies deployed to avoid development of broadly accessible web materials; the socially constructed nature of such terms as "disabled" and "accessible; the real effects of inaccessibility to students utilizing educational technologies; and implications for educators and policy makers.

Problematizing "Accessibility"

The rapid growth of the Internet has changed the ways people communicate teach and learn, while at the same time increasing the isolation of those who do not have access to these technologies.

The goal of accessibility standards is to help make the web more accessible for people with disabilities. This includes individuals with visual disabilities, hearing disabilities, physical disabilities and cognitive or neurological disabilities. Accessibility standards are intended to help web designers identify and address accessibility issues.

The World Wide Web Consortium[2] or W3C leads what is perhaps the most comprehensive web accessibility standards initiative. The W3C's Web Content Accessibility Guidelines[3] (WCAG) were the first major effort to establish guidelines for design. This standard consists of 14 guidelines, each with three levels of checkpoints.[4] The WCAG is not a legal mandate, but rather a comprehensive set of guidelines to ensure accessibility.

In addition to the WCAG guidelines, there are emerging legal mandates for accessibility. Currently, there is no direct legal mandate for university web sites in the United States, but there is strong precedent. Indeed, many states and universities are developing their own standards based on the WCAG. In the United States, Section 508 of the Federal Rehabilitation Act[5] sets standards for web pages designed or maintained by federal agencies. Section 508 requires that electronic and information technology that is developed or purchased by the federal government is accessible by people with disabilities. Section 508 does not directly apply to the private sector. While many universities have adopted the standard outlined in Section 508 as part of their accessibility policy, they are not required to do so under the current law.

Within the disability groups outlined by the WCAG, there is a spectrum of issues and technologies. The case of individuals with visual disabilities is a good example. This group includes but is not limited to blind users, users with low or impaired visibility, as well as users with color deficits. Each group has a specific set of needs and often uses a set of tools to address those needs. For example, a blind user may use a screen reader to read the content of a web page aloud. In order for a page to be read by a screen reader, the page has to have text associated with all components of the page, including images. In contrast, another user with low visibility may need the page to be rendered in large print. Another user may be colorblind and may find pages with red-blue color combinations difficult to read.

There are a variety of methods for meeting the needs of those users whether through assistive devices such as a screen reader or through presentational standards. The WCAG guidelines attempt to reflect the requirements of as many of these users as possible. What is often lost in the policy language is that users with disabilities by no means represent a uniform category, nor can they be neatly divided into subcategories.

There are multiple contradictory subject positions, ideological formations, and processes that surround and circulate throughout the conceptualization and implementation of web accessibility practices and policies. On the one hand, there are [often] progressive tendencies driving policies to make web content accessible. On the other hand, web accessibility in the United States is often linked to bureaucratic concerns such as reducing a organization's legal exposure to lawsuits and maximizing use of existing technological infrastructure and broader efforts to move instruction to the web.

Disability studies provides a new lens with which to view web accessibility (and by extension many developing educational technologies). Web accessibility as it is often conceptualized is still additive rather than a fundamental rethinking of how the technology functions and structures interactions and uses. Rather than questioning the way(s) technologies "build in disability" (Goggin and Newell, 2003), web accessibility initiatives focus on using technology to provide a solution to disability. It is important to note that I am not making a sweeping critique of web accessibility initiatives. Often, those involved in these initiatives are dedicated to the notion of providing access to all, and see this as a social justice or civil rights issue; moreover, they often face intense opposition (exemplified later in this essay) to any attempt to provide accessible content. Instead, I hope to strengthen the work of web accessibility advocates, by broadening the scope of what "disability" means, toward Alan Roulstone's (1998) assertion that the way "technology is experienced cannot be understood in a social and theoretical vacuum" (p. 7).

The concept of articulation can help us examine the complex ideological formations and understandings of disability that lie behind such initiatives as web accessibility as these ideological formations are not static, but dynamic and more than a necessary result of particular structures of power and policy. As Stuart Hall (1996, p.141) notes, "[an articulation] is a linkage which is not necessary, determined, absolute and essential for all time". When examining web accessibility and technology as examples of articulated ideological formations and various subject positions, it is crucial to recognize that such circumstances are constantly shifting. Over time, these policies will be under pressure to continue to meet the ideological pressures of various blocs affected by them. For example, there is currently a confluence of needs for universities to provide accessible content and their desire to maximize income in difficult economic times (Foley, 2003). By ensuring accessible web-based content, universities can simultaneously broaden their markets while trimming expenses. One might be led to wonder, as material and political conditions change, will this particular articulation of legal requirement and economic necessity continue to exist, and if it ends where does that leave persons with disabilities? Additionally, how does this particular articulation affect the provision of instruction at the university?

WebCT and Course Management Software (CMS[6])

The Internet has tremendous abilities to deliver instruction over great distances. It also has tremendous power to mediate the construction and re-construction of knowledge, automating and narrowing instruction (and curricula) by defining and prescribing particular pedagogic methods inscribed by particular philosophical and theoretical conceptions of teaching and learning. The vast majority of those theoretical and philosophical perspectives are those mentioned earlier—"scientific," behaviorist, etc. For example, the testing features in WebCT emphasize objective testing and timed performance.

Additionally, distance-learning technologies via the Internet construct (and re-construct) both the teacher and learner within particular discourses of power that often exist tacitly in particular technology forms. For example, WebCT structures interaction between teacher and learner in ways that are determined by the design and process of the technology. It is important to note that this is not a natural consequence of the integration of the Internet into education, but an artifact of the policies and practices that surround its use. This comprehensive view of the integration of the Internet into instruction is the basis for a broader definition of distance learning in order to better understand how these tools affect instruction. At the same time understanding the epistemologies that structure the development of these tools can offer insight into how learning at a distance may become more collaborative and less potentially oppressive.

As has been noted elsewhere (see Voithofer, 2003), the guiding principles behind most online instructional design processes represent a narrow epistemological base grounded in Tylerian curricular design or linear/sequential instructional design models. Moreover analyses of instructional software have been conducted (e.g. Streibel, 1998), but these analyses have not been applied to the particular form and function of online instructional tools. While there has been research on the development of constructivist or collaborative online learning environments, these models still rely on narrowly defined constructions of technology as a pedagogically and culturally neutral "tool" (Bowers, 1988; Postman, 1992).

The perceivable functionality (how users understand a given piece of technology to work) built into course management software presuppose particular types of learning and knowing, and by virtue of their near-exclusivity, structure how online courses are constructed and conducted. It has been noted that generally within online instructional development, emphasis is placed on delivery of content at the expense of developing a social and experiential learning context (Gilroy, 2001). Bates (1995) cautions that a directed, prescriptive model of content delivery no longer meets the changing needs of the knowledge economy workers, where communicating effectively, working in teams, analyzing information and generating new knowledge are creating complex new educational needs. Concern has been raised against creating an online instructional model that relies on assumptions and strategies derived from traditional classrooms and learning environments (e.g. Linser and Ip, 2002), but these concerns do not consider the meta-level structuring aspects of the technologies in use.

It is important to point out some concrete ways in which technology determines the form and content of the curriculum, as well as our interaction with it. These limitations within the technology are a reflection of the values of those who design, implement and maintain the instructional technology tools and are thus subject to particular [mis]understandings of disability and difference. For example, the decision to include multiple choice assessment tools into the WebCT courseware package was made on a very specific set of beliefs about teaching practices (or perhaps in ignorance of others). This decision almost certainly reflects certain understandings or misunderstandings of ability and difference.

Why Should We Do This? Excerpts From a Real Discussion

The following are examples of several legal and economic arguments deployed to avoid development of broadly accessible web materials. These examples come from a LISTSERV discussion that occurred in the late Fall of

2002 (but were still ongoing two years later). This LISTSERV is comprised of individuals involved in the design, development, and implementation of learning technologies at a large university. The themes that emerge in this particular instance are similar to other "conversations" in which the author of this chapter has participated nationally and internationally.

Legal (Compliance with the Law)

> "How does this obligation play out if a course at [University] is offered in a variety of ways? Are we obligated to make the offering over the internet [sic] completely ADA compliant if the disabled student can take the same course by another compliant means?"

This statement exemplifies the common tactic of redirecting a student with a disability to other course offerings. This statement assumes a similarity between the accommodations required by the ADA and access to online learning environments. For example, in a building with two entrances, it is common to make one entrance accessible with a ramp and automatic door and leave the other, inaccessible entrance in its original form. This is a way to meet the letter of the law while providing a "cost effective" point of entry to the building. Technically, the person with a disability has access to the building just as others have access through another entrance. This does not assume that access is equal. In the building where I work, there is a "main" entrance accessible only by two flights of stairs. Display cases are arrayed at the first landing and most people use that entrance. Conversely, the accessible entrance is at the loading dock one floor down, away from any of the entrance displays or directories. Similarly, another course offering does not provide the same type of access as an Internet based course.

From the student perspective, Internet based courses are often desirable because they provide a number of benefits over traditional face-to-face (F2F) offerings. Internet based courses often afford more flexibility in scheduling. Rather than attending a course with a set time and location, a course via Internet provides flexibility in location and time. This flexibility is of course constrained by student access to technology and course techniques (e.g. synchronous discussion where everyone must be online at the same time versus asynchronous discussion where students post independently). Internet based courses often allow students to work at a more self-directed pace accessing information when and if they need it. Specific to students with disabilities, Internet based courses offer the flexibility previously mentioned as well as the potential to more easily utilize more specialized forms of assistive technology. Because the nature of an Internet based course is so different, the assertion that offering "compliant" offerings in different settings is appropriate is specious. Assuming that another, compliant form of the class were available, the student with the disability is being forced into a narrowing of options not required of other students.

Another response to efforts to provide accessible web content can be found in policy documents themselves. Michalko and Titchkosky (2001) note that "Legislation itself insists on accessibility, but only if accommodations are reasonable" (209). Thus accessibility is mandated but only where deemed reasonable. What constitutes reasonable is highly subjective, usually poorly documented, and thus the site of incredible power. Those who determine what constitutes a reasonable accommodation determine what level and kind of access an individual with a disability has to particular web based content. Often these decisions are left to faculty who have little knowledge of the types of AT individuals with disabilities might use to access particular site or even the issues that exist with particular web-based methods. This type of "escape valve" notion exists at all policy levels and is most noticeable in focused documents like university web accessibility policies. The "draft" web accessibility policy at one university exemplifies the ways in which even policy is drafted to provide a "way out" of accessible design.

III. Exemptions
    A. Web pages are exempt from this policy if:
        1. Compliance is not reasonably attainable with current technology, or
        2. Where the content or curriculum cannot be effectively delivered in an accessible format without fundamentally altering the nature of the content or curriculum, or the content is undergoing initial development.
        3. (This provision is intended to ease the development process, but not go counter to §II(B[7]).
    B. Web authors must be prepared to justify their claims of exemption under §III(A) by demonstrating that a deliberative process was used in making this determination.

The exemptions in this policy, while well intentioned, counter the very reason for implementing a policy in the first place. Additionally, the exemptions are outlined in only the most vague terms, so there is no basis for what constitutes such conditions as "reasonably attainable" or "effective delivery."

An example of this is the clause that notes that an exemption from the policy may be granted if "compliance is not reasonably attainable with current technology." This statement is so vague that it could be utilized to exempt a fair deal of online course material from conforming to the policy. Most widely used current technology holds the potential to make almost all Web content accessible. Is it possible this clause was written specifically to address certain technologies? It can be assumed that one such technology in question is Flash animation. Flash is a popular multimedia (often called Rich Media) authoring tool used to develop animations and interactivity for websites. Flash only recently offered options for creating accessible content, and those options require a fair degree of technical skill and are not backward compatible. Moreover, the question of the appropriate use of technology is important here. Is the use of a particular technology necessary to achieve certain educational goals? For example, does something *require* being done in Flash (which is notoriously hard to be made accessible)?

All three of the conditions in this policy suggest that the framers of this policy consider web-based content intended for a context that does not consider disability as a normal or ordinary occurrence. In this context, accommodations are afterthoughts and this points to the essential orientation of the public realm—an orientation to persons within certain understandings of ordinary and commonplace (Michalko and Titchkosky, 2001).

Economic

> Much better (as various people on campus have repeated [sic] pointed out) would be to defer the cost and use the funds on providing "live" services to real disabled students when and if they materialize. This is in fact the way that disabilities were handled 20 or 30 years ago. . .In my opinion, there is no more basis for arguing that all video must be captioned than there is for arguing that all textbooks must be available in Braille. Those of us involved in online teaching need to be very vigilant regarding efforts to hold online teaching to more rigorous standards than classroom teaching. Otherwise, we give away the ball game when it comes to trying to prove that we can be cost effective.

The author of this statement draws on several common economic and cost/benefit arguments. This strategy rationalizes avoiding developing accessible web based content by constructing it as financially infeasible. Furthermore, this argument assumes that the intended audience does not include students with disabilities, and thus any effort to make accommodations is an additional and unplanned expense. Since environments often are not created with the intention of serving individuals with disabilities, then any restructuring or reorganization is unexpected and unintended. The need for rationalization of expense and accommodation is in essence a cost/benefit analysis. What is the possible benefit versus the cost to the university? This has been referred to as balancing the books on disability (Michalko and Titchkosky, 2001)–weighing any possible benefit of having persons with disabilities present against the cost to the university.

It is telling that this author chooses to identify the most costly issue in making web based content accessible captioning. Captioning is a time intensive process, but in the context of quality digital video production is less of an issue than it might seem. The primary issues involve having a good transcript from which captions can be developed. All too often what web delivered video really amounts to is nothing more than a taped lecture. Thus the issue becomes less a question of accessible technology and one of accessible teaching practice.

These are not the only two categories of techniques used to avoid compliance with web accessibility initiatives. Two other notable categories are technical arguments and rhetorical maneuver. While both of these techniques were also well evidenced in the LISTSERV discussion, there is not the space to deal with them in great detail here, but a cursory overview is in order.

Technical arguments refer to the technical overhead required to make web content accessible. These arguments are often coupled with concern that focusing on accessibility often restricts innovation or limits the tools available for content delivery.

Rhetorical maneuver involves wordplay over what constitutes "disability" (who decides, what is a fair accommodation) the actual meaning of policies (arguments to the spirit as opposed to the letter of the law), and shifting of responsibility (who actually ensures content is accessible).

Where from Here?

This chapter has considered what the conceptual work of disability studies can bring to educational technology practice as it is broadly applied and specifically with regard to distance education. As methods of teaching with Internet technologies continue to proliferate and more educational materials are placed online, it is important that educational technology researchers, theorists, and practitioners consider the social, political, and pedagogic implications of disability and difference and the Internet. What most discussions about accessibility in education fail to recognize is that access is not about the "limitations" of the individual; rather it is about society's inability to accommodate difference. Concurring with critical race theorists, Asch (2001) notes that large-scale structural societal change will be resisted unless dominant members of society perceive benefit from those changes, but that change should not be affected only because it can be justified as benefiting all, but because it is providing access to a populations previously excluded. This seemingly paradoxical approach to the issue of access and social justice informs an important conceptualization of web accessibility. Web accessibility is important because techniques and technologies involved in making content accessible benefit the broader population, but the real motivation for web accessibility initiatives (and broader educational technology development) should be informed by a desire to provide access to those previously denied and by a broader understanding of disability than found in prominent educational technology discourses.

References

Anglin, G. J. (1995). *Instructional Technology: Past, present, and future* (2nd ed.). Englewood, CO: Libraries Unlimited.

Asch, A. (2001). Critical race theory, feminism, and disability: Reflections on social justice and personal identity. *Ohio State Law Journal, 62*, 1, 391–423.

Banathy, B. (1996). Systems theory and its application in eduction. In D. Jonassen (Ed.), *Handbook of research for eductional communications and technology*. New York: Macmillan.

Bates, T. (1995). *Technology, open learning, and distance education*. New York: Routledge.

Bowers, C. A. (1988). *The cultural dimensions of educational computing: Understanding the non-neutrality of technology*. New York: Teachers College Press.

Burton, J. K., Moore, D. M., and Magliaro, S. G. (1996). Behaviorism and instructional technology. In D. Jonassen (Ed.), *Handbook of research for educational communications and technology*. New York: Macmillan.

Charlton, J. I. (1998). *Nothing about us without us:Disability oppression and empowerment*. Berkeley: University of California Press.

DeVaney, A. (1998). Will educators ever unmask that determiner, technology? *Educational Policy, 12*, 5, 568–585.

Erevelles, N. (2000). Educating unruly bodies: Critical pedagogy, disability studies, and the politics of schooling. *Educational Theory, 50*, 1, 25–47.

Foley, A. (2003). Distance, disability and the commodification of education: Web accessibility and the construction of knowledge. *Current Issues in in Comparative Education, 6*, 1.

Foucault, M. (1972). *The archaeology of knowledge; and, the discourse on language.* New York: Pantheon Books.

———. (1988). *Madness and civilization: A history of insanity in the Age of Reason.* New York: Vintage Books.

Gilroy, K. (2001). *Collaborative E–Learning: The right approach.* Retrieved February 4, 2004, from http://eveanderson.com/arsdigita/asj/elearning.

Goggin, G., and Newell, C. (2003). *Digital disability : the social construction of disability in new media.* Lanham: Rowman and Littlefield.

Hall, S. (1996) On postmodernism and articulation. In Morley, D. and Chen, K-H (eds.) *Stuart Hall: Critical Dialogues in Cultural Studies* (pp. 131-150). New York: Routledge.

Hlynka, D., and Belland, J. C. (1991). *Paradigms regained: The uses of illuminative, semiotic, and postmodern criticism as modes of inquiry in educational technology: A book of readings.* Englewood Cliffs, NJ: Educational Technology Publications.

Jonassen, D. H. (1990). Thinking technology: Toward a constructivist view of instructional design. *Educational Technology, 30* (September), 32–34.

Linser, R., and Ip, A. (2002). *Beyond the current E–Learning paradigm: Applications of role playing simulations (RPS) case studies.* Paper presented at the E–Learn 2002, Montreal.

Linton, S. (1998). *Claiming disability: Knowledge and identity.* New York: New York University Press.

Michalko, R., and Titchkosky, T. (2001). Putting disability in its place: It's not a joking matter. In J. C. Wilson and C. Lewiecki–Wilson (Eds.), *Embodied rhetorics: Disability in language and culture* (pp. 200–228). Carbondale: Southern Illinois University Press.

Peters, S. (1995). Disability baggage: Changing the educational research terrain. In P. Clough and L. Barton (Eds.), *Making difficulties: Research and the construction of special educational needs* (pp. 59–74). London: Paul Chapman.

Pfeiffer, D. (2002). The philosophical foundations of Disability Studies. *Disability Studies Quarterly, 22*, 2, 3–23.

Postman, N. (1992). *Technopoly: The surrender of culture to technology.* New York: Knopf.

Pugach, M. C., and Seidl, B. L. (1998). Responsible linkages between diversity and disability: A challenge for special education. *Teacher Education and Special Education, 21*, 4, 319–333.

Rooney, E. (1989). *Seductive reasoning: Pluralism as the problematic of contemporary literary theory.* Ithaca: Cornell University Press.

Roulstone, A. (1998). *Enabling technology: Disabled people, work, and new technology.* Philadelphia, PA: Open University Press.

Saettler, P. (1968). *The history of instructional technology.* New York: McGraw–Hill.

Smith, P. L., and Ragan, T. J. (1999). *Instructional design* (2nd ed.). Upper Saddle River, N.J.: Merrill.

Streibel, M. (1986). A critical analysis of the use of computers in the classroom. *Educational Communications and Technology, 34*, 3, 137–161.

. (1998). A critical analysis of three approaches to the use of computers in education. In L. E. Beyer and M. W. Apple (Eds.), *The curriculum; Problems, politics, and possibilities* (2nd ed.). Albany, NY: SUNY Press.

Voithofer, R. (2003). Nomadic epistemologies and performative pedagogies in online education. *Educational Theory, 52*, 4, 479–494.

Ware, L. (2001). Writing, identity, and the other: Dare we do disability studies? *Journal of Teacher Education, 52*, 1, 107–123.

Warren, J. T. (2001). Doing whiteness: On the performative dimensions of race in the Classroom. *Communication Education, 50*, 2, 91–108.

Wynn, W., and Snyder, D. (1996). Cognitive perspectives in technology. In D. Jonassen (Ed.), *Handbook of research for educational communications and technology.* New York: Macmillan.

Notes

1 http://www.webct.com

2 The W3C is the organization responsible for the standardization of a wide variety of web related technologies such as Hypertext Markup Language (HTML). The W3C also coordinates a project known as the Web Accessibility Initiative (WAI). This ongoing initiative consists of several projects including publishing a set of standards for web content, another set of standards for software used to create web pages as well as a set of standards for browsers used to view web content. URL: http://www.w3.org/

3 http://www.w3.org/TR/WCAG10

[4] Priority One checkpoints are those that the web developer must satisfy to insure that the page itself is accessible. Priority Two checkpoints are those that the web developer should satisfy to ensure that certain groups will be able to access information on the web page. Priority Three checkpoints are those the web developer may do to ensure that all content on the page is completely accessible.

[5] The regulations referred to as Section 508 are actually an amendment to the Workforce Rehabilitation Act of 1973.

[6] Course management software is often broadly defined as prepackaged computer based educational materials in which the computer mediates the educational experience. I use the term fairly specifically to refer to such software suites as WebCT, Blackboard and the like which facilitate computer-based distance education via the Internet.

[7] [University] is committed to making its World Wide Web content and other electronic information accessible to persons with disabilities.

CHAPTER 14

Accessible Information Technology in Education: Addressing the "Separate but Equal" Treatment of Disabled Individuals

Patricia A. Brown and Sharan E. Brown

The use of technology in education settings—from primary school to post-secondary institutions—has become commonplace. It is no longer a question of *if* technology is incorporated into educational curricula, it is simply a question of what type and to what degree students, their families, and instructors must interface with it. The point has often been made that technology presents unprecedented opportunities for disabled individuals to increase their independence and inclusion in society (Alpert and Rich, 2001). It is also well documented and described by others that technology can create unintended barriers to this increased access (Baker and Bellorde, 2004; Davis et al., 2002).

With the increased use of technology in education comes the opportunity to proactively design and implement information systems which provide the largest number of disabled individuals the ability to independently and seamlessly access the technology. The development and implementation of accessible information technology (IT) in education demonstrates a commitment to address the continued marginalization—social, economic and political—of disabled individuals in our society (The State of the Union, 2004). There is no question that accessible IT furthers the inclusion, equality, and independence goals articulated by the social model of disability. Failure to develop accessible IT simply continues the status quo or "separate but equal" treatment towards disabled individuals.

The existing disability rights laws—primarily Section 504 of the Rehabilitation Act of 1973 (Section 504) and the Americans with Disabilities Act (ADA)—can be used to create pressure on the schools to provide accessible IT and potentially can be successful in achieving accessible IT. However, as we describe in this essay, these laws do not require that educational institutions develop and implement accessible IT systems. Therefore, they have limited effectiveness. Accessible IT environments may eventually be introduced into educational settings as a result of the requirements of Section 508 of the Rehabilitation Act of 1973 (Section 508). Although Section 508 has no direct application to the educational setting, advocates for accessible IT are working diligently to educate developers and pre-service IT programs on the importance of addressing accessibility in the development stages of technology, and these efforts may ultimately be successful (National Center, 2002–2004). Despite these possibilities, the authors are not convinced that the civil rights laws and product development as a result of Section 508 are adequate avenues to creating an environment that allows disabled individuals access to the IT available to nondisabled individuals. Because there are no current legal mandates that educational institutions provide accessible IT, this opportunity will be missed unless educational institutions develop policies that ensure accessible IT implementation.

In recognition that existing laws are inadequate to create the equality that must be provided to truly provide equal opportunities for disabled individuals, we describe another avenue for achieving accessible IT in education—that is, the development of educational policies that mandate the implementation of accessible IT. We are not advocating compliance with current disability rights laws. We strongly believe that society should legally mandate accessible IT and disabled individuals should be able to enforce their rights to it. However, while we encourage readers to work for legal reform, we also recognize that such change requires long-term advocacy. Instead of waiting for that process to unfold, we believe that adoption of accessible IT policies in educational environments is a potentially faster advocacy approach and should be pursued concurrently with legal reform.

We now turn to a discussion of federal disability laws and accessible IT. As mentioned previously, advocating for legal change is one way that the disability rights movement works to further the goals of independence and equality. Before we explore the adoption of accessible IT policies, we will discuss the limits of this method and review how three federal disability rights laws apply to accessible IT.

Federal Disability Rights Laws and Accessible IT

There are several sources of federal law that address the rights of disabled individuals to access IT in education. The federal statutes that are relevant to public K–12 and post-secondary institutions are Section 504 of the Rehabilitation Act of 1973 (Section 504) and the Americans with Disabilities Act (ADA) of 1990, Title II. K–12 public schools must also follow the obligations under the Individuals with Disabilities Education Act (IDEA). Although IDEA, Section 504 and Title II address the responsibilities of public educational institutions to disabled individuals, none of them mentions "accessible information technology." Nonetheless, these laws are relevant in understanding the responsibilities of educational institutions to accommodate the specific IT needs of disabled individuals and can be used to advocate for implementation of accessible IT. All three of the laws we discuss are legally complex and cannot be thoroughly reviewed in this essay. Our goal is simply that you will appreciate the significant limitations of the federal disability rights laws as tools to achieving accessible IT in educational institutions.

In addition to the statutes themselves, there are regulations promulgated under all the laws that provide guidance. The federal agencies that write, interpret and enforce regulations for Section 504 and ADA are the Office for Civil Rights (OCR) in the United States Department of Education and the Civil Rights Division in the United States Department of Justice (DOJ) , respectively. These regulations address the obligations of both K–12 and post-secondary institutions. Although the regulations do not mention accessible IT, there is regulatory language as well as OCR administrative guidance that is relevant to our topic. DOJ has also issued a policy statement that is relevant to one aspect of IT and it is discussed below. Regulations interpreting IDEA come from the Office of Special Education Programs (OSEP) but do not mention or provide guidance on accessible IT.

As mentioned previously, one of the external factors that may affect the availability of accessible IT in education is the implementation of Section 508 of the Rehabilitation Act of 1973. Section 508 mandates that IT developed, maintained, used or procured by federal agencies must be accessible to disabled individuals unless doing so creates an undue burden (1998 Amendment, 1998). The law is intended to influence the development of accessible IT products of all kinds and therefore increase the commercially available options for all sectors—including educational institutions (Yukins, 2004). However, because Section 508 applies to the federal government and does not specifically affect public K–12 and post-secondary education, any influence on educational policy and practice will be indirect. We mention Section 508 later in this essay, but only as an example of achieving accessible IT through the procurement process. Another factor that may affect the development of accessible IT in education is state law. Some states have voluntarily adopted state laws that have some Section 508 features which, if the laws apply to educational institutions, can place additional responsibilities on educational institutions.

As you read this essay, please keep in mind that although there are numerous court decisions on the issue of whether a post-secondary institution needs to provide assistive technology (AT) to an individual with a disability in order to ensure that the individual has access, there are no cases specifically addressing the obligations of K–12 or post-secondary institutions to provide accessible IT.[1] And while there are several OCR resolution agreements concerning access to the Web in higher education as described below, there is no case concerning access to the Internet on a college or university campus that has been litigated and therefore no clear ruling on the duty of higher education (Hawke and Jannarone, 2002). The courts have heard a handful of cases involving disabled individuals and access to IT, but because these cases have not involved educational institutions we do not discuss them here.

Individuals with Disabilities Education Act (IDEA) and Accessible Information Technology

The Individuals with Disabilities Education Act (IDEA) is a federal law that requires states to provide eligible children (those between 3–21 years with one of 13 designated disabilities who require special education services in order to benefit from education) a "free and appropriate public education" or FAPE, in the least restrictive environment (LRE). It only addresses the rights of eligible children in primary and secondary school and not those of post-secondary students, educators or parents with disabilities. Under IDEA, FAPE means special education and related services designed to meet their unique needs. LRE means that students have access to the regular education curriculum unless, with aids and services, they cannot receive FAPE in regular education.

The IDEA requires that educators consider AT— that is, determine whether a student could benefit from AT—for all special education students during the development of the Individualized Education Program (IEP). AT may be provided under the law as part of a child's special education or as a related service. However, IDEA does not mention accessible IT, and there is no legal mandate that special education students have access to accessible IT *per se*. As mentioned above, the school district's legal obligation is to provide FAPE to each eligible child. What exactly is required to ensure FAPE should be determined on the basis of the individual needs of each student and what may be appropriate for one may not be appropriate for any other student. Because of the focus in special education of meeting the needs of the individual student to ensure that he or she benefits, in most cases, a special education student will be provided the AT that he/she needs to access the IT. The IT then becomes accessible to the student and the legal obligation under IDEA has been met— that is, the AT allows the child to benefit from the education program. Providing FAPE to students does not require that school districts/state educational agencies develop and implement accessible IT systems in any scenario that we can currently envision. A state or school district could decide to provide accessible IT in the school system and then special education students—like all students—would benefit. However, meeting the needs of an individual student under IDEA will not likely result in the development of accessible IT in schools.

Section 504 of the Rehabilitation Act of 1973

Section 504 prohibits discrimination against disabled individuals by educational entities that receive federal financial assistance, including all public K–12 schools and higher education institutions. Section 504 states that

> No otherwise qualified individual with a disability . . . Shall, solely by reason of her or his disability, be excluded from the participation in, be denied the benefits of, or be subjected to discrimination under any program or activity receiving Federal financial assistance (29 U.S.C. §794a).

This law is applicable to both K–12 and post-secondary institutions but the regulations are somewhat different. Basically, Section 504 requires school districts to provide students with disabilities benefits and services that are comparable to those offered other students. In primary and secondary schools, Section 504 regulations require schools to provide a FAPE that is equivalent to the education offered others in the LRE. In addition to some very specific requirements—such as evaluation and placement and due process protections—Section 504 regulations prohibit certain practices by the schools. These include, among others:

1. Denying a qualified person the opportunity to participate in or bene-fit from an aid, benefit or service;
2. Affording an individual an opportunity to participate in or benefit from an aid, benefit or service that is not equal to that afforded oth-ers; or
3. Providing an individual with an aid, benefit or service that is not as effective as that provided to others; providing different or separate aids, benefits or services unless such action is necessary to provide that person with aids, benefits, or services that are as effective as those provided to others.

In addition, Section 504 requires K–12 institutions to provide reasonable accommodations to qualified disabled employees or applicants unless doing so creates an undue burden.

Nowhere in Section 504—the statute or regulations—does the law men-tion AT or the phrase "accessible IT." However, in some cases schools may be required to provide AT to students in order to meet the legal standards under Section 504. In order to determine the obligations concerning IT under Section 504, the existing standards that are included in the regulations and case law are applied to IT issues—including web accessibility issues. In most cases, the questions to ask will differ somewhat depending on whether the individual is a student, community member or employee. For students and community members, the issue is whether the accommodation that the individual is requesting is necessary in order to allow the individual to have access to the school's program or service (remember, the school is not re-quired to provide an accommodation that creates an undue burden or results in a fundamental alteration). If the individual requesting the accommodation is an employee, the issue is whether it is a reasonable accommodation.

Americans with Disabilities Act (ADA) Title II

The ADA broadly prohibits discrimination "on the basis of disability in employment, programs and services provided by state and local governments, goods and services provided by private companies, and in commercial facilities." The specific language of the law is:

> [N]o qualified individual with a disability shall, by reason of such disability, be excluded from participation in or be denied the benefits of the services, programs, or activities of a public entity, or be subjected to discrimination by any such entity (42 U.S.C. §12132, 1994).

This is very similar to the language used in Section 504. Title II of the ADA is the section that prohibits discrimination by public K–12 and postsecondary educational institutions.

Like the statutory language, Section 504 and ADA Title II regulations are also very similar, although there are differences. But for purposes of our discussion, the obligations of educational institutions and the rights of disabled individuals are the same under Title II and Section 504. The regulations common to both laws that have some relevancy to accessible IT are as follows:

1. Schools are prohibited from providing different opportunities, benefits and services to people with disabilities.
2. Schools are prohibited from providing a benefit or service that is not as effective as that provided to others.
3. Schools must provide services in the most integrated setting appropriate (28 C.F.R. §35.130(b),(d); 34 C.F.R. §104.4(b)(2)).

Although Title II prohibits discrimination in employment situations, the law states that Title II covered entities (including public schools) will follow the employment rules under Title I of the ADA. Title I requires employers to provide reasonable accommodations for qualified employees and job applicants with disabilities unless doing so creates an undue burden on the employer. Again, this is similar to the obligations under Section 504.

Congress passed the ADA in 1990, and it does not specifically address access to online resources and other electronic and information technology. Neither Title II nor Section 504 requires educational institutions to provide accessible IT to disabled individuals. Both laws, as we describe in further detail below, do require access to the information technology. That requirement is typically met by providing AT to an individual so that he/she can access the information not by implementing a systems-wide change resulting in accessible IT.

The statutory language of both Section 504 and Title II covers both K–12 and the post-secondary institutions. However, the obligations towards disabled individuals are somewhat different in K–12 schools and post-secondary educational institutions because of the differences in the regulations applicable to higher education students. Generally, the expectations of the scope of modifications required of the schools are broader for K–12 students than for higher education ones and specifically, students in post-secondary education do not have a right to FAPE in the LRE.

Like the regulations relevant to K–12 education, for the most part Section 504 and Title II regulations applicable to higher education provide similar obligations on the part of schools and rights for disabled individuals. In summary, those obligations are:

1. They both require that post-secondary educational entities provide comparable access and equivalent treatment to disabled individuals.
2. Educational institutions may not exclude from a program or give different benefits or services in a program on the basis of disability.
3. Schools must provide reasonable modifications to programs and services unless doing so results in a fundamental alteration of the program or service or an undue burden.
4. Auxiliary aids and services as required to ensure effective communication with disabled individuals must be provided. Under Title II, schools must give primary consideration to the requests of the individual but are not required to provide the individual's preferred accommodation if 1) other effective means of communication exist as determined by knowledgeable experts; 2) it requires a "fundamental alteration" in the program or service; or 3) it creates an undue burden (financial or administrative) (28 C.F.R. §35.160(b)(2); Office for Civil Rights, 1997).

There are many court decisions about what "fundamental alteration" and "undue burden" mean in the educational arena. In summary, fundamental alteration has been determined to mean something more than "modification" and although always individually determined, it must be something that requires significant changes to the program or service. Something that requires fundamental alteration is not considered a reasonable modification and therefore is not required. Undue burden is defined by the regulations as "significant difficulty or expense." A court's decision as to whether something constitutes an undue burden is always determined case-by-case and is unique to the facts of the case before it. Therefore, it is really impossible to give a helpful summary of how the courts would evaluate whether a specific modification would legally create an undue burden for the covered entity.

As is true for IDEA and the regulations applicable to K–12 under Section 504 and Title II, the regulations applicable to post-secondary institutions do not mention AT or accessible IT. However, post-secondary education may need to provide AT to an individual with disabilities as a reasonable modification, to provide effective communication, or to ensure access to a benefit or service. In order to determine whether higher education institutions would ever be legally required to provide accessible IT, we need to review the guidance from OCR and DOJ.

Guidance from the Office for Civil Rights in the Department of Education

OCR is the federal agency that has responsibility to enforce several federal civil rights laws that prohibit discrimination in programs or activities that receive Federal financial assistance from the Department of Education, including Section 504 of the Rehabilitation Act of 1973 and Title II of the Americans with Disabilities Act (ADA). This enforcement responsibility includes investigating complaints by individuals concerning their rights related to accessibility of IT issues under these laws. Complaints to OCR can result in either a finding of "no cause" by OCR, resolution agreements between the covered entity and OCR, or litigation.

OCR has issued several case resolution agreement letters that provide some administrative guidance on the issue of accessible IT in post-secondary educational settings. We should note that this guidance does have some limitations. The case resolution letters involve schools that voluntarily agreed to resolve complaints brought against them by students. They are, therefore, illustrative and anecdotal; they are not binding on a court. Second, the cases involved post-secondary educational institutions which are bound by different Section 504 regulations than are elementary and secondary schools. Because of this difference, whether the guidelines will be relevant to the K–12 system remains to be seen. That said, however, they are valuable in both helping schools understand the OCR position on accessible IT—specifically web accessibility—and typically hold considerable weight in court, particularly when the law does not address the specific issue.

In one such case settlement agreement, OCR stated that institutions covered by ADA and Section 504 must "ensure that communications with persons with disabilities are as effective as communications with others." Institutions that use the Internet for communication regarding their programs, goods, or services must make that information accessible. According to OCR, the "issue is not whether the student with the disability is merely provided access, but the issue is rather the extent to which the communication is actually as effective as that provided to others." Whether the communication is via media, print, or the Internet, post-secondary institutions must "effectively communicate" with disabled individuals including students, faculty, staff and the wider community (Office for Civil Rights, 1996).

The "effectively communicate" standard was adopted by OCR to determine whether the means of communication (meaning the transfer of information, whether via media, print or the Internet) of the post-secondary institution satisfies the legal obligations under Section 504 and ADA. According to OCR, the basic considerations when evaluating effectiveness are 1) the timeliness of delivery, 2) the accuracy of the translation, and 3) provision in a manner and medium appropriate to the significance of the message and the abilities of the individual with the disability (Office for Civil Rights, 1997). For example, if a university website is inaccessible to a visually impaired student, the university is still required under federal law to effectively communicate the information on the website to the student. If the website is available twenty four hours a day, seven days a week for other users, it must be available in the same way for the visually impaired student. There are several ways this communication could be accomplished, but none is likely to be as practical or meet the effectiveness standard as well as if the website were accessible in the first place.

In addition to the "effective communication" standard, OCR has, in at least one resolution letter, cited a court decision to support the agency's statement that a post-secondary institution violates its obligations under the ADA when it only responds on a case-by-case basis to individual requests for accommodation (*Tyler v. City of Manhattan*, 1994). The *Tyler* decision itself went further to state that a public entity—in this case a local government—has an affirmative duty to develop a comprehensive policy in advance of any request (Office for Civil Rights, 1997). In this same resolution letter, a university agreed to develop a plan with input from appropriate groups, on and off campus, to devise and implement campus-wide accessibility standards for electronic and information technology. The plan was submitted to OCR for review, which had indicated that it must include a "process by which the University will ensure comparable access for students with disabilities to official University websites" (Office for Civil Rights, 1997).

OCR summarizes the principles in any consideration of web accessibility as including the following:

- Students must be provided equally effective access to the program.
- Every program and activity is covered.
- Goals are nondiscriminatory program access and effective communication.
- The law contemplates increased independence for people with disabilities through accessible technology.
- Consumer preferences need to be seriously considered.
- Failure to plan for technology access and an ad hoc approach may result in denial of access.
- Modifications are not required if fundamental alteration conflicts with essential program requirements.
- An equally effective alternative can be considered.
- OCR considers whether alternative methods of providing access to program and information are effective (on case by case determination) (Office for Civil Rights, 2002).

Guidance on Information Technology from Department of Justice

The Department of Justice (DOJ) is the federal agency with the overall responsibility to enforce Title II of the ADA and Section 504. The Civil Rights Division, Disability Rights Section, in DOJ issued a document entitled *Accessibility of State and Local Government Websites to People with Disabilities* (U.S. Department of Justice, 2003). In this document, DOJ states that State and local governments are required under the ADA and §504 to provide "equal access to their programs, services, or activities unless doing so would fundamentally alter the nature" of these programs, services or activities or "would impose an undue burden." This equal access obligation covers access to the information on governmental—that is, public educational—websites.

DOJ does not discuss the "effectively communicate" standard in this document. However, it does state that one way to ensure that governmental websites are accessible to disabled individuals is to provide "accessible features." Although DOJ acknowledges that there may be ways other than "accessible features" on the websites to provide access to the information such as a, "staffed telephone information line," the document states that:

> These alternatives, however, are unlikely to provide an equal degree of access in terms of hours of operation and the range of options and programs available. For example, job announcements and application forms, if posted on an accessible website, would be available to people with disabilities 24 hours a day, 7 days a week.

This document seems to support the OCR standard for evaluating what constitutes "effective communication" as applied to web accessibility.

To summarize, IDEA, Section 504 and Title II of the ADA do not mandate that schools implement accessible IT. These three federal disability rights laws do allow opportunities for advocating for accessible IT in education, but they are not easy ways to achieve this goal. If the vision is to create accessible IT in education—to further the goals of inclusion, equality and independence—then other strategies are probably more efficient. One such strategy is to write and implement policy on accessible IT. While educational institutions do not write legislation or regulations, they do write and implement policies, or rules, that have been formally adopted.

Accessible IT Policy Development and Implementation

The impetus to develop an IT policy may come in response to directives from top administration (federal, state or local government) or may be in response to grass roots demand (teachers, parents, students, or community members). In the best case scenario, accessible IT policy in education is some combination of government policy and institutional response from various levels, resulting in the "top down" and "bottom up" strategy that is most conducive to systemic change (Fullan, 1994). Regardless of the source of the policy, effective IT policies exhibit a common set of essential characteristics that reflect the values of inclusiveness and full participation held in common with a social model of disability (Silverstein, 2000; Shalock, 2004). These characteristics are essential to genuine, effective and meaningful access to information technology in a world in which access to IT is increasingly the norm (Yukins, 2004).

We now discuss these characteristics of effective IT policy within the context of the development and implementation phases of the policy.

Policy Development

IT policy must be inclusive, both in populations and in the technology addressed in the policy. During the policy development phase, all stakeholders, including students, parents, community members, employees with disabilities, web developers, those who train faculty and staff to develop webpages, IT support staff, procurement staff and administrators, should be consulted and actively involved in the process. Southwest Missouri State University is an example of a higher education institution that used focus groups to gather input from stakeholders and develop its web accessibility policy.

An effective policy clearly states a commitment to accessibility. The state of Arkansas, for example, states that, "The goals of the state in obtaining and deploying the most advanced forms of information technology properly include universal access so that segments of society with particular needs, including, but not limited to, individuals unable to use visual displays, will not be left out of the information age" (Arkansas Code).

In addition, effective IT policies:

- *Clearly identify the groups of people with disabilities covered by the policy.*
- *State the type(s) of technology covered by the policy.* For example, North Carolina defines IT as: "...electronic data processing goods and services, telecommunications goods and services, security goods and services, microprocessors, software, information processing, office systems, any services related to the foregoing, and consulting or other services for design or redesign of information technology supporting business processes" (North Carolina General Statutes). Note that this policy indicates the types of technology covered in general terms—e.g., "telecommunications goods and services." This allows the policy to cover rapid changes in technology without the need for frequent revisions.
- *Identify which entities are covered.* For example, in some states, educational entities are exempt from the policy. In others, only community colleges or four year state universities are covered by the policy. It is rare to see K–12 public schools included in state IT policies.

- *Identify the standards to be met, how compliance will be measured, and by whom.* Typically, state policies use either World Wide Web Consortium's Web Content Accessibility Guidelines (e.g., New York, North Carolina) or Section 508 (Kentucky). Policies at the educational institution level also typically use these standards.
- *Address how resources will be provided for the necessary training and support.*

Policy Implementation

As we stated earlier, there is no federal legally mandated access to IT in schools. Although the power to create change is limited due to the lack of a clear mandate, teachers, social workers, and social service providers, the "street level bureaucrats" (Lipsky, 1980) have considerable leeway in implementing IT policies developed at the federal, state and local levels. We suggest several things for educators to consider in their school or classroom.

1. *Develop an accessible website for your classroom or school.* Determine if your current website is accessible by using a combination of automated web accessibility evaluation and repair software tools and a Section 508 checklist.
2. *Use accessible file formats.* We often use various file formats on our classroom website to make the content more interesting and interactive for students. However, some formats are not accessible to disabled students—e.g., students who use screen readers or screen magnification.
3. *Advocate for the purchase of accessible software.* Work with school district staff and your school board to purchase accessible software. Creating accessible IT environments requires system-wide effort. To achieve the best outcomes, accessibility needs to be addressed at the procurement level, and, as stated above, needs to include all types of information technology, and to cover people with all types of disabilities.

Conclusion

Neil Selwyn and others have written convincingly that the "new computer and telecommunications technologies will transform countries into 'knowledge economies' and 'network societies'" (Selwyn, 2004, p. 342).

However, it appears that "there is considerable evidence of a so-called digital divide, namely, a growing disparity between those individuals and communities that have and those that do not have easy access to new information technologies" (Selwyn, 2001, p. 261). There are a plethora of reasons that some individuals may choose not to participate in the technological revolution, but for most individuals it is not a choice—rather they are economically and/or technologically unable to participate. Lack of participation in or exposure to technology appears to affect access to educational opportunities (Selwyn, 2001, p. 261) and therefore continues the cycle of exclusion.

Although there needs to be a great deal more research into the benefits and negative consequences of the rapid transformation of our educational systems through the adaptation of technology, it remains the case that at the beginning of the twenty first century, the ability to access technology is a requirement for full participation in American society. Although disabled individuals are increasingly accessing the "regular" education environment, if education is increasingly technology based, there is a real possibility that inability to access the technology will prevent inclusion. The goal should be to create one IT system that allows access for all students—disabled or not. The only way to achieve this is through the development of accessible IT systems which will ensure that the barriers to full participation are minimized or possibly eliminated. There is no federal law that currently requires that educational institutions create an accessible IT system, although the federal laws do require that individuals have access to the information. This access is typically provided through reasonable accommodations or modifications to the existing IT system. Until the federal laws change to mandate that schools provide accessible IT systems—or state laws are developed to do so—the authors encourage educational institutions to take the opportunity to demonstrate commitments to equality and inclusion of disabled individuals through adoption of accessible IT policies.

References

1998 Amendment to Section 508 of the Rehabilitation Act. (1998). Retrieved March 25, 2005, from http://www.section508.gov/index.cfm?FuseAction=ContentandID=14.

Alpert, D. and Rich, R.F. (2001, Fall). The Information Revolution: Implications for higher education policy. *U. Ill. Journal of Law, Technology and Policy, 291.*

Americans with Disabilities Act of 1990 §202, 42 U.S.C. S12132 (1994).

Arkansas Code (Non–annotated). Title 25. State Government. Chapter 26. Information Technology. Subchapter 2. Information Technology Access for the Blind. 25–26–201. Findings and policy.

Assistive Technology Act of 2004, Pub. L. No. 108–364, S118 Stat.1707 (2004).

Baker, P., and Bellordre, C. (2004). Adoption of information and communication technologies: key policy issues, barriers and opportunities for people with disabilities. *Proceedings of the 37th Annual Hawaii International Conference on System Sciences*, 127–136.

Davis, J., Kendall, T. and Meeks, H. (2002). The message is the message: designing information technology for inclusiveness and accessibility. *2002 International Symposium on Technology and Society,* 283–289.

Fullan, Michael J. (1994). Coordinating top–down and bottom–up strategies for educational reform. In Ronald J. Anson (Ed.), *Systemic reform: Perspectives on personalizing education.* Washington, DC: U.S. Department of Education.

Hawke, C.S., Jannarone, A.L. (2002, March 14). Emerging issues of web accessibility: Implications for higher education. *West's Education Law Reporter, 160,* 715–727.

Lipsky, M. (1980). *Street level bureaucracy: Dilemmas of the individual in public services.* New York: Russell Sage Foundation.

National Center on Accessible Information Technology (2002–2004). Retrieved March 25, 2005, from http://www.washington.edu/ accessit/index.php.

North Carolina General Statutes. State Officers. Article 3D. State Information Technology Services. Part 2. General Powers and Duties. Definitions. 147–33.81.

Office for Civil Rights (1996). *OCR docket number 09–95–2206.RES.* Retrieved March 25, 2005, from http://uwctds.washington.edu/policy/09952206.RES.htm.

———. (1997). *OCR docket number 09–97–2002.RES.* Retrieved March 25,2005,from http://uwctds.washington.edu/policy/09972002.RES.htm.

———. (2002). *Web Access Considerations under Section 504 and Title II.* Retrieved March 25, 2005, from http://uwctds.washington.edu/ocr_slides/.

Rehabilitation Act of 1973, as emended by S508, 29 U.S.C. S794d (1998).

Selwyn, N. (2001, May). Digital divide or digital opportunity? The role of technology in coming social exclusion in US education. *Educational Policy, 15,* 261.

———. (2004). Reconsidering political and popular understandings of the digital divide. *New Media and Society, 6,* 341–362.

Shalock, Robert L. (2004). The emerging disability paradigm and its implications for policy and practice. *Journal of Disability Policy Studies, 14(4),* 204–212.

Silverstein, R. (2000). Emerging Disability Policy Framework: A guidepost for analyzing public policy. Retrieved March 24, 2005, from http://www.communityinclusion.org/publications/policydocs/lawreview. doc

The State of the Union for Americans with Disabilities 2004 (2004). Retrieved March 25, 2005, from http://www.nod.org/index.cfm? fuseaction=page.viewPageandpageID=1430andnodeID=1andFeatureID=1244a ndredirected=1andCFID=1764309andCFTOKEN=82316540.

Title II of the Americans with Disabilities Act of 1990; 28 C.F.R. S35.130(b).

———. 28 C.F.R. S35.130(d).

———. 28 C.F.R. S35.160(b)(2).

Tyler v. City of Manhattan, 857 F.Supp. 800 (D.Kan.1994).

U.S. Department of Justice (2003). *Accessibility of state and local government websites to people with disabilities.* Retrieved March 25, 2005, from http://www.usdoj.gov/crt/ada/websites2.htm.

Yukins, C.R. (2004). Making federal information technology accessible: A case study in social policy and procurement. *Public Contract Law Journal, 34,* 668–819.

Note

(1) The distinction between Assistive Technology (AT) and Information Technology (IT) is important. AT includes both devices and services that allow individuals to accomplish daily living and to improve access to education, employment, and recreation. Students and employees with disabilities use a wide variety of AT devices and services, for a wide range of tasks, including those related to information technology. Accessible Information Technology (IT) is IT that meets specific technical standards. The technical standards are typically designed to make the technology usable by all people, including those with different types of disabilities and those who use AT.

This essay was supported in part by funding from the National Institute on Disability Rehabilitation Research (NIDRR), and much of the legal content has been published in various web-based publications written by Dr. Sharan Brown. Nothing in this essay is intended to provide legal advice regarding an educational institution's obligations towards a particular disabled student, employee or other individual. The authors would like to express their appreciation for the excellent research help from Nina Lang, Research Assistant with the Center on Technology and Disability Studies (CTDS), University of Washington.

CHAPTER 15

A Look at the Way We Look at Disability

Linda Ware

The question, *Why teach disability studies in education?* has surfaced at least once each semester throughout the nearly ten years I have integrated disability studies content in my education courses.[1] Whether early into the planning for a course, or during my teaching, this question emerged—notably at the points when the course content prompted collision, confrontation, and consternation. Although each semester culminated with affirming insights all around, along the way, the arc of the curriculum seemed difficult to plot—sometimes challenging students and me to stay the course.

As a professor of special education and one who is critical of traditional special education, my courses aimed to expose the mythology of "special" in education (Ware, 2004). Students read critical scholarship rather than the regulation textbooks, introducing that which I have described as "critical" special education scholars (Ware, 2001, 2004, 2006), and American critics recently characterized as special education's "dissenting voices" (Gallagher, 2004). In the past students in my classes have been awestruck by the depth and breadth of this criticism of special education, but the reaction was far from uniform in my classes. While many students began to rethink their practice informed by this critique, others voiced a clear crisis of confidence implicated by this critique that seemed to rob them of their claims to professionalism (Weatherly, 1979 for a more detailed analysis of professional claims).

Although Gallagher has suggested a return to the battle site of the "empiricism versus relativism" debate in pursuit of a resolution that might somehow put to rest the political division in special education. I suggest otherwise. Without a doubt, I agree with Gallagher that we need to enlarge the conversation among special educators across multiple perspectives; that we turn away from the mandate for training and towards the "development of intellectual autonomy" (371); however, as I have argued elsewhere, humanities-based disability studies literature provides a way to move beyond the traditional reductionist understandings of disability espoused in the special education literature. This literature invites wholly new ways to imagine disability as it authorizes accounts of the lived experience typically excised by special education research and scholarship. As evidenced by this chapter, I argue that disability studies literature engages educators in such a way as to render the "empiricism versus relativism" debate obsolete. Could it be as simple as re-examining how we "look at disability" rather than where we locate our claims to authorize our gaze? When I initially cast the question, "Dare we do disability studies?" (Ware, 2001), there was no doubt that efforts to launch this conversation among special educators would prove challenging. However, the conversations recently initiated with CCNY colleagues and our education students this chapter acknowledges the challenge as a worthy one to explore.

Informing the Conversation

The syllabi referenced here, while informed of prior teaching, remains a work in progress—an effort to integrate humanities scholarship (e.g., Davis, 1995; Thomson, 2002; Seibers, 2004); educational and curriculum theorists who extend and integrate disability studies content (Baker, 1999, 2000, 2002; Biklen, 2002; Erevelles, 2000,2002); and those who author insider accounts (Finger, 1990; Grealy, 1994; Grandin, 1995); fiction (Haddon, 2003; Stewart, 1989) and film (documentary and general audience) and other media (Beyond Affliction). In addition, classroom-based research that has the dual focus of informing awareness of disability studies scholarship and developing curriculum that draws on this content is also included (Ware, 2001). Students shape the syllabus by culling the media for disability-related content relative to both special education and disability issues. Recent contributions from the New York Times included: "The Lessons from Room 506" (Belkin, 2004)—an essay on classroom inclusion spearheaded by a father; "How About Not Curing Us? (Harmon, 2004)—one segment in a six part series on autism; and "Transported" (Linton, 2004)—an essay on public transportation in New York City sharply contrasted to, "On the Bus, Going Round and Round" (Hartocolis, 2004)—an article on parent concerns about school transportation issues in Manhattan. Current film reviews often underscored issues considered in class in both trite and surprising ways.[2]

This multi-perspectival approach to understanding disability included lectures, films, and performances assigned on an impromptu basis throughout the semester. For example, last spring the CUNY Graduate Center sponsored a panel with John Hockenberry, Leonard Kriegel, Stephen Kuusisto, and Achim Nowak—contributors in *Voices from the Edge: Narratives about Americans with Disabilities Act* (O'Brien, 2004). The Graduate Center also collaborated with the Center for Lesbian and Gay Studies (CLAGS) to host a film series exploring the intersections of queerness and disability that included *Self Preservation: The Art of Riva Lehrer* (Snyder and Mitchell, 2004). The Disability Studies Lecture Series at Columbia University included presentations by well-known disability studies activists and scholars: Michael Berube, Rosemarie Garland Thomson, Simi Linton, David T. Mitchell and Sharon L. Snyder, Harilynn Russo and Sue Schweick. Finally, a broad offering of current films served as supplemental texts throughout the semester (i.e., *Oasis, Garden State, The Sea Inside, The Keys to the House*).[3]

Taken together, our texts were multiple and varied in a purposeful effort to enlarge the discursive community that informs educators' understandings of disability. Elsewhere I have suggested that if teacher preparation coursework remains restricted to reductionist and technicist approaches exclusively, misunderstanding the lived experience is sure to follow (Ware, 2001). This chapter will consider conversations among students culled from two courses: (1) *Severe Disabilities*, a fifteen week course in the Inclusion Masters Program that enrolls both elementary and secondary special educators and leads to state certification in special education; and (2) *Issues for Secondary School Teachers: Special Education, Second Language Acquisition and Literacy,* a required course for secondary general educators who have just begun their education masters in math, science, social studies, art or English. The course is divided into three five-week components each of which is taught by CCNY faculty from Special Education, Literacy, and English as a Second Language.[4] Because this chapter draws so extensively from the work of CCNY students, what follows is a bit of background.

CCNY Students: An Introduction

The Winged Energy of Delight, Robert Bly's latest work of poetry translations, characterizes the poems of the Swedish Poet, Tomas Tranströmer as:

> [A] sort of railway station where trains that have come enormous distances to stand briefly in the same building. One train may have some Russian snow still lying on the undercarriage, and another may have Mediterranean flowers still fresh in the compartments, and Ruhr soot on the roofs. The poems are mysterious because of the distance the images have come to get there (1).

This imagery serves well to introduce the students enrolled in education at CCNY, one of the most culturally diverse campuses in the CUNY system. A colleague, Amita Gupta (2005) has reported that in a recent class of twenty-five education students, twenty-two were non-native English speakers. Students in my classes have immigrated from Africa, Argentina, Austria, Bangladesh, Canada, Dominican Republic, France, Haiti, Hong Kong, Mexico, Pakistan, Poland, Puerto Rico, Russia, and the United Kingdom. In addition, the classes included recent arrivals from California, Maryland, New Jersey, North Carolina, Ohio, Oregon, Pennsylvania, and Vermont, joining those who made their way across the 5 boroughs that constitute New York City. Unlike many American universities that market diversity as "product-placement" in glossy brochures and in billboard advertisements, diversity at CCNY informs our course offerings and curriculum. Among CCNY faculty, there is overwhelming consensus that in the instance of theories of oppression, power, and injustice in education, in particular, and society in general, our students are quick to "get it." Research by CCNY faculty suggests that much remains to be mined from the experience of minority educators teaching in urban contexts (Malone et al., 2005).

It is not my intent to rhapsodize the merits of cultural diversity per se, rather, I suggest that the diversity of experience and the subsequent interpretation of the assigned material enriched the exchange among students both in and out of class. The resulting conversation was further broadened by an existing cultural consciousness that cohered to produce a critical cultural perspective—that which I hold is essential for shifting from a clinical to a social/cultural model of disability. Certainly, the baggage of reductionism and its reliance on analytical and detached thinking was evident among students in early class discussions. However, the conversation that prevailed addressed issues and concerns relative to a common and shared humanity voiced across the "enormous distances" CCNY students expressed in their engagement with disability studies content. The conversation was less about taking sides as if in a debate, rather theirs was a conversation open to understanding and excavation of the complexity, chaos, and ambiguity that can accompany disability related issues and concerns.

Disability Studies: An Introduction in Two Courses
Severe Disabilities

Severe Disabilities began neither with a review of the syllabus nor with delineation of course requirements and other such conventions common to first night course introductions. Instead, the syllabus was issued with the promise that we would review it the following week so as to afford ample time to screen the award winning documentary film, *Face-to-Face: The Schappell Twins* (1999). The assignment was to take "good" notes as this documentary film figures into our assignments throughout the semester. The film follows the day-to day experiences of Reba and Laurie Schappell, conjoined twins who at the age of four were placed by their family in a New Jersey institution where they resided for over three decades. Through an effective filmic device, Reba and Laurie are introduced through the public gaze cast upon them as they navigate the streets of New York City. The voice over of public reaction to the twins conveys a mix of concern, curiosity, confusion, and a "purely scientific" response: one tourist justifies his intrusive demeanor with the claim, "I'm a dentist—I'm accustomed to human oddity." Interestingly, the twins return the "gaze" through their own videotaping of many of those who videotaped them. While the film leaves many critical aspects of living with disability unaddressed, it provides richly educative insights as noted by one student in his final paper:

> The film portrays a unique story of two sisters facing countless challenges in the world . . . it is a story of hope, dreams, faith . . . . a remarkable and ingenious vehicle to reflect how society views disability.[5]

Although some readers might find Gus's comments problematic, his transformation during the course was noteworthy. In an early conversation based on the homework assignment, "describe the public response that best captures your own reaction to the twins," Gus surprised his peers when he sided with the dentist and maintained that in reality, the twins' lives could amount to no more than medical curiosity. Many in class roundly challenged this view and offered a perspective informed by the meanings they brought to the class relative to disability. Many prefaced their response with the tag, "in my country disabled people" which then preceded an array of "would never" responses, including:

> In my country, disabled people like Lori and Reba would:
> . . . never be left by their families in an institution. . . . never be allowed to leave the institution.
> . . . never enjoy such independence.
> . . . never be allowed to live.

Lenny, who recently emigrated from Moscow noted:

> I was shocked the first time I saw a kneeling bus. In my country there aren't any ramps in public places, special restrooms, or motorized wheelchairs, disabled people in Moscow could not even dream about all the services I see everyday in New York.[6]

Because the classes were structured to promote critical conversation, the points made by Lenny and the others served as prompts to consider macro and micro economic and social cultural concerns. Problematizing disability was thus positioned against a broad backdrop that depicted special education as a concern of schooling when in reality, disability concerns extended beyond school-based concerns.

Claims for the "Authorized" Gaze

The film provoked tensions associated with the inevitable "stare" and its interplay with the more naive or benign practice of "looking" as many tried to tease out the differences. One student argued that by virtue of our profession and given that the twins chose to go "public" with their lives, ours was an "authorized gaze"—"invited but not intrusive." Others took immediate offense with this view of disability as spectacle—and yet none could honestly claim that they would avoid a second glance at the twins. In an effort to broaden the conversation I provided theoretical insights from the field of visual culture relative to images, representations and identity. Borrowing from the introductory text, *Practices of Looking: An Introduction to Visual Culture* by Marita Sturken and Lisa Cartwright (2001) we discussed the importance of visual representations and the images that endure in a culture. Specific to disability, the work of Rosemarie Garland Thomson's (2002) visual rhetorics for consideration of the images of disability inspired the following questions: *Does this film sensationalize disability? Does this film suggest sentimentality? Does the film characterize the twins' lives as an overcoming narrative?* From these analyses the question of culture was introduced, framed by Stuart Hall (1997) who suggests:

> It is the participants in a culture who give meaning to people, objects, and events…It is by our use of things, and what we say, think and feel about them—how we represent them—that we give them a meaning (p. 3).

How do you define severe disability?

The second written assignment was designed to build on the previous class conversation when students were asked to define severe disability. Some returned with textbook definitions, Internet references, material from their own students' individual education plans, and a few discussed vexed and multiple meanings prompted by the film and our discussions. The activity served to have the students attempt definitions in their own words, but the conversation that followed underscored the multiple ways to define this previously unproblematized term. Throughout the semester, students willingly revisited their initial definitions as in the example below.

> At the beginning of this class, the question of "What is a severe disability?" was raised. I responded with a textbook answer. This answer was one that I had been taught; yet, I had not previously taken the time or had the knowledge to think about it critically. I simply stated that a severe disability is a disability that limits the functioning of an individual in daily life to a significant level and raises concern in three main areas: access to meaningful activities, equity of education, and/or quality of education. The severity of a disability is determined by the 'norm' and how close a person is to it. Soon thereafter questions and ideologies that came up in class about the severity of a disability made me realize that my answer was completely contrived—influenced by society in order to rationalize average and normal—"the problem is the way that normalcy is constructed to create the 'problem' of the disabled person" (Davis, 1995, p. 22)[7]

Kim, like many in the class, chiseled away the rigid limits of reductionist understanding disability in schools and society. Described by Heshusius as an "inevitable struggle with the self" (2004), Kim came to recognize her own complicity as well as her volition in the meaning-making scheme that drives disability as pathology and fundamentally assumes biological rather than cultural understandings. She elaborated on this to say:

I thought that if an individual was unable to do the exact things that I felt were important, that he/she was missing out. After meeting the Schappell sisters and reading the McBryde-Johnson article, *Unspeakable Conversations*, I realized that simply because I enjoy an activity, the way that my body and mind allows, does not mean that someone else's activity is less fulfilling. McBryde-Johnson describes herself on the beach as a small child. Even though she didn't walk, run, or stand on the beach like the other children, she enjoyed herself just the same.

Shifting her concerns to her classroom, Kim described how the larger system constructed her students as failures to ensure their continued placement in a 'specialized school in a specialized class.[8] This shift to interrogate the structures that underwrite the cultural interpretations assigned to disabled people was common to those students who reported a changed view on disability. The impulse to act, to take action informed by a growing disability studies perspective soon followed for many who considered changes at the level of their own practice.

It's not enough for me to know this

Teaching disability studies in education leaves some uncertainty about how students will "apply" the content to teaching. Elsewhere I have described the application of the content as well as the perspective by teachers, and once more I found that CCNY students are far from conflicted about the application of this content into their practice. The students connect the dots that lead to change in practice for a variety of reasons, key among them their engagement with the disabled people they meet in class through richly rendered first person narratives quite unlike the case study approach common to education and social work. The texts made a lasting impression, as did the individuals they met, cited by their names and their words, readily linked to theoretical readings that in turn, informed their practice. For Maura, a social worker planning a move to education, it was easy to see the injustice common to both schools and society:

We often think that people with disabilities need to change their behavior and their approach to life. Social workers, psychologists, and teachers often speak of making people with disabilities ready for inclusion in society as if somehow they were not born into "our" society. We assume the power to include. Society focuses too much on how to change people with disabilities and not on how to change society's view of disability.[9]

Like Kim, Maura was enrolled in other CCNY classes with faculty who also integrated disability studies content into their teaching.[10] She soon wondered whether a move to education would be any less troubling than social work her frustration was obvious. Although her early concerns focused on society's misunderstanding of disability, a more personal inquiry emerged one class meeting when she declared, *"It's not enough for me to know this."* Her final class project included excerpts from interviews in which she discussed disability identity with clients on her caseload as Maura realized that her clients looked more like the forms she was asked to complete and not so much as the individuals she knew. Her interview protocol asked clients to identify their disability and their age when first diagnosed. Then she turned to more open-ended questions including: "Do you consider yourself to be a disabled person?" "What does it mean to you to be disabled?" "How do you think other people feel about your disability?"

Maura's final analysis borrowed from Eli Clare, David Mitchell and Sharon Snyder, Simi Linton, Lennard Davis, and the remarks of Peter Singer as considered by Harriet McBryde-Johnson (2003). Each underscored her take-home point, vigilant and continuous reflection on the ethics that inform professional practice. Informed by disability studies content, her understanding of her clients extended beyond the frame of medical or psychological understanding.

"There's a call and response"

Ben, a middle school English teacher who resides in the Bronx and teaches in one of the newly restructured small schools, enrolled with his colleague, the school's special education teacher. They were assigned the additional duty of planning their school's inservice days that they had hoped would focus on inclusion. They soon realized how complicated this task might prove in the absence of a more profound engagement with the faculty on disability as presented in class. Ben's growing appreciation of the nuanced lives of disabled people as presented in class increasingly impacted more than his teaching. As one half of the free-jazz duo, "Fire and Flux," Ben composed, *"You think I'm drowning but I know this is how I swim,"* inspired by *The Body's Memory*, a disability-related novel by Jean Stewart (1989). Ben borrowed this line from the disability activist, Paul Longmore who discussed the novel in the Golfus and Simpson documentary (1994). In the final class meeting "Fire and Flux" performed this composition and responded to our questions about the performance.

On the meaning of the music, in general:

> Free-jazz takes its original inspiration from multiple sources including the Civil Rights movement and because frustration, political struggle and contestation make up much of the mood of the music—it has been shunned and marginalized to loft spaces and the rare club engagement. This is a paradox, because the music's volatility and explosiveness was simultaneously the very expression of joy and the freedom that people were fighting for. What seems to violate the basic rules for listening to and for making music, is actually, from the standpoint of this music, empowering and enabling.

On the composition, in particular:

> Yes, the music is angry and chaotic sounding . . . some of our songs are about things we're angry about . . . but the dominant expression of the song is one of joy, the music is how we swim.

On the process:

> There's 'call and response' between us . . . the sound of a 'community of people engaged in a conversation in a language that no one else knows but that everyone can learn in a response to the call.'[11]

A call, a response, a community engaged in a language that no one else knows—because they have yet to learn a response, to hear the call—was apropos of everything I hoped the students would obtain. Certainly, my brief account of this fifteen-week course risks diminishing the impact of any one of these students' perspectives; however due to the limitations of space, I will move on to the conversation among the general educators.

Issues for Secondary School Teachers: Special Education, Second Language Acquisition and Literacy

Given the constraints of a five-week timeframe for *Issues for Secondary School Teachers* four readings and two documentary films formed the core content (marked with asterisks in the references). I began with an abbreviated critique of traditional special education augmented by "Special Education" (Ware and Allan, 2006). This was followed by an overview of disability studies that introduced the concept of "ableism" Linton (1998), defined as the privilege and assumed access by able-bodied and able-minded people. This frame informed the subsequent conversation on privilege and abelist assumptions that drive K–12 practice in both general and special education. One student characterized the intent of the class as a way to encourage new teachers to "express [a] willingness to serve all students and not balk at the suggestion of having special education students in my class".[12] A few class activities are outlined below in an effort to address the relevance of teaching disability studies to general educators.

Early disability memories

The first in class writing assignment considered the prompt: *recall your earliest memory of disability.* Responses included: personal experiences with siblings and relatives including those "aging" into disability; neighbors who returned home from special schools during the holidays, classmates they "sort of knew"—seen from a safe distance in school and some recalled their own "temporary" disability status following accidents from which they eventually recovered. Again, diversity informed their memories that were shared in small groups and invoked an exchange on the social construction of disability and the value of a humanities approach to understanding disability. That is, because few relied on medical or psychological language in their narratives, the absence of labels and deficit language was clear: their word choice afforded a more intimate, more humane narrative. Later in the semester, after reviewing sample special education documents, the contrastive language was obvious, especially in review of sample Individualized Education Programs (IEPs). As a culminating project students wrote anecdotal descriptions of students in a compare/contrast writing format framed as intimate/subjective or disengaged/objective representations. In preparation for this activity, samples from both fiction and nonfiction works were excerpted (e.g., Diaz, 1996; Ferris, 2004; Grealy, 1994; Haddon, 2003).

How we look at disability in schools

Students reviewed documents from the New York City Board of Education including definitions of disability categories and a delineation of the continuum of service. The document review was contrasted to the previous class conversation, as each typified the medical, clinical approach to understanding disability in educational settings. As general educators, few were familiar with these documents, within minutes they questioned how the categories were created, who was authorized to label, how the need for services was determined, and what role students had in the placement process. Educators with prior knowledge contributed their insights as we explained how the system is "supposed" to work. With examples from city schools, neighboring regions, and those with prior experience outside the state, it was evident that regardless of federal law, luck, geography, and the socioeconomic status of parents trumped the mandates to ensure a child's success in special education. Moreover, that the same variables held for success in general education served to remind us that the long-standing political battles in education were far from resolved. For these general educators new to the profession, recurring threads relative to both the myth of special education and the social construction of disability sharpened their consciousness of the complexity, chaos, and ambiguity that can accompany disability related issues and concerns.

To be sure, it is no easy task to challenge traditional special education knowledge unwittingly absorbed by novice and experienced teachers alike. In this instance, because the students remained open to confronting previously unexamined assumptions about special education in general and disability in particular, they risked powerful personal insights as in the example below:

> I have been teaching for 5 years and I have heard so many negative comments about "the inclusion students"... many students I've had myself. I must admit that I never extended a hand to go an extra mile for them. I usually let them be, saying I should treat them the same as everyone else, but knowing that they needed extra help. I assumed that the paraprofessionals extended the extra help they were supposed to get.[13]

Yecenia's comments were prompted by an article that outlined alternative approaches to literacy (Kleiwer and Biklen, 2001); however for many students, it was the authors' call for greater involvement of general educators in the education of disabled students that hooked them. These conversations were left purposefully unresolved: no absolution rendered, no claims for quick "fix" reform, and no "skills set" proffered as a means to embrace inclusion.

The documentary films

In both the films I screen the students met disabled people as human beings with their complexity intact—living richly textured lives that could greatly inform the curriculum regardless of the content area. *Self Preserva-*

tion: The Art of Riva Lehrer was particularly compelling for students who were awestruck by Riva's painting style and her insider knowledge of living with disability, making it suitable on many levels for classroom use. An in-class writing activity required the students to write a response to one self-selected excerpt from the film. Most responded to the following comment by poet and essayist Eli Clare:

> When you see disabled people in medical and scientific works, they often appear with their eyes blacked out. One thinks the eyes are blacked out on purpose. I suspect the blacking out of the eyes is on purpose to keep the disabled person from looking back, it keeps them less than human.– Eli Clare

On an overhead transparency, I borrowed an excerpt from Ben's response to help students analyze his thoughts in comparison to their own.

> This quote speaks to the way that disabled people are objectified. If they are only looked at and can never look back then they are not participating in any exchange.

> The photos Clare is talking about reinforce the idea that disabled people are to be observed, studied, written about (perhaps), but not interacted with. If disabled people are considered at all it's only in these ways, a way in which they have no voice, are purposefully excluded and as a consequence dehumanized.

The documentary succeeds on many levels to enrich understanding disability through a cultural lens as the comments from the undergraduate class suggest:[14] Given the constraints of time the theoretical insights of Stuart Hall and Rosemarie Garland Thomson (see earlier discussion) are then introduced as the course nears completion. With less time to consider a more careful integration of these analyses, it was clear, that like the students in the Severe Disabilities class, these educators possessed a formidable critique that was strengthened by the course content—evidenced by both Niculina and Mitch in the excerpts that follow. Niculina recounts:

> Here, in North American social and political contexts, one form of behavior is clearly privileged over the other, depending on a host of conditions. Not only is there a tremendous difference in the perceived level of discrimination faced by people with disabilities, but there is also wide disagreement on where discrimination is the greatest, whether it be associated with employment, education, housing, access to public places and events, or transportation.[15]

For Mitch,[16] issues of independence seemed to be the "flashpoint for the multitude of issues regarding the politics of disability." He found the curriculum lacking meaningful promotion of life-long independence on a "quality scale" similar that depicted in the documentary films. Mitch began curriculum explorations for his advisory students to address effective communication skills as he found many characters in the films as "highly effective communicators." Like many of his classmates, he reworked his definition of independence as one not easily plotted over a lifetime. He would then understand that disabled people were not easily reduced to a collective body with uniform desires, demands, abilities, and needs.

Conclusion

For many students, the readings provided not only fresh insights on disability but invited wholly unconsidered questions about their understanding of disability. Students reported a rethinking of their interactions with disabled people as well as their students. Informed by a disability studies perspective, they found multiple ways to consider disability in education as more than student pathology, and more significantly, they fully grasped the meaning of institutional abelism (Beratan, 2006). The IEP, the instructional strategies, the mechanisms for testing and labeling children, as well as the labels themselves, the training of professionals, the growth of the professions, the pathology of the organization—and more, were all carefully reconsidered in ways that ultimately challenged the epistemic determinacy of disability as a category. What to make then, of a recurring comment in the student evaluations of the course, "After this course, I'll never look at disability in the same way."

References

Baker, B. (1999). . Disabling methodologies. *Pedagogy, Culture & Society*, 7 (1), 91–115.

_____. (2000). The hunt for disability: The New Eugenics and the normalization of school children. *Teachers College Record, 104* (4), 663–703.

_____. (2002). Disorganizing educational tropes: Conceptions of dis/ability and curriculum, *Journal of Curriculum Theorizing*. Winter, 47–79.

Barton, L. and Tomlinson, S. (eds) (1984). *Special education and social interests*. London: Croom Helm.

Baynton, Douglas, C. (2001). "Disability and the justification of inequality in American history." *The New Disability History: American Perspectives.* Paul K. Longmore and Lauri Umansky (Eds.), New York: NYU Press, p. 52.

Belkin, L. (September 12, 2004) The lessons of classroom 506. New York Times Magazine.

Beratan, G. (2006). Institutionalizing inequality: Abelism, Racism and IDEA 2004. *Disability Studies Quarterly,* *26* (2). Available on line at www.dsq–sds.org.

Biklen, D. (2002). Constructing inclusion: Lessons from critical disability narratives. *International Journal of Inclusive Education*, 4 (4), 337–353.

Davis, L. J. (1995). *Constructing normalcy: Disability, deafness and the body.* New York and London: Verso.

Diaz, J. (1996). *Drown.* New York: Riverhead, 1996.

Erevelles, N. (2000). Educating unruly bodies: Critical pedagogy, disability studies and the politics of schooling. *Educational Theory*, 50 (1), 25–47.

_____. (2002). (Im)material citizens: Cognitive disability, race, and the politics of citizenship. *Disability Culture, and Education* 1(1), 5–25.

Ferris, J. (2004) *The hospital poems.* Charlotte, NC: Main Street Rag.

Finger, A. (1990). *Past due: A story of disability, pregnancy, and birth.* Seattle: Seal.

Gallagher, D. et.al. (2004). *Challenging orthodoxy in special education: Dissenting Voices.* Denver: Love Publishing Company.

Golfus, B. and Simpson, D. E. (Producers). (1994). *When Billy broke his head... and other tales of wonder* [Film]. (Available from Fanlight Productions: www.fanlight.com).

Grealy, L. (1994). *Autobiography of a face.* Boston: Houghton Mifflin.

Haddon, Mark (2003). *The curious incident of the dog in the night time.* New York: Doubleday.

Hall, S. (1997). *Representation: Cultural representations and signifying Practices.* Thousand Oaks, CA: Sage.

Harmon, A. (December, 20, 2004) How about not curing us, some autistics are pleading. *New York Times Magazine.*

Hartcolis, A. (December 3, 2004). On the bus going round and round: Parents protest treatment of special education students. *New York Times*, Sec. B, p. 1, col. 2.

Heshusius, L. (2004). Special education knowledges: The inevitable struggle with the self. In L.Ware (Ed.). *Ideology and the politics of (in)exclusion* (143–165). New York: Peter Lang.

Kliewer, C. and Biklen, D. (2001). 'School's not really a place for reading': A research synthesis of the literate lives of students with severe disabilities. *JASH*, 26, 1, 1–12.

Linton, S. (1998). *Claiming disability: Knowledge and identity*. New York: NYU Press.

Linton, S. (November, 28, 2004) Transported. *New York Times*.

Malone, C., Wilgus, G., Franklin, C., Gupta, A., and Garavuso, V., (2005). Making changes, making knowledge: Living, learning and teaching together. Paper presented at American Educational Research Association. Montreal.

O'Brien, R. (2004) *Voices from the edge: Narratives about the Americans with Disabilities Act*. New York: Oxford University Press.

Seibers, T. (2004). Words stare like a glass eye: From literary to visual in disability studies and back again. *The Modern Language Association of America (PMLA)*, 119:5, 1315–1324.

Snyder, S. (Director) and Mitchell, D. (Producer) (2004). *Self Preservation: The Art of Riva Lehrer* [Film]. A Brace Yourselves Production.

Stewart, J. (1989) *The body's memory*. New York: St. Martin's Griffin.

Sturken, M. and Cartwright, L. (2001). *Practices of looking: An introduction to visual culture*. Oxford: Oxford University Press.

Thomson, R. G. (2002). The politics of staring: Visual rhetorics of disability. In S. L. Snyder, B. J. Brueggemann, and R. G. Thomson (Eds.) *Disability Studies: Enabling the Humanities* (pp. 56–76), New York: Modern Language Association of America.

Tomlinson S. (1982). *A sociology of special education*. London: Routledge and Kegan Paul.

———. (1996). Conflicts and dilemmas for professionals in special education. In C. Christensen and F. Rizvi (eds), *Disability and the dilemmas of education and justice* (pp.175–186). Philadelphia: Open University Press.

Ware, L. (2001). Writing, identity and the other: Dare we do disability studies?" *Journal of Teacher Education*, 52(3), 107–123.

———. (2004). The politics of ideology: A pedagogy of hope. In L. Ware (ed.), *Ideology and the politics of (in)exclusion*. New York: Peter Lang.

Ware, L. and Allan, J. (2006). Special education: The histories (entry). In G. A. Albrecht (ed.), *Encyclopedia on disability, IV* (pp. 1488–1492). Thousand Oaks, California: Sage..

Weatherly, R. (1979). *Reforming special education: Policy implementation from state level to street level.* Cambridge, MA: MIT Press.

Notes

[1] *Oasis*, 2004; *The Sea Inside*, Holden, 2004; *The Keys to the House*, Dargis, 2004)

[2] Both syllabi can be found at www.ccny.cuny.edu, however, this discussion will consider only those texts that can be accessed in areas outside New York City.

[3] Currently, secondary faculty is considering how to integrate disability-related content throughout the curriculum, as there is broad agreement that this five-week course merits expansion.

[4] Gus Benjumen, *Severe Disabilities*, 2004.

[5] Lenny Sigal, *Issues in Secondary Education*, 2004.

[5] Kim Smurdon, *Severe Disabilities*, 2004.

[6] Lenny Sigal, *Issues in Secondary Education*, 2004.

[7] Kim Smurdon, *Severe Disabilities*, 2004.

[8] A recent transplant to New York from Ohio, Kim teaches in District 75, the self-contained district in Manhattan designated exclusively for special education students.

[9] Maura Rosado, *Severe Disabilities*, 2004.

[10] Students increasingly cross-reference their coursework in the classes of Professor Maysaa Bazna, Gregg Beratan, Keri Levin , Ken Male, Ayn Male, Ellen Rice. Readers can access their syllabi at www.ccny.cuny.edu.

[11] Ben Kates, Severe Disabilities, 2004. The other half of the duo, Richard Gilman-Opalsky, was not enrolled in the class, but he was fully engaged in an outside of class conversation with Ben.

[12] Carolyn Sattin, *Issues for Secondary Teachers: Special Education, Second Language Acquisition and Literacy.* Fall 2004.

[13] Yecenia Delarosa, secondary science.

[14] The students cited in footnotes 14-16 were enrolled in the undergraduate class, the majority were less than three years past high school.

[15] Niculina Guruiana, secondary mathematics.

[16] Mitch Kurtz, secondary social studies.

CHAPTER 16

Teaching to Trouble

Beth A. Ferri

As a teacher educator with background in both disability studies and gender studies, I approach teacher education from a particular theoretical standpoint. Skeptical of traditional, medical model approaches to disability, early in my career I sought out other scholars within the emerging interdisciplinary field of disability studies to inform my work in education. Most of these colleagues were working either within the humanities or social sciences. More recently I discovered an engaged and exciting group of young scholars who share a commitment to infusing disability studies in educational contexts. My work in inclusive teacher education has been directly and indirectly influenced by my many encounters with these colleagues both within education and across the academy. In this chapter I seek to articulate some of the ways that a disability studies orientation has shifted the way I design teacher education courses. Because there are no "recipes" for creating a disability studies informed course, I offer my approach as simply one example. My hope is that my experience serves to open a conversation about the potential for disability studies to transform education. I conclude by sharing a range of student responses to disability studies grounded courses and reflecting on why I believe that disability studies is crucial for both general education and special education teachers.

Enter Disability Studies

The emergence of disability studies in the academy has created a new analytic space to examine disability and normalcy from a critical lens. Disability studies scholars illustrate how the "border" between ability/disability is constructed, artificial and arbitrary, yet made to appear natural and static across time and place through the interconnected and pathologizing diagnostic, medical, and legal discourses. Such discourses, many of which are hallmarks of applied fields such as special education and rehabilitation, reify the constructed boundaries between the "normative" and the "other." Once in place, these discourses further justify the exclusion, segregation and even the eradication of people with disabilities.

In disability studies scholars question the representations of disability in cultural products, in history, and in language, but also within current educational practices and disciplinary structures—because together these perceptions, representations, and practices create and maintain disability as the devalued other. As Thomson (1995) writes, "representation shapes the reality that it supposedly reflects" (p. 20). Therefore an interdisciplinary approach necessarily draws on multiple sites and contexts for its analysis of disability. As Linton (1998) contends, "Ultimately, disability studies can be most effective as an interdisciplinary field that can bring multiple perspectives to bear on the phenomenon of disability" (p. 125).

Contemporary writers in disability studies critique medicalized and deficit-based understandings of disability in favor of more sociopolitical approaches. Disability studies, like women's studies, necessarily merges analyses of power and knowledge. Thomson (1997a), for example, describes disability studies as identifying, examining, and questioning social and political practices that regulate and control the way we think about and through the body. She challenges the myth of the normative body and also draws connections between the category of disability and race, gender, and sexuality. Thomson (1995) envisions her pedagogical role as introducing complexity into the classroom by asking students to "consider how gender, class, and disability bisect racial groupings and to interrogate the very process of social categorization according to physiological or psychological characteristics" (p. 15). Vernon (1998) also argues that moving beyond a focus on disablement as a singular system of oppression to a more intersectional model is central to disability politics and research.

Mitchell and Snyder (1997) document the "pervasive cultural and artistic dependency" (p. 12) on the disabled body in literature and film. They show how disability functions as the embodied locus for alterity and marginality. Davis' (1997) work focuses on the construction of normativity which "by definition creates the abnormal, the Other, the disabled, the native, the colonized subject, and so on" (p. 22). Like Butler's (1991) contention that "Heterosexuality. . . presupposes homosexuality" (p. 313), Davis identifies how nomativity presupposes disability. Rather than simply a symbol of oppression, however, the disabled body has also been seen as opening up radical possibilities for transgressing norms and disrupting the status quo.

Enter Disability Studies in Education

Disability studies has wide-ranging influence across many academic fields of study including history, sociology, literature, cultural studies, philosophy, and rhetoric. Scholars in disability studies in education build on this tradition, working to critically examine disability as a constructed category, interconnected to all aspects of identity and culture. Although disability studies approaches differ, scholars identifying with this model share an important commonality: a rejection of deficit based approaches to understanding disability in favor of more social, political, or discursive understandings. In this way disability studies in education shares an affinity to other critical educational approaches, including multicultural education, critical pedagogy, and social justice education. Most importantly, however, disability studies in education offers important tools for critiquing traditional approaches to educational research, policy and practice. It also provides critical insights into contemporary debates in education, such as inclusion and the overrepresentation of students of color in special education. Moreover, disability studies in education offers scholars working across the academy an example of how to link critical theory to practice. In this paper I focus on the value of designing teacher education courses from a disability studies framework. Specifically, I discuss introductory courses in disability designed for general education and special education teachers, including those seeking dual certification in general and special education. Using student responses to these classes, I illustrate both the promises and the challenges of integrating disability studies in education.

(Re)Thinking Dis/ability and Inclusion

As someone whose work bridges disability and gender studies, I often find traditional approaches to teaching about disability and difference to be problematic and limiting. In an attempt to dislodge the medical/deficit model of disability, I typically frame my courses with several interrelated goals in mind. First, I seek to trouble rather than reify identity categories and expose the interconnectedness of issues of disability, race, class, gender, and sexuality. Second, through the use of autobiography, narrative, and even fiction, I aim to broaden and complicate students' ideas about sources of expertise about disability. Third, I seek to trouble students' taken-for-granted assumptions about disability by highlighting the constructedness of both ability and disability categories.

Dislodging dominant paradigms requires a critical rethinking of foundational assumptions. For example, many advocates of disability studies in education, myself included, identify as being pro-inclusion. Yet, because even in inclusive models the dominant group retains the power to include or exclude, inclusion in and of itself does not automatically dislodge the privilege maintained by the dominant group. As Spelman (1997) writes, inclusion entails "adding voices but not changing what has already been said" (p. 162–3).

Thus, a particular challenge in teaching inclusive education is not simply working to get disabled students in the door, but rather finding ways to encourage general education teachers to rethink their basic perceptions about who *their* students are. This often requires making students conscious of their working definition of student—and asking them to think about who their definition includes and excludes. For example, many general education teachers in inclusive settings still talk about "their" students as distinct from special education students who are supposedly included in their class. When describing their classroom they might say things like, "I have twenty seven students, plus three special education (or inclusion) students in my classroom this year." Thus, disabled students are physically included, but not conceptually included in the teacher's mind. True inclusion, therefore, requires more than physically adding disabled students, but rather a more foundational rethinking one's very definition of student.

Conceptual separation between identity categories is also fostered in many traditional approaches to teaching about difference. Chapters in special education introductory texts, for example, are almost always divided into disability categories. These books are designed to neatly fit into a semester, provided that you cover roughly one broad category per week. In introductory courses throughout the U.S., students (in both general and special education) first learn about various disabilities through descriptive "case" studies (a poster child approach to disability) that focus on how that week's particular group differs from the "normal" or typical student. There is no chapter on the "normate" student, nor any analysis of how this signifier came to be

(Thomson, 1997b). Instead, the norm—the typical, general, generic student—remains transparent, unexamined, and unnamed.

Likewise, little attention is paid to variations within any of the categories; individuals are not described as multiply-situated in terms of race, class, gender, sexuality, or other social markers. Although recent texts sometimes include a chapter on diversity or multiculturalism, these topics tend to be neatly contained within "special interest" chapters, not allowed to permeate the other disability-specific chapters. In other words, by hyperfocusing on disability, other differences and identities are often elided or relegated to the margins. Students are not encouraged to think about how social class or race, for example, radically changes how any disability is experienced. As Spelman (1988) argues, such texts ignore "How one form of oppression is experienced is influenced by and influences how another form [of oppression] is experienced" (p. 123).

Within disability studies, the case study has been linked to the medical model of disability and even to a modern-day form of the freak show (Thomson, 1997a). Connecting the objectifying gaze of the freakshow spectacle to the clinical gaze of the medical specimen, Thomson (1997) highlights the oppressive ideologies that undergird both practices. The case study, so ubiquitous in special education, highlights and exaggerates differences between groups of students and fails to question the constructedness of the normative center. Moreover, objectification, categorization, and containment all work together to justify exclusion, segregation, and social inequality of disabled people based on the supposed meritocracy of the "normal" (Erevelles, 2000). By essentializing and reducing disability, these approaches to difference fail to trouble ableism and society's investments in the fictional category of the "normal" student.

In *Learning to Divide the World*, Willinsky (1998) links related kinds of exhibition with the "colonial imagination," which is founded upon a voyeuristic relationship that fetishizes and exoticizes the other (p. 19). Knowing the other as object, as spectacle, can only be achieved by "keeping one's distance" (p. 81). By constructing and reinforcing boundaries between self and other, between margin and center, we are schooled in difference; and, in a distant relation to those differences, we define ourselves.

A particularly troubling way to keep one's distance is achieved through disability simulation, another common feature employed to teach non-disabled people about disability. In disability simulations non-disabled participants are asked to try on disabilities, as if they were trying on someone else's coat (Spelman, 1997). Simulations, like case studies, exploit and exaggerate difference. By eliciting either pity or sentimentality, simulations reinforce subject/object relations and a distant regard for an "unfortunate inferior" (Spelman, 1997, 118–9). Moreover, because disabled people invariably learn adaptive strategies to deal with obstacles, non-disabled students, who have no time to develop these skills, gain a very distorted view of disability. Instead, simulations encourage non-disabled people to appropriate disabled people's experiences, asserting an authority that leaves no room for disabled people to define their own experiences or realities (Spelman, 1997, p. 70). As Spelman (1997) explains in her analysis of Linda Brent's rhetorical strategies in *Incidents in the Life of a Slave Girl, Written by Herself,* "being the object of charity is hardly to be compared with being the subject of freedom (p. 71).

Of course, such models are not confined to special education. The clinical and case study approach differs very little from liberal multiculturalism's "tourist models" (Erevelles, 2000, p. 35). These models continue to operate within some introductory women's studies classes and multicultural classes, where identity categories are also offered up in weekly installments adding up to a quilt of identities by the end of the semester. Courses and textbooks separating and safely containing specific identity categories into chapters or weeks of study are problematic in that they refuse the possibility of intersections among or differences within categories. Similarly, diversity week programs and activities organized around discrete identity categories reproduce the same dynamic. In the *Tunnel of Oppression,* a common feature on many campuses during diversity week or month, spectators move from room to room—stopping at each one to gaze at a victim of a particular kind of oppression. The walls of each room safely demarcate both the distance between the viewer and the objects of oppression, as well as between the various types of oppression portrayed. Spelman (1988) illustrates how talking separately about sexism and racism, for example, erases the experiences of black women who experience both racism and sexism simultaneously. Such analyses also ignore the complicated and varied intersections among privileges and oppressions and replicate us/them dualisms between the self and the other. Spelman illustrates how disentangling multiple and layered identities reduces each identity to discrete beads like those found in a pop-bead necklace. Moreover, rarely is the white, heterosexual, middle-class, able-bodied exemplar (or bead) included as a category of analysis, reproducing an unstated and unexamined norm by which all others deviate.

Likewise, efforts at diversity and inclusion that adopt a collector's model, in which identities are gathered up and displayed, are similarly exploitive, objectifying, and colonizing. Both Lather (1998) and Willinsky (1998) trouble these kinds of practices for fostering a cannibalizing impulse to "know [or have] the other" (p. 496). I am reminded of an instance when a prospective disabled student on a visit to a college campus was actually stalked by a university photographer who finally admitted to her that she wanted to "capture" her image for public promotion materials for the college. Her experience highlights the invisibility of disabled students who were already on campus and demonstrates the desperate desire of the college to reduce this "not yet" student to the role of poster girl, all in the name of communicating to outsiders a climate of campus diversity and inclusiveness.

Similarly troubling is the "embarrassing etc." approach to theorizing identity in which differences are tacked onto an ever-lengthening list of self-consciously stated, yet under-theorized categories—similar to Spelman's (1988) pop bead necklace. This type of inclusion calls to mind general education classrooms where the disabled students are included but only nominally. They are invited into an existing structure, but the structure is not changed or modified in any substantial way. They are expected to assimilate. Similarly, although it is now more common to find disability tacked onto the end of categorical lists which include race, class, gender, and sexuality, rarely is it made clear what difference this difference makes in the analysis or how various systems of oppression interdepend. This amounts to what Utall (1990) calls "inclusion without influence" (p. 42).

I do not deny that identity-based pedagogical models are rooted in the desire to include rather than exclude. Such models are also powerful in that they make focused political work and sustained scholarly engagement possible. Yet, identity models are also paradoxical because they uphold the very kinds of universalizing and essentializing practices they seek to undo. So, although theoretical debates on identity politics are not new, some of the most recent critiques are occurring at the pedagogical level where authors are attempting to "go beyond the rearrangement of scholarship around a given materiality—the disabled body [for example]—to contest the very notion of any such fixed object of concern" (Price and Shildrick, 1998, p. 224). In this regard, disability studies in education offers a place for a more complicated view of disability and inclusion.

(Re)Teaching Dis/ability

Like all critical theories, disability studies is better at critiquing dominant models and understandings than offering clear cut solutions or alternatives. A particular challenge in operationalizing a disability studies approach to teacher education, for instance, is the limited number of textbooks (and even readings), particularly at the undergraduate level, that begin with a disability studies perspective to education. Moreover, teacher education faculty must often operate within very traditional educational programs and be accountable to state and federal guidelines or lose the ability to certify teachers. Scholars in disability studies in education, therefore, are often left to their own devices in trying to integrate disability studies into their teaching. Despite limited resources and lack of available models, disability studies scholars have begun the task of infusing disability studies into all of education, including teacher education. In the next section I will briefly describe how I approach teacher education courses from a disability studies lens and how students have responded to these courses. I believe their responses illustrate the transformative potential of disability studies in education.

Curriculum Matters

Students often take a disability course to learn about disability as a discrete set of knowledge. They anticipate studying particular disabilities and learning what they must do to meet each type of student's needs in the classroom. I like to complicate these expectations right up front. In planning my teacher education courses I typically begin each course with an activity aimed at curriculum transformation. In other words, I hope to help them see that disability connects to all curricular areas and is not simply a problem, inherent in students, that they have to identify and solve before they can cover their content areas.

For example, in a secondary education course where I have students from a range of different curricular backgrounds, I group students into curricular areas and assign a particular reading that bridges their curricular background and disability studies scholarship. I might assign an article about the history of euthanasia of people with disabilities as a precursor to the Holocaust or a reading about the history of the disability rights movement to students in social studies education. Students in math or science might receive a reading linking the rise of statistics and the bell curve with eugenic ideas about race and ability. I might assign English education majors an article about the representation of people with disabilities in contemporary works of fiction. Finally, students in Art or Music education might receive a reading about representations of disability in popular culture, art, or film.

In courses where I have special education or elementary education students, I typically assign students a particular era in the history of disability to research and then present to the class. Students are asked to construct a group timeline of meanings of disability and discuss how the various meanings given to disability throughout history influenced how individuals with disabilities were "treated." In each of these examples, I aim to illustrate how disability is not confined to a particular curricular area or something that is static across time or place. I also introduce the idea that disability is not simply about who we teach, but also what we teach. Finally, as a group we brainstorm other possible curricular topics that would lend themselves to infusing disability perspectives.

Students often comment in course evaluations that they had never been exposed to thinking about disability in terms of curriculum. I am always struck by the number of students who discuss this activity, which typically covers only the first and second class meetings, in their final course evaluations. They often write, for example, that this project helped them to think about disability in ways they "had not previously been exposed to" or presented material that was "all new to them." One special education student was so motivated by learning about the disability rights movement, for example, that s/he wrote, "I want to take this information to my students so they can become young soldiers for the movement...so they can learn more about changing society." This student also wrote that learning more about disability rights would encourage teachers to be "less likely to see people with disabilities as helpless and in need of lower standards."

I find in their feedback an important statement about a lack of attention given to disability across the curriculum. Thus, a central task of disability studies scholars in education is to begin to fill in some of these gaps and help teachers see where disability could be infused across the curriculum. One particularly promising web based project called *Disability Studies for Teachers*, provides sample lesson plans and links to materials to help teachers in grades 6–12 to integrate disability studies into the curriculum (see http://www.disabilitystudiesforteachers.org/). More resources like this are needed to help address the many gaps in our knowledge base about disability.

Breaking Silences

Another activity that I tend to do early in the semester is to have students do a spontaneous in-class free write about their earliest memory of disability. When students begin to share their experiences the class in general is often surprised to see how many of them had personal experiences with a family member or friend with a disability. Despite the fact that disability is often a common occurrence in their neighborhoods or families, however, few of the stories told are school stories. In other words, in sharing these stories students find they were often shielded from disability once they entered school. Some students share their experiences with a disabled sibling, often to the surprise of their classmates with whom this aspect of their background had "never come up." Others take this opportunity to discuss their own experiences with getting labeled as having a learning disability or ADHD, for example. These students are sometimes emboldened by this disclosure and end up taking leadership roles in the classroom, sharing insider perspectives and critiques on topics such as labeling and inclusion.

Sometimes students report feeling confused about whether or not a particular relative or friend was *really* disabled. This opens the door for a discussion about how disability has always been a rather elastic category that expands and contracts depending on context. Reminding them of the history of eugenics, for example, when the "unfit" might include individuals who were considered disabled, but also those who were poor, or women who were promiscuous, I then introduce the idea that disability is really a constructed category—each cultural context ultimately decides where the line between ability and disability lies. I like to talk about the line between disability and ability as being like the equator—a line that only exists on a globe. Often this line seems quite arbitrary—as in learning disabilities, in which the same student can be deemed eligible for special education in one state, but not another. We then discuss other kinds of disability categories like mental retardation where definitions have shifted over time or disability categories like blindness or deafness, where the line is a number and entirely arbitrary. We also consider whether or not individuals with facial disfigurement, for example, are disabled and why or why not. Finally, we consider episodic disabilities—and how we define people who are disabled some-times. In each of these examples I try to get students to unpack some of their most basic assumptions about disability and ability. By troubling their no-tions of disability, I am also hoping to spark questions about the constructed-ness of normalcy.

Drawing on deconstructivist thinking, Price and Shildrick (1998) call for a radical disability pedagogy that critiques binaries and boundaries, troubles the illusion of a stable or secure self, and exposes "the failure of…norms to ever fully and finally contain a definitive standard of normativity" (p. 228). In refusing to focus on disability as a single, isolated system of oppression, Price and Shildrick show how all categories are leaky and unstable— requir-ing constant reiteration by disciplinary regimes to patrol their borders. Be-cause all bodies contain traces of the other "neither separation or closure is possible" (Price and Shildrick, 1998, p. 246) and all identities and all bodies are themselves performative (Butler, 1990).

A Pedagogy of Disruption

Such destabilizing moves in the classroom can be troubling to students and teachers alike. I find that when students take a disability-related class they are seeking what they describe as "practical knowledge" about what to *do* in the classroom—they do not typically expect it to be a "political" class. This is one important difference between disability studies and other identity studies courses, like gender studies or race studies. Thus, when students first encounter the term ableism and concepts such as able-bodied privilege and the social construction of ability/disability they must confront their own attachments and identifications to these categories and trouble their own ways of knowing about disability. As two students write:

> It's interesting to take an introductory course in LD and then to doubt its very existence. I guess that's what its all about. It's time for me to question all that I know or thought I knew.

> I was sure that she wasn't connecting information and that something was off. I was sure that there was a red flag saying that she needed outside support. I was sure that she was having trouble learning the information being presented. I was sure that she needed to be evaluated for special services. Now I am not so sure.

Admittedly my overall goal *is* to create a disruption in students knowing about disability and, as a result, to make the normative strange. I find that I, too, struggle with how to deconstruct the categories of disability and ability without silencing or erasing the experiences of people with disabilities themselves—and how my own relation to disability as someone with a chronic, but episodic health condition is blurry at best. Rather than having students conclude that, *"everyone has a disability,"* I ask them to stay mindful of Spelman (1997) who questions those

> who claim the right to point out commonality, who assert or exercise the privilege of determining just what it means in terms of other's identities, social locations, and political priorities (p. 138).

She reminds us that it is important to think through what is said to follow from an asserted commonality or difference, especially when such assertions are made across unequal access to power, authority, or rights.

In other words, we try to honor the opening lines of Pat Parker's *For the White Person Who Wants to Know How to Be My Friend*:

> The first thing you do is to forget that I am Black.
> Second, you must never forget that I'm Black (in Spelman, 1988, p. 123).

In class we struggle together with what it means to define oneself as an advocate or ally working to make change within a system that is highly invested in maintaining the status quo. We think together about how to work towards making general education more accessible—using concepts like universal design, yet recognizing that treating students fairly sometimes means treating them differently. We experiment with alternative ways of thinking about disability—such as disability as adaptation rather than deficit, and how we as teachers can honor and build on students' abilities and resilience rather than trying to fix them or make them more like some rigid definition of normalcy. Often deeply identified with the role of helper, students are often most challenged to think about the politics of care—and ways care often replicates and depends on subject/object relations (Spelman, 1997). They do not like thinking about making a living off disability. About the time I attempt to introduce the idea of spatial politics and the physical location of special education classrooms, students complain that I see *everything* as political.

An often lively discussion begins with naming the kinds of things people commonly say to them about their desire to become special education teachers. Deconstructing the meanings behind such statements—for example, what does it mean to be told that you must be "extra special" or "so patient" to work with special education students? How does this discourse construct disabled students? One student writes:

> I hate to admit it, but I came into this class with that "I'm a special education teacher, so I must be extra special" attitude. It has been important for me to look at disabilities from the perspectives of the disability community because my attitudes have changed. This new perspective will affect my teaching by showing me the prejudice in my own thinking.

This discussion usually leads to a debate about what teachers really need to know to work with special education students? Is it medical knowledge about causes and lists of characteristics associated with disability categories, is it specialized pedagogy, or is it a critical consciousness about disability? And what is considered an important source of information about disability—what kind of knowledge about disability counts? A student writes:

> It makes you see and hear the child or person as a whole being—to go to them [as sources of information] about what they need.

We also work at ways to shift the object of remediation from "defective" students to inaccessible classrooms—a necessary shift for any school reform that is based on an ethic of social justice.

> Children with disabilities do not need to be segregated from other learners, and [they] do not need a watered down curriculum, but instead need a stimulating, challenging, and supportive environment.

> There are certain projects that will need to be altered..., but in general I think it would be great for all students to feel as though they are getting a fair chance to learn the curriculum.

Unaccustomed to thinking about how various systems of oppression interconnect, students do not expect to discuss how racism, sexism, and classism *are* disability issues (and vice versa). Even students who have taken gender and multicultural studies classes, find that ableism complicates their ideas about difference. Disability, because it is often considered biologically determined, is often seen as a different kind of difference. Assignments that connect the history of segregated special education classes to the discourse surrounding *Brown v. Board of Education*, however, require students to consider how different systems of oppression interdepend. As one student wrote, "I don't think I'll be able to think about one identity alone again."

Students also do not expect interdisciplinary assignments asking them to analyze disability images and representations in cultural products and the media. They sometimes question how these assignments are relevant to learning about how to teach special education students. However, I include these assignments because I want my students to think critically about how their own understandings of disability have been shaped by the cultural context in which they live. Because of employment discrimination, segregation, and exclusion, non-disabled students (and even disabled students for that matter) may have had very little direct experience with disabled people. Thus their knowledge of disability can be limited to stereotypical portrayals they encounter in books, on TV, or in film.

When using autobiographies, I tend to assign students to literature circles where they chose among a list of first person accounts of disability. Wanting to make sure students do not mistake any one narrative as *the* authentic account of a particular disability, I usually select a few narratives of individuals who share the same disability, but differ in terms of other identity markers. I also want them to understand that we are all inside culture. Thus, individuals with disabilities are subject to the same cultural understandings of disability and often fall into familiar tropes, such as the overcoming script that is so ubiquitous in portrayals of disability in film. An overall goal of this assignment is to expand students' ideas about sources of expertise or authority about disability.

I hope that students take away from this and other assignments, that students themselves can be important sources of expertise about their learning. Moreover, because non-disabled students often grow up without sustained contact with disabled people, autobiography and cultural representations take on an even more important role. Yet, students accustomed to a steady diet of the medical-model may question how required readings that draw from autobiography, novels, film, poetry, or even their students or classmates can be "reliable" sources of information.

> I was unsure how some of the readings were relevant to the class.

> I could tell you all the issues surrounding it [inclusive education] but as far as methods go, I could only tell you what I saw my classmates present.

Although I typically get a range of student responses to my classes (both positive and negative), one thing I can say for certain is that I tend to confound their expectations for the course. In fact, I have learned to introduce the course with a summary of how the course would most likely be taught from a traditional standpoint and why I take an alternative path. I find that students appreciate when I make my theoretical orientation explicit and are more open to thinking about why they might have certain kinds of expectations. And, although students may not immediately make the connection between ableism and other oppressive social relationships or gain an ability to critique the politics of representation, or multiple and interrelated practices of othering on both individual and social levels, I do find they have amazing insights. I find that students do recognize the interlocking nature of disparate forms of power and begin to refuse the reductionism inherent in oppositional ways of thinking about difference. If students come away from the class with a more complicated view of dis/ability and normalcy, a more expansive notion of who *their* students will be, and shift to thinking about their own classroom practices as either creating or removing barriers, then I usually feel that I have achieved what I set out to do.

Teaching Through Trouble

To be sure, teaching disability studies in education can be both exciting and frustrating. Our work remains marginalized within the academy and even within education. Most scholars in disability studies work without established degree programs, like-minded colleagues, or high status outlets for their scholarship. In fact, disability studies remains more marginalized within the academy than fields like women's studies or other area studies. Disability studies scholars in education face a particular set of exclusions—seen as too practice oriented by humanities-based disability studies scholars and too theoretical/not practitioner enough by colleagues in education. Thus, even within education, disability studies scholars can be perceived as threatening or simply irrelevant. However, in recent years tremendous gains have also been made—in terms of programs, courses, publications, professional organizations, and conferences.

Certainly teaching disability studies in education has its own unique challenges. Yet, I find student resistance and disbelief just as important as student transformation, because I believe that the places of conflict and friction represent some of the most troubling and productive times I have had in the college classroom. Despite students (and sometimes my own) resistance to destablizing categories and deconstructing normativity, I concur with Lather (1998), Ellsworth (1997), Kohli (1998) and others, that it is in these "stuck places"—when we are challenged by "ruptures, failures, breaks, and refusals"—that we find our most promising pedagogical moments (Lather, p. 495). Both Lather and Ellsworth (1997) call on us to ask the "hard questions" (p. 496), which become most visible during what she calls "pedagogical meltdowns" or when things go "wrong" in the classroom (Lather and Ellsworth, 1996). It is in these moments of resistance and disjuncture that we find spaces to trouble our taken-for-granted ways of knowing, being, and acting.

In moving from traditional and deficit-based models to more intersectional disability studies approaches in education—we ask students (and ourselves) to give up certainties but in the process we gain complexity, we give up having easy answers but get better at asking hard questions, we ask for trouble in the classroom and in our own thinking but in so doing we end up with a pedagogical model that is both more than and different from any sum of identity-based parts. In the process we gain "different, strategic possibilities for ethical, political, and relational work" (McCoy, 2000).

The emerging discourses of disability studies in education reveal some of the stuck places in our thinking about difference. Disability studies troubles existing theories at the same time it offers alternative counternarratives that complicate any easy conceptions of difference and normativity (Erevelles, 2000). Destablizing "what has been deemed natural, normal, normative, and true" (Collins, 2000, p. 41) makes visible the way discourse determines what can be said and understood, as well as what can be done (McCoy, 2000, p. 252). Certainly more cross-disciplinary dialogue among disability studies and other critical scholars across the academy would exponentially expand the transformative potential of disability studies. I believe disability studies scholars in education have a critical role in such conversations.

References

Butler, J. (1990) *Gender trouble: Feminism and the subversion of identity.* New York: Routledge.

———. (1991). Imitation and gender in subordination (307–320). In H. Abelove et al. (Eds.). *The lesbian and gay studies reader.* New York: Routledge.

Collins, P. H. (2000). What's going on? Black feminist thought and the politics of postmodernism. In E.A. St. Pierre and W.S. Pillow (Eds.) *Working the ruins: Feminist poststructural theory and methods in education.* New York:Routledge.

Davis, L. (1997). Constructing normalcy. In L. Davis (Ed.) *The disability studies reader* (pp. 9–28). New York, NY: Routledge.

Ellsworth, E. (1997). *Teaching positions: Difference, pedagogy, and the power of address.* New York, NY: Teachers College Press.

Erevelles, N. (2000). Educating unruly bodies: Critical pedagogy, disability studies, and the politics of schooling. *Educational Theory, 50*:1, 25–47.

Kohli, W. (1998). Critical education and embodied subjects: Making the poststructuralist turn. *Educational Theory, 48*, 4, 511–519.

Lather, P. (1998). Critical pedagogy and its complicities: A praxis of stuck places. *Educational Theory, 48*:4, 487–497.

Lather, P. & Ellsworth, E. (1996). Situated pedagogies: Classroom practices in postmodern times. *Theory into Practice, 35*(2), 70-71.

Linton, S. (1998) *Claiming disability: Knowledge and identity.* New York, NY: Routledge.

Mayo, C. (2000). The uses of Foucault. *Educational Theory, 50*, 1, 103–116.

McCoy, K. (2000). White noise—the sound of an epidemic: Reading/writing a climate of intelligibility around the "crisis" of difference. In E.A. St. Pierre and W.S. Pillow (Eds.) *Working the ruins: Feminist poststructural theory and methods in education.* NY: Routledge.

Mitchell, D. and Snyder, S. (Eds.) (1997). *The body and physical difference: Discourses of disability.* Ann Arbor, MI: University of Michigan Press.

Paterson, K. and Hughes, B. (1999). Disability studies and phenomenology: the carnal politics of everyday life. *Disability and Society, 14*, 5, 597–610.

Price, J. and Shildrick, M. (1998). Uncertain thoughts on the dis/abled body. In M. Shildrick and J. Price (Eds.). *Vital signs: Feminist reconfigurations of the bio/logical body.* Edinburgh: Edinburgh UP.

Sedgwick, E. K. (1990). *Epistemology of the closet.* Berkeley, CA: University of California Press.

Spelman, E. V. (1988) *Inessential woman: Exclusions in feminist thought.* Boston: Beacon Press.

———. (1997) *Fruits of Sorrow: Framing our attention to suffering.* Boston: Beacon Press.

Thomson, R. G. (1997a). Body criticism as a context for disability studies. *Disability Studies Quarterly, 17*, 4, 297–300.

———. (1997b). *Extraordinary bodies: Figuring physical disability in American culture and literature.* New York: Columbia University Press.

———. (1995). Integrating disability studies into the existing curriculum: The example of 'Women and Literature' at Howard University. *Radical Teacher 47*, 15–21.

Utall, L. (1990). Inclusion without influence: The continuing tokenism of women of color. In G. Anzaldua (Ed.). *Making face, making soul: Creative and critical perspectives by feminists of color* (pp. 42–45). San Francisco, CA: Aunt Lute Books.

Vernon, A. (1998). Multiple oppression and the Disabled People's Movement. In T. Shakespeare (Ed.). *The disability studies reader: Social science perspectives.* London and New York, NY: Cassell.

Willinsky, J. (1998) *Learning to divide the world: Education at empire's end.* Minneapolis, MN: University of Minnesota Press.

CHAPTER 17

Internationalization and the Impact of Disability Studies: Scholarly Work or Political Project?

Susan Peters

Before responding to this question, it may be instructive to put forth some observations about the status of disabled people globally. For the last twelve years, the International Disability & Human Rights Information Network (a branch of the UK-based Disability Awareness in Action or DAA) has been tracking the status of disabled people worldwide and documenting their conditions. In this organization's penultimate December 2004/January 2005 issue of the *Disability Tribune*, the DAA observed that since the International Year of the Disabled in 1981, the status of the estimated 600 million disabled people in the world has not substantially improved:

> Disabled people are STILL known to be the poorest of the poor in every country. Many disabled people STILL lead isolated lives without adequate support. Disabled people are STILL often denied access to public places because of architectural barriers or discriminatory attitudes....98% of disabled children in developing countries STILL have no access to education. Even in richer countries, education for many disabled children is still segregated and inadequate....The democratic voice of disabled people is STILL rarely heard in the formulation of policies and programs that directly affect us (*Disability Tribune*, 2004/2005, p. 5).

At the outset then, given this current state of affairs, it is difficult to make claims for Disability Studies' influence on education when most of the world's disabled population do not even have access to schooling. Further, several other factors make it difficult to discern the impact, if any, of Disability Studies on education at the international level. These difficulties lie, first, in the ways in which one conceives of disability studies and education. If Disability Studies is conceived of as the product of scholarly writing and its impact on the academy, the impact appears especially minimal. On the other hand, if Disability Studies is conceived of as a *political project* for developing a social model of disability with a concomitant philosophy of oppression acting on a minority group, then the impact may be more substantive. Specifically, the 'social model' does indeed appear to have had an influence, at least at the international policy level in education. For example, the discourse inherent in the social model has begun to filter its way into the language of major international policy documents related to education, such as the Salamanca Statement of 1994 and the work of the newly established United Nations Flagship on Disability and Inclusive Education. Second, in terms of education, if an analysis of influence concerns itself only with formal schooling, then the impact is similarly bleak. Specifically, it is estimated that as much as 75% of the world's disabled population live in developing countries (DFID, 2000 as reported in Baylies, 2002). Further, as early as 1984, the UN Secretary General estimated that 20–25% of the populations of developing countries were disabled (UN, DESA, 2000). And in these countries, it is further estimated that only 1–5% of 120–150 million children and youth are enrolled in school (Peters, 2003). However, casting a broader net to examine spheres of influence outside of schooling, in nonformal sectors may reveal a more positive picture. Finally, it is difficult to discuss education (whether in terms of formal schooling or in terms of nonformal education outside of schools) without considering its dependency on other sectors, such as transportation, employment, health, human rights, and social welfare. Examining the influence of Disability Studies on practices and knowledge acquisition in these related sectors can provide a clearer and more holistic picture of impact.

In answering the question, then, concerning Disability Studies' influence on education at the international level, this response will address each of these difficulties in turn, and then cast a broader net. First, the response will consider the impact of Disability Studies' scholarly writing in the field of education and in the academy. Second, areas of possible influence in the nonformal education sector will be discussed. Third, the impact of Disability Studies in related fields will be analyzed. When these three ways of thinking about Disability Studies' impact on education are utilized, one can begin to map some of the influence at the international level.

The Impact of Scholarly Writing

The first way to investigate the impact of Disability Studies on education is to look at scholarly writing in international journals. This type of investigation presupposes that publications will have an impact on the academy, as dissemination of intellectual ideas occurs within institutions of higher education, particularly those related to education and whose work influences teacher training and practice in schools. However, if one looks only at scholarly publications in Disability Studies and education, the impact is problematic, at best.

Two prominent journals that specifically focus on the intersection of disability and education at the international level are the *International Journal of Disability, Development and Education (IJDDE)*; and the *International Journal of Inclusive Education (IJIE)*. An examination of articles published in these two journals for a randomly selected year reveals publication records and editorial board compositions heavily skewed in favor of OECD (Organization for Economic Cooperation and Development) or advanced industrialized countries. Table 1 provides a summary of publications for these two journals in the year 2003.

For both journals in Table 1, the editor's country of origin is Australia, with editorial board members and reviewers originating predominantly from OECD countries. Articles published also reflect this bias. Topics of the articles included in this review also tend to be narrow in scope and lacking in cross-national or comparative perspectives. For example, an Australian study in the IJDDE is entitled "Self-Esteem of Greek Mothers of Children with Intellectual Disabilities."

An examination of a third leading journal, *Disability & Society*, and across multiple years (2000–2005) yields more diversity in terms of country studies, but also does not focus on education, as its mission is broader. However, across these five years, articles published include only a handful of cross-national comparative studies that shed light on global conditions and trends or that discuss implications for practice at the international level.

The examples given above only scratch the surface and are meant to be illustrative of possible problems with respect to the level of influence Disability Studies may have on the academy at the international level. However, one would expect that IJIE and IJDDE, focusing as they do on disability and education, would be concentrated sources for cutting edge work in the field, and that this work would be more balanced globally in every published issue of the journal. If it is not, one must ask, why not? For example, an investigation into the ways in which global submissions by disability scholars in developing countries could be supported and encouraged might be of assistance in addressing the current imbalance.

Table 1: Articles published in 2 leading journals of
disability and education in 2003

Country of Study	IJDDE # of studies	IJIE # of studies	Total articles in both
Australia	12	9	21
United Kingdom	0	11	11
EUC	3	4	7
USA	3	1	4
Sub-Saharan Africa	2	0	2
Israel	1	0	1
Turkey	1	0	1
New Zealand	1	0	1
Malta	0	1	1

To extend this inquiry, a genealogical and historical study of scholarly works with Disability Studies perspectives in mainstream journals and other sources (e.g., books, web-based sources, monographs, and commissioned studies by international organizations such as UNICEF) would need to be conducted to definitively answer the question of influence. Another line of inquiry might examine the extent and nature of readings from these sources that can be found in academic course syllabi of higher education institutions across the five continents. There is a rich literature, for example, in Spanish language journals emanating from Latin America that would need to be included in this inquiry as well. Finally, one would need to examine the readership of these journals and their utilization in practice to determine the extent of impact and the distribution of knowledge across the continents.

The Impact of Disability Studies as a Political Project

Meekosha (2004) argues that Disability Studies has evolved as an integral part of the emergence of the social movement of disabled people and that this movement parallels the intellectual struggles of Disability Studies within the academy.

> Disability studies has developed as part of a *political project* (emphasis added), where the recognition of the discursive power of the old order to disable people with impairments leads to an alternative world view and analytical pathway. As such it has been closely tied to the nature of the social movement of disabled people in various countries—themselves affected by the social structures and histories of particular societies (Meekosha, 2004, p. 724).

Another way, then, to consider the impact of Disability Studies in education at the international level is to cast a net broadly to include the political projects that educate disabled people outside of academia or formal primary schooling. Largely excluded from schooling, disabled people worldwide have taken on the task of educating themselves. Examples of this education, in what has been called 'nonformal' sectors, includes sanghams in India, development cooperatives in Africa, and community-based integration projects across South East Asia, Latin America, and postcommunist countries of Central and Eastern Europe. At the international level, this conception of education as embracing nonformal sectors is particularly important, since the majority of disabled people in the world still do not have access to formal schooling.

Non-governmental organizations (NGOs) have burgeoned over the past two decades. A large number of NGOs have grown out of grass-roots activism of disability groups. Literally every country in the world today has registered NGOs run by these groups. It is impossible, in this short space, to adequately describe the depth and scope of their work. However, a few examples of their work in relation to education are given here.

After Zimbabwe's independence from Rhodesia in 1980, disabled people in that country organized a national NGO, the National Council of Disabled People in Zimbabwe (NCDPZ). The Council's initial work focused on organizing each province into membership groups and conscientizing individual members as to their rights. A number of projects subsequently evolved at the grass-roots level in rural areas. A Rural Membership Development Program supported members in setting up practical projects to increase disabled people's self-reliance. The underlying goal of these projects was a "gradual change in people's consciousness and ability to manage themselves and their environment successfully" (Coleridge, 1996, p. 141).

Sanghams (village disability groups) in India provide an example of similar work. These independent living centers provide disabled people, and especially disabled women, some independence from the disabling caste system. An NGO—the Association of the Physically Handicapped—in Bangalore, India runs training programs for disabled women. These training programs teach communication and leadership skills, including management and administration of sanghams. The goal is "to mobilize disabled people to take action on their own behalf, and to use existing structures to secure services and benefits" (Coleridge, 1996, p. 164).

In the Slovak Republic, the Alliance of Organizations of Disabled People in Slovakia is an umbrella organization for more than 35 local, regional and national disability NGOs. According to Holland (2003), the Alliance (as part of the Slovak Humanitarian Council) provides community-based services that include educating Slovak people regarding their legal and social rights and enhancing community re-entry services for individuals with acquired disabilities. As the work of the NGOs has grown in Slovakia, it has become necessary to train NGO leaders. This training has taken the form of integrating management courses in university curriculum, and providing continuing education services to enhance the knowledge base and management skills of NGO leaders.

The work of these NGO's constitutes a significant potential source of resources and influence on education in schools. Community-Based Rehabilitation (CBR) programs have become essentially educational. Kisanji (1999) discusses the links between CBR and inclusive education for students with disabilities and provides some examples of initiatives in this area. In Kenya, for example, itinerant CBR workers conduct an 'open education' program in rural areas. These workers visit blind children in their homes and work with the parents to provide early stimulation activities that will assist them in entering school. The workers also provide Braille lessons in schools and attend teacher staff meetings to assist in planning and curriculum adaptation. Tanzania uses a similar model of itinerant CBR workers in schools, funded by the Tanzanian Society for the Blind. In the West Bank and Gaza Strip, disabled people's CBR Centers began by providing education classes for those excluded from school, then expanded to helping 'slow learners' in 'normal school' with supplementary lessons and tutoring after school (Coleridge, 1996, p. 184).

All of these examples of direct services grew out of grass-roots political projects grounded in the basic tenets of Disability Studies and a social model of disability inherent in its discourses and scholarly work.

The Impact on Related Fields

A third way to cast a broad net in relation to the focus of this response is to turn the gaze towards the influence that Disability Studies has had on fields related to education. This consideration is particularly important because disability is an issue that cuts across health, education, social welfare (human rights) and employment sectors, and all of these sectors are interdependent. A good example of this interdependency is the impact Disability Studies has had on the World Health Organization in terms of conceptualizing disability as an interaction between the person, the impairment and the environment.

The new International Classification of Functioning and Disability (ICF) developed by the World Health Organization (WHO) reflects the social model of disability in its realization that the environment plays a significant role in disablement. The WHO adopted this new classification system in 2001 under concerted pressure from international disability rights organizations. The ICF organizes disability along two dimensions: functioning and disability (including body functions/structures and activities/participation in society) and contextual factors (environmental and personal). This conceptual model of disability encourages focus on kinds and levels of interventions appropriate to the disablement needs of individuals within specific contexts, and is consistent with the social model of disability that lies at the core of Disability Studies. Ingstad (2001) reports that this ICF classification system was developed using a process of consensus involving both developed and developing countries. Ingstad argues that the ICF distinctions are particularly important in many developing countries, where personhood depends more on social identity and the fulfillment of family obligations than on individual ability.

The importance of the ICF classification for education carries enormous implications and possibilities. Focus on the environment means that schools and teachers must accommodate the environment to individual learners, not the other way around.

Another example of the influence of Disability Studies on education is the work that has been done in the area of human rights. Education is a basic human right that cannot be achieved without access to adequate health care, housing, nutrition and transportation. In more advanced industrialized countries, basic human rights such as these are more or less taken for granted. By contrast, many disabled people in developing countries must consider survival their first priority, and education is seen as a luxury.

The work of Disabled People's Organizations (DPOs) has made critical inroads on human rights. In particular, over the past decade, the momentum for disability rights pertaining to education has grown exponentially. The literature also makes clear that the impetus for inclusive education of people with disabilities has been put on the agenda of the United Nations and other international organizations working in the field of education (e.g. UNICEF and UNESCO). Specifically, the 2000 World Declaration on Education for All affirmed the notion of education as a fundamental right and clearly identified inclusive education as one of the key strategies to attain Education For All: "Inclusion was seen as the fundamental philosophy throughout UNESCO's programs and the guiding principle for the development of EFA" (UNESCO, 2002, p. 17).

Education for disabled people has been put on the agenda and propelled forward by disabled people's organizations, beginning critically with the 1993 UN Standard Rules on Equalization of Opportunities for Persons with Disabilities. UN Standard Rule #6.1 declares that general education authorities are responsible for education of persons with disabilities in integrated settings. The rule further states that education for persons with disabilities should form an integral part of national educational planning, curriculum development and school organization. This standard rule is one of the most comprehensive international standards for inclusive education that exists.

Disability Studies as a political project has achieved these gains through organized political pressure and mobilizing allies. Organizations such as SHIA (Swedish Organizations of Disabled Persons International Aid Association) and DAA (Disability Awareness in Action) have provided critical monitoring reports aimed at keeping this pressure active. For example, in 1999, the SHIA Human Rights and Disability Network, which constitutes DPOs from the North, South and East, conducted a study that found efforts toward human rights of disabled people were "beneath contempt." In the area of education, the report highlights examples from Tanzania, Uganda and in countries of Central and South America where evidence of theoretical opportunities for education exist, but in most cases the actuality was ruled out because of physical access and curriculum barriers.

Also, in 1999, the DAA launched its Human Rights Database. This database is one of two systematic attempts to provide an international record of human rights abuse directed at people with disabilities. DAA is a collaborative among DPI (Disabled People International), IMPACT, Inclusion International and World Federation for the Deaf. Violations are categorized according to the thirty Articles contained in the UN Universal Declaration of Human Rights. With respect to violation of rights pertaining to education of disabled persons, the DAA has collected 118 documented cases affecting 768,205 people in 67 countries (Light, 2002). DAA's database includes testimony invited for submission to the UN Human Rights Commission as part of its Global Rights Campaign. The number of violations in the area of education constitutes the sixth largest category of the Articles.

The work of these groups has uncovered violations as well as gaps in services, safeguards and monitoring strategies. The newly constituted UN Flagship on EFA and Rights of Persons with Disabilities will work on this gap as a strategic objective. The data that this group gathers on children and youth with special education needs and disabilities will be critical to future planning.

In summary, progress in the area of education for disabled people at the international level has been slow but steady. This progress may be encapsulated by comparing the discourse between the 1975 Universal Declaration of Human Rights and the 2000 Dakar report on Education for All. In 1975, the United Nations Declaration of Human Rights focused on assisting the 'disabled individual' to develop abilities, capabilities and self-reliance for functioning in 'normal' life. By contrast, the Dakar report on Education for All progress since Jomtien (2000), states:

> Concern about inclusion has evolved from a struggle in behalf of children 'having special needs' into one that challenges all exclusionary policies and practices in education...Instead of focusing on preparing children to fit into existing schools, the new emphasis focuses on preparing schools so that they can deliberately reach out to all children (UNESCO, 2000, p. 16).

Remaining Challenges

Some children start school with more advantages than others—advantages of wealth and health among the most influential. Children in poverty and with impairments, and all marginalized children (whether due to language, religion, race, ethnicity, gender) do not have to be disadvantaged by their treatment in schools or by exclusion from schools. Judy Heumann, head of the Disability Group for the World Bank, has said, "If you deny disabled people educational opportunities, then it is the lack of education and not their disabilities that limits opportunities." Today's inequalities and state of progress toward education for persons with disabilities provide both challenges and opportunities. If we are to improve the conditions of disabled people at the international level, then we are challenged to commit ourselves to investing our beliefs, our resources, and our intellectual problem-solving abilities in education. Our opportunities will manifest themselves in the day-to-day tasks that we undertake with teachers enrolled in the academy, and with children in classrooms, and in society.

References

Baylies, C. (2002). Disability and the notion of human development: Questions of rights and capabilities. *Disability & Society, 17*, 7, 725–739.

Coleridge, P. (1996). *Disability, liberation, and development.* Oxford: Oxfam Publications.

Department for International Development (2000). *Disability, poverty and development.* London: Stairway Communications.

Disability Awareness in Action (2004). The status of disabled people. *Disability Tribune.* December 2004/January 2005. London: Disability Awareness in Action.

Holland, D. (2003). Grass roots promotion of community health and human rights for people with disabilities in post–communist Central Europe: A profile of the Slovak Republic. *Disability & Society, 18*, 2, 133–143

Ingstad, B. (2001). Disability in the developing world. In *Handbook of disability studies.* G. Albrecht, K. Seelman & M. Bury (Eds). London: Sage Publications. Pp. 772–792.

Kisanji, J. (1999). Models of inclusive education: Where do community based support programs fit in? Paper presented at the Workshop on "Inclusive education in Namibia: The Challenge for Teacher Education,"

24–25 March 1999. Rossing Foundation: Khomasdal, Windhoek, Namibia.

Light, R. (2002). *A real horror story: The abuse of disabled people's human rights*. England: Disability Awareness in Action.

Meekosha, H. (2004). Drifting down the Gulf Stream: Navigating the cultures of disability studies. *Disability & Society, 19,* 7, 721–733.

Peters, S. (2003). *Inclusive education: Achieving education for all by including those with disabilities and special education needs*. Washington, D.C.: World Bank.

United Nations, Division for Social Policy and Development (DESA) (2000). *The United Nations and disabled persons: The first 50 years*. Available at: http://www.un.org/esa/socdev/enable

UNESCO (2000). *World education forum final report. Part II: Improving the quality and equity of education for all*. Subsection entitled "Meeting special and diverse education needs: making inclusive education a reality." Paris: UNESCO.

———. (2002). *Education for all: Is the world on track?* Paris: UNESCO.

CHAPTER 18

Transgressing Noncrossable Borders:
Disability, Law, Schooling, and Nations

Bernadette Baker and Fiona Campbell

> The passion to eradicate alterity from the earth is also the passion for the home, the
> country, the dwelling, that authorizes this desire and rewards it. In its nationalism,
> parochialism and racism it constitutes a public and private neurosis. So, unwinding
> the rigid understanding of place that apparently permits me to speak, that guarantees
> my voice, my power, is not simply to disperse my locality within the wider coordi-
> nates of an ultimate planetary context. That would merely absolve me of responsibil-
> ity in the name of an abstract and generic globalism, permitting my inheritance to
> continue uninterrupted in the vagaries of a new configuration. There is something
> altogether more precise and more urgent involved. For in the horror of the unhomely
> pulses the dread for the dispersal of Western humankind: the dread of a rationality
> confronted with what exceeds and slips its grasp.
> (Iain Chambers, *Culture after Humanism*, 2001, p. 196)

During his time as a high school student in New South Wales, Australia,
Daniel Hoggan was suspended on five occasions for "unacceptable behavior." He was described by teachers' aides in their "Communication Book" as
becoming increasingly violent towards other students and teachers (*Purvis*,
2000, EOC 93–117, para 2.5.4.). This included kicking, pushing, punching,
and biting his aides, other students and teachers, and using obscene language.
After multiple suspensions, the school eventually expelled Daniel Hoggan,
rejecting his foster father's claims of disability discrimination.[1] Daniel's
foster father, Alexander Purvis, took the school to court. The case run by
Purvis, on behalf of Daniel Hoggan, was one of direct disability discrimination (as opposed to indirect discrimination). This meant that Purvis had to
prove that the school, by suspending and expelling Hoggan, had discrimi-

nated against him, by treating him less favorably than it would have treated a person without Hoggan's disability, in circumstances that were "the same or not materially different." In juridical terms, then, the dispute in the case was the relationship of behavior to disability and whether Daniel's exclusion from school constituted direct disability discrimination under the *Disability Discrimination Act* 1992 (DDA) of Australia (202 *ALR* 134 at para 1, Gleeson J).[2] The long-running dispute between the applicant (Purvis) and the New South Wales Department of Education and Training (representing the state high school) ended when the High Court of Australia ruled in favor of the school.

The biomedical narrative relayed around Daniel's case located the behavior as "his," placing it at a discrete site of origin and invoking an evolutionary, if not teleological structure: At about 6 months of age, Daniel Hoggan experienced a severe illness that resulted in brain injury, manifesting itself in intellectual disabilities, vision impairment and epilepsy. The intellectual disabilities also affected Hoggan's thought processes, his perception of reality and his emotions; His impairments were also manifested by unusual individual mannerisms such as rocking, humming and swearing and by aggressive behavior, such as hitting or kicking.

This chapter is an analysis of the above pivotal High Court case, as an instance of how "disability" is produced and experienced as aporia in and around the borderlines of nations, disciplines, and the subjectivities attributed to the young. Drawing on Derrida's analysis of three different levels of aporia and three kinds of borderlines—anthropological borders (territories, languages, or cultures), problematic closures (the exclusivity of disciplines or fields), and conceptual demarcations (the borders separating concepts or terms), we argue that the (non)experience of aporia within a nation-law-education nexus have not been innocuous, neutral, or innocent, nor have they been "sealed up." Rather, the responses persistently demonstrate what we call, a *performative passion for sameness* (cf. Stiker, 2000). We are, however, not talking about *any* sameness, but paradoxically and deliberately a sameness underpinned by shifting constitutional divides that enact an ontological separation between "abled" and "disabled," where "mixtures" are expiated through processes of fabrication and simulation. Similarly, we are not speaking of any version of passion but that which resembles *haecceity*, a process, event or effect of individuation through waves of intensity in continuous variation (Deleuze and Guattari, 1987, pp. 262–63).

A plateau of differential intensities does not automatically link passion to desire but instead sees a multiplicity of "suffering-pleasure" beyond binary, beyond simplistic representations of longing. Such a plateau foregrounds a mutual and reciprocal connection across individuations that seem to repeat, fall short, and shift (Robinson, 2003, p. 120). In Foucault's (1996, p. 313) terms:

> Passion arrives like that, a state that is always mobile, but never moves toward a given point. There are strong and weak moments, moments when it becomes incandescent. It floats, it evens out. It is a kind of unstable time that is pursued for obscure reasons, perhaps through inertia. In the extreme, it tries to maintain itself and disappear.

Far from referring to a phenomenological inscription, then, a performative passion for sameness is understood here as both historical and without singular origin, as coming from nowhere in particular but seeking place, as has having no simple destination but heading toward something. The "something" in the *Purvis* case includes the enactment of certitude against liminal or pluralized backgrounds that uphold the continuous effort to sort:

> Passion gives itself all the conditions necessary to continue, and, at the same time, it destroys itself. In a state of Passion one is not blind [*sic*]. One is simply not oneself. To be oneself no longer makes sense. (Foucault, 1996, p. 313).

We argue in this chapter, then, that a performative passion for sameness operates at multiple levels in the figurings and responses to *Purvis*. These levels include efforts to plug up "disability" as a kind of imperfect "leaky body", make discrete the postcolonial identity of "uncertain nations" and regulate "bad boys' behaviour" as symptomatic of the failure of closure in the former two. *Purvis* invokes and exemplifies a performative passion for sameness, or as Latour (1993, p. 100) puts it makes lisible the effort "...to extirpate ourselves from those horrid mixtures as forcibly as possible by not confusing what pertains to mere social preoccupations and what pertains to the real nature of things." Indeed, the case of *Purvis* exposes the fabrication of fixity of "disability" and unveils "disability" as a signifier that may be understood in terms of *catachresis*. That is, there is no literal referent for this concept, for as soon as we discursively interrogate "disability", its meaning loses its fixity, generality, and ultimately collapses (Baker, 1998; Campbell, 1999)[3].

We conclude by considering an ethics of affirmation, of retaining the alterity of the other, that a sensibility of aporia invites. We lay out how it is simultaneously impossible and necessary to cross borderlines that the *Purvis* case brings to noticeability. We elaborate how the persistent figuring of "disability" as ambiguous and elusive keeps open dual-edges (at least); on the one hand making disability-as-embodied a suspect retreat to the biological and on the other affirming disability-as-desirous and as an alterity of the integral and not of the integrable (Stiker, 1998). Recognizing such dual-edges requires dwelling within what Foucault (1961/1988) calls "an uncomfortable region." It requires intuiting, as Chambers (2001) already has, how continuous efforts at inscribing and defining "disability" are implicated within the politics of place which are not adequately addressed by shifting the analytical gaze from body to "the body", nation to international, or citizen to global citizen. In short, our analysis calls upon a rethinking of justice that is not the same as right or law. We suggest instead that the figurings and responses to *Purvis* marshal us toward an alternative conceptualization of justice where justice "is a relation to the unconditional that, once all the conditional givens have been taken into account, bears witness to that which will not allow itself to be enclosed within a context" (Derrida and Ferraris, 2001, p. 17).

Aporia, Borderlines, (Non)Experience

The Greek word *aporia* (singular *aporos*) indicates impassable crossings. Playing on *pas* as both "step" and "not" Derrida (1993, p. 8) describes crossing an impossible threshold as "the 'coming to pass' of an event that would no longer have the form or the appearance of a *pas*: in sum, a coming without *pas*." The path of aporia is "the difficult or the impracticable, here the impossible passage, the refused, denied, or prohibited passage, indeed the non-passage, which can in fact be something else, the event of a coming or of a future advent which no longer has the form of the movement that consists in passing, traversing, or transiting" (Derrida, 1993, p. 8).

Where the step across lands is a difficult question. Derrida deployed *aporia* as a descriptor "without really knowing where I was going, except I knew that what was going to be at stake in this word was the 'not knowing where to go'" (Derrida, 1993, p. 12). He describes three versions of aporia that embody and structure the experience of *pas* as step and not.

First, a state of non-passage is reflected in the "opaque existence of an uncrossable border," the border that cannot be passed (Derrida, 1993, p. 20). Second, aporia stem from the fact that "the limit is too porous"; aporia emerge when the limit is so indeterminate and permeable that there is no border to cross—the dividing line between two opposite sides has become invisible. Third, aporia reside in "themselves." There are aporia because there is not even any space for an aporos determined as experience of the step or of the edge: "the impossible, the antinomy, or the contradiction, is a non-passage because its elementary milieu does not allow for something that could be called passage, step, walk, gait, displacement, or replacement" (Derrida, 1993, p. 21).

The (non)experiencing of aporia is conjured as neither avoidance nor deficiency. It requires openness to an other and a view of paralysis or frozenness as the condition of responsibility. The (non)experiencing of aporia may be "paralyzing [sic] us in this separation in a way that is not necessarily negative; before a door, a threshold, a border, a line, or simply the edge or the approach of the other as such" (Derrida, 1993, p. 12). In other words, "disability" instead of invoking the more common response of crises or tragedy, may be-come a moment of invocation or opportunity.

An ethical sensing of an aporos thus requires belief in borderlines, of which Derrida describes three: the first is an *anthropological border* separating "territories, countries, nations, States, languages, and cultures" (Derrida, 1993, p. 22). Its edge is always artificially determined, such as distinctions between American or Australian. The second is a *problematic closure*, dividing domains of discourse such as respective disciplines. The exclusive unity of a certain inquiry is assured, such as distinctions between theology, education, and law as fields. The third is a *conceptual demarcation*, the borderline separating concepts or terms (Derrida, 1993, p. 22). It defines concepts and places them into opposition, such as childhood and adulthood or ability and disability. Every borderline is problematic (from the Greek *problema*) in both senses of projection and protection: as the projection of a project or task to accomplish and as the protection created by a substitute, a "prosthesis that we put forth in order to represent, replace, shelter or dissimulate ourselves, or so as to hide something unavowable" (Derrida, 1993, p. 11).

The three borders overlap and determine one another. As borderlines they are not fixed, however, but are capable of being open to another border. In so being, the hierarchy implied in the delimitation of the anthropological border, the problematic closure, and the conceptual demarcation is under question. The borders of territory/language/culture, field, and concept are not closed but always open to those that are not themselves. This risks unhinging existing ontological, hierarchical and territorial apparati. In this openness to the other, the demarcation of the boundary is not overthrown but neither does it stay within the settled territory, so that it is *both* impossible to pass the border and necessary to cross it. The juridical-political borders contained by traditions, cultures, and law are unsettled and displaced in this "both-and." In the movement of displacement, identity and non-identity connect, intertwine, but do not coincide.

Unruly Nations, Regulatory Disciplines, and Bad Boys

The languages of nation-making, law, and education require entification to do their work; A cannot be B and A can only occupy one place in space at a time. Michael Sells (1994) argues that there is a long history to the language and logic of entities within Western prose (as defined through the cross-fertilization of the Abrahamic traditions). As Sells notes, however, there has been a tendency to say and unsay such entification under a perceived pressure of meeting a limit and hoping to transcend it, inciting multiple efforts historically to transgress noncrossable borders.

Our argument is that insofar as nations, laws, educational institutions, and boys appear "visible," as kataphatic sayings of the obvious, there is also simultaneously a tendency to unsay "the" self-evidence and certitude of such categories, even from within "their own" operations. This vacillation between the saying of an obviousness and an unsaying immediately following it suggests the (non)experience of aporia in "Derridean" terms. The perception of a solidified entity such as Australia, the *DDA*, a high school, or bad boys is mitigated by the intuition of complexity, paradox, and liminality, the latter of which is both quashed and required for systems-maintenance. That is, belief in the propriety of discrete entities sustains and makes possible perceptions of liminality which in turn incite efforts at sorting, which in turn structure further intuitions of liminality. The non-originary mutual rhythms of containment and excess, of confinement and slippage give institutions something to work on and with.

In this case, the saying and unsaying of entities characterize and structure the discursive moves around the *Purvis* case, and their real and reality effects especially for Daniel Hoggan in at least three interrelated ways we discuss in detail below. First, in terms of the "opaque existence of an uncrossable border" we suggest that the anthropological border drawn around "Australia" acts in ways that are homologous to that of "disability" in the *DDA*. As a sliding signifier that has historically occupied liminal if not negative and eradicable locations on broader scales that seem to come from nowhere "Australia" works off of a series of indices that generate slippery meanings—indices that attempt to mark a specificity of place that eventually leaks and escapes such efforts at pinning down or closure.

In the second aspect of aporia, aporia emerge when the limit is so indeterminate and permeable that there is no border to cross—the dividing line between two opposites sides becomes invisible, inciting efforts to reestablish a constitutional divide. *Purvis* needs to be viewed against the backdrop of wider moves (at least in "the West") to rein in legal definitions of disability by adopting reductionist strategies that attempt to rid "disablements" of their leakiness, relationality, and ambiguity. Such juridical fabrications of ontologies of disability are policed by law, which has the authorizing space to say what disability *is* and *is not* and to thereby resecure law's status as the legitimate field of arbitration. As an instance of problematic closure—the effort to divide domains of discourse such as respective disciplines–the *Purvis* case is highly significant. *Purvis* has changed the landscape as to how disability is uttered in Federal law and thereby institutes a new kind of legal fiction, reterritorializing both law and education as related fields of citizen-production.

Third, the High Court of Australia exposed the contestability and decided purview of legal disability under the *DDA* in ways that have explicit ramification for how the young are treated in or out of schools and who is entitled to speak about it. The *Purvis* judgment is important for educationalists with an interest in inclusive education, especially concerning those students existing under the burden of the ascription of "challenging behavior." The case has implications for the usage of "tick and flick" sheets based around regulatory norms of exclusion. It suggests how borderlines between conceptual demarcations can generate the (non)experience of aporia in relation to what is a behavior, a bad behavior, and a form of discrimination.

Anthropological Borders: Making "Australia," Making "Disability"

In "Australia" the central piece of Federal legislation related to protection from discrimination based on disability is the *DDA*. Skouteris (2004) argues that the art of government requires that the good and perfect citizen, who is both performative and contributory, is one who can be well-counted, mapped, and divided along a multitude of dimensions. The definition of disability set out in section 4 of the DDA exemplifies this passion. The section provides a broad and expansive definition that has come to be seen as a national benchmark. Section 4 states that disability, in relation to a person, means:

(a) total or partial loss of the person's bodily or mental functions; or
(b) total or partial loss of a part of the body; or
(c) the presence in the body of organisms causing disease or illness; or
(d) the presence in the body of organisms capable of causing disease or illness; or
(e) the malfunction, malformation or disfigurement of a part of the person's body; or
(f) a disorder or malfunction that results in the person learning differently from a person without the disorder or malfunction; or
(g) a disorder, illness or disease that affects a person's thought processes, perception of reality, emotions or judgment or that results in disturbed behavior;

It includes a disability that:

(h) presently exists; or
(i) previously existed but no longer exists; or
(j) may exist in the future; or
(k) is imputed to a person.

This section of the *DDA* is interesting on a number of accounts. Whilst sub-sections (a) to (g) incorporate and continue to reinforce an etiological and functionalist tradition, sub-sections (h) to (k) not only invoke the fluid and temporal aspects of "embodiment"; they recognize the constructed and relational dynamics of disability as a signifier. The extensive definition of disability incorporated within the *DDA* reflects an underlying tension and contestation between advocates who suggest that disablement has an objective reality that can be functionally measured and universally ascribed and those advocates who believe that a universal definition of disablement is impossible as notions of disability are enacted in relation to other discourses, for example, other scaled human bodies, the use or non-use of technologies, or coverage under various administrative regimes (Altman, 2001).

The simultaneous fixity and fluidity attributed to the figuration of "disability" in legal discourse is homologous to the theorization of "Australia" in the social sciences, humanities, and policy realms—no one seems quite sure what "it" really is in terms of a universal resting place, hence multiple efforts to delimit, clarify, and reassert, performed within differential frames of reference.

In Sinclair's (2004) terms, for instance, what dominates an "Australian imaginary" are subjectivities that link the secular to the Ordinary.[4] The characterization of Australia as a secular nation functions to differentiate Australia historically from its two dominant colonizers, England and the United States. The rhetoric of "God Bless America" Sinclair argues "is commonplace and legendary (to Australians) and is read as constitutive of an essentialized US national identity," in particular one obsessed with Christianity (Sinclair, 2004, p. 283). In contrast, "the idea of Australia as secular is also closely linked to the idea of Australia as 'ordinary,'" meaning a dislike of anything seen as symbolic, excess, and emotional. The secular Ordinary Australian imaginary that Sinclair contests is thus depicted as a community of people who both valorize the Ordinary and perceive themselves to *be* ordinary (Sinclair, 2004, p. 284). The Ordinary Australian is here not simply associated with White Australia, with masculine, rural Australia, with One Nation, but with a range of sites in which "plain speech" is valued, where limited emotional or affective expression is preferred, and where together these confer a sense of entitlement to manage national space and represent the interests of "Ordinary Australians." Among the categories of exclusion that a valorization of the Ordinary produces are the "extra-ordinary" or the "non-ordinary," and it is to either of these categories that the spiritual and the religious—and we would argue "disability" —also belong when ordinariness is privileged.

In Burney's (2004) terms, however, "Australia" is something else; it is constituted in part by over 300 different nations that are now pooled under the term "indigenous." Among other differences, each nation has its own welcoming rituals. The rituals prevent anyone not from the home nation from speaking for the home nation. Explaining how when she was born she was officially considered part of the fauna and not counted as a person or citizen, Burney (2004) argues that Australia can never be seen as just one thing, whether the focus is "indigenous," "white," or "immigrant." This dual-edged movement between seemingly monolithic federal policies and inherent, longstanding diversity paradoxically marks "Australia," making it seem both more of the same and something different. As Duncanson (2001, p. 3) similarly notes: "Oxfam International points out the uniqueness of the Australian constitution in specifically authorizing racial discrimination. After 1901, the White Australia policy was inaugurated and Aborigines were literally not counted until after the referendum of 1967 included them in future populational censuses."

In diametric opposition to Burney's openness to difference was a recent antipodean moment, witnessed as the *Tampa* crisis, where a ship of refugees was refused entry into "Australian waters." It became possible and permissible for Prime Minister John Howard to invoke a passion for sameness and proclaim in defense of the refusal "One of the greatest things about living in Australia is that we're essentially the same. We have a great egalitarian innocence" (Howard, cited in Rundle, 2001, p. 26).

"Australia," then is subjected to multiple significations that seem to emerge out of disparate non-originary locations that are contradictory and contemporaneous, as site of invasion, as a colonial society now in a post-colonial moment, as having suffered from "cultural lag" and "cultural cringe" mentalities, as multicultural, as monochromatic, as egalitarian, as secretly Second and Third World desperately seeking First World status on someone else's scale, as secular and down-to-earth, as fearing invasion and unwelcoming, as eradicable because economically irrelevant on a "global" scale, and as that which eradicates the extra-ordinary in order to "purify" from within. What is "truly" Australian amid these "dangerous coagulations" (and why it should even matter), then, is difficult to determine—the anthropological border operates as both open and closed, loose and solid, permeable and impregnable.

It is not toward resolving or asserting definitive characteristics, or filling in an open referent, that is of most interest here so much as the vacillation around perceived borders. The vacillation around the "authenticity" of "Australia" is homologous to the play around "disability" in the *DDA*. Just as "disability' is torn in the definitional sections between an obvious and inherent biomedical condition and that which inheres in social relations and amid other signifiers so too does "Australia" suffer the same fate; the contestation over the universality, self-evidence, security, or otherwise of "its" location speaks volumes regarding the difficulty of placement—neither a person with a "disability" or "Australia" have quite made it yet to that false sense and site of "independence." The "inferiority complex" coincides around a second-order norm, pivoting on a fulcrum of incompleteness that both mobilizes a further chase and sees that chase itself *as* the defining quality, as by default identificatory. Thus, amid the very effort to say what is uniquely Australian and to call forth a chain of signification that solidifies the particularity, there is the continuous play of perceived liminality, inciting moments that race toward clarification of the ambiguous. These are moments, like the *Tampa* crisis, that seek phantasmic identifications against what Judith Butler (1993, p. 105) calls "ambiguous and cross-corporeal co-habitations."

The implications of such fuzziness around anthropological borders has direct consequence for Daniel Hoggan, for the fear of the unhomely pulses through the legal figurings and responses—what kind of citizen do "Australian" schools want to produce and who should be allowed to go to one on that basis? What kind of legal systems "protect" the interests of some "Australians" (remaining students and teachers) against the actions of other "Australians" (bad boys)? What kind of legal systems "protect" persons with disabilities from discrimination? We suggest below that there is a subtle yet energetic interpenetration between aporia around "Australia" and those sensed around the role of law and education as problematic closures. As responses to aporia sensed but never quite articulated, the two fields sustain or reinvigorate a constitutional divide between "abled" and "disabled" that play out on Daniel Hoggan's existence, reterritorializing the disciplines' discursive domain's on the (non)basis of *différance*.

Problematic Closures: Law, Education, and Burning Down the School

[We must] … embark on a disease defense build-up similar to that undertaken in the 1980s to respond to the perceived military threat of the Soviet Union. We must reorder our nation's budget priorities from programs that destroy life to those that will preserve and enhance life. It is ironic that we can defend our country from a foreign foe but we cannot defend our people from disease….I will continue to challenge those who believe that our national defense lies solely in our military arsenals. They are missing the point—if we cannot protect our citizens from disease and disability, the true enemy lies within our borders (Hatfield, 1995, p. 1077).[5]

Students cast as "disabled," especially those deemed as being of the unruly or outlaw kind incite a degree of hysteria that requires vigorous policing and border control—just in case an "alien body" disturbs the solace of sameness. Rooting out the possible invader (to build on Hatfield's semantics) is achieved through a rhetoric of moral panic. The passion for hysteria is only possible by invoking an imaginary of sameness. Such a frenzied reaction is more than a mere dread of falling into the abyss of "disability," it is what Laplanche and Pontalis (1973, p. 194) term a "paroxystic [event] (e.g. emotional crisis accompanied by theatricality)." The crisis is exemplified in a catchcry reminiscent of xenophobia amid perceived waves of immigrants or refugees crashing onto the shore: "If we let Daniel in, how many more will come? There'll be mayhem in the classroom!"

Brenda Brueggemann et al. (2001) document other versions of backlash against perceived borders that have become too porous—in this case it is backlash against the "mainstreaming" of students designated with learning disability (LD) in the United States. They cite the famous instance of Jon Westling, provost of Boston University who manufactured a case history of a student he called Somnolent Samantha, who repeatedly dozed off in class and needed updating by her professors on the missed content. It was only after a lawsuit that Westling owned up to inventing the "extreme" story as part of a campaign of opposition to educational accommodations for people with LD. As Brueggemann et al. put it "the rhetorical strategy of finding, or, if necessary, inventing, an extreme example of LD students' 'demands' has become routine practice in a growing learning disability backlash" (p. 376).

Across hemispheres, the High Court of Australia continues the tradition; the "monstrous body" of Daniel Hoggan becomes a site that admonishes and warns of an impending penetration of a border as well as threatens the collapse of institutions that govern and subjectify proper citizenly conduct. New theatrics then circulate and what "takes place" as part of the outcome is the reorganization of territory, in this case the landscapes "owned" by law and the "bodies" (dis)owned by education—in short, a reformulation of the never-settled bodyscapes of citizen-production and being "Australian."

There is an alchemy of governmental effects when law and education meld to consider what separates out the abled from the disabled, the proper from the improper, the compulsory from the excluded, the citizen from the non(contributory)citizen. In the *Purvis* case, descriptions of Daniel Hoggan's behavior become exemplary sites for reaffirming perceived borders that had been transgressed and for reinvigorating the illusion of control over bureau-cratic conduct, institutional objectives, and subjectivities of the young. The illusion of reaffirming hard lines around disciplinary fields and their "docile" subjects is achieved in part through rhetorical strategies that most efficiently capture what Chambers (opening quote) calls "the horror of the unhomely" and "the dread of a rationality confronted with what exceeds and slips its grasp." In this case it entails reinforcing as a solid entity images of criminal behavior such as pyromania and using that as a benchmark against which to fabricate and discuss Daniel's "place."

For example, several documents including the High Court *Application for Special Leave to Appeal (HCA, Special leave to Appeal,* 5 November 2002)*, the transcript of proceedings in *Purvis* (HCA No S423 of 2002, *Proceedings*, 2003) and the High Court judgment itself *Purvis v New South Wales (Department of Education and Training)* 2003 (202 *ALR* 133), contain legal narratives that indicate a slippage between the unruly subject (in this instance Daniel Hoggan) and the criminalized anti-citizen (a fictitious fire bug). In an interplay between Daniel's transgression of behavioral norms and imagined school burnings a constitutional divide between disability and ability, between criminal and citizen, is reenacted. Daniel's behavioral trans-gressions were noted in the legal texts but perhaps weren't considered trans-gressive enough. There was still a degree of uncertainty around whether what he did was so horrendous even if it was already considered "bad." To procure and explain how compulsory schooling is only compulsory schooling for some and tentative and provisional for others, enacted under a limited ethos of citizenly performance and contribution, a "badder" version of Daniel had to be implied—a version which pins the pyromaniac as unquestionably deviant and that moves Daniel closer to a stricter limit that ought not be transgressed. The effect is not just what bubbles over for Daniel—rather, it remakes "state schools" in "Australia" as exclusive sites, set up not so much in opposition to the private but more in consonance with "the human," "the citizen," and "the Ordinary."

A most effective, even if not intended, way to achieve the reorganization of borders, to reestablish a dividing line that may have lost its visibility temporarily, is to invoke the specter of violence as rationale for marked and unmarked change. Themes of violence featured significantly in the *Application for Special leave to Appeal (HCA, Special leave to Appeal,* 5 November 2002)*: Justice Gummow argues (at lines 70–71) that s.5 of the DDA requires the courts to find the "true basis for the activity" [the source of the problem] and swiftly concludes that "on one view of it anyway…It was violence (per Gummow at lines 75–76)." The heart of the matter is whether Daniel's behaviors, translated into symbols of violence, resulting in exclusion are read as constituting discrimination (see Gleeson at lines 81–82). But not just any violence will do. It has to take a form that arouses different intensities distributed across a state of passion—a form that incites moral panic in excess of the acts under deliberation. Justice Gleeson plays on such a sense of moral panic, for instance, by asking "Now if his [Daniel's] behaviour had included repeated attempts to burn down the school, could he have been excluded lawfully?" (per Gleeson at lines 108–109).

Despite the fact that there was never any suggestion that Daniel Hoggan had attempted or had a propensity to attempt to burn down the school Gleeson persistently enflames legal argument by returning to the trope of the dangerous fire bug within the appeal application, in the proceedings, and traces of the image do appear in his final judgment. The strategy is not individualizable; however, the image proved seductive and traveled further into the heart and hearth of the legal dispute in other instances as well, for example when Gummow curtly asked counsel for Alexander Purvis, Mr S. J. Gageler: "It is my question, too: Could this kid have been excluded if he had burned down the school?" (per Gummow at lines 124–125). Gleeson observes further that "disability seems to be a negative concept. The part to which you are refering seems to be limited to an inability to do something" (per Gleeson, at lines 744–746). He then asks "Does this [definition of disability] apply to someone who is, for example, a pyromaniac? A child who enjoys setting fire to premises…." (per Gleeson, at lines 755–757). The rhythm of repetition increases with Calligan asking "How many schools would he be allowed to burn down?"(per Calligan at line 772). The line of reasoning and order of questioning bespeak a fit of pyro-manic fantasies that wed Daniel's kicking, biting, and swearing "naturally" to arson. This in turn constitutes a new kind of *problema* for the system—pyromania can be comfortably posited as behavior which undoubtedly projects a task to be done (a soul to "correct") and that protects from something unavowable (an imagined child who hates school so much).

There are crucial discursive shifts in the reasoning here, then, that move from simulation to unquestioned reality, creating a new kind of "disabled student" and authorizing a new response. That is, while Daniel's behavior did not suggest any preoccupation with fire, the repetition assures that burning down the school—a fantasy of law and education's "inability" to fully close the system of citizen-reproduction—becomes the point of reference for territorial reorganization—of law's purview for what counts as disability and as discrimination and of compulsory education's range of acceptable students. What is tolerable in or as "Ordinary Australia" or "proper" Australian citizenship interpenetrates, then, what can or cannot be accepted as a function of "disability." Put another way, the decisions and judgments made about Daniel's behavior are not simplistically a function of deciding what is good or bad conduct within a given school or what is workable or not workable within a classroom. Rather, Daniel's behavior is always and everywhere something beyond "his" at the very moment it is paradoxically pegged to his "body" and individualized as his own:

The appellant points out that an aspect of the pupil's disability was his disturbed behaviour, it is said that he was suspended and expelled because of his disability. The same would apply if the disturbed behaviour resulting from a pupils' disorder has taken the form of attempting to burn a school down, or attempting to kill somebody. On the appellant's argument, to suspend or expel such a pupil because of his or her behaviour would be to treat the pupil in that way because of his or her disability (per Gleeson, at 202 *ALR* 137, para 10).

The misreading of Daniel's body and reconfiguration of Daniel's persona as violent and therefore onto-deviant masks the tropes that law itself has deployed in the instituting of trauma and violence. This is a violence where, as Van Oenen (2004, p.140) puts it "legal decisions are always haunted by undecidability, and by traces of the original violence that installed the law."[6] Daniel's behavior is entrapped in a loop, oscillating between embodiment and disembodiment, revealing the contrariness and ambiguity of "the disabled body," which via Leder (1990), is taking flight and "dys-appearing."

There is little doubt that those "humans" on the receiving ends of Daniel's hitting, kicking, and swearing felt that they had been subjected to violence, a violence they would rather not encounter as part of going to class or doing their job. Anyone who's taught in "volatile" situations knows the feeling and would probably rather be home watching television than ducking and weaving blows. Whilst we acknowledge multiple levels of duty of care to different stakeholders by the school (other students, teachers and Daniel Hoggan), we suggest that once launched overtly into the institutions of the Court, the legal transcripts fabricate a subject, arbitrate an ontology, and determine a life chance in ways that exceed what was anterior to their entering a court of law and in domains beyond their purview. In short, we suggest that the institution of law aggressively gains new territory for itself as arbiter of matters ontological especially when the subject being remorphed is young and is marked as "disabled," that this includes the arbitration of what a school is and who should or should not attend, and that this in turn acts back upon the sliding signifier of "Australia."

We suggest further that it is such (non)experiences of aporia that seek to resecure "Australia," "law," and "education's" domains through clarifying the dividing lines around ability and disability, that it is "the disabled body" that is torched more so than any school building. The transformation of the disabled body into another fabrication called "the suspect class" is a restatement and transmogrification of an historical association of "disability" with dishonesty, deception, and more broadly with the criminal body (Stone, 1984). This association rears its head in discussion of what a criminal behavior actually is: "Do you accept that 'disturbed behaviour' when referred to in (g) [s. 4, *DDA*], will include some behaviours which are criminal behaviours?" (HCA No S423 of 2002, *Proceedings*, 2003, per Hayne at lines 1371–1374). Thus, for Justice Callinan the *primary basis* for rejecting the Appeal concerned the potential for the *DDA* to condone criminal actions:

> (T)he Act cannot be sensibly read, in my opinion, as extending to behavior which constitutes criminal or quasi-criminal conduct. If it were intended to include, as a disability behaviour which was criminal, itself a startling proposition, then the legislation would surely have said so in clear terms, if of course constitutionally it could operate to impose toleration of criminal conduct on a state educational authority ... And by criminal behaviour I do not mean only behavior not excusable by reason of an absence of mens rea [knowable intent]. Whether there may or may not be such a defense available is a different matter from the nature of the physical acts which, on the face, involve unlawful behavior. If it were otherwise, behavior with a capacity to injure, indeed even kill someone, or to damage property (by, for example burning a school down) could be excused (202 *ALR* 196, per Callinan at para 271).

Yet, this aggressive and even violent effort at shoring up what belongs to legal systems fails to close the door completely. Aporia are sensed not just within the to and fro around what standard, principle, or primary basis to apply to Daniel's (non)place within a school (and perhaps more chillingly on earth) but more specifically in what does and what *could* operate as a "body" mediated in legal texts. That is, neither law nor education could operate in the same mode as they do now if they could not objectify, individualize, count, and sort "bodies" as independent entities amenable to administration, governance, reward, and blame. Thus, the reterritorialization of law and education in the *Purvis* case, and we would argue beyond it, is dependent upon a particularly paradoxical discourse of *body*.

Specifically, this is a conception of body as a mechanical structure with clear demarcations between functionality and exteriorized voliticious actions, a functionalist biomedical ordering that is not just repressive but that is ultimately productive; such orderings tell "us" stories, they contain narratives as to "whom" we are and how we "should be." Yet, if such conceptions of body were so encompassing, self-evident, and logical then different and competing conceptions could not be articulated. The loss or marginalization of competing conceptions of body (repression) is what *Purvis* is dangerously implicated in.

For instance, in his analysis of contemporary American law that draws inspiration from Judith Butler's *Bodies That Matter*, Alan Hyde offers three principal theses concerning *body* and legal discourse. First, *body* means an inconsistent and incoherent assortment of representations and visualizations, deployed to solve political problems internal to legal discourse. Second, there is no attractive alternative to this practice of representation. In particular, there is no "real" or "material" body that is available as a standard for political or legal theory, even when the precise question to be answered involves defining boundaries of, or intrusion into, or use of, that body: "We have literally no way of grasping cognitively the most intimate aspects of our bodies except through words and images of legal, that is political discourse, developed to serve political purposes." Third, legal thinkers should recognize and confront the constructed nature of their representations of body, and not, as they often do, inappropriately naturalize those constructions: "Such inappropriate naturalizations of what are really discursive artifacts include localizing in the body of such apparently natural or objective factors such as race, sex, and disease" (Hyde, 1997, p. 4).

Hyde locates the ethical sensibility of his project in proliferation, then, not in repression: "the proliferation of competing discursive constructions and the acquisition of a particular psychological attitude toward our constructions, under which they come to be experienced as made, not natural" (p. 8). An instance of such an alternative conception would be Elizabeth Grosz's (1994) discussion of body as möbius strip. The notion of a möbius strip represents corporeality in terms of a two-fold, yet non-dualist schema of "the inside out" and "the outside in" covering two dimensions, physicality/flesh and figuring/discipline, that foreground the limitations of a traditional interior/exterior problematic and body/mind dualism. In addition, a number of feminist post-structuralist legal scholars have argued over just how much legal discourse can handle alternative conceptions of body or corporeality. Despite the elusive, contradictory, and even conflicted representation of body in legal discourse of which Hyde speaks, there is another sense in which a "benchmark" legal body is observable, thoroughly saturated with a history in specific locales that has not been erased even if invisible (Grbich, 1992; Thornton, 1996; 2000). In these accounts, even if ontological figurations are understood as fabricated standards, something normative is still operating to form identities, social meaning and values, and to structure particular kinds of subjectivities. Thornton (1996, p. 72) calls this something "benchmark man"—a convenient carapace that occludes the identity of its typical beneficiary.

In Daniel Hoggan's case, while perhaps qualifying as a "typical beneficiary" on the fabricated grounds of race, class, and gender the haunting of legal and educational imaginaries by a performative passion for sameness disqualified him from greater proximity to the preferred location—at desk at the local state high school. In the following section, then, we consider how conceptual demarcations around behavior, bad behavior, and discrimination both inscribe and exceed discourses of body or shifts into theorization of "the body."

Conceptual Demarcations: Bad Behavior, Disability, and Discrimination in Schools

One of the central questions (points of dispute) in *Purvis* and the preceding cases concerned the matter of whether Daniel Hoggan's "behavior" was part of his disability or whether the behavior that was seen as a part of him was not part of his disability. The High Court found that Daniel had not been discriminated against on the basis of his disability. The Court also found that his behavior was not planned or motivated by ill intent (202 *ALR* 164 at para 128, per McHugh and Kirby). The judgment of Justices McHugh and Kirby were in dissent. The Court found that the definition of disability in section 4 (g) of the *DDA* includes behavior that may arise from underlying conditions. However, the majority also found that Daniel needed to be compared to a student who was not disabled but who had acted as Daniel had acted (i.e. "violently"). This meant that there would have been no discrimination.

The conceptualisation of the comparator ties directly into how constitutional divides between "able-bodied" and "disabled" are performed and renewed as a passion for sameness. Indeed, the notion of treating "likes" with like, an Aristotelian ethos, undergirds anti-discrimination law and leads to a focus on procedural rather than substantive "equality." Before exploring this matter further, though, it is important to state that in s5(1) of the *DDA* a person is considered to have discriminated against another, if because of that person's disability, they treat the disabled person less favorably "than, in circumstances that are the *same or are materially different*" (emphasis added) and in regard to the treatment of a person without a disability. So there are two points of reference—similitude in the situation and a person without a disability.

In their deliberations, counsel for the appellant and the Judges debated the basis of the attributes of the comparator—should the comparator be a student with unruly behavior or delinquency problems or a student without an impairment? As Gleeson remarks, if we compare the "treatment" of Daniel with another hypothetical person without a disability, "What if anything is the other pupil to be assumed to have done?" (202 *ALR* 136, para 8). The issue of "doing" raises the vexed question of agency and volition—old Western theological preoccupations with will and free will—and whether, for instance, the meaning of unruly behavior changes depending upon the onto-status of the person concerned: Would the student have been expelled sooner if they were marked as indigenous or female? In legal terms, however, the vexed question is slightly different—it relates to whether the comparator should have the characteristics of "the disabled person" (in this case Daniel). The debate thus turned implicitly on what counted as a characteristic, on whether the point of reference should be a white boy deemed to have a disability such as emotional disturbance (ED) or a white boy who simply "*chooses*" to be "bad?" The most pivotal decision, then, was in terms of who the comparator should be as predicated on perceived presence or absence of disability.

The issue of *how the comparator is chosen* has been contentious since the commencement of the *DDA*. In their report *Federal Discrimination Law 2004,* the Human Rights and Equal Opportunity Commission (HREOC 2004) noted that although the question appears to be settled in the decision of *Purvis*, that contestation will continue.[7] For instance, Blind Citizens Australia argued in a submission into the *Inquiry* into the DDA, that the usage of a comparator (who is "abled" [with disablement]) has led to difficulty pursuing cases of direct discrimination under the DDA by blind people: "There are situations in which the aggrieved person's disability is material to the unfair treatment but it still cannot be said that treatment is the case of the aggrieved person's disability" (Blind Citizens Australia, 2003, p. 7).

While one legal authority indicated that the characteristics of the person were not to be imputed to the comparator,[8] the Full Federal Court (*Purvis v New South Wales (Department of Education and Training)* (2002) 70 ALD 609) in reviewing the original (*Purvis*) decision made by the HREOC rejected this line of argument:

> The proper comparison ... in order to test the relevance of disability, as such, is between the treatment of the complainant with the particular brain damage in question and a person without that brain damage but in like circumstance. This means that like conduct is to be assumed in both cases (70 ALD 618, para 29).

And later:

> The task then is to ascertain whether the treatment or proposed treatment is based on the ground of the particular disability or 'on another (and non-discriminatory) ground. There must always be that contrast. To be of any value, the hypothetical illustration must make assumption as to *all factual integers* (70 ALD 618, para 32; emphasis added).

Although the High Court rejected the Full Federal Court's understanding of disability, arguing that disability includes all its behavioral manifestations, they nonetheless approved of the Federal Court's argument about the comparator. They held that the comparator was to be a student *without* a disability but also a student who displayed violent behavior. As Gleeson puts it:

> What for him, was disturbed behavior, might be, for another pupil, bad behavior. Another pupil "without the disability" would be another pupil without disturbed behavior resulting from a disorder, not another pupil who did not misbehave....The required comparison is with a pupil without the disability; not a pupil without the violence (202 *ALR* 137, para 11).

This approach by the High Court silences the differences between Daniel and the comparator in ways that exceed commonsensical discourses of body and theorization of "the body." It denies the existence of a different *moral* landscape that eclipses disparities in volition. The approach arbitrates what a behavior is and what a "bad behavior" is before the case has really begun. It implies that "bad behavior" and "disability" are inherently linked and therefore unlinkable in ways that exceed whether body is seen as interior, exterior, both, or neither. In so doing, however, it attempts to locate the origins of school-based interactions within a discrete and singular site—Daniel—while eliding his particularity, his input (Daniel was never called upon to speak at the trial—an "invisible" limit), and his unique biographical constellation. Through a passion for sameness that circularly constructs deviation the performance of authorizing the comparator slides beyond consideration of "body" and "the body"-blanching differences into a vision of similitude and pegging distinctions on behavior that is already deemed isolatable, observable, and individual.

We argue that this invoking of the comparator draws on an erroneous analogy of "benchmark boy" where the variable upon which comparison pivots is not a debate over the school's atmosphere, the teachers' attitudes, the teasing by other children, a poor curriculum, or any other such variable that may constitute "all factual integers." Instead, the invocation of the comparator as "without disability" suggests the ultimate paradox and (non)experience of aporia—body becomes irrelevant at one level, yet it must be inherently significant for "without disability" to be recognized at another. The decision thus presumes what ought to be explained and diminishes precisely what is being contested back into a liberal semantic. The establishment of a particular kind of norm, against which to rate Daniel's normalcy one more time, reduces all the paradoxes, complexities, and ambiguities of the case to a metric of equivalence predicated on a single, obscure variable—"bad behavior" as a function of "volition." Adherence to the norm leaves the "ableist body" of law intact and veiled—points of entry are only possible by arguing for assimilating into a fictive standard, creating points of impassibility for certain "bodies." This in turn controls what counts as "difference" and as "sameness" or similitude in the comparator's case—difference is not that which cannot be known, ungraspable, but that which is produced *only* in relation to a pre-established norm, amenable to being pegged on a scale, and governed in terms of its distance from a silent or unquestioned center.

We suggest further that in Daniel's case, then, even in legal terms the comparator mobilized is not "matching like with like" and conflates descriptors such as "disturbed behavior" with an a priori yet unarticulated presumption of "bad behavior." The implications of such conceptual demarcations and efforts to both transgress and block the step across into a site unknown are serious. It establishes a precedent that reduces being to segregable units and depicts lives of children labeled as disabled as simply variations of a theme which, ironically, have no other "theatrics" attached to them except what is "granted" as a point of comparison with another fabrication, "the able-bodied." As Thornton argues "a model predicated on comparability is particularly unsuited to the ground of impairment because the complainant simply cannot be said to be similarly situated to an able-bodied person" (Thornton 1996, 79). The saying and unsaying of "disability" and its "difference" secure the temporary solidity of a (temporary) center or reference point. "Disability," conceptualized as "neither-this-not-that" in terms of citizenship and belonging is thus called upon to confer solidity on "this-and-that."

The line of reasoning that refuses to unthink either the comparator process in theories of justice as well as the very historicity of the operation of the norm (Davis, 1997) helps structure the fine-grained interpretations of the *DDA* that were eventually delivered in the *Purvis* case. In contrast with the initial HREOC findings against the school[9] the High Court decision shifted discursive emphasis away from school liability towards the onto-deviancy of Daniel. In short, law's authorizing eye positioned its gaze on the student and not on the actions of other available entities or "factual integers" such as principal or curriculum. An onto-deviancy focus thus obscured alternate approaches to reading dis/ability and the issues at hand in a case like *Purvis*.

In sum, the multiple conceptual demarcations invoked around *Purvis* and efforts to transgress and block them in legal texts simulate yet exceed "the uniqueness of the Australian constitution" that legitimized discrimination based on constructions of race. According to the legal decisions made, discrimination against "disabled people" in this case "disabled students" may occur and not necessarily be *illegal*—and in the end becomes *permissible*.

It is not accurate, however, to say that s5 (2) of the Act imposes an obligation to provide accommodation. *No matter how important* a particular accommodation may be for a disabled person or disabled persons generally, *failure to provide it is not a breach* of the Act per se. Rather, s5 (2) has the effect that a discriminator does not necessarily escape a finding of discrimination by asserting that the actual circumstances involved applied equally to those with and without disabilities. *No doubt as a practical matter* the discriminator may have to take steps to provide the accommodation to *escape a finding* of discrimination. But that is different from asserting that the Act imposes an obligation to provide accommodation *for the disabled* (per McHugh and Kirby at 158, para 104; emphasis added).

We are not engaging here, though, in a competition for oppression that pits race against disability against gender against class to win the prize of the most oppressed under static or sovereign theories of power. Instead, we suggest that what underwrites conceptual demarcations, populational reasonings, entifications, objectifications, essentializations, and generalizations about "ontology" is not a "poor will" or "false consciousness," nor an intended repression or conspiracy theory, but a *metric conception of equality, discrimination, and justice predicated upon a language and logic of entities* that has met its limits in the figurings and responses to *Purvis*. Once "ontologies" are presumed discrete and thought amenable to calculation, the limits of the discursive field are set and "society" is thought to speak for itself (Ewald, 1991). Ontological politics, embedded particularly in legal texts between poles of life and death, which are not to be questioned, establish ideas of risk and risk-management. Only certain recombinations become possible when life is thought one thing, death another, and disability is constantly refigured as somewhere "in-between." A serialized ontology and flat chronology structure belief in a middle, in liminality, in ambiguity. Entification functions, then, to rein in the very "excess" that a language and logic of entities structures and makes possible—that symbolic excess thought so offensive to "Ordinary Australians."

As such, something still seems to escape the "settlement" that *Purvis* appeared to render. Daniel's mediated presence in the legal text, drawn through his silencing, screams. What is really "Australian" in terms of corporeality, citizenship, and schooling still seems unclear, for the scenario could seemingly be played out in multiple locations, with appeals to global citizens, globalization or the global economy not fully explaining how this could be; and what transcendental authority law and education make appeal to as well—their comparator or point of reference as *fields*—maintains an important ambiguity. For what else would such disciplines do or rely upon if the continuous organization of dissent and the governance of the out-of-joint was no longer available to them?

(Non)Concluding Thoughts

The (non)experience of aporia at the levels of anthropological borders, problematic closures, and conceptual demarcations are not cases of intellectual gymnastics without effects and nor are they cases suggesting completion. We suggest through this analysis that openness and closure around leaky borders operate as relations of intensification rather than of opposition

(Luhmann, 1995). Such orientations to borders may present new ways of understanding normalization and the construction of the disabled body that is in a constant state of unfinishedness. This state of unfinished is not that which upsets the system, however, but that which *allows* it (Derrida and Ferraris, 2001). In this light, there are several political implications of the *Purvis* case worth elaborating in conclusion.

First, as the *Purvis* case indicates, "disability" has no literal referent. It is formed dialogically, is continually engaged with the processes of subjectification, differential corporeal markers, and indices of "the human," "the citizen, and "the Ordinary." As such, our analysis also suggests, then, that there is no "inside" and "outside" of disability. The central question in *Purvis*—whether and to what extent should a distinction be drawn between disability and "its" manifestations—highlights instead that what is at stake is a peculiar form of rationality that draws confidence from identifying causal links in order to correct them when they go "awry." More specifically, we suggest that the figurings and responses to *Purvis* index a juridico-philosophical crossover point in arguments over "human relations"—that which is shifting from a metaphysical obsession with absence/presence (suspension/expulsion/inclusion) to a new chaotics of pattern/random (the comparator/bodies/nations).

Second, the figurings and responses to *Purvis* also marshal us toward an alternative conceptualization of justice that does not draw upon theories of justice as distributive, corrective, right, or law. The *Purvis* case forces consideration of seeming binary positions: whether "disability" is that which has to be *surrendered and disavowed* (integrated, included, mitigated,[10] mainstreamed and thereby eradicated) or *defended* (left uncontested as embodiment that is and is not "biological"). If there is such an ethics of affirmation that aporia invite us to consider, then it implies that one is attentive to "otherness," to the alterity of the other, to something new and other, and to an unforeseeable future.

Such affirmative action is not in order to harness something back toward the same. The affirmation is an openness to a difference that seems impossible to imagine, grasp, or even know; a difference that does not emerge out of deviation from "the same" or from a norm, an openness to difference that is the other's unique forms without knowledge of the constitutional divide that props up perceptions of "uniqueness." This attentiveness to difference without a priori anchor may also frighten, appear risky, seem dangerous—the fear of saying "yes" arises when the most is thought to be at stake. The ethical responsibility that the paralysis of paradox establishes does not elevate embrace over fear or fear over embrace but intuits the unknowability of where the step across might land, with an optimism toward the possibility of new forms of relations when the edges are admitted and engaged.

The *Purvis* case avidly tests such an emergent conception of relations, ethics, and justice, straining "the environment's" willingness to hold all within its loving arms: Who wants to be hit? Who wants their child to be hit? Who wants their child expelled for hitting? Yet in focusing solely on the hitting (and on a presumed homogeneous "who") and not on the possibilities for experiencing (or even designing) the world very differently such forms of alterity become construed as problems of the integrable rather than of the integral--an orientation to "disability" as that which must be identified in order to be effaced, as that which enables the performance of a passion for sameness so that other temporary identifications can be reconstituted as solid and as "at home."

Third, the analysis lends reconsideration and breadth to the politics of place beyond the simplicity of identifying "nations"; under an aporetic conceptualization of ethics "home" is up for grabs. Because aporia cannot be fully experienced they refuse arrival at a final universalized place. Home may not be so much what is returned to but what is carried and travels. This is precisely what Chambers (2001) notes is at stake in new appeals to globality—he fears the resecuring of a final destination, a place which authorizes my speech in the name of some other fabrication and that again occludes recognition of the "typical beneficiary"—a dispersal, a spread, a diffusion of "the same"—a change without difference.

Thus we suggest that it is simultaneously impossible and necessary to cross borderlines that the *Purvis* case brings to noticeability in rethinking disability, law, education, and nations. The persistent figuring of "disability" as ambiguous and elusive keeps open dual-edges that create the conditions of paralysis necessary for responsibility. If, on the one hand, appeals to disability-as-embodied are a suspect retreat to the biological and on the other affirming disability-as-desirous and as an alterity of the integral and not of the integrable is a romantic illusion that elides a history of eradication then we are pushed toward a new conceptualization of home. But instead of finding new homes to inhabit, colonize, homogenize, and straighten, new sites in which to ground "voice," we can perhaps recognize how an uncomfortable region, an unhomeliness, dwells within and makes us into an "us" and "we" in the first "place."

References

Altman, B. (2001). Disability definitions, models, classification schemes, and applications. In G. Albrecht, K. Seelman and M. Bury (Eds.), *Handbook of disability studies* (pp. 97–122). Thousand Oaks, CA: Sage.

Baker, B. (1999). Disabling methodologies. *Pedagogy, culture and society, 7*(1), 91–116.

———. (2002). The hunt for disability: The new eugenics and the normalization of schoolchildren. *Teachers College Record, 104*, 663–703.

Brueggemann, B. J., Feldmaneier White, L., Dunn, P., Heifferon, B., and Cheu, J. (2001). Becoming visible: Lessons in disability. *CCC (College, Composition, and Communication), 52*(3), 368–398.

Burney, L. (2004). *Keynote address at a meeting of the Australian Association for Research in Education (AARE)*. Melbourne: University of Melbourne.

Butler, J. (1993). *Bodies that matter: On the discursive limits of "sex."* New York: Routledge.

Campbell, F. (1999). Refleshingly disabled: Interrogations into the corporeality of "disablised bodies." *Australian Feminist Law Journal,* 12 March, 57–80.

———. (2001). Inciting legal fictions: "Disability's date with ontology and the ableist body of the law." *Griffith Law Review, 10*(1), 42–62.

Carlson, D. (2003). The traumatic dimension of law. *Cardoza Law Review, 24*(6), 2287–2329.

Chambers, I. (2001). *Culture after humanism: History, culture, subjectivity.* London: Routledge.

Deleuze, G., and Guattari, F. (1987). *A thousand plateaus: Capitalism and schizophrenia* (B. Massumi, Trans.). Minneapolis: University of Minnesota Press.

Derrida, J. (1993) *Aporias*. Stanford, CA: Stanford University Press.

Derrida, J. and Ferraris, M. (2001) *A Taste for the Secret.* Cambridge: Polity Press.

Duncanson, I. (2001). *A (re)turn to race in Australian politics.* Melbourne: 19th annual Law and Society Conference: Forms of Legal Identity.

Ewald, F. (1991). Insurance and risk. In G. Burchell, C. Gordon and P. Miller (Eds.), *The Foucault effect: Studies in governmentality*. Chicago: University of Chicago Press.

Foucault, M. (1961/1988). *Madness and civilization: A history of insanity in the age of reason* (R. Howard, Trans.). New York: Vintage Books.

———. (1996). *Foucault live: Interviews, 1961–1984*. New York: Semiotext(e).

Grbich, J. (1992). The body in legal theory. *University of Tasmania Law Review, 1*, 26–58.

Grosz, E. (1994). *Volatile bodies: Toward a corporeal feminism*. St. Leonard: Allen and Unwin.

Hatfield, M. (1995). The war against disease and disability. *The Journal of the American Medical Association, 274*, 1077.

Human Rights and Equal Opportunity Commission (HREOC). (2004). *Federal Discrimination Law 2004*. Sydney: Author.

Hyde, A. (1997). *Bodies of law*. Princeton, NJ: Princeton University Press.

Laplanche, J., and Pontalis, J. B. (1973). *The language of psycho–analysis*. London: Hogarth Press.

Latour, B. (1993). *We have never been modern*. New York: Harvester Wheatsheaf.

Leder, D. (1990). *The absent body*. Chicago: Chicago University Press.

Luhmann, N. (1995). *Social systems*. Stanford, CA: Stanford University Press.

Robinson, K. (2003). The passion and the pleasure: Foucault's art of not being oneself. *Theory, Culture, and Society, 20*(2), 119–144.

Rundle, G. (2001). The opportunist: John Howard and the triumph of reaction. *Quarterly Essay, 3*.

Sells, M. (1994). *The mythical languages of unsaying*. Chicago: University of Chicago Press.

Sinclair, J. (2004). Spirituality and the (secular) Ordinary Australian imaginary. *Continuum: Journal of Media and Cultural Studies, 18*(2), 279–293.

Skouteris, V. (2004). Statistical societies of interchangeable lives. *Law and Critique, 15*, 119–138.

Stiker, H. J. (2000). *A history of disability*. Ann Arbor, MI: University of Michigan Press.

Thornton, M. (1996). *Dissonance and distrust: Women in the legal profession*. Melbourne: Oxford University Press.

———. (2000). Neo–liberalism, discrimination, and the politics of ressentiment. *Law in Context Special Issue, 17*, 8–27.

———. (2001). EEO in a neo–liberal climate. *Journal of Interdisciplinary Gender Studies, 6*(1), 77–104.

Van Oenen, G. (2004). Finding cover: Legal trauma and how to take care of it. *Law and Critique, 15*, 139–158.

Notes

[1] *Purvis v New South Wales (Department of Education and Training)* 2003 (202 *ALR* 133).

[2] S.22 of the *DDA* specifically concerns education and makes it unlawful for any educational authority to discriminate against a person with a disability by denying or limiting a student's access to any benefits provided by the authority, by expelling the student or subjecting them to any other detriment.

[3] Yet "disability" endures as a category. See Greg Eghigian's analysis in *Making Security Social* of the coming-into-being of disability as a term in relation to and yet beyond paid employment in Bismarckian Germany and the subsequent efforts by governments, most notably in the USA and Japan, for instance, to simulate such social insurance schemes for injured workers.

[4] This is a linkage Sinclair unpacks and around which she suggests alternatives.

[5] Senator Mark Hatfield was a Republican from Oregon and the extract is from a speech *The War Against Disease and Disability he* made when awarded the 1995 Albert Lasker Public Service Award, American Medical Association.

[6] For a fuller discussion of this theme, see Carlson (2003), *The Traumatic Dimension of Law.*

[7] In common law jurisdictions judges have acknowledged that it is often not possible to locate a comparator (for instance in the case of pregnancy) and when it is possible to find a "match" that comparator as an analogous ontology is of little use. As Thornton notes (2001, p. 94) "equality is blanched of meaning in the absence of a dialectical relationship with inequality." Resorting to a comparator masks the fact that not all-differential treatment induces inequality, just as a passion for sameness may promote "inequalities."

[8] See *Doplink v Department of Defence* (1995) EOC 92 -669;*IW v City of Perth* (1997) 191 CLR 1 *Alex Purvis on Behalf of Daniel Hoggan v State of NSW (Department of Education)* (2000) HREOC, Digested in (2001) EOC 93 -117.

[9] HREOC noted failure on the school's part to adjust the Draft Welfare and Discipline Policy, a failure to provide teachers with training or an awareness program, and a failure to obtain the assistance of experts) (summarized in 202 ALR, paras 49–55).

[10] See Campbell (2001) on the US Supreme Court's ADA decisions to introduce the motion of "elective" or "mitigated" disability.

CHAPTER 19

Conversations Across Disability and Difference: Teacher Education Seeking Inclusion

Julie Allan

"What is this strange desire for words?" (van Manen, 2002)

"Do not read me" (Derrida, 1979, p. 145)

Attempting to answer the last of the "vital questions facing disability studies in education" caused some trouble. At first this trouble seemed associated with writing in the normative realm and with the task of outlining what disability studies in education should be doing. Then the trouble seemed to relate to a lack of certainty about what this thing called disability studies in education was and whether its scholars were characterised by consensus or by "dialectical tensions between coherence and hybridity or between homogeneity and variability" (Artiles, 2004, p. 551). Much later I realised the trouble was with a reification of disability studies in education, treating it as if it has a life of its own, and with the very task of writing *to* disability studies in education and setting *it* challenges, as if it has the capacity to respond to these. This essay is instead directed at the scholars who locate themselves within what Davis (1997) reminds us is both a field of inquiry and a political activity. This is not a semantic point: talking about what a discipline does or should do allows for a displacement of responsibilities. It also sets up exclusions by giving the sense of disability studies in education being a (particularly clever) club to which people either belong or do not. Talking about ourselves, on the other hand, allows for a recognition of our own capacities to act and to think strategically about how—and where—we might *do* disability studies in education. I will begin by exploring the relationship between disability and other arenas of exclusion, including race, ethnicity, gender, religion, class and sexual orientation. I will then consider ways in which scholars might be able to use disability studies in education to promote and extend conversations across these different contexts in their writing and research and in teacher education.

Disability and, and, and...

Scholars of disability studies in education have expressed much pride in their discipline, viewing it as "a field of study whose time has come" (Davis, 1997, p. 1) or "an emergent field with intellectual roots in the social sciences, humanities and rehabilitation sciences" (Albrecht, et al., 2001, p. 2) and the "theoretical armamentaria" (Albrecht, et al., 2001, p. 2) from these areas. Williams (2001) declares that since the advent of disability studies in education "theorizing disability is no longer a dry intellectual or technical task" (p. 123). In spite of this evident pleasure at being associated with such a bold and innovative discipline, there have been many plaintive cries that disability studies is largely unnoticed by the academic world and that the impact of disability studies has been relatively limited. Davis (2002), for example, bemoans the fact that in spite of the prevalence of literature from disability studies "the majority of academics do not consider disability as part of their social conscience" (p. 35). Davis illustrates his argument with examples of hate crimes in which disability is overlooked by the focus of attention being given to race, which legal theorists have named "intersectionality" (p. 148). This "eclipse of disability by race occurs because anti-discrimination legislation revolves around a single axis framework" (Crenshaw, 1994, p. 40), but it could be argued that this is also how academics orient themselves in the world, only able to handle one form of oppression at a time. Berubé (1997) sees the refusal to acknowledge disability as part of what he calls the "politics of disavowal" (p. 5) or a form of ableism which sits alongside other forms of oppression such as sexism or racism but expresses a hope that scholars are moving disability studies from being a "sideshow to midway" (Berubé, 2002, p. xi). Berubé (2002) reminds us, however, that "the importance of disability as a category of social thought may depend more on the practices and politics of people with disabilities than on the work of academic disability studies" (p. x).

Concerns about the eclipse of disability by race have been somewhat overshadowed by a recognition that ethnic minorities are overrepresented within special education (Artiles et al., 1997; Ferri, 2004), and suspicion has turned on special education and its role in preserving education in the face of ever increasing diversity (Dudley-Marling, 2001). In spite of the convincing empirical evidence of the problem of overrepresentation of particular groups of students, Artiles (2004) questions the appropriateness of the focus on "representation" of any group, the result of which, he argues, is that "these students are seen as the passive carriers of categorical markers of difference (e.g., race, class, gender) and their assumed nefarious consequences (e.g., low achievement, dropout, delinquent behaviour)" (p. 552). This reductive tendency and the obsession with the physical presences and essences of students generate "myopic understandings of the role of culture and history" (p.552) and ensure that agency is denied.

The pernicious influence, especially in the US, of special education scholars such as Fuchs and Fuchs (1994) and Kauffman and Hallahan (1995) has kept conversations of any kind, never mind those across disability, race, ethnicity, gender, class, sexual orientation and other social constructs to a minimum. Slee (2001) notes an "astonishing lack of reflexivity by some special education researchers" (p. 120), such as Kauffman and Hallahan (1995), about the nature of their research and "an appalling ignorance of the scope of inclusive education" (Slee, 2001). Brantlinger (1997) can be credited with initiating the first of a series of challenges to "attackers of inclusion" (p. 426), who claimed that inclusion was being used as an ideological weapon with which to beat special education. She and others have been rewarded with vitriolic attacks which Danforth (2004) has analysed playfully—and successfully—using the sociological literature of "heresy". Brantlinger, (2004a) however, has remained puzzled that her values orientation rather than an empirical orientation has met with such hostility. Such crass attacks in which the opponents talk past one another ensure that inclusive education continues to be "about special children ... who will prove problematic as they are resettled in the mainstream" (Slee, 2001, p. 170).

The dominance in teacher education by special education has been hard to shake off, and Slee (2001) has noted the continuation of the "teacher training imperative" (p. 173) in which teacher educators continue their former practices under the guise of "inclusion" and shape new teachers into "card carrying designators of disability" (p. 171). The training of student teachers requires them to rehearse the "official scripts" of teaching (Smyth and Hattam, 2002, p. 392), which are "dominant and restrictive" (Smyth and Hattam, 2002, p. 392) and emphasise "the physical control of students' bodies...that is their movements, whereabouts and silence" (Gutierrez et al, 1995, p. 413). As Brantlinger (2004b) has observed, education policy has replaced theory as a source of guidance for practitioners and consists mainly of bland platitudes about students who are "different." At the same time as they are required to buy into a version of teaching which encourages them to control students' behaviours by modifying their own, they are kept under a veil of uncertainty about whether they will "make it" as teachers, by ensuring that their knowledge of teaching is always partial:

> Incompleteness, often valorized in textual politics as ambiguity which exposes the limits of the metaphysics of voice, in the discourse of corporate training (which in a way has colonized the discourse of education) becomes another tactics of control in human resource management (Gregoriou, 2002, p. 230).

Student teachers are thus controlled by being perpetually in training (Deleuze, 1992), never finished with education, in the sense of not yet having proved themselves as competent, and remain, according to Deleuze (1992, p. 3) "in debt."

The standards which new teachers must achieve are part of what Strathearn (2000) has called the tyranny of transparency, a regime of accountability which emphasises proving rather than improving. Elliot (2001) suggests that "colonisation through audit fosters pathologies of creative compliance in the form of gamesmanship around an indicator culture" (p. 202) and creates substantial mistrust. The standards have been recognised as invalid indicators of good teaching generally (Smyth and Shacklock, 1998; Hextall, 2000) and as part of the "struggle over the teacher's soul" (Ball, 2003, p. 217); when the standards have been applied to inclusion and participation, the effects have been sinister, pushing the new teacher towards the management of, rather than engagement with, difference. They envelop the student teacher within rigid stratifications (Roy, 2003) which deny complex thinking and firmly establish the territories of teacher and taught, knowledge and knower.

The mandate for new teachers to show that they can "address issues of diversity proactively to promote equity and to ensure that their students — regardless of race, nationality, ethnicity, religion, exceptionalities, primary spoken language, socioeconomic status, sexual orientation, body image, or gender—receive equal opportunities to participate in, enjoy, and benefit from instructional activities and resources" (National Board for Professional Teaching Standards, 2001) creates a problem and a spectacle of difference and conveys three messages to new teachers. The first is that all that is required of them is a *performance* of inclusive values, without actually having to commit to them in practice. The second message is that one can never know enough about students' pathologies to be able to deal effectively with them. Thus, they come to regard their responsibilities towards students who exhibit any kind of difference with guilt, fear and the sense they will inevitably let them down. The third message is that they can evade these responsibilities by deferring to apparently more competent individuals— those who hold "specialist" knowledge about children's difficulties or difference.

Spaces for "Doing" Disability Studies in Education

Disability, according to Albrecht et al.(2001), is an enigma which is both public and private and disability studies in education has the capacity to respond by seeking to understand "the ways in which we produce the *private room* of disability in our most public discourses" (Mitchell and Snyder (1997, p. 17). Perhaps most importantly, there is scope within disability studies in education to take up Artiles' (2004) challenge of "ending the innocent notion of essentialism" (p. 553) and restoring the notion of agency. There are four significant spaces in which scholars of disability studies in education can do their most productive work. The first is within universities, where disability studies can be established as an academic, interdisciplinary discipline; the second is in schools where young people can be assisted in thinking about difference positively and creatively; the third is in research and writing, where disability studies in education scholars can attempt to generate new debates and foster new kinds of politics; the fourth space is in teacher education, where disability studies in education can be used to challenge special education orthodoxies and cultivate student teachers who recognise their own implication in exclusion. Other contributors to this volume will have direct experience of the first of these and will be able to comment effectively on the development of disability studies in education within universities and scholars such as Ware (2001) will have much to say about the successful work with teachers and students in schools; I will concentrate on the productive spaces for change which exist in relation to research and writing and to teacher education.

Research and Writing

The challenge for scholars of disability studies in education to contribute to the on-going education conversation about race, ethnicity, gender, religion, class, sexual orientation and other social constructs is a paradoxical one. On the one hand, researching and writing about generic constructs of "social reciprocity and redistributive justice" (Brantlinger, 2004b, p. 497) or analysing the "five faces of oppression" (Young, 2000, p. 39)—exploitation, marginalisation, powerlessness, cultural imperialism and violence—take us out of the essentialist trap and reduces concerns about privileging one area over another or about the silencing effects produced in discourses; on the other hand, it is necessary also to trouble the way in which, for example, race and identity become entangled in discourses (Reid and Valle, 2004). A key question is "whose voices are validated, acknowledged and taken into account in defining the future of the field" (Artiles, 2004, p. 553). Ferri (2004) also calls for more self-conscious practices:

> LD scholars and researchers must turn the research gaze back on ourselves; a reflexive turn is necessary in order to transform our past and present complicity with racist hierarchies and agendas (p. 512).

The self-proclaimed "positivists" (Danforth, 2004) have demanded empirical evidence that special education is ineffective (Kauffman, 1999) and/or proof that inclusion is a better alternative. Those who have been unable to resist such pressures and have gone in search of *what works* have either failed to produce answers or these answers have reduced inclusion–again–to a technical problem (Sebba and Sachdev, 1997). As Ferri (2004) recommends, we should "stay with the questions rather than moving so quickly to answers" (p. 514), and it is vital that researchers refuse to give answers. We should resist the accountable but not the empirical and should undertake the kind of research which addresses the gaps caused by a failure to engage disabled people. Linton (1998) spells out what is required:

> New scholars of all stripes must recognize their moral and intellectual obligation to evaluate gaps and faults in the knowledge base they disseminate to students that result from the missing voices of disabled people (p. 142).

These missing voices are required to provide an understanding of what good inclusion looks and feels like and is more concerned with *consequences* than with outcomes (Allan, 2003; Slee and Allan, 2001).

Those writing in the field of disability studies in education are united, according to Williams (2001), by a rejection of the medical model of disability and a desire to situate difference more positively. The politicised nature of disability studies in education scholars is evident in their espoused goals of interrupting (Ferri, 2004), confounding (Brantlinger, 2004b) and exposing (Ware, 2005), adopting a "sociopolitical vision" which makes it possible to "resist and eventually change the discourse itself" (Reid and Valle, 2004, p. 478). Yet educational policy appears to be devoid of politics and disability studies in education is well placed to bring politics back (Gewirtz, 2000). This requires us to "foreground the struggles between competing interest groups over key concepts such as accountability, performance indicators and quality" (Vidovitch and Slee, 2001, pp. 450–451). We need to be vigilant and to "fight against accumulation, concentration and monopoly; in short, against all quantitative phenomena that might marginalize or reduce to silence anything that cannot be measured on their scale" (Derrida, 1992, p. 99).

One of the most exciting features of disability studies in education is that it is not limited to academic texts but has embraced a variety of art forms and modes of communication. These enable practitioners to tackle the thorny issue of representation (Artiles, 2004) in novel ways but also offer a radical form of critique in which difference is engaged with playfully and through which the gaze turns on the non-disabled viewers, forcing them to confront the banality of their own existence and their implication in disability and exclusion (Allan, 2005). Films such as *Self Preservation* and others produced by Snyder and Mitchell (2004) convey how "a new mode of *being disabled* is taking shape. This work disrupts *and* disturbs. More generally, the arts can have a positive influence on disability studies in education scholars, by encouraging them to resist closure and endings: Beckett's (1958) declaration: "the end's the beginning and yet you go on" encourages us to see inclusion as having no fixed point to which we aspire, but as a process that has to be constantly performed and with vigilance for whatever threatens it.

Although the work of scholars of disability studies in education embraces a multitude of perspectives including Marxism, feminism, postmodernism and poststructuralism, their critics have tended to portray them as postmodernists. Somewhat perjoratively branded as an "academic cult"

(Sasso, 2001, p. 188) these postmodernists have been accused of being dismissive of competences on the grounds that they are too difficult and of being a danger to children (Kauffman, 1999) Disabled researcher Mike Oliver (1999) has also been highly critical of the "pessimistic postmodernist approach to life as survival among the ruins" (p. 190), viewing it as part of the "sociological drift to irrelevance" (p. 190). Such branding is, of course, part of the reductive essentialism that disability studies in education scholars have set out to challenge. Nevertheless it is worth acknowledging that the perspectives of postmodernism and post-structuralism are particularly useful to disability studies in education. The main reason for this is that they offer tools for generating the kind of disruption practitioners of disability studies in education might aspire to, the most effective of which is deconstruction.

Deconstruction is a particularly useful tool for the practice of disability studies in education. It can help to undermine or subvert the "ideology of expertism" (Troyna and Vincent, 1996, p. 142) disrupting the "decidability" (Patrick, 1996, p. 141) in what professionals say, do and write, and exposing the exclusionary pressures which continue to be inscribed within texts (Slee and Allan, 2001). This way of reading how policy texts "get into trouble, come unstuck, offer to contradict themselves" (Eagleton, 1993, p. 134) invites us to "think again and afresh" (Biesta, 2001, p. 34) about justice and "keeps an inventionalist eye open for the other to which the law as law is *blind"* (Caputo, 1997, p. 131; original emphasis). For Derrida (1997) deconstruction *is* justice because it always "has to do with the other" (p. 17; original emphasis). The "findings" of deconstruction can be presented, not as a destruction of the well-intentioned products of the writers, but of an illustration of the impossibilities we face, framed as a series of aporias which highlight dual responsibilities:

> That is not easy. It is even impossible to conceive of a responsibility that consists in being responsible *for* two laws, or that consists in responding *to* two contradictory injunctions. No doubt. But there is no responsibility that is not the experience and experiment of the impossible (Derrida, 1997, pp. 44–45; original emphasis).

Derrida provides an example of an aporetic reframing of responsibility by asking how might we respect and respond to, on the one hand, differences and minorities and, on the other hand, the "universality of formal law, the desire for translation, agreement and univocity, the law of the majority, opposition to racism, nationalism and xenophobia" (Derrida, 1997, p. 78). Rather than seeking to reduce these double-edged responsibilities to a single set of recommendations, with the inevitable erasure this will generate, the divergent nature of these obligations can be acknowledged. Relating this to student teachers, we can think about supporting them through a series of contradictory obligations, such as demonstrating the necessary standards to qualify as a teacher *and* understanding themselves as in an inconclusive process of learning about others; maximising student achievement *and* ensuring inclusivity; or understanding the features of particular impairments *and* avoiding disabling individual students with that knowledge. Helping students to see how these obligations may pull them in different directions could enable them to recognise the significance of contingency and uncertainty in teaching and to focus their attention more constructively in the way that Brantlinger (2004b) has urged:

> We educators are entangled in complex and sometimes disturbing practices that may not benefit those we claim to serve. I ask not only that we think hard about practices that harm but also that we turn to a morality of social reciprocity and distributive justice, in which the school and life circumstances of the most vulnerable are considered first (p. 497).

I turn now to a further consideration of how teacher education might be informed and enhanced by disability studies in education.

Teacher Education

Much of the work required in teacher education is an unravelling of the existing special needs knowledge base and opening students up to difference as complex and interesting rather than as something to be managed. They need to be veered away from knowledge about students' pathologies and to be not allowed to "fix the world concretely and reductively" (Brantlinger, 2004b, p. 497).

Student teachers could be encouraged to engage in a kind of learning which Deleuze and Guattari (1987) describe as rhizomic and in which they are made to experience and experiment with inclusion and difference. The rhizome, which grows underground, differs from typically "aborescent" tree structures—comprising rigid hierarchies—of knowledge and power. These aborescent structures emphasise factual knowledge and construct learning as a process of representation, requiring performances of the *good* student or the *good* teacher. Learning to be a teacher, in the rhizomic sense, is not a journey towards a fixed end, as denoted by the standards, but wanderings along a "moving horizon" (Deleuze, 1994, p. xxi). As well as creating new knowledge, these wanderings provide opportunities for student teachers to establish new assemblages and new selves as teachers:

> A rhizome, a burrow, yes–but not an ivory tower. A line of escape, yes–but not a refuge (Deleuze and Guattari, 1987, p. 41).

Student teachers" empirical wanderings will inevitably take them into new territories in their relationships with children and, following Levinas (1998), they will have to contend with the ethics of their encounter with the other. They will have to learn how to engage with the marginalised or silenced other without trying to assimilate or acculturate that other (Levinas, 1998; Moss and Petrie, 2002). Derrida (1996) suggests that this relationship is characterised by an "infinitude of responsibility . . . with regard to the other" (p. 86), a concern to prevent injustice which is without limits.

Adopting the rhizome as the means for exploring pedagogy would privilege experimentation and experience over the interpretation of theory (Deleuze, 1995). Instead of absorbing, and later replicating, content, student teachers would be involved in:

> experimenting with pedagogy and recreating its own curricular place, identity, and content; expanding its syllabi and diversify its reading lists; *supplementing* educational discourse with other theories; deterritorializing theory of education from course based to interdisciplinary directions (Gregoriou, 2001, p. 231; original emphasis).

Student teachers' knowledge and understanding might be fashioned as a series of maps, "entirely oriented toward an experimentation in contact with the real" (Deleuze and Guattari, 1987, p. 12). These maps do not replicate knowledge; rather, they perform and create new knowledge:

> The map is open and connectable in all of its dimensions; it is detachable, reversible, susceptible to constant modification. It can be torn, reversed, adapted to any kind of mounting, reworked by an individual, group or social formation. It can be drawn on a wall, conceived as a work of art, constructed as a political action or as a mediation (Deleuze and Guattari, 1987, p. 12).

Student teachers" wanderings need to be supported and responded to in a way which does not entrench further their novice and incompetent identity. The undecidable is experienced by students as an ordeal and sustained as evidence of non-mastery, yet Deleuze and Guattari (1987) contend that "it is through loss rather than acquisition that one progresses and picks up speed" (cited in Roy, 2003, p. 56). The function of the teacher educator, in Deleuzian terms, is to create pedagogical spaces which are open and smooth, in contrast with the closed and striated spaces of conventional approaches. They would establish a form of apprenticeship which encourages students to "read everyday reality in a *foreign language* with a hesitancy and a stuttering, keeping in abeyance our everyday modes of apprehension" (Roy, 2003, pp. 172–173). Students' "creative stammerings" (Deleuze and Guattari, 1987, p. 98), questions and searches for links would be engaged with, rather than closed down as indicative of their failure to grasp content. It is in these spaces or schisms where complex thinking would take place and where "a new experiment in thought could be inserted…that might help teachers get an insight into the generative possibilities of the situation" (Roy, 2003, p. 2).

Finality Without End: Going on with Inclusion
Much of what has been suggested here has been concerned with privileging uncertainty, contingency and openness. The kinds of conversations across different arenas of exclusion—disability, race, ethnicity, gender, religion, class, sexual orientation—can be achieved, it is argued, through the kinds of practices in research and writing and in teacher education which involve "finding connections without erasing the differences" (Ferri, 2004, p. 513). These processes are, as Deleuze (1998) remarks, "a question of becoming, always incomplete ways in the midst of being formed" (p. 1). It may, however, be easier to proclaim oneself as a practitioner of the contingent than to achieve this in practice, and Baker (2002) warns us that the hunt for disability is irresistible and that a negative ontology forces all of us—despite our best intentions—to find the pathological in order to function. We may also find the pressure of the positivist sceptics waiting to see evidence that inclusion works too difficult to handle. Perhaps we can find affirmation in Beckett (1958), whose characters fail to reach an end definitively by attempting to end repeatedly. As the narrator of *Unnamable* puts it: "The search for the means to put an end to things, an end to speech is what enables the discourse to continue"(Beckett, 1958, p. 15). Can we conceive of our work within disability studies in education as a form of endless repetition which enables

us to function as constant irritants who refuse to be silenced and who are the harbingers of inclusion to come?

References

Albrecht, G., Seelman, K. and Bury, M. (2001) The formation of disability studies in G. Albrecht, K. Seelman and M. Bury (Eds). *The handbook of disability studies.* California/London/New Delhi: Sage Publications Inc.

Allan, J (2003) Introduction in J Allan (Ed). *Inclusion, participation and democracy: What is the purpose?* Dordrecht: Kluwer.

———. (2005) Encounters with exclusion through disability arts. *Journal of Research in Special Educational Needs,* 5 (1), 31–36.

Artiles, A. (2004) The end of innocence: historiography and representation in the discursive practice of LD. *Journal of Learning Disabilities,* 37 (6), 550–555.

Artiles, A., Trent, S. and Juan, L. (1997) Learning disabilities empirical research on ethnic minority students: an analysis of 22 years of studies published in selected refereed journals. *Learning Disabilities Research and Practice,* 12, 82–91.

Baker, B. (2002) The hunt for disability: The new Eugenics and the normalization of school children. *Teachers College Record,* 104 (4), 663–703.

Ball, S. (2003) The teacher's soul and the terror of performativity. *Journal of Educational Policy,* 18 (2), 215–228.

Beckett, S. (1945) *Molloy.* New York: Grove Publishers.

———. (1958) *The Unnamable.* New York: Grove Publishers.

Berubé, M. (1997) The cultural representation of disabled people affects us all. *Higher Education Chronicle,* May, 85.

———. (2002) Foreword: side shows and back bends. In L. Davis *Bending over backwards: Disability, dismodernism and other difficult positions.* New York/London: New York University Press.

Biesta, G. (2001) "Preparing for the incalculable": Deconstruction, justice and the question of education. In G. Biesta and D. Egéa–Kuehne (Eds) *Derrida and education.* London: Routledge.

Brantlinger, E. (1997) Using ideology: Cases of nonrecognition of the politics of research and practice in special education. *Review of Educational Research,* 67 (4), 425–459.

―――. (2004a) Ideologies discerned, values determined: getting past the hierarchies of special education, in L. Ware (Ed). *Ideology and the politics of in/exclusion.* New York: Peter Lang.

―――. (2004b) Confounding the needs and confronting the norms: An extension of Reid and Valle's essay. *Journal of Learning Disabilities,* 37 (6), 490–499.

Caputo, J. (1997) *Deconstruction in a nutshell: A conversation with Jacques Derrida.* New York: Fordham University Press.

Crenshaw, K. (1994) Demarginalizing the intersection of race and sex: A black feminist critique of antidiscrimination doctrine, feminist theory, and antiracist politics, in A. Jagger (Ed) *Living with contradiction: Controversies in feminist social ethics.* Boulder: Westview.

Danforth, S. (2004) Orthodoxy, heresy, and the inclusion of American students considered to have emotional/behavioral disorders. Paper presented at the Inclusive Education Colloquium, Montreal, 19–21 July.

Davis, L. (1997) *The disability studies reader.* New York/London: Routledge.

Davis, L. (2002) *Bending over backwards: Disability, dismodernism and other difficult positions.* New York/London: New York University Press.

Deleuze, G. (1992) *Postscript on the societies of control,* Accessed 30 October 2000 from: http://www.dds.nl/~n5m/texts/deleuze.htm.

―――. (1994) *Difference and repetition,* Trans P. Patton. London: Athlone Press and New York: Columbia University Press.

―――. (1995) *Negotiations 1972–1990,* Trans M. Joughin. New York: Columbia University Press.

―――. (1998) *Essays critical and clinical.* London: Verso.

Deleuze, G. and Guattari, F. (1987) *A thousand plateaus: capitalism and schizophrenia.* London: The Athlone Press.

Derrida, J. (1979) Border lines. In Bloom et al. (Eds) *Deconstruction and criticism.* New York: Seabury Press.

―――. (1992) *The other heading: reflections on today's Europe,* trans. P Brault and M Naas. Bloomington/Indianapolis, Indiana University Press.

―――. (1996) Border lines in Bloom et al (Eds) *Deconstruction and criticism.* New York: Seabury Press.

―――. (1997) The Villanova roundtable: A conversation with Jacques Derrida, in: J. Caputo (ed.). *Deconstruction in a nutshell: A conversation with Jacques Derrida.* New York: Fordham University Press.

Dudley-Marling, C. (2001) Reconceptualizing learning disabilities by reconceptualizing education. In L. Denti and P. Tefft-Cousin (Eds). *New ways of looking at learning disabilities*. Denver: Love.

Dyson, A, Howes, A and Roberts, B (2002) A systematic review of the effectiveness of school–level actions for promoting participation by all students. London: Evidence for Policy and Practice.

Eagleton, T. (1993) *Literary theory: An introduction.* Oxford: Basil Blackwell.

Elliot, J. (2001) Characteristics of performative cultures: Their central paradoxes and limitations of educational reform. In D. Gleeson and C. Husbands (Eds). *The performing school.* London: Routledge.

Ferri, B. (2004) Interrupting the discourse: A response to Reid and Valle, *Journal of Learning Disabilities,* 37 (6), 509–515.

Fuchs, D. and Fuchs, L. (1994) Inclusive schools movement and the radicalization of special education reform. *Exceptional Children,* 60 (4), 294–309.

Gewirtz, S. (2000) Bringing the politics back in: A critical analysis of quality discourses in education. *British Journal of Educational Studies,* 48 (4), 352–370.

Gregoriou, Z. (2001) Does speaking of others involve receiving the "other"? A postcolonial reading of receptivity in Derrida's deconstruction of Timaeus. In G. Biesta and D. Egéa–Kuehne (Eds). *Derrida and education.* London: Routledge.

Gutierrez, K., Larson, J. and Kreuter, B. (1995) Cultural tensions in the scripted classroom: The value of the subjugated perspective. *Urban Education,* 29.

Hextall, I. (2000) *Reconstructing teaching: Standards, performance and accountability.* London: RoutledgeFalmer.

Kauffman, J. (1999) Commentary: Today's special education and its message for tomorrow. *Journal of Special Education,* 32 (4), 244–54.

Kauffman, J. and Hallahan, D. (1995) (Eds) *The illusion of full inclusion: A comprehensive critique of a current special education bandwagon.* Austin: Pro–Ed.

Levinas, E. (1998) *On thinking of the other: Entre nous.* London: Athlone.

Linton, S. (1998) *Claiming disability: Knowledge and identity.* New York: New York University Press.

Mitchell, D. and Snyder, S. (1997) *The body and physically difference: Discourses of disability.* Ann Arbor: University of Michigan Press.

Moss, P. and Petrie, P. (2002) *From children's services to children's spaces: Public policy, children and childhood.* London: RoutledgeFalmer.

National Board for Professional Teaching Standards (2001) Professional Teaching Standards. Washington: NBPTS.

Oliver, M. (1999) Final accounts and the parasite people. In M. Corker and S. French (eds.). *Disability discourse.* Buckingham: Oxford University Press.

Patrick, M. (1996) Assuming responsibility: or Derrida's disclaimer. In J. Brannigan, R. Robbins, and J. Wolfreys (Eds). *Applying: to Derrida.* Basingstoke: Macmillan.

Reid, K. and Valle, J. (2004) The discursive practice of learning disability: Implications for instruction and perent-school relations. *Journal of Learning Disabilities,* 37 (6), 466–481.

Roy, K. (2003) *Teachers in nomadic spaces: Deleuze and curriculum.* New York: Peter Lang.

Sasso, G. (2001) The retreat from inquiry and knowledge in special education. *Journal of Special Education,* 34 (4), 178–93.

Sebba, J. and Sachdev, D. (1997) What works in inclusive education? Barkingside: Barnardo's.

Slee R. (2001) Social justice and the changing directions in educational research: The case of inclusive education. *International Journal of Inclusive Education* 5 (2/3), 167–178.

Slee, R (2003) Teacher education, government and inclusive schooling: The politics of the Faustian waltz. In J Allan (Ed). *Inclusion, participation and democracy: What is the purpose?* Dordrecht: Kluwer.

Slee, R. and Allan, J. (2001) Excluding the included: A reconsideration of inclusive education. *International studies in the sociology of education,* 11 (2), 173–191.

Smyth, J. and Hattam, J. (2002) Early school leaving and the cultural geography of high schools. *British Educational Research Journal,* 28:3, 375–398.

Smyth, J. and Shacklock, G. (1998) *Remaking teaching: Ideology, policy and practice.* London, Routledge.

Snyder, S. and Mitchell, D. (2004) *Self preservation: the art of Riva Lehrer.* A BRACE YOURSELVES production. DVD.

Strathearn, M. (2000) The tyranny of transparency. *British Journal of Educational Research,* 26 (3), 309–321.

Troyna, B. and Vincent, C. (1996) The ideology of expertism: The framing of special education and racial equality policies in the local state. In C. Christensen and F. Rizvi, (Eds). *Disability and the dilemmas of education and justice.* Buckingham, Open University Press.

van Manen, M. (2002) *Writing in the dark: Phenomenological studies in interpretive inquiry.* London, Ontario: The Althouse Press.

Vidovitch, L. and Slee, R. (2001) Bringing universities to account? Exploring some global and local policy tensions, *Journal of Educational Policy,* 16 (5), 431–453.

Ware, L. (2001) Writing, identity and the other: Dare we do disability studies? *Teachers College Record,* 52 (2), 107–124.

———. (2004) *Ideology and the politics of in/exclusion.* New York: Peter Lang.

Williams, G. (2001) Theorizing disability. In G. Albrecht, K. Seelman and M. Bury (Eds). *The handbook of disability studies.* Thousand Oaks, CA: Sage Publications Inc.

Young, I. (2000) Five faces of oppression. In M. Adams, W. Blumenfield, R. Castaneda, H. Hackman, M. Peters and X. Zúñiga (Eds). *Readings for diversity and social justice: An anthology on racisim, anti–semitism, sexism, heterosexism, ableism and classism.* New York/London: Routledge.

CHAPTER 20

Deconstructing Difference: Doing Disability Studies in Multicultural Educational Contexts

Nirmala Erevelles

Ten years ago, almost midway through my doctoral program, I found myself participating in a series of non-conversations in the two academic areas I was passionately interested in—special education and third world/postcolonial feminist theory. In the special education program in which I was enrolled, I—a non-disabled former special education teacher from India—had been taught by my professors to re-conceptualize disability as a social construction and to radically challenge the "normalizing" practices of schooling. At the same time, as an international graduate female student of color enrolled in a university in the United States and experiencing the process of first being constructed as racialized subject and then experiencing the oppressive impact of this racialization, I was struggling to obtain the knowledges that would help me theorize the complexities of my postcolonial, gendered, and racialized subjectivity. In the special education program, there were no faculty and very few students of color, and thus, even though issues of race were often acknowledged and sometimes discussed, these discussions lacked the passionate urgency that I yearned for. However, when I introduced disability as a political construct into discussions of postcolonialism, feminism, and race with graduate students and faculty outside my program, my interjections were often greeted with a polite disinterest. The irony of this disconnect, however, was not lost on me. Here I was, a doctoral student of color engaged in studying the marginalization experienced by disabled students in educational contexts, while at the same time experiencing my own marginalization as a politicized, racialized, and gendered subject at a higher educational institution in the United States. Yet, notwithstanding several apparent commonalities, it looked like ne'er the twain shall meet.

Ten years later with Disability Studies as a recognized field of study, this disconnect between disability and other constructs of social difference— namely race, class, ethnicity, gender, and sexual orientation—in educational contexts can no longer be defended. In contrast to the medical/clinical definitions of disability traditionally prevalent in educational contexts, the field of Disability Studies has theorized disability as a social and political construct and disabled people as a minority group engaged in a political struggle for civil rights. According to Disability Studies scholar, Simi Linton (1998):

> Disability [S]tudies takes for its subject matter not simply the variations that exist in human behavior, appearance, functioning, sensory acuity, and cognitive processing but more crucially, the meaning we make of those variations. The field explores the critical divisions our society makes in creating the normal versus the pathological, the insider versus the outsider, or the competent citizen versus the ward of the state (p. 2).

Linton's definition foregrounds social difference as the critical analytic that is central to a Disability Studies perspective and, in particular, the construct of normality. The construct of normality is also central to the everyday practices of educational institutions in their functions of sorting, organizing, educating, and evaluating students. In fact, the historian of education, Lawrence A. Cremin has argued that education is the "deliberate, systematic effort to transmit, evoke, or acquire knowledge, attitudes, skills, or sensibilities, as well as any outcomes of that effort" (quoted in Sadovnik, Cookson and Semel, 2001; p. 19) in the attempt to create the "ideal" citizen (Spring, 2001). However, according to Disability Studies scholar Lennard Davis (2002), whereas the ideal was perceived "not as an absolute but part of a descending continuum from top to bottom" (p. 101), this notion of the "ideal" was transformed in the nineteenth century (with the birth of statistics), into the concept of the "norm"—a concept that has since served as an imperative to the population to conform/to fit/ "to huddle under the main part of the [normal] curve" (p. 101). Thus, for example, one of the central ideologies of the Common School Movement of the 1840's, as articulated by the

Father of U.S. public education, Horace Mann, was to socialize all children into a common political and social ideology, notwithstanding their heterogeneous origins and capacities so that they would be able to live up to the normative principles prescribed by the new Republic (Spring, 2001).

Educational institutions have become very adept in this task of disciplining the student population into conformity. This has been achieved by comparing students to a normative code of behaviors, attitudes, skills, and dispositions through the use of standardized, objective, and scientific evaluations that demand homogeneity from a heterogeneous student population. As a result of such practices, students differing on the basis of race, class, gender, sexual orientation, and disability have had qualitatively different experiences in educational institutions and have, therefore, also experienced qualitatively different educational outcomes (Kozol, 1991; Harris, 1997; Orenstein, 1994; Valenzuela, 1999; Jones, 2004) It is in this context then that a Disability Studies' perspective is necessary when responding to the following questions: (a) Why and how is the social construction of the disabled Other connected to issues related to race, class, ethnicity, gender, and sexual orientation?; (b) What are the material consequences of organizing social difference along the axes of normative ability in educational contexts?; (c) In what ways can an analysis from the critical standpoint of Disability Studies have transformative potential not just for disabled students but for all students marked oppressively by race, class, gender, ethnicity, and sexual orientation?

Narrating Difference: Educational Discourse as Prosthesis

The disciplinary function of public education as a mode of social control has been well documented (Foucault, 1979; Sarason and Doris 1979; Noguera 1995; Spring 2001; Watts and Erevelles, 2004). For example, the French philosopher, Michel Foucault (1979), in his book *Discipline and Punish*, has drawn analogies between the birth of the prison and the social organization of schooling in the eighteenth century. According to Foucault, institutions such as schools regarded the student body as both "an object and target of power" and utilized various technologies of discipline and punishment so as to make the body completely docile. Those whose bodies challenged the rigidity of this discipline and proved to be "unruly bodies" (Erevelles, 2000), were subjected to the "ceremony of punishment" — "an act of terror" (Foucault, 1979, p. 54) that was utilized to make everyone aware of the unrestrained presence of disciplinary power in the school. In this way, schools just like the prison/asylum became very effective in their attempts to regiment, control, and discipline those who came to be known as "social outcasts of education" (Noguera, 1995, p. 194).

Student populations who are designated as "social outcasts of education" are as heterogeneous as the identities they embody. In a society where white supremacy still rears its ugly head, students of color (African American, Latino/a, Native American), particularly those from low income neighborhoods, are often segregated on account of presumed academic and behavioral "deficiencies" that are seen to run counter to expectations of white suburban aspirations and lifestyles (Ferguson, 2001; Fordham, 1995; Kozol, 1991; Valenzuela, 1999). Pregnant teens (especially those who are girls of color from low income neighborhoods), are believed to embody moral deviance and are often shunted out into alternative programs outside the school because their pregnant condition is seen as socially contagious to other teenage girls (Saphire, 1996; Pillow, 2003a; Luttrell, 2003). Legislation such as Proposition 187 passed in California in 1994 to deny public benefits and therefore public education to the children of "illegal" immigrants as well as the debate about the legitimacy of bilingual education programs across the country (Valenzuela, 1999; Valencia and Solarzano, 1997; Macedo and Bartolome; 1999) have made linguistically diverse students cultural outcasts in public school contexts. Lesbian, gay, bisexual, and transgendered students are often enshrouded in educational discourses of deviancy and isolation, even by those policy makers who have attempted to combat the violence they face in school on a daily basis (Talburt, 2004). And last but not least, notwithstanding IDEA, students labeled as disabled continue to be ostracized and warehoused in self-contained classrooms on account of their significant physical/cognitive/ behavioral differences.

In each of the cases mentioned above, what is clearly apparent is that public education has used the concepts of difference, deviance, and disability synonymously to justify the exclusion of certain student populations in an attempt to adhere to demands of normativity, even while claiming that their practices are democratic. It is here then that deploying the Disability Studies perspective is critical in exposing the normalizing practices of schooling, especially the way these practices oppressively engage social difference.

Unfortunately, however, theorists of race, class, gender, and sexual orientation, rather than seeing some commonality with disability have, instead, actively sought to distance themselves from disability, fearing that associating with disability will imply that their difference would equate with a biological deviance/deficit—an association they assume will be even more difficult to critique. This is because, despite the critical interventions of Disability Studies in Education, disability continues to be theorized via a deficit model that associates disability with "physiological deviance" and/or "lack of intelligence" in educational contexts where the social constructs of "intelligence" and "ability" are seldom questioned. Thus, for example, distinguished intellectuals like Stephen J. Gould (1995), Henry Louis Gates (1995), Howard Gardner (1995), and Jacqueline Jones (1995), among others, in critiques leveled against Herrnstein and Murray's (1994) controversial book, *The Bell Curve: Intelligence and Class Structure in American Life* have argued against making any linkages between disability and race because such linkages erroneously demonstrate the "collective *stupidity* [emphasis added] of the group" (Jones, 1995, p. 81). Similarly, queer students, pregnant teens, working class students, and linguistically diverse students have claimed that their bodies/minds reflect almost all aspects of normativity, and the only differences they manifest have been either superficial (e.g. skin color, language, sexual choice) and/or temporary (pregnancy). This is an argument that disabled students can seldom make because their differences are definitely not superficial and are, in fact, often permanent. As a result, even though issues of intersectionality of difference are avidly pursued in educational contexts (McLaren, 1997; Nieto, 2000), disabled students are often left out in the cold. In this sense then, the disabled student is an embodiment of the "abject Other" (Erevelles, in press), where according to Kristeva (1982) the abject is:

> ...the jettisoned object....A massive and sudden emergence of uncanniness, which, familiar as it might have been in an opaque and forgotten life, now harries me as radically separate, loathsome. Not me. Not that. But not nothing, either. A "something" that I do not recognize as a thing....[but] which crushes me (p. 2).

Even though both hegemonic and counter-hegemonic educational discourses isolate disability in their analyses, disability is nevertheless an intimate part of contemporary educational discourses. This is because educational discourses shore up their adherence to normativity by constructing disability as the very antithesis of "regular" educational practice and therefore a condition that must be either rejected, avoided, and (if need be) excluded. However, because difference (on the basis of race, class, gender, sexual orientation, and disability) is also an integral part of public education in a democratic society, educational practices support difference if and only if difference can be controlled, disguised, and/or rendered invisible—in other words if difference is "prostheticized."

According to Disability Studies scholars, Mitchell and Snyder (2000) a prosthesis is a device that accomplishes the illusion of enabling an individual to fit in and de-emphasize his/her differences so that s/he can return to a state of imagined normativity. In other words, in most educational contexts, students identified as different from the norm because of their race, class, gender, ethnicity and/or sexual orientation are validated if and only if they can deploy "prosthetic practices" that enable them to "pass" as not really that different from the norm by hiding their dis/ability. As a result, disability becomes the discursive link that simultaneously explains and exposes the social construction of difference in education along the axes of race, class, gender, ethnicity, and sexual orientation.

It is for these reasons I argue here that disability IS the organizing logic utilized by the educational bureaucracy as the "master trope of disqualification" (Mitchell and Snyder, 2000, p. 3) to legitimate exclusionary and oppressive practices meted out against students marked by race, class, gender, ethnicity, and sexual difference. It is easy enough to recognize this logic in the daily workings of the educational bureaucracy—the battery of standardized tests that students are forced to take on a daily basis; the detailed records of any infringement of school policy that teachers are required to complete; the carefully spelled out and rigidly controlled curriculum that disallows any deviation from the master text; and the rigid codes of (un)acceptable behavior that are monitored even in extracurricular activities such as the school prom.

Each of these bureaucratic functions take up a large part of an administrator's and teacher's working day, interrupting the pedagogical functions of education, and all this for the purpose of ensuring that students conform to the normative requirements of schooling or risk being labeled (dis)abled. To be labeled as disabled in an educational context implies that one is both a disruptive presence as well as an embodiment of deficiency. Disability, therefore, serves as the raw material that is utilized to make other differences visible by requiring all students to exhibit particular skills/behaviors/ dispositions (prosthetics) that minimize their difference/distance from the norm. Failure to do so results in punishment, segregation, and/or expulsion.

Mitchell and Snyder (2000) describe comparable practices within the literary domain as "narrative prosthesis" — a concept that they argue "situates the experience and representational life of disability upon the ironic grounding on an unsteady rhetorical stance [i.e. the prosthesis]" (p. 6). Shifting from the literary domain to the educational, I borrow from Mitchell and Snyder's work to describe "educational discourse as prosthesis" in its narration of social difference in educational contexts. In doing so, I argue that "educational discourse as prosthesis" foregrounds the pervasiveness of disability as the central device in the organization of social difference in narratives of public education. However, the demand for the deployment of prosthetic practices in educational contexts foregrounds another irony. Even though, educational discourses struggle to keep the unruly dis/abled body outside the mainstream in order to obliterate its challenge of the norm, this very struggle is always undermined by the fact that these prosthetic practices are artificial and therefore (re)signifiable.

For example, this irony is evident in the ways that educational institutions constantly struggle to find appropriately descriptive ways to label nonconforming students (e.g. emotionally disturbed; behaviorally disordered; learning disabled; mentally retarded; autistic) in order to segregate them from the "normal" student population even though these labels are often unstable and therefore meaning-less (Brantlinger, 2004; Reid and Valle, 2004). However, the continuous repetition of this representational formula of disability in educational contexts only reifies the association of disability with deviance/deformity such that any attempts to distance disenfranchised educational communities marked by race, class, sexual orientation, and ethnicity from the fantasy of deformity/deviance further entrenches the disabled student as the "real abnormal from which all other non-normative groups must be distanced" (Mitchell and Snyder, 2000, p. 6). As a result, in the final analysis, all students labeled disabled experience the most brutal social violence in educational contexts—a violence that is legitimated even by those who may claim to be educators of social justice.

Deconstructing the Biological/Social Binary:
A Disability Studies Perspective

During her research on teen pregnancy, Wanda Pillow (2003b) reported a school administrator's comment that "bodies are dangerous" (p. 145). She, therefore, argues that, in educational institutions, paying attention to bodies seems taboo because bodies "remain uncontrollable in many ways, receptive to and disruptive of power" (p. 146). Part of this dangerous uncontrollability attributed to the body is because it is seen as a "fixed system of muscle, bone, nerves, and organs...amenable to scientific examination...a site of established fact" (Kirk quoted in McWilliam, 1996; p. 17). Such logic supports the distinction between the biological (nature) and the social (nurture) bases of difference based on the assumption that those differences associated with the biological body are, in fact, inalienable and therefore inviolable. In educational contexts this translates into seeing as educationally salvageable only those dis/abled students whose differences are socially based. Education for all other bodies whose dis/ability is seen to be biological is considered a futile venture. It is therefore important to explore the possibility of deconstructing the biological(nature)/social(nurture) binary because it has real material consequences for the educational lives of students labeled disabled.

In my attempts to deconstruct the biological/social binary, I draw on feminist critiques of the sex/gender dichotomy (Butler, 1993) to make an analogical deconstruction of the disability/impairment dichotomy that has been avidly debated in Disability Studies (Corker and French, 1999; Thomas, 1999). Feminist theorist Judith Butler (1993) has critiqued feminists who theorize "sex" as a natural/biological and therefore ahistorical concept, as opposed to "gender" that they theorize as a social construct. Butler has argued that "sex" is also a social construct, and she uses as her example a particular moment in a person's history—one's birth—when an infant's gendered identity is seemingly identified solely through its biological make up (nature) at the moment the doctor utters the infamous words, "It's a girl." Butler argues that at that very instance of utterance, the infant (it) is medically interpellated as "she"—a process that Butler describes as "girling"— this naming that "is at once setting a boundary and also the repeated inculcation of a norm" (8). "Girling" occurs, through incessant (re)iterations (repetitions) emerging out of a chain of foreclosures, erasures, and/or boundary conditions that make it appear to be natural. Any deviations from this "natural" trajectory (e.g. transsexual/intersexual) will "not only produce the domain of intelligible bodies [bodies that matter], but produce as well a domain of unthinkable, abject, unlivable bodies [those that do not matter in the same way]" (xi).

Butler's argument is appealing to Disability Studies scholarship because it problematizes our taken-for-granted interpretation of the natural. Disability studies scholars have also struggled with the biological versus social debate, producing their own dichotomy of impairment versus disability that mirrors in many ways the feminist debates regarding sex versus gender (Corker and French 1999, Linton 1998; Thomas, 1999). Disability Studies scholars have had to struggle with the conundrum that even though they argue that disability is, in fact, a social construction, they are also eager to recognize the unique phenomenological experiences of having an impairment— experiences that mark their bodies as irreducibly different from "normal" bodies and yet, at the same time, are integral to their identity as disabled people. This is because even though de-linking disability from impairment will expose the social construction of oppression on the basis of disability, at another level this de-linking will be unable to adequately account for the complexity embedded in the formation of disabled identity (Thomas, 1999).

Butler's analysis becomes useful here. Impairment, just like sex, is associated with the medical interpellation of subjects into the semiotics of difference. At the moment of interpellation, the actual act of "naming" the impairment immediately triggers off an entire semiotic chain of meaning that draws on an already historically situated discourse that links "impairment" with the "defective body" that needs to be "normalized" rather than a "different body" that has "different" needs. For example, the very moment of labeling a student disabled on account of an identified impairment (e.g. mental retardation; autism) immediately interpellates the student into a whole subset of educational discourses that mark the student as outside the norm, and therefore, the student may experience segregation, subjection, and/or expulsion—a decision that has real material consequences for the educational future of the student. In that sense then, the issue of "impairment" can never be thought of as a completely biological category that is radically separate from its social counterpart, disability. It is for this reason that I argue that how educational institutions engage with the disabled body is still mediated by the social.

Additionally, Butler argues that the boundaries that form identity are merely unstable discursive constructions that masquerade as the norm through the action of performativity. Performativity, according to Butler, is not constituted by a single voluntaristic act, but is, in fact, a series of (re)iterations that cite authoritarian conventions of normality that are themselves social constructions. Consequently, these normative constraints that map out the limits of the "natural/normal" body are now exposed as discursive constructions/performances, and in doing so challenge the hegemonic cult of normativity (Erevelles, 2002). This notion of performativity is especially relevant to this discussion. In fact, I argued earlier that in educational institutions, students are expected to "pass" as "normal" through the deployment of what I termed "prosthetic practices." These practices are nothing other than a "performance" of normality—a performance that renders the cult of normality as unstable, illusory, and at the same time extremely transgressive. Thus, what would happen, if the students see that the battery of tests they are forced to take and the rigid codes of normality that they are forced to obey are illusory constructions based on a highly unstable category of dis/ability? What if students, realizing that being "normal" is just a performance, reject drawing on the use of prostheses that force them to "pass?" The discursive possibilities of transgression are exciting....But what about the material consequences of challenging the norm?

Bringing Materiality Back: (Re)Theorizing Education, Disability, and Difference

Up until this point in this chapter, I have described how educational discourses have been instrumental in constructing, organizing, and mediating difference and have also suggested discursive linkages between disability and other constructs of difference namely race, class, ethnicity, gender, and sexual orientation. I have argued that disability IS the organizing logic utilized by educational institutions in the government of these constructs of difference. I have also argued that because the biological is always also shaped by the social, the normality/disability binary is both unstable and illusory and therefore has transgressive possibilities. It is to these transgressive possibilities that I now turn.

Acting on transgressive possibilities in educational contexts is not an unusual occurrence. This is evidently true especially in public schools where students' active resistance against normative school regulations happens on a daily basis. This is because, as philosopher Foucault (1984) has argued, the repressive requirements of normality actually allow for radical possibilities. As Foucault (1984) explains:

> [T]he notion of repression is quite inadequate for capturing what is precisely the productive aspect of power....If power were never anything but repressive, if it never did anything but to say no, do you really think one would be brought to obey it? What makes power hold good, what makes it accepted is, simply the fact that it doesn't only weigh on us as a force that says no, but that it traverses and produces things, it induces pleasure, forms knowledge, produces discourses (p. 61).

Foucault's recognition of the deconstructive possibility in disciplinary institutions like schools is a cause for celebration. But, I also argue here that celebrating student resistance within the discursive realm without exploring the real material consequences of such transgressions on the educational lives of students is problematic. For example, the very fact that segregated educational programs such as special education classrooms and alternative schools are dominated by students of color (African American and Latino Males, in particular) mostly because they have been diagnosed and labeled emotionally disturbed, violent, and or behaviorally disordered testifies to the reality that behavior that flouts the norm has zero tolerance in public schools (Fordham, 1995; Noguera, 1995; Watts and Erevelles, 2004; Ferguson, 2001). Furthermore, these zero tolerance policies have devastating effects on the future lives of these students who because they receive a sub-standard education often find themselves in low paid service jobs, or as dependents on state welfare or in the prison industrial complex that is yet another violent segregational institution (Watts and Erevelles, 20004).

It is also important to know why educational institutions support these oppressive practices and it is here that a materialist Disability Studies perspective becomes useful. I have argued elsewhere that in the current context of transnational capitalism disability as an ideological category is utilized to justify an oppressive social division of labor (i.e. along the axes of race, class, and gender) in the interests of the maximum accumulation of profits (Erevelles, 2000). In the social context of the United States, that celebrates the free market and liberal democratic rights, the social construction of disability-as-lack is utilized to justify why a vast majority of disenfranchised U.S. citizens struggle on a daily basis to these "inalienable" rights to life, liberty, and the pursuit of happiness.

Critical race theorist, Cheryl Harris (1995) has argued that historically the notion of individual rights that emerged during the founding period of the new republic was rooted in the protection of one's property where property as described by John Madison "embraces every thing to which a man may attach a value and have a right" (quoted in Harris 1995, 279). Because rights in property became "contingent on, intertwined, and conflated with race" (p. 277), Harris argues that whiteness as property became significant because it provided the ideological justification to exclude people of color from the privileges of owning property. Expanding on Harris' argument, I have suggested elsewhere that whiteness as property was also the ideological discourse that has been used to justify the racial superiority of white people over people of color by using the logic of dis-ability (e.g. inferior genes, low IQ) to decide who has the rights to citizenship (Erevelles 2002). As such, it became critical that, in addition to whiteness, "ability" (both cognitive and physical) was also an important property right that had to be safeguarded, protected, and defended in the attempt to decide who could or could not be a citizen.

Ferri and Connor (2005) echo this position when they argue that in the post-*Brown* world "discourses of racism and ableism have bled into one another permitting forms of racial [re]segregation under the guise of 'disability'" (p. 454) in United States public schools. Similarly, Baker (2002), also describes how disability as an "outlaw ontology" was used to justify the exclusion of individuals on the basis of race, class, gender, and sexuality, drawing on what she terms the "new discourses of eugenics as 'quality control'" (p. 663). Watts and Erevelles (2004) describe these segregated settings as "internal colonies" —spaces of exclusion, segregation, and enclosure that are overpopulated by poor students of color, many of whom are labeled emotionally disturbed, behaviorally disordered, and/or potentially violent.

Additionally, as per the NCLB guidelines, educational institutions are charged with the efficient production of future workers, and so student behaviors that are deemed disruptive to this mission are under close administrative scrutiny. One such context is student sexuality, where once again the logic of disability-as-lack is deployed to regulate student sexuality by valorizing certain expressions/practices of sexuality as normative while labeling others as deviant/disabled. Thus, for example, certain institutionalized school activities like senior prom, the Beauty Walk, and cheerleading that support patriarchal and heterosexual norms are actively encouraged while other practices of sexual expression that are disruptive of dominant ideologies are actively repressed.. For example, the discourses deployed in sex education programs across the country set up codes of sexual behavior that determine who can have sex (e.g. only heterosexual able-bodied adults) and what forms of sexual expression are acceptable in educational contexts (e.g. participation in the heterosexual school prom). Interjecting discourses of morality into these discussions contributes to the organization of sexual subjects into a hierarchy of identity that separates "us" (the moral normative majority) from "them" (the deviant disabled minority).

Claiming and/or passing as normal while maintaining a dis-stance from the "real" aberrancy of disability is amply rewarded in educational contexts. Put simply, "we," therefore, try really hard not to be like "them." In the context of sex education and the related HIV/AIDS education programs, the discourses of morality are instrumental in assigning the following populations to the category "them": pregnant teens, gay/lesbian/bisexual youth, transgendered youth, disabled youth, and youth living with HIV/AIDS. These students who express themselves outside of the prescribed norms experience social and educational isolation—experiences that have devastating consequences on these students' future lives as citizens (Harris, 1997; Thomas, 1999; Luttrell, 2003; Pillow, 2003b; Jones, 2004; Talburt, 2004). Oppressively marked thus by race, class, gender, sexuality, and disability, many of these students struggle in their later years in low-paid service jobs, dependent on the social welfare, and often incarcerated in the nation's prisons. It is in this context then the material violence waged against those who reject the cult of normativity and therefore get labeled disabled.

Conclusion

In this chapter, I have argued that disability is the central logic that organizes hierarchies of social difference in educational context. Disability Studies is therefore crucial to any discussion of social difference as it relates to issues of social justice. In fact, Disability Studies is well poised to challenge the unquestioned authority of (special) education practices to legitimize, expose and control the boundaries between normality and abnormality (Brantlinger, 2004). Failure to do will only reify the cult of normativity. And that we know has devastating consequences for *all* of us.

References

Baker, B. (2002) The hunt for disability: The new eugenics and the normalization of school children. *Teachers College Record*, 104(4): 663–703.

Brantlinger, E. (2004). Confounding the needs and confronting the norms: An extension of Reid and Valle's essay. *Journal of Learning Disabilites*, 37(6): 490–499.

Butler, J. (1993). *Bodies that matter: On the discursive limits of sex*. New York: Routledge.

Corker, M. and French, S. (Eds) (1999). *Disability discourse*. Philadelphia: Open University Press.

Davis, Lennard (2002) Bodies of difference: Politics, disability, and representation. In S. L. Snyder, B. J. Brueggemann, and R.Garland Thomson (eds.) *Disability studies: Enabling the humanities*, pp. 100–106. New York: The Modern Language Association.

Erevelles, N. (2000). Educating unruly bodies: Critical pedagogy, disability studies and the politics of schooling. *Educational Theory, 50*(1), 25–47.

———. (2002). (Im)Material citizens: Critical race theory, disability studies, and the politics of education. *Disability, Culture, and Education, 1*(1), 5–26.

———. (in press). Understanding curriculum as normalizing text: Disability Studies meets curriculum theory. *Journal of Curriculum Studies*.

Ferguson, A. A. (2001). *Bad Boys: Public school in the making of black masculinity*. University of Michigan Press.

Ferri, B. A. and Connor, D. J. (2005). Tools of exclusion: Race, disability and (re)segregated education. *Teachers College Record*, 107 (3); 458–474.

Fordham, S. (1995) *Blacked out: Dilemmas of race, identity and success at Capital High*. Chicago: University of Chicago Press.

Foucault, M. (1979). *Discipline and punish: The birth of the prison*. New York: Vintage Books.

———. (1984) Truth and power. In P. Rabinow, (ed.) *The Foucault reader*, pp. 51–75. New York: Pantheon Books

Gardner, H. (1995). Cracking open the IQ box. In S. Fraser (ed.) *The bell curve wars: Race, intelligence, and the future of America*, pp. 23–35. New York: Basic Books.

Gates, H. L (Jr.). (1995). Why now? In S. Fraser (ed.) *The bell curve wars: Race, intelligence, and the future of America*, pp. 94–96. New York: Basic Books.

Gould, S. J. (1995). Curveball. In S. Fraser (ed.) *The bell curve wars: Race, intelligence, and the future of America*, pp. 11–22. New York: Basic Books.

Harris, C. I. (1995) Whiteness as property. In Crenshaw, K., Gotanda, N., Peller, G., and Thomas, K. (Eds.). *Critical race theory: The key writings that formed the movement* (pp. 276-291). New York: New Press.

Harris, M. (1997). *School experiences of gay and lesbian youth. The invisible minority*. New York: Harrington Park Press.

Herrnstein, R. J. and Murray, C.. (1994). *The bell curve: intelligence and class structure in American life.* New York: Free Press

Jones, J. (1995). Back to the future with the bell curve: Jim Crow, slavery, and G. In S. Fraser (ed.) *The bell curve wars: Race, intelligence, and the future of America*, pp. 80–93. New York: Basic Books

Jones, M. M. (2004). *Whisper writing: Teenage girls talk about ableism and sexism in School.* New York: Peter Lang.

Kliewer, C. and Fitzgerald, L. M. (2001). Disability, schooling, and the artifacts of colonialism. *Teachers College Record*, 103 (3) 450–470.

Kozol, J. (1991). *Savage inequalities.* New York: HarperCollins.

Kristeva, J. (1982) *Powers of horror: An essay on abjection.* New York: Columbia University Press.

Linton, S. (1998). *Claiming disability: Knowledge and identity.* New York: New York University Press.

Luttrell, W. (2003) *Pregnant bodies, Fertile minds: Gender, race, and the schooling of pregnant teens.* New York: Routledge.

Macedo, D. and Bartolom, L. I. (1999). *Dancing with bigotry: Beyond the politics of tolerance.* New York: St. Martin's Press.

McLaren, P. (1997). *Revolutionary Multiculturalism: Pedagogies of Dissent for the New Millenium.* Boulder, Colorado: Westview Press.

McWilliam, E.. (1996). Pedagogies, technologies, bodies. In E. McWilliam and P. G. Taylor (eds.) *Pedagogy, technology, and the body*, pp. 1–22. New York: Peter Lang.

Mitchell, D. and Snyder, S. (2000). *Narrative prosthesis: Disability and the dependencies of discourse.* Ann Arbor, MI: University of Michigan Press.

Nieto, S. (2000). *Affirming diversity: The sociopolitical context of multicultural education.* New York: Longman.

Noguera, P. (1995). Preventing and producing violence: A critical analysis of responses to school violence. *Harvard Educational Review, 65,* 189–212.

Orenstein, P. (1994). *Schoolgirls: Young women, self–esteem, and the confidence gap.* New York: Doubleday.

Pillow, W. (2003a) *Unfit subjects: Educational policy and the teen mother.* New York: Falmer Press.

———. (2003b) "Bodies are dangerous": Using feminist genealogy as policy studies methodology. *Journal of Educational Policy*, 18(2): 145 – 159.

Reid, D. K. and Valle, J. W. (2004). The discursive practice of learning disability: Implications for instruction and parent–school relations. *Journal of Learning Disabilities*, 37(6): 466–481.

Sadovnik, A. R., Cookson, Jr., P. W., and Semel, S. F. (2001). *Exploring education: An Introduction to the foundations of education*. New York: Allyn and Bacon.

Sapphire. (1996). *Push: A novel*. New York: Random House.

Sarason, S., and Doris, J. (1979). *Educational handicap, public policy, and social history: A broadened perspective on mental retardation*. New York: The Free Press

Spring, J. (2001). *The American school: 1642–2001*. New York: McGraw Hill

Talburt, S. (2004) Construction of LGBT youth: Opening up subject positions. *Theory into Practice*, 43(2): 116–122.

Thomas, C. (1999). *Female forms: Experiencing and understanding Disability*. New York: Taylor and Francis.

Valencia, R. R. and Solarzano, D. G. (1997). Contemporary deficit thinking. In R. R. Valencia (ed.) *The evolution of deficit thinking: Educational thought and practice*, pp. 160–210. New York: Falmer Press.

Valenzuela, A. (1999). *Subtractive schooling: U.S. Mexican youth and the politics of caring*. Albany: State University of New York Press.

Watts, I. and Erevelles, N. (2004). These deadly times: Reconceptualizing school violence using critical race theory and disability studies. *American Educational Research Journal*, 41(2): 271–299.

Contributors

Julie Allan, University of Stirling (Scotland)

Bernadette Baker, University of Wisconsin, Madison

Alicia A. Broderick, Columbia University

Patricia A. Brown, University of Washington

Sharan E. Brown, University of Washington

Fiona Campbell, Griffith University (Australia)

David J. Connor, Hunter College

Scot Danforth, The Ohio State University

Nirmala Erevelles, University of Alabama

Dianne L. Ferguson, Western Oregon University

Philip M. Ferguson, University of Missouri, St. Louis

Ron Ferguson, Louisiana Tech University

Beth A. Ferri, Syracuse University

Alan Foley, University of Wisconsin System

Susan L. Gabel, National College of Education, National Louis University

Deborah J. Gallagher, University of Northern Iowa

Chris Kliewer, University of Northern Iowa

Kagendo Mutua, University of Alabama

Susan Peters, Michigan State University

D. Kim Reid, Columbia University

Nancy Rice, University of Wisconsin, Milwaukee

Phil Smith, Eastern Michigan University

Robin M. Smith, State University of New York, New Paltz

Santiago Solis, Columbia University

Steven J. Taylor, Syracuse University

Claire Tregaskis, University of Plymouth (England)

Jan Weatherly Valle, City College of New York

Linda Ware, City College of New York

Index

Disability Studies in Education

GENERAL EDITORS: SUSAN L. GABEL & SCOT DANFORTH

The book series Disability Studies in Education is dedicated to the publication of monographs and edited volumes that integrate the perspectives, methods, and theories of disability studies with the study of issues and problems of education. The series features books that further define, elaborate upon, and extend knowledge in the field of disability studies in education. Special emphasis is given to work that poses solutions to important problems facing contemporary educational theory, policy, and practice.

To order other books in this series, please contact our Customer Service Department:

(800) 770-LANG (within the U.S.)
(212) 647-7706 (outside the U.S.)
(212) 647-7707 FAX

Or browse by series:

WWW.PETERLANG.COM